WANTED
DEAD OR
ALIVE

WANTED DEAD OR ALIVE

THE AMERICAN WEST IN POPULAR CULTURE

EDITED BY

RICHARD AQUILA

UNIVERSITY OF ILLINOIS PRESS   URBANA AND CHICAGO

This book is printed on acid-free paper.

Library of Congress Cataloging-in-Publication Data

Wanted dead or alive : the American West in popular culture / edited
  by Richard Aquila.
      p.   cm.
   Includes bibliographical references and index.
   ISBN 0-252-02224-6 (alk. paper)
      1. Popular culture—West (U.S.) 2. Popular culture—United
States. 3. West (U.S.) in mass media. 4. West (U.S.) in art.
5. West (U.S.)—In literature. I. Aquila, Richard, 1946– .
F596.W28 1996
306'.0978—dc20   95-32476
                                                                CIP

FOR MY PARENTS,
Mary and Philip L. Aquila

Contents

Preface

Most Americans can readily identify Billy the Kid, George Armstrong Custer, Jesse James, Crazy Horse, Wyatt Earp, Annie Oakley, Geronimo, Calamity Jane, and a host of other figures from the Old West. These legendary heroes and villains are all major players in one of America's longest-running and most successful dramas, the "pop culture West." This action-packed tale features an exciting cast of cowboys, Indians, gunslingers, and other colorful western characters and is set against an exotic backdrop of jagged mountains, big skies, and wide-open spaces.

Over the years scholars have explored various territories of the pop culture West. There have been excellent studies of individual western genres, including movies, literature, and television. However, no one volume has ever presented an overview of the birth and growth of the pop culture West. This book is an attempt to fill that gap.

Each chapter in this volume is written by a specialist in the field and focuses on a different area of popular culture. Each author surveys the history of a particular western genre or field, summarizing its origins, main developments, and themes and analyzing its relationship to American life and thought. This anthology is not meant to be the final word on the pop culture West. Instead, it is designed as a starting place. The chapters offer an introduction to the subject and overviews of several of the most important aspects of the pop culture West. The introduction examines the birth and growth of the pop culture West in the context of American history. Part 1 surveys main developments in popular Western fiction. Part 2 focuses on major forms of live Western entertainment. Part 3 explores major trends in Western movies and television shows. Part 4 explains images of the West in popular music. Finally, part 5 investigates visual images of the West in popular art and advertising. Suggestions for further reading are included at the end of each section so that the reader can explore in detail various themes or topics introduced in individual chapters.

Together the chapters paint an overall picture of the pop culture West. Obviously, the painting is incomplete. Space limitations and other considerations preclude additional chapters on dude ranches, comic books, Broadway shows, outdoor dramas, living museums, toys, fashions, folklore, or other possible topics. Nevertheless, the result is more than just a sketch; it constitutes a one-volume survey of the main areas of the pop culture West, providing valuable information about the significance of the West in American history and culture.

This book could not have been completed without the help of many people. In particular I would like to thank the contributors to this volume, who took time out from their own research and teaching to write chapters. Additional thanks go to Ray White, chair of the Ball State history department, and to Ball State University for providing resources and release time to complete this project. Last, but definitely not least, I wish to thank my family for making this book both possible and worthwhile. My wife, Marie, was there, as always, for support and editorial advice. My kids, Stephen and Valerie, helped to keep everything in perspective. A long time ago my brother, Phil, shared and encouraged my enthusiasm for cowboys and Indians. And over the years, my parents, Mary and Phil Aquila, have contributed in numerous ways to make everything possible.

WANTED
DEAD OR
ALIVE

INTRODUCTION

Richard Aquila

The Pop Culture West

LIKE JESSE JAMES or Billy the Kid, the mythic West has long been wanted dead or alive by the American public. For over two centuries the West has been an extremely popular and profitable subject of popular culture. It has been marketed through numerous books, songs, illustrations, movies, television shows, and other mass-produced products.[1] Although western images in popular culture have varied greatly, one thing has remained constant. Whether fact or fiction, story or place, the "pop culture West" has struck a responsive chord in audiences of every generation.

The diverse images of the West found in popular culture reflect the ambiguity of American attitudes toward the West itself. The American West has long represented different things to different people. For some it was an actual location; for others it was a concept or hope. George Catlin, who journeyed to the West in the 1830s to paint American Indians' portraits, tried to come to terms with the real and mythical aspects of the American West. Catlin observed, "Few people even know the true definition of the term 'West'; and where is its location?—phantom-like it flies before us as we travel."[2]

Later scholars have come no closer in their attempts to locate the West. In 1893 Frederick Jackson Turner used the terms *West* and *frontier* interchangeably to describe a process of westward movement. More recent historians, calling for a "new western history," maintain that the West is a specific place, a region, not a process.[3]

A 1992 survey of 480 historians, writers, editors, and publishers tried to provide some specific answers to the "process versus place"

question. Three basic questions were asked: (1) what are the boundaries of "the West"; (2) where do you have to go to get to the West; and
(3) what characteristics set the West apart from other regions? Most re-
spondents defined the West in geographic terms, although they could
not agree on its location. About one out of every six, however, said
that the West is "a state of mind," a "myth," an "idea," or a "mental
construct."⁴

Most likely, people will never agree on one definition. Literary
scholars Frank Bergon and Zeese Papanikolas explain, "More than
other American regions, the West eludes definition because it is as
much dream as a fact, and its locale was never geographical. Before it
was a place, it was a conception."⁵

The West evokes numerous images in the American mind. Foremost
is the image of the mythic West as a Garden of Eden. There are several variations of this theme. Sometimes the West is described as a land of
abundance and the source of economic, political, and social content-
ment. Other times the West appears as a land of opportunity, where
one can achieve happiness, spiritual rejuvenation, equality, universal
brotherhood, and social, religious, and individual freedom while living
in a climate so healthy and vibrant as to dispel all doubts that the West
must truly be "God's country." These images of the West as a land of
milk and honey contributed to the American Dream of success and the
good life. Stressing individualism and self-reliance, they gave Americans hope for a better future. During hard times Americans looked to
the West as an avenue of escape. They might never actually break free
from the chains of economic or political oppression, but the western
Garden of Eden gave them hope that the future might be better. The
mythic West made all Americans the masters of their own destinies.⁶

Americans also thought of the mythic West as a faraway, romantic,
and exotic land. It was a place of adventure and thrills, where one had
to face natural dangers from the rocky terrain, wide-open spaces, and
ferocious beasts, as well as human threats from Indians and desperadoes. It was a land of heroes and romance, a place where legendary
good guys like Buffalo Bill, Kit Carson, and Wild Bill Hickok rode
across the Big Sky country to thwart the evil designs of villains before
riding off into the sunset. The western story became an exciting morality play, teaching Americans how to succeed through rugged individualism and aggressive behavior.⁷

At the same time there has always been a dark side to the mythic
West. Although the West offered the potential for immeasurable success, it also held the possibility of abysmal failure through dashed
hopes, broken dreams, financial ruin, or even tragic death at the hands

of brutal bad guys or unrelenting forces of nature. Well-known tales about Custer's Last Stand, Billy the Kid, the James gang, and the Donner party lurked in the shadows as reminders of the nether side of the mythic West. This West of the imagination reflected the tensions within American culture between civilization and wilderness, the past and progress, realism and nostalgia, and ultimately, between good and evil.[8]

The Birth and Growth of the Pop Culture West

The American West in all its shapes and varieties proved to be an ideal subject for popular culture. The roots of the pop culture West can be found in pre-nineteenth-century folklore and popular writing, including almanacs, magazines, broadsides, histories, diaries, journals, sermons, and pamphlets. Many folktales, reflecting the colonists' fears and prejudices, focused on the strange new land, its animals and its natural wonders. They told of giant wild horses that slept leaning on tall trees, rattlesnakes that bit chunks out of axes, snakes that could hypnotize victims, "love flowers" with phallic appearances, and a natural environment that could be both divine and satanic. Other folklore dealt with Indians, usually describing them as barbaric, semihuman heathens who were drunkards, buffoons, sorcerers, or treacherous, bloodthirsty warriors.[9]

Similar tales could be found in colonial writing. Early histories such as John Smith's *Description of New England* (1616), William Bradford's *Of Plymouth Plantation* (1650), or William Byrd's *History of the Dividing Line* (1728) offered fascinating descriptions and analyses of the wonders of the new land. Almanacs and broadsides (verses that were printed on sheets of paper and sold by street peddlers) also kept readers informed about life in early frontier settlements.[10]

Colonial writing paid close attention to the native inhabitants of the New World. Some histories, reflecting the primitivist tradition of sixteenth- and seventeenth-century Europe, depicted Indians as noble savages. In 1584 Arthur Barlowe described the native inhabitants of North Carolina as "gentle, loving, and faithful." Similar images of Indians could be found in André Thevet's *Cosmographic* (1575), as well as in the engravings in Theodore de Bry's edition of Thomas Hariot's *Briefe and True Report of the New Foundland of Virginia* (1590). These images, according to historian Robert Berkhofer, became "standard illustrations for texts about Native Americans for two centuries." For example, in 1766 Robert Rogers, who gained fame as the leader of Rogers's Rangers during the French and Indian War, published the play *Ponteach; or the Savages of America,* which treated Pontiac and his followers as noble savages duped by scheming whites. During the Enlightenment French philosophes and other writers used the image of the noble savage to critique society and culture.[11]

Not all writing from this time treated Indians so kindly. Richard Johnson's *Nova Britannia* (1609) claimed that Virginia was "inhabited with wild and savage people," whereas Alexander Whitaker's *Good News from Virginia* (1613) maintained that Indians worshiped the devil. Increase Mather's *Illustrious Providences* (1684) recorded divine providences such as a red snow that preceded an Indian attack, a small-pox epidemic sent by God to destroy Indians, and a partial eclipse that stopped a militia attack during King Philip's War. William Hubbard's *Narrative of the Troubles with the Indians* (1677) and Thomas Prince's *History of King Philip's War* (1716) gave eager readers accounts of Indian warfare on the early frontier that were part history, part diary, part sermon, and part adventure novel.[12]

Captivity narratives were especially popular. The *Narrative of the Captivity and Restoration of Mrs. Mary Rowlandson* (1682) may have been the first best-seller in American literary history. Written in the first person, it told the frightening tale of a bloody Indian attack on the early New England frontier. Mary Rowlandson's compelling account described in gory detail what it was like to be captured by Indians. A unique blend of fact, fiction, sensationalism, and religion, the book went through thirty-one editions, spawning approximately five hundred similar accounts, such as John Williams's *The Redeemed Captive* (1707). Along with teaching that Christian devotion was the key to New World survival, these frontier morality plays helped to establish a formula for popular literature that stressed Indian warfare, white captivity, and eventual redemption.[13]

By the late eighteenth and early nineteenth centuries stories about Indians and the frontier were well-established in American popular culture. Citizens of the new republic, eager to learn about their heritage and national identity, found clues in a variety of places. Popular histories such as Francis Parkman's *Conspiracy of Pontiac* (1851) and *Jesuits in North America* (1867) detailed the ferocity of Indian-white warfare on the early frontier. Lewis Henry Morgan's *League of the Ho-dee-no-sau-nee, or Iroquois* (1851), Henry Schoolcraft's *Algic Researches* (1839), and the popular *McGuffey's Reader* presented romanticized accounts of American Indian history and culture.[14]

Indians and the frontier also proved to be popular subjects for stage plays and melodramas. Although some plays from this time treated Indians as villains, most portrayed Native Americans as benign, if not benevolent, children of nature. For example, Ann Julia Kemble Hattan found great success in 1794 with *Tammany, a Serious Opera,* which depicted Indians as noble savages. Joseph Croswell had similar success with *A New World Planted* (1802), a play about a Pilgrim who had fallen in love with an Indian princess. Wanting to marry her but troubled by miscegenation, he rationalizes, "I know she's browner than European dames, But whiter far, than other natives are." Perhaps the most popular frontier/Indian play was John Augustus Stone's *Metamora, Or the Last of the Wampanoags* (1829). The lead character, Metamora (King Philip), was the ideal noble savage: he had statuesque good looks and was the perfect husband and father, a wise chief, a principled warrior, and a man of integrity who went to war only after being tricked by unscrupulous whites.[15]

Along with melodramas numerous magazine stories, popular poems, and historical fiction of the late eighteenth and early nineteenth centuries focused on Indians and the frontier. Noble savages can be found in Philip Freneau's poems of the 1780s, which dealt with the tragedy of vanishing Indian tribes, or Henry Wadsworth Longfellow's epic romantic poem *Hiawatha* (1855). Ignoble savages commonly appeared as villains in popular historical fiction, such as Ann Eliza Bleecker's *History of Maria Kittle* (1793) or Samuel Drake's *Indian Captivities; or Life in the Wigwam* (1839). According to Robert Berkhofer, "the blood-and-gore sensationalism" of these fictional captivity narratives "led directly to the dime novels and the later cowboy and Indian movies of popular culture."[16]

A prototype for the western hero emerged shortly after the founding of the United States. John Filson helped to establish the character with *The Discovery, Settlement and Present State of Kentucke* (1784), which related the story of Daniel Boone, intrepid explorer, frontiersman, and Indian fighter.

James Fenimore Cooper expanded the frontier-hero construct. Between 1826 and 1841 the New York native wrote five historical novels, known collectively as the Leatherstocking Tales: *The Last of the Mohicans* (1826), *The Pathfinder* (1840), *The Deerslayer* (1841), *The Pioneers* (1823), and *The Prairie* (1827). Not only did the Leatherstocking Tales fully develop Cooper's vision of the frontier hero and setting, but they helped to establish Natty Bumppo as the quintessential frontiersman, a romanticized hero of the wilderness whose action-packed exploits involved Indians, villains, and daring rescues. Professor Roy Harvey Pearce explained Leatherstocking's appeal: "At the center of the Tales is neither a savage nor a civilized man, but rather Natty Bumppo, Leatherstocking, somewhere between savagism and civilization, the 'beau ideal' of the frontiersman, with all the goodness and greatness that the pioneer could have in the circumstances of pioneering. Yet even he, no Indian, is steadily pushed westward until he dies on the prairies; and the progress which makes for his death is known ultimately to be good."[18]

The frontier hero was soon appearing in a variety of pop culture disguises. He gained tremendous popularity as Davy Crockett, the real-life hero immortalized through folktales and numerous editions of *The Davy Crockett Almanac.* He provided inspiration for James Kirke Paulding's *Lion of the West,* a popular play of the 1830s that featured a Crockett-like character named Nimrod Wildfire, described as "the yellow flower of the forest" and "a human cataract for Kentucky." In addition, he became the protagonist of Robert Montgomery Bird's tale of frontier vengeance, *Nick of the Woods* (1837).[19]

By the 1800s all the ingredients for the making of the pop culture West were in place. Building on earlier traditions, popular forms of expression continued to deal with frontier heroes, settings, and American Indians. This time, however, the focus was on the lands west of the Mississippi.

Nineteenth-century folklore about the West followed the lead of earlier frontier tales. Many reports—transmitted either orally, through song, or by written speeches, letters, newspapers, and almanacs—described the exotic landscapes or adventures to be found out west. Easterners learned about Indian fights, exciting heroes, and life on the western frontier through folktales, ballads, or published accounts such as *The Personal Narrative of James Ohio Pattie* (1831) or George F. Ruxton's *Life in the Far West* (1849).[20]

Oral tales and newspaper articles made easterners aware of the fertile soil or perfect climates to be found out west. One orator described Oregon as a "pioneers' paradise," adding, "the pigs are running about under the great acorn trees, round and fat, and already cooked, with knives and forks sticking in them so that you can cut off a slice whenever you are hungry." Letters from overland travelers praising the West were reprinted in newspapers or passed hand to hand, adding further credibility to the western myth. Oregon, California, and other western locales were depicted as virtual Gardens of Eden. Historian Ray Allen Billington reported the following about the perfect health to be found in California: "A traveler in Missouri told of one [California] man who, tired of life at the age of 250 years, finally made his will and moved to another spot, requesting only that he be brought back for burial. That was a mistake, for no sooner was he safely in his grave in that health-giving land than 'the energies of life were immediately restored to his inanimate corpse!'"[21]

Popular guidebooks, narratives, and reports contributed to the rise of the pop culture West. Lansford W. Hastings's *Emigrants' Guide to Oregon and California* (1845) described the West in glowing terms, eventually luring the Donner party to its fate. Published reports and journals of western explorers and adventurers such as Lewis and Clark, Stephen Long, John C. Frémont, Jedediah Smith, and Osborne Russell also helped to popularize the West.[22]

By the mid-nineteenth century the American West had found its niche in popular literature. The young historian Francis Parkman found a ready and eager audience for his epic travelogue/history, *The California and Oregon Trail* (1849). Other accomplished writers as diverse as Edgar Allan Poe, Henry David Thoreau, Walt Whitman, Washington Irving, Bret Harte, Richard Henry Dana, and Mark Twain also turned to the West for inspiration.[23]

Even more important to the rise of the pop culture West was the popular writing aimed at the mass market in the mid-to-late 1800s. Penny press newspapers, almanacs, magazines, and journals such as the *National Police Gazette* provided lurid western tales for public consumption. The western-influenced verses of Joaquin Miller, who gave poetry readings dressed in buckskins, brought the mythic West to life. Western novels written by Charles Webber and Emerson Bennett applied Cooper's Leatherstocking formula to the Far West. Most popular of all were the sensational story papers and dime novels patterned after England's "penny dreadfuls." One of the earliest was Charles Averill's *Kit Carson, Prince of the Gold Hunters* (1849), which helped to establish Carson's reputation as an Indian fighter and western hero extraordinaire. Dime novels became extremely popular during and after the Civil War. These inexpensive, disposable volumes capitalized on the public's insatiable appetite for sensational, action-packed stories about the American West. Cranked out by the hundreds by experienced hack writers such as Ned Buntline or Prentiss Ingraham, and mass produced by publishers such as Beadle and Adams, these books focused on either historical figures such as Buffalo Bill and Kit Carson or fictional characters such as Deadwood Dick or Seth Jones. As historian Richard W. Etulain has pointed out, the heroes of early Western dime novels were based on Cooper's Leatherstocking but eventually became "more adventurous and less reflective."[24]

Public interest in the American West was furthered by popular illustrators. F. O. C. Darley gained wide recognition for his sketches illustrating Parkman's *Oregon Trail* and various editions of Cooper's Leatherstocking Tales. Painters such as George Catlin, Karl Bodmer, Albert Bierstadt, Frederic Remington, and Charles Russell reinforced and often shaped public attitudes toward the West through their popular paintings of Indians, cowboys, landscapes, and other images of the mythic West. Currier and Ives prints brought images of the West to millions of Americans. For example, the popular 1866 Currier and Ives lithograph *The Rocky Mountains: Emigrants Crossing the Plains,* based on a painting by Fanny Palmer, could be found hanging in hotels, saloons, and homes across the United States, providing viewers with a glorious look at the imagined grandeur of the Rocky Mountains. Even photographers became popular purveyors of the pop culture West. William Henry Jackson, whom historian Richard White calls the "preeminent nineteenth-century photographer of the American West," attracted a large audience through photographs that depicted the West as a Garden of Eden, a land of opportunity, or a mythic source of learning and inspiration.[25]

The pop culture West expanded its audience through live performances of cowboys, Indians, folksingers, and other western-influenced entertainers. William F. Cody, better known as "Buffalo Bill," developed the most successful live western act. After gaining fame as the hero of numerous dime novels, Cody became the star of a stage play entitled *Scouts of the Plains,* written by Ned Buntline in 1872. In 1883 Cody secured financial backing to produce a traveling show, "Buffalo Bill's Wild West," which at various times featured sharpshooters, cowboys, stagecoach holdups, shoot-outs, battles with Indians, buffalo hunts, and other exciting episodes associated with the mythic West. According to scholar Don B. Wilmeth, the Wild West show "evolved in part from the 'specs' (or spectacular pageants) of the circus, the old traveling menageries, early exhibitions of cowboys skills and Indians dating from the 1820s, and the numerous plays, novels, and cheap popular literature of the nineteenth century." The phenomenal success of Cody's Wild West show gave birth to numerous imitators. Between the 1880s and World War I over one hundred different Wild West shows toured the United States. These shows, which historian Robert V. Hine has called "dime-novel western[s] come to life," contributed greatly to popular images of the American West.[26]

By the turn of the century the American West had established itself as one of pop culture's top draws. For the most part popular culture spotlighted positive images of the American West, providing comforting memories and a clear national identity for nostalgic Americans facing rapid change at century's end. The pop culture West glorified the western landscape and its colorful inhabitants, serving as a psychological safety valve for city dwellers back east. It offered vicarious thrills and escape from economic and social concerns. Its idyllic setting reminded urban and industrial America of its rural past, reinforcing America's belief in the Jeffersonian ideal. Its legendary tales echoed Jacksonian democracy and taught lessons of self-reliance, morality, nationalism, and heroism. And its wild setting and potential for rugged individualism appealed to a popular mood influenced by the rise of literary naturalism.

The dawning of the twentieth century ushered in a "Golden Age" for the pop culture West. The new era began with the publication of Owen Wister's Western novel *The Virginian* (1902), which pulled together all the elements of the pop culture West. The book, which firmly established the Western as a literary genre, featured the nameless, self-reliant western hero/cowboy, as well as the climactic showdown between the good guy and bad guy.[27]

The success of *The Virginian* made the West an obvious subject for early filmmakers. Edwin S. Porter's *The Great Train Robbery* (1903) is generally regarded as the first Western movie. Featuring the first western hero on film, Bronco Billy Anderson, the ten-minute "epic" included holdups, chases, posses, horses, and a climactic shoot-out. The film's tremendous popularity quickly established the Western as a staple of the movie industry, leading to classics such as Cecil B. DeMille's *Squaw Man* (1913) and *The Virginian* (1914), William S. Hart's *Hell's Hinges* (1916), and James Cruze's *The Covered Wagon* (1923).[28]

The Golden Age of the pop culture West lasted until the early 1960s and produced numerous pop culture products, including classic Western novels by Max Brand, Clarence Mulford, Zane Grey, and Louis L'Amour; Western movies with stars such as William S. Hart, Tom Mix, Buck Jones, Randolph Scott, and John Wayne; "singing cowboys" such as Gene Autry and Roy Rogers; and popular television shows such as *Gunsmoke, Have Gun Will Travel, Maverick, Wagon Train*, and *Bonanza*.

As in earlier days some pop culture products of the twentieth century critiqued the mythic West. For example, films such as William Wellman's *Ox-Bow Incident* (1943) and Nicholas Ray's *Johnny Guitar* (1954) questioned western-style justice and morality, whereas John Sturges's *Bad Day at Black Rock* (1955) exposed the racism in the West that contributed to the internment of Japanese-Americans during World War II.

For the most part, however, pop culture products that critiqued the mythic West were the exception rather than the rule. Overall the years between 1900 and the early 1960s witnessed the triumph of positive images of the mythic West in Western pulps, pop songs, novels, B Westerns, feature films, television shows, and other forms of popular culture. The mythic West provided the perfect symbol for Americans to rally around when confronted by progressive reforms, World War I, the Great Depression, World War II, and the cold war. The myth not only provided temporary escape from life's problems, but it taught Americans how to cope with reality. The mythic West demonstrated that Americans could succeed if they remained true to the spirit of the Old West. Like mythic westerners, Americans had to retain their self-reliance, independence, and sense of mission and adhere to the morality inherent in the code of the West. At the same time the myth taught that all problems could be solved through cooperation, action, and dedication to the nation's quest for truth, justice, and the American Way. These lessons provided the ideal unifying myth in an era when national crises demanded consensus.

The mythic West remained a staple of popular culture until the mid-1960s. By then Americans were becoming increasingly divided over civil rights, the Vietnam War, and other social and political issues. At that point the pop culture West began offering its audiences a revisionist approach to the mythic West. A new duality of western images emerged in popular culture, in keeping with the revisionist times. Alongside the traditional images were alternative images that either challenged the mythic West or used traditional western images in new ways to critique American life and thought. For example, traditional western heroes could still be found in the novels of Louis L'Amour, in the popular country music of Marty Robbins, on television programs such as *Bonanza*, or in movies such as John Wayne's *True Grit* (1969). But less traditional heroes became equally popular through movies such as Sergio Leone's *A Fistful of Dollars* (1967), novels such as Thomas Berger's *Little Big Man*, and pop songs such as the Eagles' "Desperado" (1973).

The new duality of western images in popular culture reflected both continuity and change, as well as the growing polarization of American society. Familiar western images demonstrated that the mythic West with its traditional values was still very much alive in contemporary America. At the same time, however, the rise of nontraditional images of the West reflected newer attitudes and the end of consensus behavior. After the mid-1960s the pop culture West provided alternative images of a more pluralistic American society and culture; it explored issues of race, ethnicity, gender, and class; and it revealed that oppression and exploitation were common elements of the western experience.

The Significance of the Pop Culture West

The chapters in this volume demonstrate that the pop culture West—like the American West itself—has played an important role in American life and thought. The pop culture West enables us to explore the development and meaning of the mythic West, which has been one of America's most enduring national myths. This myth reveals how Americans view themselves. It reflects the American experience not so much as it really was but as how Americans would like it to be. It speaks directly to American ideals, values, needs, and goals. It combines other American beliefs involving national purpose, individual freedom, success, the superiority of common people, and the quest for perfection. It is nothing less than the American Dream set against the quintessential American backdrop.

The pop culture West provides evidence to study continuity and change in the western myth, demonstrating that the myth is still very much alive in modern America, albeit in altered form. Many experts have focused on the unique qualities of America's mythic West, stressing its particular setting, identifiable story, and unmistakable characteristics. Others have established a link between American and European cultures by demonstrating the similarities between the western myth and the epics of Homer or the legends of King Arthur and his knights, popularized by Sir Walter Scott and other writers of historical fiction.[29] Western writer Shirl Henke recently commented on the staying power of the western myth: "The West is a dream, the freedom to begin again. As such it is the stuff of primal myth and will never be defined absolutely. I do not believe it accidental that Star Trek has become a classic. Its opening line says it all: 'Space, the final Frontier.'"[30]

America's ever-changing face is mirrored in the birth and growth of the pop culture West. The emergence of the pop culture West in the eighteenth and nineteenth centuries reflected industrialization, urbanization, immigration, technology, the rise of mass culture, and other forces that gave birth to modern America. Ironically, at the very moment when those forces were establishing the pop culture West in the American mind, they were bringing to a close the real frontier West. But if the West's frontier phase was over, the pop culture West continued to mirror historical trends of the twentieth century. Its changing images revealed corresponding shifts and tensions in American politics, society, and culture and reflected important issues and events.

The pop culture West not only reflected the times, but it also helped shape them. Ray Allen Billington explains: "image and legend have played a role in shaping human behavior no less influential than facts and events: what a people thought took place, or believed to exist, was only slightly less important to them than what did happen, or did exist."[31] Many Americans learned lessons about life from the pop culture West. They adopted its notions of justice, rugged individualism, and opportunity, and they acted accordingly. In effect the pop culture West was etched into Americans' collective memory, influencing who they were, how they thought, and how they behaved.

The pop culture West also served as a mirror and a matrix for American attitudes toward gender, race, ethnicity, and class. Prior to the 1960s popular culture usually portrayed the West as a wild, untamed land ready to be conquered by European Americans. Quite often its story was told in optimistic, patriarchal terms similar to those found in national epics involving Manifest Destiny, rugged individualism, or progressivism. The pop culture West frequently served as a metaphor for the superiority of white, Anglo-Saxon, Protestant culture, idealizing middle-class Anglo males at the expense of women, new immigrants, Hispanics, Indians, and other people of color. After 1960 the pop culture West changed with the times. As movements for civil rights and women's rights raised public awareness of minorities and women, and political and social protests questioned the common wisdom of the day, the pop culture West became more responsive to people and topics traditionally ignored by the mythic West.

At the same time, the pop culture West was never monolithic. The malleability of the mythic West guaranteed its continued success in popular culture, enabling several generations of audiences to reshape the myth to meet specific needs or fit the changing times. The pop culture West always provided audiences with the opportunity to read the mythic West in a variety of ways, depending on the medium, the text, or individual needs and goals.[32] It often became a cultural battleground between oppositional forces representing a variety of economic, social, and political interests. Through it all the pop culture West offered hope to every "good guy," regardless of gender, race, ethnicity, class, or creed. Moreover, it gave everyone—ordinary people, social bandits, and outsiders alike—the chance at life, liberty, and the pursuit of happiness.

Over the years the pop culture West has served several important functions. It has provided entertainment and vicarious thrills for countless numbers of people, making it one of popular culture's most profitable products. If it has offered some audience members escape, it has provided others with solutions to their problems. The pop culture West has also provided a public forum wherein Americans could reaffirm or reconsider shared beliefs. At times it has served as a morality play, helping several generations of Americans deal with social change or various political and economic crises. On other occasions it has reminded Americans about their own national identity, forcing them to consider ideas related to rugged individualism, Turner's frontier thesis, Social Darwinism, and the notion of progress.

The evolution of the pop culture West sometimes followed the same path as the writing of western/frontier history in the twentieth century; at other times it anticipated historiographical change. The early pop culture West, like early western history, was a product of the nineteenth and early twentieth centuries. As such, it generally reflected hegemonic attitudes that often neglected complex historical forces, as well as the important roles women and minorities played in western history. By the mid-1960s, however, a new pop culture West had emerged, one more in keeping with the era's rapid social and political change. This new pop culture West, while not ignoring older western themes, probed newer social, economic, and political topics. It offered its audiences a critique of the mythic West that reinterpreted the roles played by women, minorities, and the working classes, and it investigated the exploitation of the West's native peoples and resources. Significantly this "new pop culture West" actually predated—by at least two decades—the rise of the "new western history."

The pop culture West offers glimpses of America's self-identity, providing insights into American values, beliefs, and actions. It shows where Americans have been, where they are, and perhaps, where they are headed. Each generation has viewed the West differently, sometimes swinging wildly between romanticism and reality, or hope and despair. Through it all, however, the pop culture West has survived, providing a unifying symbol for Americans divided by race, ethnicity, gender, class, religion, or region. Although the frontier may be closed and the geographical West may be settled, the mythic West continues to exist in the thoughts, dreams, and popular culture of the American people.

Notes

1. There have been numerous studies of various genres of the pop culture West. Studies of Western movies include Jenni Calder, *There Must Be a Lone Ranger: The American West in Film and in Reality* (New York, 1975); George N. Fenin and William K. Everson, *The Western from Silents to the Seventies* (New York, 1973); Jon Tuska, *The Filming of the West* (New York, 1976); and

John H. Lenihan, *Showdown: Confronting Modern America in the Western Film* (Urbana, Ill., 1980). For books on Western literature see Richard Etulain and Michael T. Marsden, *The Popular Western: Essays toward a Definition* (Bowling Green, Ohio, 1974); John Milton, *The Novel of the American West* (Lincoln, Nebr., 1980); and Henry Nash Smith, *Virgin Land: The American West as Symbol and Myth* (Cambridge, Mass., 1950). For books on television Westerns see Ralph Brauer, *The Horse, the Gun, and the Piece of Property: Changing Images of the television Western* (Bowling Green, Ohio, 1975); and J. Fred MacDonald, *Who Shot the Sheriff? The Rise and Fall of the Television Western* (New York, 1987).

2. Frank Bergon and Zeese Papanikolas, eds., *Looking Far West: The Search for the American West in History, Myth, and Literature* (New York, 1978), 59.

3. Frederick Jackson Turner, "The Significance of the Frontier in American History," *American Historical Association Annual Report for the Year 1893* (Washington, 1894), 199–227; For information about the "new western history" see Patricia Nelson Limerick, *The Legacy of Conquest: The Unbroken Past of the American West* (New York, 1987); Patricia Nelson Limerick, Clyde A. Milner II, and Charles E. Rankin, eds., *Trails: Toward a New Western History* (Lawrence, Kans., 1991); and William Cronon, George Miles, and Jay Gitlin, eds., *Under an Open Sky: Rethinking America's Western Past* (New York, 1992).

4. Walter Nugent, "Where Is the American West? Report on a Survey," *Montana: The Magazine of Western History* 42, no. 3 (Summer 1992): 2–23.

5. Bergon and Papanikolas, *Looking Far West*, 2.

6. For discussions of this theme see Smith, *Virgin Land*, 17, 32, 45, 52, 81, 123, 124, 136, 142, 169, 247; Ray Allen Billington, *The Far Western Frontier, 1830–1860* (New York, 1962), 85–88; Clark Spence, ed. *The American West: A Source Book* (New York, 1966), 420–21, 444; Bergon and Papanikolas, *Looking Far West*, 1–14, 59–139, 191–237, 239–342; and Ray Allen Billington, ed., *The Frontier Thesis* (New York, 1966), 41–62.

7. Bergon and Papanikolas, *Looking Far West*, 240–44, 147–49, 166, 170, 171, 190; Spence, *American West*, 420; Charles W. Harris and Buck Rainey, eds., *The Cowboy: Six Shooters, Songs, and Sex* (Norman, Okla., 1976), 157; Robert V. Hine, *The American West: An Interpretive History* (Boston, 1973), 268–82, 130–32.

8. Clyde A. Milner II, *Major Problems in the History of the American West* (Lexington, Mass., 1989), chaps. 9 and 11; for specific examples of western violence and defeat, see B. A. Botkin, *A Treasury of Western Folklore* (New York, 1980), 110, 337, 592, 584; Botkin, *A Treasury of American Folklore* (New York, 1948), 49–68, 177, 178, 179, 196.

9. Richard M. Dorson, *American Folklore* (Chicago, 1977), chap. 1.

10. Dorson, *American Folklore*, 12, 14, 17; Russel Nye, *The Unembarrassed Muse: The Popular Arts in America* (New York, 1970), chap. 1.

11. Robert F. Berkhofer Jr., *The White Man's Indian: Images of the American Indian from Columbus to the Present* (New York, 1978), 72–73; Roy

Harvey Pearce, *Savagism and Civilization: A Study of the Indian and the American Mind* (Los Angeles, 1988), 170; Berkhofer, *White Man's Indian,* 76.

12. Pearce, *Savagism and Civilization,* 12, 13; Nye, *Unembarrassed Muse,* 13–15.

13. Robert K. Dodge, "Almanacs," in *Concise Histories of American Popular Culture,* ed. M. Thomas Inge (Westport, Conn., 1982), 14; Suzanne Ellery Greene, "Best Sellers," in *Concise Histories,* ed. Inge, 49.

14. Pearce, *Savagism and Civilization,* 163–68, 130–34; Berkhofer, *White Man's Indian,* 88, 90.

15. David Grimsted, *Melodrama Unveiled: American Theater and Culture* (Los Angeles, 1968), 194, 215–17; Pearce, *Savagism and Civilization,* 172.

16. Berkhofer, *White Man's Indian,* 88; Janice Radway, "Verse and Popular Poetry," in *Concise Histories,* ed. Inge, 417; Pearce, *Savagism and Civilization,* 191–94, 198; Berkhofer, *White Man's Indian,* 85.

17. Richard W. Etulain, "Westerns," in *Concise Histories,* ed. Inge, 425.

18. Pearce, *Savagism and Civilization,* 201–2.

19. Dodge, "Almanacs," 14; Grimsted, *Melodrama Unveiled,* 190; Pearce, *Savagism and Civilization,* 229.

20. Billington, *Far Western Frontier,* 85–88; Dodge, "Almanacs," 14; Bergon and Papanikolas, *Looking Far West,* 175–77, 172, 324, 158–62, 417.

21. Billington, *Far Western Frontier,* 85–88; The pioneers' paradise quotation comes from Edward H. Lenox, *Overland to Oregon in the Tracks of Lewis and Clarke. History of the First Migration to Oregon in 1843* (Oakland, Calif., 1904), 13; quoted in Billington, *Far Western Frontier,* 85. The story about the Californian who could not die comes from Edwin Bryant, *What I Saw in California* (New York, 1848), 16–17; quoted in Billington, *Far Western Frontier,* 88.

22. Bergon and Papanikolas, *Looking Far West,* 163, 170.

23. Ibid., 44, 88, 116, 118, 139, 123, 204, 261, 262, 265.

24. Bill Blackbeard, "Pulps," in *Concise Histories,* ed. Inge, 291; Etulain, "Westerns," 426, 425; Smith, *Virgin Land,* 54; Richard White, *It's Your Misfortune and None of My Own: A History of the American West* (Norman, Okla., 1991), 617, 620.

25. James J. Best, "Illustration," in *Concise Histories,* ed. Inge, 172–73; Hine, *American West,* 302, 303, 310, 312, 314, 315; Richard White, *It's Your Misfortune,* 627.

26. Hine, *American West,* 293–94; Don B. Wilmeth, "Circus and Outdoor Entertainment," in *Concise Histories,* ed. Inge, 67–68.

27. Hine, *American West,* 286–88; Greene, "Best Sellers," 52.

28. For information about *The Great Train Robbery* see Gerald Mast, *A Short History of the Movies* (Indianapolis, 1981), 32–34; an excellent chronology of Western films can be found in Jack Nachbar, ed., *Focus on the Western* (Englewood Cliffs, N.J., 1974), 129–37.

29. Richard W. Etulain, "Cultural Origins of the Western," in *Focus on the Western,* ed. Nachbar, 19.

30. Shirl Henke, quoted in Nugent, "Where Is the American West?" 23.

31. Ray Allen Billington, "The Plains and Deserts through European Eyes," *Western Historical Quarterly* 10 (October 1979): 467, 486.

32. Popular culture often acts as a cultural battleground. Several recent studies demonstrate how various audiences have interpreted the same pop culture products in different ways to satisfy individual needs or specific agendas. For examples, see John Fiske, *Understanding Popular Culture* (Boston, 1989); Randy Roberts and Steven Mintz, eds., *Hollywood's America: United States History through Its Films* (St. James, N.Y., 1993); and Dick Hebdige, *Subculture: The Meaning of Style* (London, 1979).

Suggestions for Further Reading

The Pop Culture West

For books about specific areas of the pop culture West, see the suggested reading list at the end of each section in this book.

Athearn, Robert. *The Mythic West in Twentieth-Century America.* Lawrence, Kans., 1986.

Billington, Ray Allen, and Martin Ridge. *Westward Expansion: A History of the American Frontier,* 5th ed. New York, 1982.

Cronon, William, George Miles, and Jay Gitlin, eds. *Under an Open Sky: Rethinking America's Western Past.* New York, 1992.

Davis, Robert Murray. *Playing Cowboys: Low Culture and High Art in the Western.* Norman, Okla., 1992.

Goetzmann, William H., and William N. Goetzmann. *The West of the Imagination.* New York, 1986.

Limerick, Patricia Nelson. *The Legacy of Conquest: The Unbroken Past of the American West.* New York, 1987.

Limerick, Patricia Nelson, Clyde A. Milner, and Charles E. Rankin, eds. *Trails: Toward a New Western History.* Lawrence, Kans., 1991.

Milner, Clyde A., Carol O'Connor, and Martha A. Sandweiss, eds. *The Oxford History of the American West.* New York, 1994.

Nash, Gerald D. *Creating the West: Historical Interpretations.* Albuquerque, N.M., 1991.

O'Neill, Paul. *The End and the Myth.* Alexandria, Va., 1979.

Prassel, Frank Richard. *The Great American Outlaw.* Norman, Okla., 1993.

Rosenberg, Bruce A. *The Code of the West.* Bloomington, Ind., 1982.

Savage, William W., Jr. *The Cowboy Hero: His Image in American History and Culture.* Norman, Okla., 1979.

Slatta, Richard W. *Cowboys of the Americas.* New Haven, Conn., 1990.

Slotkin, Richard. *Regeneration through Violence: The Mythology of the American Frontier, 1600–1860.* Middletown, Conn., 1973.

———. *The Fatal Environment: The Myth of the Frontier in the Age of Industrialization, 1800–1890.* Middletown, Connecticut, 1986.

———. *Gunfighter Nation: The Myth of the Frontier in Twentieth Century America.* New York, 1992.

Turner, Frederick Jackson. "The Significance of the Frontier in American History." *American Historical Association Annual Report for the Year 1893.* Washington D.C., 1894. 199–227.

White, Richard. *It's Your Misfortune and None of My Own: A New History of the American West.* Norman, Okla., 1991.

PART ONE

Fiction

ONE

CHRISTINE BOLD

Malaeska's Revenge; or, The Dime Novel Tradition in Popular Fiction

READ COLLECTIVELY DIME novels and their descendants tell the story of the frontier West's commodification in popular literature. This process was mediated by changing historical circumstances and individual authorial contributions, from the first intersection of mass literature and westward movement in the mid-nineteenth century to the "nostalgic remorse" for the frontier West of late twentieth-century capitalist culture.[1] Early and late, however, the commercial frameworks within which cheap Westerns were produced left their imprint on this fiction's format, formulaic action, narrative voice, and reception.

The mass production of American cheap fiction took off in the 1830s as part of the explosion in America's market economy.[2] The commodification of literature was facilitated by a huge increase in urban population, the spread of literacy, and rapid advances in transportation, industrialization, and print technology. The newly invented rotary press and the fanning out of a railroad network made possible, for the first time, fast, voluminous production of low-priced literature and transcontinental distribution to a mass audience. The new technology also dictated the appropriate form of this reading material. Story papers' large folio sheets with serials set in cramped columns of diminutive typeface, few illustrations, and a very low price—three to six cents per issue—were the result of a narrow calculation about how to attract and hold the largest audience as cheaply as possible. The meshing of cheap literature with a range of commercial interests and pressures was established.

With the beginning of the dime novel, these developments bore down on—and were refined in—Western fiction, the dominant genre of adventure story in the dime format.[3] Irwin and Erastus Beadle and Robert Adams began dime novels in 1860 when they produced uniformly packaged series of complete, predominantly American novels in compact pamphlets priced at five or ten cents. The Beadles' major innovation was gearing their marketing strategies to the period's trends: the portable format suited escalating rail travel; the distinctive cover designs, uniform for each series and "library," and the increasingly lurid illustrations made effective displays at the recently developed newsstands; and the very low price for stories of 35,000 and 70,000 words ("A DOLLAR BOOK FOR A DIME!!" the publicity blared) was affordable even for the poorer industrial workers and immigrants. These mass publishers attempted to regulate not only production, advertising, and distribution but writing as well. Beadle and Adams regimented authors' production mainly in terms of quantity, speed, length, and fixed payment rates, supplying only general instructions on content. The results were massively successful; before they folded in 1898 Beadle and Adams published 3,158 separate titles and sold copies in the millions. By 1879 W. H. Bishop could declare that dime novel literature was "the greatest literary movement, in bulk, of the age, and worthy of very serious consideration for its character." He concluded, "the phenomenon of its existence cannot be overlooked."[4]

A host of imitators sprang up. The most successful were Frank Tousey, George Munro, Norman Munro, and Street and Smith (the last transferring from the story paper to the dime novel field late, in 1889, but immediately becoming the Beadles' main rival and surviving as pulp magazine and comic book publishers until 1950). These later publishers extended the network of commercial pressures bearing down on cheap fiction by introducing advertising and cutting prices to produce competitive "nickel novels"; furthermore, by narrowing the output to juvenile fiction and by supervising their writers much more closely, they systematized the production line more rigorously than Beadle and Adams had. Dime publishers came to commodify authors, denying them decision-making powers: by 1896 Ormond Smith dictated character, plots, and scenes to the author who was ostensibly "inventing" Frank Merriwell.[5] Writers in dime and nickel stables lost their individualized signatures, too. Publishers and editors shunted authors around from one house pseudonym to another; at Street and Smith multiauthored series under one trademark name came to be the rule.

This emphasis on standardization left direct and indirect textual imprints on dime novel Westerns. The conservatism of the Western's fictional formula can be explained in a number of ways: by the political conservatism of frontier society that is represented—to however mediated a degree—in these adventure stories, by the slowness with which large-scale popular tastes change, or by the imitative tendencies of individual authors. Nonetheless, publishing calculations clearly encouraged caution and the reproduction of proven successes. Typical of the mass publishers' shrewd commercial strategies is Erastus Beadle's choice of the first dime novel: *Malaeska: The Indian Wife of the White Hunter,* by Ann S. Stephens, which was reprinted from its serialization in the *The Ladies' Companion* of 1839 to appear as number 1 of Beadle's Dime Novels in June 1860. Not only did Erastus Beadle begin with a proven bestseller, but he grafted an example of sentimental or women's fiction—the most popular genre of the mid-nineteenth century—onto a new format and new publicity that exploited public interest in the westward movement. *Malaeska* is a decidedly woman-centered frontier narrative. Set in the early wilderness of the Hudson Valley, the story traces the fate of a Native American woman who is left widowed by the death of her white soldier husband, robbed of their son by her aristocratic in-laws in New York City, forced to witness his suicide when his Native American heritage is revealed to him years later, and finally killed by her own grief on her boy's grave. That this is a distinctively female, as well as Native American, experience is suggested by the narrator's comment on Malaeska's self-sacrifice: "It was her woman's destiny, not the more certain because of her savage origin. Civilization does not always reverse this mournful picture of womanly self-abnegation."[6]

Although *Malaeska* sold at least a half-million copies in its dime format, its plot did not become the dominant formula for Western dime novels. Later in 1860 Edward S. Ellis, a young schoolmaster, brought to the Beadles a wilderness adventure with clear sales potential. *Seth Jones; or, The Captives of the Frontier* tells the frontier story from a perspective different from *Malaeska*'s, focusing on a white hunter who saves various white captives from the Mohawks in a series of melodramatic adventures in the wilderness of western New York State. Orville J. Victor, Beadle's editor, called *Seth Jones* "the perfect Dime Novel."[7] Publishing it as number 8 of Beadle's Dime Novels, the firm puffed it with a massive advertising campaign in which newspaper advertisements, billboards, and handbills carried the tantalizing question "Who is Seth Jones?" followed by lithographs of a coonskin-capped hunter declaring, "I am Seth Jones." The public response was even more massive than that to *Malaeska,* and the story of male heroism became entrenched as the dominant dime novel formula.

This paradigm shift, from a centrally female to emphatically male Western, carries cultural and political resonances. In direct contrast to *Malaeska, Seth Jones* and its imitators articulated the West in the optimistic, patriarchal terms of Manifest Destiny then in the ascendancy in public rhetoric. Whereas *Malaeska* to a degree exposed the human cost of the western movement, the male-centered dime novel drew on the same fund of triumphant images and nationalistic narratives as did newspapers and politicians. At the same time the Beadles' preference for the Ellis version of frontier adventure can be read as one beachhead in the attack on women's sentimental, religious culture. Jane Tompkins has tracked brilliantly how men seized the public imagination in the post–Civil War Western and into the twentieth century. It may be that what Tompkins names "the deauthorization of women" profited from an early, explicitly commercial boost.[8]

Although *Seth Jones* was a new story, it strongly resembled an earlier series of bestsellers—James Fenimore Cooper's Leatherstocking Tales (1823–41)—in terms of plot, setting, character types, and the representation of social roles.[9] Like Cooper, Ellis chose an attack by "savage" Native Americans on a family of white settlers as the framework for his plot and an avuncular, Indian-slaying hunter as their rescuer. If Ellis's disposition of gender and race is recognizably conventional, his configuration of class is modified. Whereas Cooper's backwoodsman, Natty Bumppo, is unfit for the romantic role because he lacks social standing, Seth Jones casts off his hunter's disguise at the end of the tale to reveal himself as a young, aristocratic easterner suited to marry the white heroine whom he has saved from captivity. Both authors play out European social hierarchies in the American wilderness, but Ellis's frontier hero transcends class stratifications in a way that Cooper's does not. This sunny, optimistic ending erases the tension between East and West evident in Cooper: a shift of register with particular symbolic power in a time of national strife. Ellis's adaptation of Cooper also serves patriotic nationalism by simplifying the ethics of white settlement: demonizing the Native Americans justifies white conquest, and the elision of backwoodsman and aristocrat harmonizes competing economic interests. (By 1868 an obvious imitation of *Seth Jones* had made this message explicit. Percy St. John characterizes white frontier settlers thus: "Never weary, never conquered, they advanced still onward toward the setting sun, laying first the foundations of home and then of empire.")[10]

This version of the frontier adventure, appropriating the wilderness for the glorification of white men rescuing white women and killing

Native Americans, held sway thereafter in the Beadle production line and its imitators. Over time a combination of publishers, editors, and authors adapted the scenes, character types, and political rhetoric in response to changing historical circumstances, but the familiar narrative line of the formula survived. This strategy of innovation contained within repetition is perceptible in the development of heroic types in dime and nickel Westerns. The imperative to produce a hero transcending class and region remained paramount, but as the figure was inserted into different cultural environments, his specific lineaments changed: the hunter gave way to the scout, the cowboy, the outlaw, the frontier detective, and the freelance law-enforcer. In different accents these heroic types voiced their commitment to a certain brand of democracy and nationalism.

Buffalo Bill extended the Western hero's range, both fictively and commercially. Bill Cody was working as a buffalo hunter and scout for the Western army when he was discovered in 1869 by E. Z. C. Judson, a prolific popular author, entrepreneur, and sometime political activist better known by his most famous pseudonym, Ned Buntline. Buntline recognized Cody's commercial potential. He wrote him up as a heroic scout, Sioux fighter, freelance law-enforcer, and rescuer of captive maidens, first in *Buffalo Bill, the King of Border Men!* (which was serialized in Street and Smith's story paper *New York Weekly* of 1869–70) and then in dime novels; Buntline also briefly put Cody on the New York stage.

When Prentiss Ingraham took over authorship of Buffalo Bill stories in 1879, the figure became more violent, slaughtering scores of Native Americans in defense of whole communities instead of picking off single attackers in the style of Seth Jones, and more flamboyant, dressing in rich, elaborate costumes. In Ingraham's formulation the violent plainsman's gentlemanly demeanor and exotic appearance endowed Buffalo Bill with the marks of gentility necessary to the romantic hero. Ingraham also worked the figure up as nationalist icon: anticipating the Turner thesis by fifteen years, Ingraham depicted Buffalo Bill as "a barrier between civilization and savagery, risking his own life to save the lives of others."[11] When Cody began to star in his own Wild West show from 1883, he extended his dime novel persona into the historical and political arena by incorporating America's imperialist ventures into his act, while Ingraham continued to produce melodramatic dime and nickel fiction as tie-ins to the performances.[12] Gradually a commercial constellation emerged around the imperialist frontier hero (fig. 1.1).

Figure 1.1. Buffalo Bill was featured in numerous dime novels,
such as this Beadle and Adams
issue from 1896. (Ball State
University Photo Services.)

Overlapping this development was the construction of another version of the dime novel hero. Edward Wheeler promoted the popularity of the Western outlaw when he introduced Deadwood Dick in the
first number of Beadle's Half Dime Library in 1877. Deadwood Dick
is the familiar amalgam of savagery, culture, nationalism, and individualism but inflected in a new direction. An easterner, Deadwood Dick
has been forced to flee west under threat of imprisonment through the
depredations of a pair of eastern financiers. Disguising himself in a
black costume and mask, Dick gathers a hardy band around him and
undertakes a series of violent adventures whose ethical status is ambiguous. On the one hand, the reader is told that Dick has abandoned
himself to illegal pursuits; on the other, Dick is repeatedly shown rescuing innocent, genteel easterners, dispatching villains who are more
often crooked businessmen than savage Native Americans, and becoming entangled in a number of romantic attachments. These melodramatic adventures play out class interests more explicitly than earlier
dime novels, partly because the site of the action is the frontier boom-
town rather than the sparsely settled wilderness. Dick frequently op-
poses "purse-proud aristocrats," who are clearly censured by the democratic narrative voice: in *Deadwood Dick's Device or, The Sign of the*

Double Cross (1879), the scheming Howells are "a leading family, both financially and socially—for Leadville, mind you, has its social world as well as its Eastern sister cities, formed out of that class whom fortune has smiled upon. And surrounded by great superfluity of style, pomp and splendor, they set themselves up as the 'superior class,' ye gods!"[13] But the social bandit's alignment with the laboring classes does not extend to political activists: "on a visit to Chicago soon after the Haymarket Riots of 1886, Deadwood Dick, Jr., denounces the anarchists who are on trial because they are an undesirable foreign element. He declares that all the accused persons deserved to be hanged."[14] A number of dime publishing firms capitalized on the popularity of the outlaw hero by developing entire libraries devoted to increasingly sensational tales of actual and fictional bandits. As the thrills became more exaggerated, the explicit sociopolitical commentary waned.

In the early twentieth century this sensationalizing of outlaws drew the wrath of some concerned citizenry and public bodies. One cultural institution in particular acted on this outcry against dime and nickel publishers: the office of the postmaster general determined what material could be sent through the mail and at what rates. This office, perhaps in response to concerns over worker unrest and rising socialism, censored inflammatory outlaw stories from 1883 through the turn of the century by refusing mailing privileges.[15] In response dime publishers turned to moralistic adventure stories, fastening particularly on the heroic cowboy.

The cowboy had emerged gradually as a cultural hero; partly through the intercession of dime fiction, his image shifted over the 1880s from hell-raiser to half-wild, half-cultured frontier hero and democratic individualist who could function equally adroitly on the open range and in the frontier town.[16] The decisive gentrification of the cowboy occurred beyond the dime novel genre, in the fiction of Owen Wister, the political rhetoric of Theodore Roosevelt, and the art of Frederic Remington.[17] That development was reincorporated, in turn, into the juvenile nickel Westerns of the twentieth century, which transformed the gentlemanly cowboy into a clean-cut boy. Frank Tousey's *Wild West Weekly*, a series about a gang of boys in the West (again led by a displaced easterner) that began in 1902, was the most popular version of this formula. In 1904 Street and Smith produced a close imitation, *Young Rough Riders Weekly* (later, *Rough Rider Weekly*), authored under the house pseudonym "Ned Taylor." These stories played on associations with Teddy Roosevelt, who was beginning his second term as president when the series began: the leader of this gang of boys is Ted Strong, an easterner who inherits two ranches in the

Dakotas and one in Texas, and each gang member wears "a neatly-fitting khaki uniform such as those worn by the Rough Riders during the Spanish-American War."[18] Although the standard captivity-and-rescue ritual survives, the action is modernized and heavily influenced by marketplace issues: battles revolve around corporate trust busting, the regulation of property rights, technological advancement, and sporting competitions, not the killing of Native Americans. Ted Strong's pervasive influence functions primarily to eradicate the wildness from the West.

What these shifts and turns in dime fiction share is the location of power in the white hero. In the dime and nickel Western white women and all nonwhite figures are relegated to providing the occasion for the excitement but are permitted no agency in its momentum or consequences. White women are typically passive victims saved by the hero's courage and wilderness skills; Native Americans, the threatening savages whom he destroys; Mexicans, the lustful degenerates whom he drives off; and blacks, the comic childlike incompetents whom he protects. (The most extreme reification of an African American occurs in Buntline's *Red Ralph, The River Rover; or, The Brother's Revenge* [1870]. The black figure, Tony, is servant to the aristocratic villain. Repeatedly doing his master's bidding, his punishment is a stark dehumanization: catching Tony in an assassination attempt, the hero first cuts a cross into his forehead and then returns him to his master with a letter pinned to his breast. Red Ralph the sailor later carves anchors into the servant's cheeks, and the heroine finally scalds him white.)

Variations to these flat caricatures appear, but ultimately they seem contained by the heroic imperative. For example, when Deadwood Dick defends the land rights of a peaceful Crow Indian in *Deadwood Dick's Claim; or, The Fairy Face of Faro Flats* (1884), the point is more the extent of the hero's protective powers than American Indians' rights. Wheeler also produced a series of female figures who transcend the passive gentility of the typical dime novel heroine: Hurricane Nell, Wild Edna, Rowdy Kate, and most famously, Calamity Jane, who figures briefly as Dick's wife but more regularly as his sidekick in the Deadwood Dick series.[19] These women adopt masculine attire, display prowess on horseback and in gunplay, and often save the hero from fatal danger. Ultimately, however, their ostensible power is negated: either the masculine role is only a stage in a woman's maturation toward adult domesticity, or her masculinized behavior results in her death, or (as in the case of Calamity Jane, who has lost her chastity) she leads a kind of living death, forever branded a degenerate and outcast from respectable society. In lip service to women's changing social roles in the early twentieth century, Stella, Ted's companion in *Rough Rider Weekly,* is empowered in gradual, limited ways: she initiates and conducts her own adventures, and her western costume is practical yet feminine; ultimately, however, she depends on Ted for her safety. With these stereotypes the fictional narratives entrenched a disposition of gender and race that was reflected in the demographics of the publishing houses, where white men predominated in all professional roles.

However simplistic the dime—and nickel—novel formula, the embedding of topical references in the narratives and their responsiveness to changing cultural climates suggest that these melodramas were offered as prisms through which to view current affairs. Implicitly and explicitly the frontier wilderness came to be aligned with modern society, to the extent that the dime Western could be read, in Daryl Jones's words, "as a vehicle for addressing social problems associated with urbanization and industrialization."[20] Public discourse and cheap fiction symbiotically supported a vibrant, optimistic political rhetoric that characterized the Far West as site of national, economic, and personal regeneration. On a number of fronts dime and nickel Westerns seem to support the dominant rhetoric of the era by mimicking and extending it into frontier melodrama.

Complicating the easy alignment of text to sociopolitical arena, however, is the author-reader relationship. Inscribed in these formulaic Westerns are authorial voices that attempt to circumvent the regulation of the marketplace by insisting on their individual contributions to narrative production and by recovering an oral relationship with their readers. The details of both mass-publishing history and textual developments suggest that, ultimately, these voices were circumscribed by the culture industry. Nevertheless, they can be read as limited but significant challenges to the powerful institutions of cultural production, as signs that the fictional West was not completely homogenized by commerce.[21]

Some Beadle and Adams authors forged a facsimile of a storyteller's relationship with their audience by talking to their readers about the commercial paraphernalia of the dime novel. Buntline, for example, mounted a running commentary on his place in the production line, as well as a defense of his populist politics, within his repetitive dime tales of captivity, chase, and rescue on the frontier. In a typical acknowledgment of the competitive commercialism of his task, he ended a stirring frontier tale with "I hope you feel as if you had got your money's worth."[22]

Edward Ellis and Prentiss Ingraham implicated authors, characters, and readers in self-conscious codes, conventions, and sign systems, thus moving the fiction closer to an acknowledgment of its status in the publishing field. In Ellis the narrative commentary is supplemented by characters simultaneously enacting and discussing the formulaic plots: series characters typically cite by title their appearances in earlier publications, and they explicitly acknowledge their participation in ritualistic, somewhat predictable action. Ingraham's fiction insists that the production and decipherment of codes are at the heart of Western adventure. In *Buffalo Bill's Redskin Ruse; or, Texas Jack's Death-Shot* (1895), for example, characters spend much time translating secret messages, "reading signs" on trails, devising "talking papers" (as maps are called), and interpreting key clues on clothing and bodies, all the while identifying their adventures as types of games.

Edward Wheeler's characters emphasized the constructedness of the formula further by becoming independent of their author to the extent that they wrote their own plots, devised their own identities, and fought their own publishing battles. For example, just at the time that Street and Smith marketed an imitation of the Deadwood Dick Series, Wheeler had his hero declare, "I see that counterfeits are being shoved on the market—that is, sham Deadwood Dicks. We have one here in Eureka. . . . I wish to meet this chap and learn where he obtained the right to use my copyrighted handle?"[23] The voice that recognizes the rules of the marketplace and the systematic interchange between producer and the consumer now belonged to the characters. The shift in rhetorical power is a textual illustration of the diminution of authorial power, just around the time when authors were losing more of their autonomy in the publishing hierarchy.

As dime publishers became more interventionist, these authorial gestures disappeared from the text. In Street and Smith juvenile nickel series an editorial voice at the end of the story comments on the construction of the fiction, encourages readers to distribute it for financial rewards, and in time, invites the audience to participate in its composition. The most emphatic example of this process occurred in the letters pages of *Rough Rider Weekly*, significantly revolving around the social construction of gender. In response to conflicting advice from readers about whether Ted Strong should marry Stella, the editor threw open the author's study and invited in all the readers: "So you think Ted and Stella should marry? What do the rest of our readers think about it? . . . There are two sides to this question, and we should like to have it decided by our readers."[24] The fiction thus became an overt bargaining tool between publisher and public; the only role left to the author was to carry out the audience's demands.

The question of how all these textual signals—of topicality, authorial presence, and reader power—were received by readers is linked to the equally knotty question of who constituted the massive new audience for dime and nickel Westerns.[25] The Beadles avowedly aimed at a large and diverse audience, attempting to transcend class division in audience as well as hero; they announced in 1860 that they "hoped to reach all classes, old and young, male and female."[26] They advertised dime novels in the nationally influential *New York Tribune,* and some of their publications were reviewed (favorably) in the highbrow *North American Review.* The Civil War produced a captive audience of soldiers, who were highly responsive to the sensational adventure that some publishers became adept at producing. Later, industrialization, urbanization, and economic calculations seem to have delivered the working classes as the main audience for cheap fiction. Frederick Whittaker specifically enumerated the audience: "The readers of the dimes are farmers, mechanics, workwomen, drummers, boys in shops and factories"; extrapolating from this and other evidence, Michael Denning has averred that "the bulk of the audience of dime novels were workers—craftworkers, factory operatives, domestic servants and domestic workers."[27] Retrospectively commentators tended to style dime novels as "part of the youth of many of us" (this from an editorial in the *New York Sun* in 1900). In fact, however, it was only toward the end of Beadle and Adams's life and throughout Street and Smith's dime career that a specifically juvenile audience was targeted. Within these reading groups for dime novels, more males than females seem to have been attracted to Westerns, and readers developed different interpretive strategies according to their level of investment as "Committed, Regular, or Casual" readers.[28] Hypothetical reconstructions of these readers' responses to authorial and narrative signs suggest that working-class readers, at least, read dime fiction in ideologically charged ways, not as simple escapism dissociated from their daily lives. Piecing together evidence from a patchwork of autobiographies, diaries, and reports by social reformers, Michael Denning has argued that workers read cheap novels allegorically or typologically, interpreting a range of scenarios as microcosms of their social world. Thus, especially at times of industrial agitation and strikes in the late nineteenth century, workers could read the triumph of labor in stories of western outlaws, such as Wheeler's *Deadwood Dick, The Prince of the Road; or, The Black Rider of the Black Hills* (1877). One way of understanding the authorial gestures toward the commercial constructedness of the work is as invitations to what John Fiske labels a "producerly reading":

the producerly text has the accessibility of a readerly one . . . but it also has the openness of the writerly. . . . It offers itself up to popular production; it exposes, however reluctantly, the vulnerabilities, limitations, and weaknesses of its preferred meanings; it contains, while attempting to repress them, voices that contradict the ones it prefers; it has loose ends that escape its control, its meanings exceed its own power to discipline them, its gaps are wide enough for whole new texts to be produced in them.[29]

Both empirical evidence and theorized hypothesis suggest, then, that the audience of dime and nickel Westerns was not undifferentiedly passive. Some readers could respond to textual hints and ambiguities according to their own agendas, contributing their own meanings to the complex multiple authorship of these cheap forms.

In their ritualistic adventures of attacks, captivity, and pursuit, dime novels encode a West where nationalism and commerce intersect regeneratively. The market operates visibly on the manufacture of the dime novel as product, on the textual representation of the West—which develops from untamed wilderness to site of business opportunities—and on the narrative voices that deliver those images. Within this representational space a hierarchy of gender and race is formulaically inscribed. Distributed by the millions, this version of the West could claim a democratic voice on many levels.

The pulp magazines and comics that succeeded dime and nickel novels display similar strategies, although potentially to different rhetorical effect. The production process became slicker and more intense as the technological and commercial environment heated up, distribution increased exponentially, and certain narrative features became increasingly exaggerated. Encoded within these changes, however, is a familiar story of white male supremacy impelled by a democratic ethos that conflates nationalism and commerce.

Partly because of the postal restrictions on series of complete novels, pulp magazines took over from dime novels after World War I, bringing with them a new format and different editorial methods.[30] These weekly and monthly magazines were miscellanies of short and long fiction with various features like quizzes, letters pages, and factual articles, printed on cheap pulp paper and selling for ten or fifteen cents. Pulps were invented in 1896, but they reached the height of their popularity only once they began to specialize after 1919: Street and Smith were first with this innovation, with their all-Western *Western Story Magazine*. Within the Western genre further subdivision (into, for example, romance Westerns—*Ranch Romances, Romantic Range*—and

adventure Westerns—*Ace-High Western Stories, Double Action Western*) enabled publishers to target specific audiences. This precision was
important because of the attempts to raise advertising revenue; advertisers wanted assurance that notice of their products was reaching appropriate audiences. The run of pulp authors was slotted into this reg-
ulated scheme, with uniform payment rates—two cents and, later, one
cent per word—and manuscript lengths—5,000 words for a story,
30,000 words for a novelette, and 60,000 words for a serial. The reign-
ing climate was imitation and reproduction, the editorial consensus
being that "if there is one trait that the pulpwood reader has it is his
predilection for sameness."[31] The pulps died as a popular form around
1950, partly because of competition from the more seductive media of
television and cinema and from the boom in slick magazines and paperback books when paper quotas ended after World War II. In at least
one pulp editor's opinion, however, pulps suffered also because the
automation of production became too oppressive for the writers, artists, and editors involved in their making.[32]

By and large pulp magazines recycled the formulaic narratives and
character types of the twentieth-century nickel novels, dispensing with
the juvenile emphasis and adding some violence and sex to the action.
For example, when Street and Smith turned *Wild West Weekly* into the
pulp magazine *Wild West* in 1927, the lead story simply took the characters from the nickel novel and turned them into mature young men, enlarging the scope of their violent action and romantic entanglements.
Although the subgenre of the romance Western seems to privilege wom-
en figures, by endowing them with economic power (typically portraying them as ranch owners) and positioning them in the center of the adventurous action, the female sphere is ultimately limited in familiar
ways. In "Hearts and Saddles," by J. Edward Leithead—the lead story
of *Ranch Romances* for July 1931—the heroine is contained by the es-
sentialist marks of femininity; Sally Kerrigan is "a very pretty girl in
overalls and brass-studded buzzard-wing chaps, a gray curled-brim
sombrero drawn low on her head. Unless one looked closely, noting the
wholly feminine cast of brown features and the soft, well rounded con-
tours of a girlish form, she might be mistaken for a rider of the opposite
sex."[33] It is not surprising that, despite her contribution to the vanquish-
ing of rustlers, the crises of the cattle drive, and the hard work of the
ranch, Sally Kerrigan ends the tale in the hero's arms, "her eyes . . . shining in proclamation of surrender."[34] Figures from minority cultures
within America continue to function as appendages to the white male
hero, too. Occasionally a more distinctive narrative emerged from the
mass, from a "star" writer who succeeded in parlaying his or her work

into paperback book format. The pulp fiction of Zane Grey and Frederick Faust (better known by one of his twenty pseudonyms, Max Brand), for example, has marked characteristics. Both authors worked up the Western's mythological associations, shaping familiar adventures into an archetypal pattern of separation-initiation-return; Grey emphasized sexual thrills and lavish scenic descriptions; and Brand came to reverse the dominant trend, turning from the Virginian type of romantic hero to the Leatherstocking type of extrasocietal loner. Ultimately, however, these variations seem primarily structural, not challenging the ideological limits of the pulp formula.

The diminution of the authorial voice continues in the textual dynamics of the pulp magazines, with the further impression that readers, too, are being articulated as component parts of a commercial scheme run for the benefit of the publishers. Generally the stories lack even the limited individuation of the dime narrative voices, although occasional stars like Grey and Brand sustained characteristic accents in their work. Story functioned as product in this format more explicitly than ever; in the words of one pulp editor, "Serials are nothing more than sales promotion efforts."[35] The power of the editorial voice was institutionalized in departments such as "The Round-Up" in Street and Smith's *Western Story Magazine* and "The Wranglers' Corner" in the same firm's *Wild West,* where editors orchestrated characters' responses to readers' letters in a facsimile of direct contact. Authors, particularly star authors, were intermittently given a voice in this conversation, but it was heavily mediated by editorial invention and the injunction that authors are "just common folks, same as you and me."[36] This device served not only to induce community identification in the reader but to gauge and manipulate audience response for financial profit. As part of this rhetoric, in 1924 readers of Street and Smith's *Western Story Magazine* were enlisted in the effort to drum up advertising revenue: "We know you read the advertisements in our magazines, and that you can help us prove it to the advertisers."[37] In a final sign of commodification, when the latter-day pulp *Far West* was launched in 1978, the readers' responses were limited to a multiple choice questionnaire that explicitly controlled the range of responses available to them. The implication is that publisher-editors were attempting the ultimate rationalization of labor, incorporating authors and readers as component parts of their smoothly operating machine. Given Henry Steeger's judgment that "pulps were the principal entertainment vehicle for millions of Americans," the circulation of such traditional images of the West and the attempt to reify their readers potentially marked a large sector of American cultural life.[38]

The genre that finally linked the written Western to the movie and television version was the comic.[39] According to Maurice Horn, "the birth of the comics as a distinct medium"—as strips with sequential narrative, continuing characters, speech balloons, onomatopoeia, and frame-enclosed pictures—occurred in 1896, with the panel *Yellow Kid* by Richard Outcault in Joseph Pulitzer's Sunday supplement to the *New York World*.[40] By the early years of the twentieth century comic strips were a regular feature in daily newspapers, too. Over time these strips expanded from juvenile to adult forms; from about 1929 many privileged adventure action over comedy; and from the early 1920s, they increasingly imitated the "syntax" of movies with much cross-fertilization of content between comics and animated cartoons. American comic books took off in the 1930s, first with reprinted comic strips, and then with original material, mainly addressed to young readers. Since World War II the development of comic strips and books has been intermittent, with periods of censorship, decline, and renewed innovation, especially from underground "comix."

The economics of comic production were distinct from dime and pulp calculations because strips were controlled by a syndicate distribution system that rationalized production and centralized control more fiercely than any publishing house. There is diverse evidence of syndicate editors seizing the creative initiative from artists and authors. For example, Joseph Patterson, founder of the Tribune-News Syndicate, "often took average artists, suggested titles, changed characters and outlined themes, to create classic comics."[41] Especially after the consolidations of the 1930s, syndicates also managed energetic cross-fertilization among the entertainment media. In the 1970s the Field Newspaper Syndicate developed features and continuities on the basis of quasi-scientific planning and polling, including canvassing newsagents' responses to new titles. Audiences were massive: in 1938 a Gallup survey stated that 63 percent of adults read daily comics and 73 percent of adults read Sunday comics.[42]

Strips devoted to the Wild West appeared in the late 1920s, and flurries of humorous and adventure Western stories occurred throughout the 1930s, 1940s, and 1950s, both in newspaper strips and in comic books. By 1965 comic Westerns kept pace with developments in the cinematic Western with such irreverent anti-Western comics as *Tumbleweeds*. The hand of the syndicate is evident in these developments. The Tribune-News Syndicate initiated many Western titles; *Texas Slim*, for example, which ran from 1925 to 1928 and then from 1940 to 1958, arose in response to Patterson's request for a humorous Western. The comic strip *Bronc Peeler*, drawn by Fred Harman from the early 1930s, was transformed into *Red Ryder* by New York entrepreneur Stephen Slesinger, who then parlayed the figure into movie serials, comic books, novels, radio shows, and advertising. With the Lone Ranger the commercial diversification operated in the opposite direction. Beginning life as a radio serial in 1933, the figure's massive success led editors at King Features to initiate Lone Ranger comic strips and comic books, which survived until the 1970s; there was also highly successful marketing of Lone Ranger guns, Lone Ranger costumes, Lone Ranger books, and Lone Ranger movie serials (fig. 1.2). There were comic strips of Zane Grey's novels and of screen cowboys such as Tom Mix and Gene Autry.

The narratives of these Western comics remain recognizably formulaic. The following summary of *Broncho Bill* (begun by Harry O'Neill for United Features in the late 1920s as *Young Buffalo Bill*, later *Buckaroo Bill*) suggests their debt to the dime and nickel formulas of an earlier era: "The stories in *Broncho Bill* came to center around the activities of a Bill-led group of youthful vigilantes calling themselves the Rangers, sort of gun-toting boy scouts. O'Neill's idea of suspense was to have some innocent, a hapless infant or a golden-haired little girl, about to fall over a cliff or be eaten by a grizzly bear."[43] The positioning of Native American sidekicks—speaking, at least in *Bronc Peeler* and *The Lone Ranger,* the most ludicrous "You Betchum!" patois—is familiar, too. Some suggestive exceptions to the formula appeared, however; the protagonist of *White Boy* (from 1933) was raised among Native Americans, and *Ghost Rider* (from 1950) was a supernatural Western. Moreover, the graphic articulation of comics served, in time, to heighten the sensationalism of both violence and voyeuristic sex. Even more resonantly than earlier forms, the comics speak to the political world; they not only incorporate topical references (during the World Wars, for example), but the strips' position within newspapers links them to cultural events, however dissociated their fantasy world may seem. Western comics survive to an extent today, although, as with movie Westerns, they are no longer the dominant genre; perhaps their heritage is most strongly imprinted in the individualistic "superheroes" such as Superman and Spiderman.

Within this matrix of production authors' and artists' choices and roles were heavily determined by the syndicate machine. When entrepreneurial forces took over Fred Harman's comic strip, for example, the artist was turned into an economically productive celebrity: "Harman appeared in the ads along with his characters. 'Fred Harman, famous cowboy artist who draws the popular NEA newspaper cartoon RED RYDER COMIC STRIP, was a sure 'nough Colorado cowboy

Figure 1.2. The Lone Ranger's initial success on national radio helped him become a popular comic book hero after 1948. (Ball State University Photo Services.)

before hittin' the trail to New York City. Fred helped Daisy design this genuine Western-style saddle carbine an' hopes you get your RED RYDER CARBINE right away!'"[44] The Daisy Manufacturing Company (a maker of BB guns) also conducted competitions, with the artist as first prize: "SEE Fred Harman DRAW his famous Cartoon Strip." In a familiar ironic juncture Harman was puffed as the originary talent just at the time when his strip was being scripted by a number of ghost artists. Most syndicate employees enjoyed less exposure than this, being shuffled from strip to strip as market forces dictated.

Despite all these structural similarities between comic narratives and modes of production and those of earlier mass-produced Westerns, readers' responses may have made different meanings out of comics. Martin Barker's nuanced reading of non-Western comic books suggests that an increasingly sophisticated and knowing rhetoric—on the cover, in the editorial matter, and within the strips themselves—plays with the slippage between fantasy and reality and with self-reflexive commentary in ways much more complex than, though still recognizably related to, the rhetoric of dime novels. Barker reads these socially embedded signals as offering readers a "contract" involving resistance to authority (adult authority, in the case of juvenile audiences); working with a more textual interpretation, Horn argues that "if the medium is the message, then the message of the comics, with their flouting of the rules of traditional art and of civilized language, can only be subversion."[45] This hypothesis can be extrapolated to Western comics. As early as 1939 the comic strip *Little Joe* emphatically parodied the genre's reliance on racial stereotypes. Utah, the old frontiersman, seeks to cheat "an Injun" out of his fine horses in exchange for what Utah believes is a defunct automobile:

> UTAH: Howdy! Right nice pair o' hosses you got thar—care to sell?
>
> "INJUN": Ugh! No sellum!
>
> UTAH: Ah—I see you like-um automobile—nice car—swap cheap! Have look-see anyway—
>
> "INJUN": Ugh! Heap fine smell buggy!
>
> UTAH [*sotto voce*]: Heh! Heh! Look at him! Them simple red men is all suckers fer bright paint—jest watch me git him—[to "Injun"] Done! I git th' hosses! You git th' car . . . all even—no backin' out! (Heh! Heh! Jest wait'll th' illiterate cuss tries drivin' it!)
>
> "INJUN": Ugh! [driving off in car] Yes—a very snappy job—superb lines—abundant power—much improved over the model I had while in college—nice to have met you—adios!
>
> [Utah collapses in astonishment, mouth agape.][46]

Marvel Comics' *Kid Colt Outlaw* plays up the parody of its "BLAM! WHUMP! WHAM!" action with pointed editorial comments: Kid Colt's "Deadly Double" is a "Wild and Wooly Western Masterpiece! . . . Lettered by: Al Kurzrok . . . Villain Booed by: Sagebrush Irv."[47] Such reminders of comics' artifice and their melodramatic absurdities proliferate throughout the recognizably formulaic tale of robbery, vengeance, and justice. These textual gestures can be interpreted as inviting a resistant reading of the plot, thereby undermining the narratives of law and order. Such subversion is, of course, significantly contained by the syndicate machine producing and profiting from these publications. Nevertheless, at the rhetorical level comics offer readers the opportunity to challenge the codes and hierarchies of the Western genre (and the society that it represents). The comics' pronounced foregrounding of parody is largely foreign to the pulp magazines and promises more subversion than the "producerly readings" or space for contestation opened up by the dime novels.

Evidence that these subversive gestures in comics are matched by readerly resistance, expressed as critical distance, comes in the reading practices of the comic audience most studied to date: children. Working from various case studies, Barker identifies "children's handling of the 'hidden curriculum' of adult power" in their reactions to weekly comics.[48] Reflecting more personally on his son's response to 1950s comics, Robert Warshow speculated that the boy's fascination with the publishing house, the staff, and the drafting processes indicated a specific strategy on the part of the juvenile reader: "I think that Paul's desire to put himself directly in touch with the processes by which the comic books are produced may be the expression of a fundamental detachment which helps to protect him from them; the comic books are not a 'universe' to him, but simply objects produced for his entertainment."[49] Again, a critical leap is required to extrapolate from this evidence specifically to Western comics. Nevertheless, the potential is clearly there for comic readers to construct a West of the imagination more self-consciously parodic or knowingly limited than any mere plot summary might suggest.

In this chapter I have tried to read the frames of production and reception that mediate narratives of the Wild West in dime, nickel, pulp, and comic publications. The image of the West that results is shifting and, to a degree, fractured. On the one hand, at the level of textual representation, the West of the majority of cheap fiction seems unremittingly masculinist, racist, and nationalistic, whether represented as savage wilderness, vanguard of American civilization, wellspring of imperialist energy, limitless playing field, home of entrepreneurial capitalism, or a dehistoricized, moralistic environment that legitimizes violence and, later, sexual titillation. Yet the reading of this simple triumphalism is complicated by the contradictory voices that emerge as part of the commodification process. The most dynamic developments in the fictional formula seem to occur in the nineteenth and early twentieth centuries, when dime and nickel Westerns adapted their lineaments to changing cultural and political climates, partly by incorporating the market economy into their fictional action. Thereafter, repetitions in plot, character, setting, and language saturate the fictive material. At the same time, however, editorial gestures to readers become more knowing and sophisticated; whereas the formulaic fiction petrifies in the later twentieth century, the rhetorical devices framing that fiction become increasingly suggestive, offering readers various kinds of resistance to the heroic narratives. Audiences of different classes and periods seem to have followed their own agendas, their interpretations sometimes running counter to and sometimes colluding with the manifest story lines and the commercial paraphernalia. The "meanings" of mass-produced Western fiction can be read as the product of all these forces in contention and collusion with one another, contested terrain playing out a range of economic, national, and personal interests.

Notes

1. Umberto Eco, *Travels in Hyperreality,* trans. William Weaver (London, 1987), 10.

2. I address this period at greater length in Bold, "Popular Forms I," in *The Columbia History of the American Novel,* ed. Emory Elliott, 285–305 (New York, 1991). Sources include Mary Noel, *Villains Galore: The Heyday of the Popular Story Weekly* (New York, 1954); Madeleine B. Stern, ed., *Publishers for Mass Entertainment in Nineteenth Century America* (Boston, 1980); and Jane Tompkins, *Sensational Designs: The Cultural Work of American Fiction, 1790–1860* (New York, 1985).

3. The proportion of dime novels devoted to western topics is documented in Philip Durham, "Introduction," *"Seth Jones," Edward S. Ellis and "Deadwood Dick on Deck," Edward L. Wheeler: Dime Novels* (New York, 1966): "approximately three-fourths of the [Beadle and Adams] dime novels deal with the various forms, problems, and attitudes of life on the frontier, and . . . more than half are concerned with life in the trans-Mississippi West" (ix). The details of dime novel production and formulas are drawn from Christine Bold, *Selling the Wild West: Popular Western Fiction 1860 to 1960* (Bloomington, Ind., 1987); Michael Denning, *Mechanic Accents: Dime Novels and Working Class Culture in America* (London, 1987); Albert Johannsen, *The House of Beadle and Adams and Its Dime and Nickel Novels: The Story of a Vanished Literature,* 2 vols., supplement (Norman, Okla., 1950, 1962); Daryl Jones, *The Dime Novel Western* (Bowling Green, Ohio, 1978); Quentin Reynolds, *The Fiction Factory; or, From Pulp Row to Quality Street: The Story of 100 Years of Publishing at Street and Smith* (New York, 1955); and Madeleine Stern, *Publishers for Mass Entertainment.*

4. W. H. Bishop, "Story-Paper Literature," *The Atlantic Monthly,* September 1879, 383.

5. Reynolds, *Fiction Factory,* 88–89.

6. Ann S. Stephens, *Malaeska: The Indian Wife of the White Hunter,* Beadle's Dime Novels no. 1 (New York, 1860 [1839]), 57.

7. Henry Nash Smith, *Virgin Land: The American West as Symbol and Myth* (Cambridge, Mass., 1950), 93.

8. Jane Tompkins, *West of Everything: The Inner Life of Westerns* (New York, 1992), 42.

9. For more information, see John Cawelti, *Adventure, Mystery, and Romance: Formula Stories as Art and Popular Culture* (Chicago, 1976); and Smith, *Virgin Land.*

10. Jones, *Dime Novel Western,* 22.

11. Prentiss Ingraham, *Buffalo Bill, from Boyhood to Manhood. Deeds of Daring, Scenes of Thrilling Peril, and Romantic Incidents in the Early Life of W. F. Cody, the Monarch of Bordermen.* Beadle's Boy's Library of Sport, Story, and Adventure no. 2 (New York, 1878), 2.

12. Christine Bold, "The Rough Riders at Home and Abroad: Cody, Roosevelt, Remington, and the Imperialist Hero," *Canadian Review of American Studies* 18 (Fall 1987): 324–30; Richard Slotkin, "The 'Wild West,'" in *Buffalo Bill and the Wild West,* 27–44 (Brooklyn, 1981).

13. Jones, *Dime Novel Western,* 84–87.

14. Smith, *Virgin Land,* 101.

15. Bold, *Selling the Wild West,* 6–7; Jones, *Dime Novel Western,* 79.

16. Warren French, "The Cowboy in the Dime Novel," *Studies in English* 30 (1951): 219–34.

17. G. Edward White, *The Eastern Establishment and the Western Experience: The West of Frederic Remington, Theodore Roosevelt, and Owen Wister* (New Haven, Conn., 1968).

18. Ned Taylor, "The Young Rough Riders in the Rockies; or, a Fight in Midair," *Young Rough Riders Weekly* no. 38 (1905), 1.

19. For further information about dime novel heroines, see Smith, *Virgin Land,* 112–20.

20. Jones, *Dime Novel Western,* 127. Various articles in *Reckless Ralph's Dime Novel Round-Up* (1931– ; retitled *Dime Novel Round-Up* in 1953) document examples of topical references.

21. I develop this argument in much greater detail in Bold, *Selling the Wild West.*

22. Ned Buntline, *The White Wizard; or, The Great Prophet of the Seminoles,* Beadle's Dime Library 2, no. 16 (New York, 1879 [1858]), 32.

23. Edward L. Wheeler, *The Phantom Miner; or, Deadwood Dick's Bonanza* (Cleveland, 1899 [1878]), 17.

24. "A Chat with You," *Rough Rider Weekly* no. 140 (1906), 30.

25. That this audience was new and massive is confirmed by Smith, *Virgin Land,* 91, and Jones, *Dime Novel Western,* 8, 14.

26. Johannsen, *House of Beadle and Adams,* 1:9.

27. Frederick Whittaker, "Reply," *New York Tribune,* March 16, 1884, 8; Michael Denning, *Mechanic Accents,* 27.

28. Martin Barker, *Comics: Ideology, Power, and the Critics* (New York, 1989), 51.

29. John Fiske, *Understanding Popular Culture* (Boston, 1989), 104.

30. These details of pulp magazine production are drawn from Bold, *Selling the Wild West;* John A. Dinan, *The Pulp Western: A Popular History of the Western Fiction Magazine in America,* I. O. Evans Studies in the Philosophy and Criticism of Literature, no. 2. (San Bernardino, Calif., 1983); Tony Goodstone, ed., *The Pulps: Fifty Years of American Popular Culture* (New York, 1970); Ron Goulart, *Cheap Thrills: An Informal History of the Pulp Magazines* (New Rochelle, N.Y., 1972); Frank Gruber, *The Pulp Jungle* (Los Angeles, 1967); and Harold Brainerd Hersey, *Pulpwood Editor: The Fabulous*

World of the Thriller Magazines Revealed by a Veteran Editor and Publisher (New York, 1937; reprint, Westport, Conn., 1974).

31. Hersey, *Pulpwood Editor,* 2.

32. Daisy Bacon, "The Golden Age of the Iron Maiden," *The Roundup,* April 1975, 7–9.

33. J. Edward Leithead, "Hearts and Saddles," *Ranch Romances,* July 1931, 169.

34. Ibid., 215.

35. Hersey, *Pulpwood Editor,* 23.

36. "The Round-Up," *Western Story Magazine,* October 27, 1927, 135.

37. "A Chat with You," *The Popular Magazine,* February 1905, n.p.

38. Goodstone, *Pulps,* v.

39. Information about comics is drawn from Barker, *Comics;* Herb Galewitz, *Great Comics* (New York, 1972); Goulart, *Cheap Thrills;* and Maurice Horn, ed., *The World Encyclopedia of Comics,* 2 vols. (New York, 1976).

40. Horn, *World Encyclopedia of Comics,* 1:10–11.

41. Richard Marschall, "A History of Newspaper Syndication," in *World Encyclopedia of Comics,* ed. Horn, 2:726.

42. Galewitz, *Great Comics,* vii.

43. Goulart, *The Adventurous Decade* (New Rochelle, N.Y., 1975), 184.

44. Goulart, *Adventurous Decade,* 187.

45. Barker, *Comics,* 61; Horn, *World Encyclopedia of Comics,* 1:50.

46. Galewitz, *Great Comics,* 244.

47. Gary Friedrich, Werner Roth, and Herb Trimpe, "The Deadly Double," *Kid Colt Outlaw,* August 1978, 1.

48. Barker, *Comics,* 86.

49. Robert Warshow, *The Immediate Experience: Movies, Comics, Theater, and Other Aspects of Popular Culture* (Garden City, N.Y., 1962), 87.

TWO

William Bloodworth

Writers of the Purple Sage:
Novelists and the American West

In 1980 John R. Milton's study *The Novel of the American West* presented the case for serious fiction about the American West, holding up for particular admiration the works of Vardis Fisher, A. B. Guthrie Jr., Frederick Manfred, Walter Van Tilburg Clark, Harvey Fergusson, and Frank Waters. These writers found deep significance in western landscape and history. As a result, Milton explains, they have portrayed the West in elemental or even sacred terms. Such novels as Waters's *The Man Who Killed the Deer* (1942), Guthrie's *The Big Sky* (1947), or Fergusson's *The Conquest of Don Pedro* (1954) thus tend to be symbolic and archetypal, paying attention "to man's psychological and spiritual relationship with the land."[1]

There are other traditions and categories of Western novels. Willa Cather's work in such books as *O Pioneers!* and *My Antonia* stands on its own as a recognized literary accomplishment, for critics and scholars have long admired her complex renderings of the pioneer experience. Virtually every region of the West can claim novels dedicated in one way or another to realistic depiction of its places and times; even broad-scale popular novels such as Edna Ferber's *Giant* or James Michener's *Texas* are eligible for consideration, as are many novels (including those by Laura Ingalls Wilder) aimed at younger readers. Novels by American Indian authors, such as James Welch's *Winter in the Blood* or Leslie Silko's *Ceremony,* represent a special and rich subcategory of Western fiction. The hard-boiled California detective stories of Ross McDonald are also Western novels, as are works by writers as diverse as Mark Twain, Frank Norris, Mary Austin, Jack Kerouac, Wallace Stegner, and Edward Abbey.

Thus "Western novels" as a category can include literary works that vary greatly in intent, setting, audience, and popularity. The general use of the term is more restrictive, however. In common parlance "Western novels" means "Westerns," that is, popular stories that incorporate conventional or formulaic elements of plot, character, and setting. Western novels in this sense came into existence after the beginning of the twentieth century for a variety of reasons, but one stands out above all others: the existence of large numbers of readers. As with other aspects of American popular culture, the creation of Westerns depended on the interaction of authors, publishers, and audiences. Westerns therefore have literary, commercial, and cultural dimensions. Above all else, they comprise a complex means by which the history and geography of the West have been interpreted within the system of values and attitudes that we refer to as American culture.

The historical roots of the Western prior to the twentieth century are open to interpretation. Some scholars prefer to see the Western as a continuation of the so-called dime novel that provided cheap mass entertainment, often in the form of exaggerated stories about Buffalo Bill Cody and other legendary frontier figures, for several decades following the Civil War. Others have found loftier origins in the Leatherstocking novels (1823–41) of James Fenimore Cooper or even in the earliest accounts of European contact with the new world of North America. Richard Slotkin's *Regeneration through Violence: The Mythology of the American Frontier, 1600–1860* is a particularly good example of the latter, claiming that basic "mythopoeic" elements of American frontier stories, including the imaginative dimensions of the frontier hero, began to take shape in seventeenth-century Puritan narratives of captivity and Indian wars.[2]

Such a deep view of the Western's roots is hard to disregard. It is entirely possible that the cultural lineage of the popular Western story derives from early Indian-white conflict, the legendary status of frontiersmen such as Daniel Boone, and such literary ancestors as Natty Bumppo. Nevertheless, the reason for the Western's popularity may have less to do with older mythic material than with the anxieties of its own time. Westerns began to flourish during the first two decades of the twentieth century, a time when the frontier itself had virtually, but only recently, disappeared. The closing of the frontier contrasted sharply with the move to cities and towns, as increased urbanization, immigration, and industrialization marked the coming of twentieth-century America. To a large extent, then, the rise of the Western was a popular literary response by both authors and readers to the closing of the frontier and opening of a new, urban environment. Suddenly lacking an actual frontier as a place to demonstrate the triumph of civilization, Americans turned to imaginary frontier experiences. It is likely for this reason that Westerns exhibit great nostalgic affection for the final twenty-five years of the actual frontier, roughly 1865 to 1890—the era of the open cattle range that came to a dramatic end after the Great Plains were swept by severe blizzards during the winters of 1885 and 1886.

In any event, the rise of the popular Western thereafter represents a collective act of imagination by which writers and their audiences precisely separated off a geographic region and a period of history for special treatment. In this manner the Western has served to preserve mythic, even epic, assumptions about the American past. But the Western has not been uniformly nostalgic. As one historian has written, "the roots of the Western . . . were nourished by cultural and intellectual currents that rippled through American experience between the end of the nineteenth century and the Depression."[3] From its beginning the Western has incorporated a complex relationship with its own times, reflecting social change and the defined cultural roles of men and women.

The history of the popular Western begins with the dramatic appearance of Owen Wister's *The Virginian: A Horseman of the Plains* in April of 1902. The novel went through six printings in six weeks and sixteen printings in its first year. It was the top seller in fiction for 1902 and fifth for 1903.[4] Before *The Virginian* there had been other novels of the West, even other novels about cowboys, but nothing with the impact of Wister's book. In capturing the nation's fancy, *The Virginian* had a decided effect on the commercial publishing industry. It identified a wide adult readership for Western fiction that followed in a myriad of variations spun out of the basic materials of *The Virginian*.

Owen Wister was born in 1860 to an aristocratic Philadelphia family with southern roots and an interest in artistic and literary matters. Henry James and Robert Browning were personal friends of the family. Wister graduated from Harvard in 1882, hoping to become a composer of operas. When his physician father encouraged a more conventional career, Wister tried his hand at banking, which he found dull and depressing. Never in robust health, he began to show alarming symptoms, including vertigo, hallucinations, and recurring nightmares. For relief he went west, where he became friends with an aristocratic Wyoming rancher and experienced a sense of personal rejuvenation. He returned east to study law at Harvard but continued thereafter to visit frequently in the West, eventually becoming a writer of Western stories.

The Virginian was thus a very personal book growing out of the author's experience. It is also a complicated and discursive novel. The central feature is the character of the Virginian himself, identified as a cowboy but also serving as a skilled poker player, hunter, tale-teller, lover, manager, hangman, and even literary critic. To list these roles is to identify the heroic, larger-than-life qualities of Wister's cowboy protagonist.

Cowboys interested Wister. He described them in his journal as "the manly, simple, humorous, American type which I hold to be the best and bravest we possess. . . . They work hard, they play hard, and they don't go on strikes."[5] In *The Virginian,* however, Wister did not present a realistic, historical image of the cowboy. His "Horseman of the Plains" was a highly idealized portrait. As Ben Merchant Vorpahl has pointed out, Wister "seemed incapable of coming to terms with the cowboy except by transforming him into something else."[6]

In *The Virginian* the primary means of transformation is romance. The Virginian, described by the narrator as "a slim young giant, more beautiful than pictures," encounters Molly Wood, a schoolmarm recently arrived on the Wyoming plains from Vermont.[7] The young cowboy falls in love with Molly and sets out confidently to win her heart. To prove himself worthy of an educated eastern woman, the Virginian must discuss literature and confess that he is of the proper southern stock, born in the state of Virginia. All along he introduces Molly to the ways of the West, including the necessity of lynching rustlers.

The Virginian's long pursuit of Molly parallels a second major focus in the novel: the Virginian's quarrel with the villain Trampas, which leads ultimately to a showdown and the killing of Trampas. Molly, engaged to the Virginian by now, objects strenuously to his way of dealing with Trampas. She tells her lover that he must either avoid bloodshed or give her up. He chooses to do his duty and kills Trampas, only to find that afterward Molly will still have him. "Thus did her New England conscience battle to the end, and, in the end, capitulate to love."[8] Wister's cowboy hero is thus an agent of both justice and love. In future Westerns by writers who followed Wister's lead, capitulation to love almost always redeems the violent acts of the hero (fig. 2.1).

Wister also attached connotations of class and nationalism to his Western in a way that appealed to his 1902 readers, residents of a nation facing ever-increasing immigration and still lacking a fully cohesive sense of national unity. The Virginian is not the typical working-class cowboy of the bunkhouse. He is described by the narrator as a true gentleman from Anglo-American stock in the Virginia Piedmont

Figure 2.1. Illustration from Owen Wister's *The Virginian* (1902) that depicts Molly begging the hero to avoid a showdown. (Ball State University Photo Services.)

with aristocratic inner qualities. The impact of Wister's novel suggests that the character and his story touched some deep-seated dialectical national attitudes. The Virginian synthesizes both wildness and civilization, both individual freedom and loyalty to others. The primitive conditions on the frontier allow the Virginian to use violence, even lynch law, to champion civilization. When necessary, to rid society of the evil represented by Trampas, he has the requisite fortitude to kill in cold blood. But he is also a lover, a loyal employee, and ultimately, in the closing pages of the novel, a successful and wealthy rancher.[9] The novel is an amalgam of American geography, values, and behavior.

After writing the first Western novel of great national popularity, Owen Wister turned next to the South for inspiration, publishing *Lady Baltimore* in 1906. He wrote no more Westerns. The Western field was left to other and more prolific writers, such as B. M. Bower, Clarence Mulford, Charles Alden Seltzer, William McCloud Raine, Zane Grey, and Max Brand, who became Wister's chief heirs until the late 1920s. Max Brand alone published over three hundred Western serials and novelettes between 1919 and 1938.

The proliferation of Westerns after *The Virginian* was more a commercial than a literary trend, but it is important to note that the Western gained popularity at a time when American literature was in the doldrums. The glittering decade of the 1890s, with writers like Stephen Crane attracting interest, was past. As Larzer Ziff has pointed out, the 1890s were followed in American letters by a "dull transition" and "the calm of a pleasant senility."[10] By the time of *The Virginian* American literary realism had faded as a trend, the critical voice of William Dean Howells was only a whisper, Mark Twain had turned his interests toward the past and the faraway, and Hamlin Garland had taken up real estate as an avocation. Crane the literary naturalist was dead; Frank Norris would die six months after the appearance of Wister's novel. It was a time lacking in artistic direction and distinctiveness. For writers of Westerns this was an advantage, for they could respond freely to audience interests and develop a variety of styles.

There was the other matter as well: the disappearance of the frontier and all that it represented in American experience. As historian Frederick Jackson Turner had noted dramatically in an 1893 essay entitled "The Significance of the Frontier in American History," Americans no longer observed an advancing frontier line with its powerful symbolic message of civilization's triumph over wildness. Instead, muckraking journalists and progressive reformers drew their attention to city slums, corrupt politics, and oppressive industrial working conditions. Wister, however, had defined an alternative. If the physical frontier had once served as a kind of safety valve for American development, a place to go when the population grew dense in the East, the Western story could provide psychological relief from the problems of urban life. Writers could turn, in imagination, to the American West. Given the right configurations of plot, character, and setting, readers would follow eagerly, perhaps to escape from urban and industrial woes or to recapture an alleged more pastoral "Golden Age."

The first writer to lay claim to the territory of the Western after *The Virginian* was a woman, Bertha Muzzy Bower. Hiding her gender under the byline of B. M. Bower, she established herself as a steady, popular producer of Westerns that projected an image of the West as a place where women were neither rare nor fragile. Unlike Wister and most other Western writers, B. M. Bower, the wife of a Montana rancher, actually lived in the West.[11] Bower began her career writing for magazines, and her first Western appeared as a story, "Chip of the Flying U," in 1904. Two years later it was expanded into a novel. By 1940 Bower had published more than sixty books, most of them Westerns. Her Westerns, although sentimental and melodramatic at times, had a realistic tone that did not idealize the cattle country of the West.

Bower's best-known Western is her first book, *Chip of the Flying U* (1906). The Flying U ranch is also the setting for other Bower novels involving the Flying U cowboys, whom she called the "Happy Family." Although these stories were generally humorous, developing comedy out of bunkhouse speech and antics, they also touched on serious issues. *Chip of the Flying U,* for instance, depicts the entrance of a female doctor, Della Whitmore, into the daily life of her brother's Montana ranch. This eastern woman turns out to be a person of wit and skill who, like many of Bower's women, adapts well to the same landscape that Wister's Molly had difficulty accepting. In *Chip* the woman's first act is to shoot a coyote dead; her second is to see through a fake lynching staged by cowboys who hope to frighten her away. Her response to the latter ploy is to tell the cowboys, "Hurry up . . . so I can be in at the death."[12] Bower's novel, like Wister's, moves toward the marriage of the cowboy hero (Chip himself) and the eastern woman, but the tone of the novel is much different, with the woman given far more stature in the plot.

Bower's stories often reveal that the Western is amenable to the concerns of women. Choosing to write under the byline of B. M. Bower as a cover for her gender, Bower still made effective raids on prevailing attitudes toward women. One of Bower's best novels, *Lonesome Land* (1912), pays particular and serious attention to the role of women in the West. In this novel a genteel eastern woman follows her husband west, bringing with her a set of romantic expectations about life in the region, "a viewpoint gained chiefly from current fiction and the stage."[13] Ultimately she manages to adapt. Her husband, however, falls prey to alcoholism as the comic clichés of western saloons and red-eye whiskey become the stuff of potential tragedy. The husband degenerates to the point where his wife seeks a divorce, but before this can happen, the husband turns violent and is shot to death by the local sheriff.

Although most of Bower's work was less serious than *Lonesome Land,* her novels often made humorous but critical references to the treatment of the West in print, on the stage, or in movies. Bower was particularly fond of alluding to *The Virginian,* and her Westerns reflected a strong self-consciousness of being Westerns. Several novels even included the making of Western movies as part of the story, thereby producing a sense of a Western within a Western. For example, after the title character of *Jean of the Lazy A* (1915) discovers a film crew making a Western on her father's Montana ranch, the cowgirl (who knows how to rope and shoot) becomes a movie star in her own Westerns. The title of her first film is the title of Bower's novel. This situation gives Bower's movie star protagonist an opportunity to criticize the popular treatment of the West. In another novel Bower has a protagonist, who is an author of Western novels, bemoan the fact that most people who write about the West "sit back East and write it like they think maybe it is; and it's a hell of a job they make of it."[14]

Clarence Edward Mulford was one of those writers who made a hell of a job of the Western. He began shortly after Bower with a novel entitled *Bar 20* (1906), drawn not from personal experience in the West but from his reading and imagination. This novel and others dealt with the exploits of a group of cowpunchers cum gunmen on a mythical west Texas ranch (the Bar 20). Chief among the Bar 20 gang was a gritty young puncher with a limp, a clever tongue, and a proclivity for violence surpassing anything ever imagined by Owen Wister. The character's name was Hopalong Cassidy.

Mulford, writing from the perspective of Brooklyn, where he worked in the county clerk's office, published six novels about Cassidy and the Bar 20 gang between 1906 and 1913. He ceased writing for several years, reentered the field in 1918, and continued as a Western author until 1941.[15] His widely read works were the sources of later movie and television treatments.

Mulford's Westerns do not exhibit the freedom and experimentation of Bower's. Instead, they show a tighter formulation emphasizing violent conflict and superhuman heroics. They also make extensive use of what Mulford took to be western vernacular. His characters, despite their violent heroics and Mulford's own lack of contact with the West, actually work with cows. They do not quote Shakespeare (as do Wister's Virginian and Bower's Chip) or even give much evidence of knowing how to read. Nor is there any real sense of social or economic relationships around them. Mulford's cowboys are residents of a wild, mythical West who are concerned not so much with society or progress but only with the joys of working and fighting. They are killers, too, even though their killing takes place in a world of absolute moral values where the bad men always deserve the deaths lavishly meted out by Hopalong Cassidy and other Mulford heroes.

The Bar 20 stories celebrate violence and fuse it with cowboy humor. Mulford's characters fire bullets and jokes with equal accuracy. In *Hopalong Cassidy* (1910) readers are told that for Hopalong, "life was a humorous recurrence of sensations, a huge pleasant joke instinctively tolerated, but not worth the price cowards pay to keep it."[16] In *Bar-20 Days* (1911), when Cassidy and his sidekick are apparently about to be killed by renegade Apaches, Mulford takes time to explain that even in the most desperate straits, Hopalong "could find something at which to laugh."[17] Such statements suggest a kind of protoexistentialism, almost as though Mulford had adapted a Jack Kerouac character to saddle and sagebrush. But the central feature of Mulford's Westerns is not humor or nonchalance. It is violence.

Mulford's depicted violence puts his work in a class with the *Iliad*. His very first Western story recounts a barroom brawl of such proportions that it becomes, in later stories, a legendary source of references. The aftermath of the fight includes "ruined furniture, a wrecked bar, seared and shattered and covered with blood," and "bodies as they had been piled in the corners."[18] In another novel Mulford describes a genial, avuncular sheriff as a person who "did his shooting as an unavoidable duty—a business, a stern necessity. . . . When he shot at a man he did it with becoming gravity, but nevertheless he radiated pride and cheerfulness when he hit the man's nose or eye or Adam's apple at a hundred yards."[19] This is violence of a kind that goes several steps beyond the "serious orientation towards violence" that Robert Warshow claims to be the chief feature of the Western film.[20] A work like Jack Schaefer's *Shane* (1949), where only with great reluctance does the hero take up his gun to kill, seems mild by comparison.

Mulford's West is also a place of special, epic qualities that would echo through the works of other writers in the decades to follow. As he explained it at the beginning of *Hopalong Cassidy*, it was "the raw and mighty West, the greatest stage in all the history of the world for so many deeds of daring which verged on the insane . . . seared and cross-barred with grave-lined trails and dotted with presumptuous, mushroom towns of brief stay whose inhabitants flung their primal passions in the face of humanity."[21] Although not all later writers saw the West in such terms, Mulford's words aptly describe a central image of the West that persisted in American popular culture until at least the 1970s.

B. M. Bower and Clarence Mulford represent two different directions taken by the Western in the early years of its popularity, and it is important to recognize that the genre was accessible to many writers. The dominant writer of Westerns between 1910 and 1930, however, was a former baseball player and dentist named Zane Grey, born Pearl Zane Grey, the middle name deriving from his mother's illustrious Ohio family.

Zane Grey played a major role in American popular culture. He began writing about the West when he was thirty-five, displaying a seriousness at least equal to Wister's twenty years before. His productivity matched that of Bower. And his vision of the West, formed as a result of personal experience and romantic yearning, was probably of greater consistency than that of any of his contemporaries. His appeal to general readers was considerable, and he found greater public acceptance than probably any other writer of Westerns prior to Louis L'Amour. In nine of the ten years between 1915 and 1925, a Zane Grey novel was among the top ten best-selling novels of the year. Unlike the works of many of his peers, Grey's books remained in print more than a half-century after his death in 1939.

Grey became a writer because he was bored by dentistry. He began by turning out three novels between 1903 and 1909 about the Ohio frontier and some of his own ancestors. None of these books attracted much attention. In 1906, however, Grey took a honeymoon trip to Arizona and began a lifelong romance with the landscape and history of the trans-Mississippi West. By 1906 he had also read *The Virginian* and come to realize the literary value of his response to the West. In his Ohio novels Grey had produced dark plots with clear distinctions between wildness and civilization. His heroes, for instance, were eastern military and political heroes. In the Southwest, however, where there was less history of settlement to draw on, Grey was free to turn his considerable descriptive powers on the landscape itself. For Grey, the Southwest was a place of expansiveness and color; it suggested openness and elation, not confinement and danger. As a result he turned out entirely different kinds of stories, beginning with *The Heritage of the Desert* in 1910.

The Heritage of the Desert is a romance in which a sickly easterner falls in love with a part-Indian woman in Arizona. The woman, whose name—Mescal—is also the name of a desert flower, represents the land that Grey himself had come to love. The story is ultimately one of physical and spiritual rejuvenation of the eastern male. As Grey explains it in the novel, "The desert regeneration had not stopped at turning weak lungs, vitiated blood, and flaccid muscles into a powerful man; it was at work on his mind, his heart, his soul."[22]

Grey continued this pattern, with variations, in dozens of novels between 1910 and the mid-1930s, becoming one of the wealthiest of all American writers. The secret of his success can be found not in action or shoot-outs (which appear with some frequency) but in the quasi-spiritual value of the West itself; this value leads Grey almost unfailingly to romance and regeneration. Even in one of his most famous novels, *Riders of the Purple Sage* (1913), the themes of romance and regeneration ultimately emerge from scenes of fast action, complicated behavior, and the spilling of much blood. The novel is one of extreme passions and powerful descriptions of human emotions and western landscape. In the end, however, the most powerful force is love, and the western gunman, Lassiter, the hero of the novel, is transformed by it.

Specific themes and character types reappear in later works. Protagonists are regenerated spiritually by their contact with the West and what Grey considered its central fact of life: "the wild passions of wild men in a wild country."[23] The same West, in Grey's stories, produces villains who represent moral retrogression. In this manner Grey's Westerns resemble Clarence Mulford's. But Grey was far more romantic than Mulford, and for him the difference between heroes and villains, between good and bad, often seems to be a quality of responsiveness to landscape and love. Moreover, Grey incorporates obvious erotic overtures in his treatment of love. Grey's heroes and heroines are generally drawn together by intense feelings and strong, covert sexual urges.[24]

The novels of Zane Grey contain strong primitivistic urges beneath a surface moralism. They share with Mulford's stories a romantic evocation of violence, but the violence is joined by a strong erotic impulse tied symbolically to western landscape. As such, Grey's Westerns have a medieval sense to them and bear resemblance to the romance as much as to the novel. They were a powerful imaginative lure to mass American audiences facing the complexities of urban life and the cultural aftershocks of World War I. There is nothing minimalist about a Zane Grey novel; the scale of his materials and the often overdrawn style of his prose were the basic ingredients for a strong sentimental antidote to the equally powerful forms of change in American society.

Grey's reputation was initially built on the novels he published between 1910 and 1915: *The Heritage of the Desert, Riders of the Purple Sage, Desert Gold* (1913), *The Light of Western Stars* (1914), *The Lone Star Ranger* (1914), and *The Rainbow Trail* (1915). Afterward he wrote novels about a variety of western events and situations. In every case he visited the locale, conducted historical research, and interviewed residents, always seeking to get the details of history and landscape right. Between 1912 and 1928 alone he published twenty-five Western novels, as well as six books about hunting and fishing, two juvenile novels, and dozens of magazine articles. Beginning in the 1920s many of his novels were turned into movies through contracts in which Grey specified that filming had to take place on location. Grey not only helped to popularize the Western, but he also gave the American West a romantic prominence and significance it otherwise would not have had.

Although Zane Grey was possibly the most important early writer of Westerns, he was not the most productive. That honor belongs to Max Brand. The name "Max Brand" deserves quotation marks, because it was only one of twenty-one pen names used by Frederick Schiller Faust; in fact, it was one of eight pseudonyms that Faust used for his Western stories alone, for he also published historical adventures, detective stories, spy thrillers, medical dramas (including the original Doctor Kildare novels), and other kinds of popular fiction. He wrote more Westerns than anything else, however. For instance, between 1917 and 1925 Faust published 204 works in various magazines, a high percentage of his titles being either single-issue novelettes of about 25,000 words or multi-issue serials ranging from 50,000 to 90,000 words. More than 150 of these were Westerns. In less than twenty years, from 1918 to the mid-1930s, he published well over 350 Western stories in popular magazines, especially *Western Story Magazine.*

Frederick Faust died in 1944, but his stories continued to appear thereafter, as they had during his life, in book form. By 1986 over 150 of his Western novels had been published as books, most appearing under the by-line of Max Brand even when they had been first published under one of Faust's other pseudonyms. From 1919 to 1986 a new Faust book was published on the average of every four months.[25] Faust, then, stands out as a Western novelist whose popularity began with magazine readers in 1917 and continued for more than seventy years on the bookracks of the United States.

Faust was a unique Western writer because he claimed to dislike the West and to despise not only Westerns but virtually all the popular genres he produced. His fondest literary interest was traditional poetry in the mode of Milton and Shakespeare. His many attempts at poetry were not especially good, however, but his popular fiction was. As a result, with the encouragement of editors and motivated by the money he could earn, which was considerable until the magazine market came to an end in the mid-1930s, Faust wrote Western novels. He kept his identity a secret to all but a few persons, though, and quite unlike Zane Grey, he avoided publicity altogether. Although he had been born in Seattle and had grown up on farms and ranches in the San Joachin Valley in California, he preferred to live in Europe. Many of his Westerns were written in Italy, where Faust rented a luxurious villa from 1926 to 1938.

In spite of his stated dislike of popular fiction, Faust had a genuine flair for creating stories and possessed a keen sense of style. Beginning with the appearance of *The Untamed* in 1918 (then as an *All-Story Weekly* serial, which was published a few months later as a hardcover book), he turned out Westerns quite unlike those of other writers. The uniqueness of Max Brand Westerns lies in the absence of serious pretensions to dealing with the actual West. Settings are rarely identifiable geographical places, and plots are almost never based on historical events. Moreover, Max Brand Westerns often contain elements from other literary genres, including heroes and plots drawn from classical and northern European mythology and legend. They are also action oriented to an extreme degree, with complicated, fast-paced plots. "Action, action, action is the thing," Faust once wrote about his Westerns.[26]

Although *Destry Rides Again* (1930) can lay claim to being the best known of the Max Brand Westerns, thanks to the film version starring James Stewart and Marlene Dietrich, others are more typical. In *The Untamed*, for instance, which was followed by two sequels, *The Night Horseman* (1920) and *The Seventh Man* (1921), the Max Brand hero is a strange young man named Dan Barry, who turned up as a child one day following a flock of wild geese and whistling an odd tune. As he grows up he develops a close companionship with a wolf and a black horse named Satan. Known as "Whistlin' Dan," he seems to have an imperturbable personality until one day when he is struck on the face by the leader of an outlaw gang. Having tasted his own blood, he is then overwhelmed by an instinctual desire for revenge. An inhuman yellow light begins to glow in his eyes, and he pursues a quest for revenge unimpeded by his affection for Kate Cumberland, the daughter of a rancher. Slim and somewhat feminine in stature, Dan Barry shows preternatural skill with a six-gun and, as the plot develops, eventually uses his bare hands to choke the outlaw leader to death. In the sequels to *The Untamed* Faust created other situations where Barry's animalistic instincts are unleashed by the actions of antagonists, eventually putting him in conflict with the law and even with Kate Cumberland, who by the final novel has become his wife. In that book, *The Seventh Man*, Barry kills six men to avenge the killing of a horse. The seventh man to be killed is Barry himself, finally shot to death by his own wife in a powerful and ironic act of love and understanding.

In his final series of Western novels Faust produced a neoproletarian story about the Montana Kid, a nonchalant Anglo roamer in Mexico. The Kid joins a jolly band of Mexican revolutionaries who battle constantly and joyfully against the military dictatorship. Aided by the guns and wits of the Montana Kid in *Montana Rides!* (1933), *Montana Rides Again* (1934), and *The Song of the Whip* (1936), the lower class is irresistibly victorious. Despite explicit scenes of violence and gore, these Robin Hood–like stories provided freewheeling merriment and exotic characters.

The hundreds of Max Brand Westerns lack literary and historical pretensions even though many of them contain literary allusions and some of the best prose produced in the genre before World War II.

They were originally written for public entertainment and printed in inexpensive pulp magazines meant to be read and then thrown away. Within the history of the Western novel they demonstrate the remarkable degree of narrative freedom enjoyed by the Western at the height of its popular appeal.

Max Brand Westerns reveal the market forces that sustained popular Western stories in the 1920s and 1930s. These forces originally were unleashed by other writers, especially Grey, and to some extent by Hollywood. Writing as Max Brand, Frederick Faust discovered readers more than he created them. Since he was an admittedly commercial vendor of his narrative talent, Faust's writing of Westerns was neo-experimental, its purpose being to find what would sell. He produced a wide variety of story types and hundreds of individual "yarns" (a term he liked) that defy efforts to discern unifying features beyond good telling and an avoidance of specific historical and geographical content. Max Brand novels often take the mythological West for granted. They assume western trappings as part of the stage set, devote little attention to the significance of events or places, and move forward into stories, generally of revenge and pursuit, told in tight prose with few extraneous features.

By 1935 the Western was in full flourish as a part of American popular culture. Bower, Mulford, Grey, and Brand had by then produced the majority of their work. Thereafter the Western was shaped by new writers whose careers began after World War I and by two external developments. One was the enormous popularity of the film Western, which took audiences away from print stories and created new interest in the kind of stories that Hollywood produced. A second and closely related development was the decline of pulps, the cheaply printed magazines that had provided the initial outlet for much Western fiction prior to the Great Depression of the 1930s. The typical route for a popular Western had been first appearance as a magazine serial (or a single-issue novelette) and then publication as a hardcover book, followed sometimes by a screen adaptation. The disappearance of the pulps, such as *Western Story Magazine,* left the magazine market in the hands of the so-called slick magazines (such as *The Saturday Evening Post*), which published less Western fiction to begin with and fewer novel-length works in general and which maintained different editorial expectations.

These changes, from the late 1930s into the 1960s, did not diminish the Western novel. Writers such as Ernest Haycox, Nelson Nye, Wayne Overholser, Luke Short, Will Henry, and others produced Westerns with regularity; in the early 1950s Louis L'Amour entered and then virtually dominated the field. These writers, Haycox in particular, brought considerable literary talent, especially in matters of style, to the Western. Competing against the powerful visual techniques of Hollywood, the medium of print fiction called for more attention than it did in the heyday of Zane Grey's florid style. In *Nevada* (1926), for instance, Grey described the western landscape as seen by his heroine in the following terms:

> Every time Hettie moved her absorbed gaze from one far point to another of the valley, the outlines, the colors, the distances, the lines of lonely cedars, the winding black threads of gullies—all seemed to change, to magnify in her sight, to draw upon her emotion, and to command her to set her eyes upon that sublime distance, that ethereal blending of hues and forms, that stunning mystery of the desert, of that magnificent arid zone which gave this country its name.
>
> "I can only look—and learn to worship," whispered Hettie, in a rapture. "It awakens me. What little have I seen and known! ... Oh, lonely wild land—Oh, Arizona!"[27]

Later, in novels by Ernest Haycox and other writers less romantically inclined, descriptions of the landscape tend to be unsentimental reflections of emotions and tensions deriving from the plot of the story. Note, for instance, the following passage from Haycox's *Starlight Rider* (1933), set in Nevada:

> He crossed to the west end of the porch and stared toward the higher elevation of land where the spur made jointure with Mogul's plateau. In that direction the glare of the down-plunging sun rose like the red guttering of a mountain fire, and broad bands of gold swept overhead. Thinking to himself, "In the morning I'll trace these cattle tracks," he turned back to unsaddle his horse; and it was then, hard on the heels of the thought, that the still, hot peace of the ridge was broken by the spanging echo of a rifle shot. The bullet went through the house wall a good ten feet from him with a quick and small and crushing sound.[28]

Ever since *The Virginian* Westerns have functioned as morality plays of good in conflict with evil, with the results portrayed in such a way as to idealize the past in contrast to the present. Many early Westerns, including *The Virginian,* involved epic confrontations in which violence was the means by which evil is removed and civilization firmly established. (Trampas emerges in Wister's novel as a threat to social order, not just to the Virginian himself.) This kind of story was joined by other stories that took up conflicts at a later point in the settlement of the West, often involving villains such as corrupt public officials or avaricious bankers whose origins are from within society. Overall the general nature of the Western story was formulaic.[29] Conventions of the genre almost always demanded a male hero whose heroism is based on some formative experience with western wildness outside that of the settled or settling community itself. With this basic feature of the story expected, the challenge to writers of Westerns was to develop a particularly effective style (as seen in Haycox's description of the "quick and small and crushing sound" of a bullet) or else to elevate the general significance of the formulaic story.

Most writers of popular Westerns were in the business for the long haul, and after the demise of the pulp magazines, many depended heavily on the paperback book market, hoping to produce steady incomes through publishing several titles per year. Such conditions did not encourage great experimentation or wide variation from traditional plot lines. In fact, they created additional tensions for those hoping to earn a living by writing Westerns. Even though the paperback book market was large in terms of the number of titles published per year, especially until the 1980s, the profit margin was small. Strained relationships between authors and publishers frequently resulted. Nelson C. Nye, for example, stopped writing in 1969 after producing more than a hundred books because, as he said in an interview twenty years later, "the publishing business began holding up writers' money."[30]

One writer did particularly well in this environment, however, outstripping his competition and becoming what his paperback covers eventually claimed to be "the bestselling western writer of all time." Louis L'Amour became a famous Western writer almost overnight in 1953 when an editor at Fawcett Publications recommended that he expand into a novel a short story he had just published in *Collier's*. The resulting book, *Hondo*, was soon bought by John Wayne and made into a feature film. Then, according to L'Amour, "everyone wanted Westerns."[31] Forty-six years old at the time he wrote *Hondo*, and with little prior experience in the Western genre, L'Amour began to produce what readers and editors wanted. Between 1953 and his death in 1988 he published over seventy Western novels, achieving great popularity and even receiving a Presidential Medal of Freedom from Ronald Reagan.

In *Hondo* L'Amour combines the Western formula with a Mickey Spillane–like writing style. The tone is set in the second paragraph of the novel: "He was a big man, wide-shouldered, with the lean, hard-boned face of the desert rider. There was no softness in him. His toughness was ingrained and deep, without cruelty, yet quick, hard, and dangerous. Whatever wells of gentleness might lie with him were guarded and deep."[32] Hondo Lane is a roamer at this point, with a reputation as a gunman, but he soon runs into a widow and her children on a southwestern ranch threatened by an Apache uprising. The woman, Angie Lowe, is as strongly attracted to Hondo as he is to her.

Hondo is complete with graphic violence. Near the end of the story Hondo Lane kills a renegade Apache leader, Silva, who is portrayed as thoroughly evil, especially in his needless earlier killing of Hondo's faithful dog. In the final struggle Hondo "gutted the Indian as the Indian had gutted the dog."[33] In L'Amour's hands this is justified action, however, and in the final paragraph of the novel, one page later, the reader learns that the "wells of gentleness" in Hondo have been tapped by Angie Lowe. The Apache threat now removed, he thinks of a new life in "a home where smoke would soon again arise from the chimney," where "a woman would be there with him, in that home, before that hearth."[34]

L'Amour made both violence and hearth key features of his later novels. Over the years, however, he moderated his style, toning down the violence and stressing the value of hearth and family. His novels kept pace with readers trained by television to expect easy reading and clearly articulated themes. It was a lesson L'Amour himself had learned from reading the pulps.[35] But L'Amour's talents were given a great boost by the publicity efforts of his publishers, especially Bantam Books, which by 1975 became the sole purveyor of his novels.

In the 1950s L'Amour concentrated on action novels like, but not always as good as, *Hondo,* with little reference to anything beyond the immediate story. Later, however, L'Amour wrote novels with obvious historical trappings in which protagonists travel widely or migrate to the West from places far in the East, even from Europe. In such novels as *Under the Sweetwater Rim* (1971) the western hero serves also as a representative of family heritage reaching back to earlier American and European traditions. With the publication of *Sackett* in 1961 L'Amour also began writing the kind of story that would dominate his work after the mid-1970s. *Sackett* was the first novel to feature as its hero a representative of a family from which other members would be chosen to appear in later stories (fig. 2.2). Eventually L'Amour wrote novels chronicling the exploits of three families, each demonstrating a different aspect of the frontier experience. The Sacketts are portrayed generally as trailblazers; the Talons are settlers and builders on the land; and the Chantreys are persons of sophistication and reason. L'Amour's novels thus provide a collective expression of the frontier process.[36] Shortly before his death L'Amour stated the obvious general theme of his Westerns: "I am concerned with building a nation, learning to live together, with establishing towns, homes, and bridges

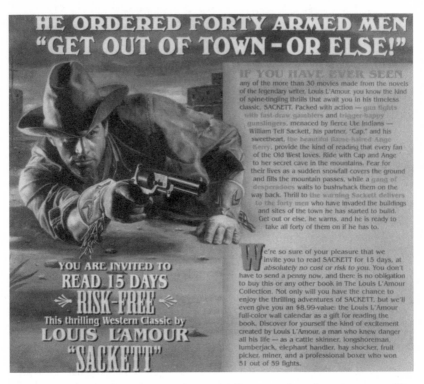

Figure 2.2. Western images straight out of dime novels and B Westerns still exist, as evidenced by this 1995 advertisement for Louis L'Amour novels. (Ball State University Photo Services.)

to the future."[37] Such an emphasis aptly expressed the domestic hopes of the cold war world where the source of present greatness was an imagined, positive sense of community in the past.

The richest and most literary Westerns, however, were written not by journeyman writers like L'Amour but by authors who took seriously the subject of the Western, especially the historical experience it represented, and elements of the formula. Writers as various as Edward Abbey, Jean Stafford, and E. L. Doctorow have drawn literary inspiration from the Western.[38] But the best example of a novel that elevated the significance of the Western, drawing to it the serious attention of later writers, is Jack Schaefer's *Shane*, published in 1949 and made into a major motion picture starring Alan Ladd in 1953. Schaefer was familiar with the West, although he was not a practicing writer of Westerns. In *Shane* he combined the elements of the popular story in a way that was enormously attractive to post–World War II readers, and he showed other writers that the popular or formula Western could be an effective medium for art, as well as popular entertainment.

In *Shane* Schaefer created the ultimate western morality tale, rich in meanings associated with community, sexuality, family, and violence. The story is relatively simple in outline. A mysterious, armed stranger rides into a struggling farming community adjacent to cattle ranges; the stranger, known only by the single name "Shane," puts aside his gun and assists a small family (husband, wife, and young son) in their efforts. When the family and the community are threatened by a rancher and his hired gunman in a dispute over access to water, Shane eventually straps on his six-gun again, kills the rancher's hired gun, is badly wounded himself, and rides off into the mysterious western space from which he has come.

This summary fails almost entirely to note the effect of Schaefer's narrative style, in which the family's young son, Bob, grown older, tells the story retrospectively as a tale of his own childhood. Moreover, no summary can adequately indicate the powerful emotions, many of them covertly sexual, that flow among Shane, Marian Starrett (the wife), Joe Starrett (the husband), and even little Bob; nor can it adequately convey the theme of reluctant violence in the story. When Shane ultimately is forced to take up his gun again, Schaefer's story seems to echo the decision of the United States to use atomic weapons in the recently concluded world war. It is as if Shane himself knows full well that his use of deadly force will render him unsuitable for further participation in the society to which he has chosen to throw his lot. He and his rancher antagonist, Fletcher, are both anachronisms— one of them good, the other bad—but neither with a chance to survive the transformation of the West from open range to fenced-off agriculture. Bob notes at one point that Shane seems to have been destined for violence, for his weapons "were part of him, part of the man, of the full sum of the integrate force that was Shane."[39] The "integrate force" apparently derives from some distant point in the frontier past.

At the end of the novel the character of Shane, now gone and possibly dead, having knowingly sacrificed himself for the sake of others, takes on Christlike qualities in the thoughts and memories of the Starrett family. In this way *Shane* provides the apotheosis of the American Western in the form of a cold war morality play about the use of force to combat evil.

While the popular Western was flourishing in the 1940s and 1950s, the West as a place of reality rather than myth became of increasing interest to serious novelists. Writers such as Idaho's Vardis Fisher and

Montana's A. B. Guthrie Jr. took their regions of the West as appropriate subjects for serious fiction. Wallace Stegner, in novels such as *The Big Rock Candy Mountain* (1943), *Angle of Repose* (1971), and *Recapitulation* (1979), made similar and, in the eyes of many critics, better literary use of the West.

According to critic John R. Milton, many of the works that can be considered regional novels of the West are based on some intrinsic value found in the geography and history of the West. Often this value is connected with western Native American cultures. Willa Cather, for instance, attributed great significance to the vanished cliff dwellers of the Southwest, as if such facts gave the region an unusually powerful sense of antiquity not available elsewhere in America.

Nevertheless, the central feature of Western novels since World War II has been not the West itself—the unmediated West, so to speak—but the power of prior perceptions of the West deriving largely from popular culture. Western novels, that is, have been about the Western as often as they have been about the West. Such perceptions of what the West once seemed to be have frequently served as material for ironic novels that twist the Western story into new shapes. In Edward Abbey's *The Brave Cowboy* (1956) the cowboy of the tale is an out-of-his-time hero, Jack Burns, who struggles on horseback against a modern sheriff armed with automobiles and helicopters. Although Abbey's character remains the lone, noble individual pitted against a repressive government, he falls victim to a highway accident in which he and his horse are run over by a tractor-trailer hauling bathroom fixtures. "Poor Jack," a friend says of him in the story, "poor old Jack—born too late, out of place, out of time. Look at him, the scheming atavist, all wound up in reality looking for a tunnel back to his boy's dream world of space and horses and sunlight."[40]

Such a sense of how things once were—or seemed to be—flows through a minor but important tradition of Western novels, works that tell stories of westerners who are "out of place" and "out of time." In fact, this theme of historical displacement is an undercurrent even in *The Virginian*, for Wister knew that he was dealing with a world that had already disappeared. Yet the Virginian himself was able to change, marry the eastern woman, and take advantage of progress. The sense of being at odds with historical progress sometimes appears in Zane Grey in the guise of contemporary eastern characters, both male and female, who are converted by the values of the West in such a way as to cause them to turn almost viciously against contemporary trends. In some respects the passing of the West is the central subject of all popular Westerns.

Several Western novels in recent decades have made particularly effective use of this theme. These include Schaefer's *Monte Walsh* (1963), about the life and death of an ordinary cowboy who, like Abbey's Jack Burns, prefers horses to fences and automobiles; Robert Flynn's *North to Yesterday* (1967), about an attempt to drive cattle from Texas to Trail's End in Kansas some twenty years after the closing of the cattle trails; and, above all else, several novels by Larry McMurtry: *Horseman, Pass By* (1961), *Lonesome Dove* (1985), *Anything for Billy* (1988), and *Buffalo Girls* (1990).

McMurtry deserves a special note in any discussion of the Western novel, because *Lonesome Dove,* winner of the Pulitzer Prize, rejuvenated interest in the epic Western at a time when it was generally considered moribund. McMurtry's long story of two aging former Texas Rangers is one writer's testimony to the continuing value of the Western as a literary form, yet it is also a commentary on the Western. Augustus McCrae and Woodrow Call, the graying protagonists of the novel, do not function as formulaic western heroes. Instead, they are fallible humans, perhaps more fallible than most. "All you two done was ruin one another, not to mention those close to you," says the woman whom McCrae has loved most of his life.[41] Still, they sustain a thousand pages of contemporary fiction in McMurtry's book and many hours of a television miniseries, serving as vivid reminders of the Western's appeal as both form and subject almost nine decades after *The Virginian.*

McMurtry shows the contemporary dilemma of the Western novel. Deriving to some extent from such historical roots as the passing of the frontier and the anxieties of urban life in twentieth-century America, the Western itself has become a feature of what it once sought to describe. Conventions and character types in the Western not only have shaped views of the West but now exist as such pervasive features of literary culture that writers are hardly free to ignore them.

Western novels have always explored territories shaped more by imagination than by nature. William S. Hart, a working cowboy who became a Hollywood star, with one screen version of *The Virginian* to his credit, may have sized up the popular Western better than anyone else. Referring to Wister's novel, Hart said that it was "a beautiful story" but also "a monument to the fact that a truly great writer can make the moon look like green cheese and get away with it."[42] *The Virginian,* that is, was not particularly realistic, and neither were the Westerns that followed. Even though writers like Zane Grey and Louis L'Amour took pride in historical details and the trivia of western lore, they, too, had to make the moon look like green cheese. Cowboy life itself, to take a chief subject of the Western, was in reality dirty and tiresome. Historian William W. Savage Jr. has pointed out that such life simply "could not be portrayed accurately and interestingly at the same time."[43] The writers of Westerns were shapers of myth, not recorders of reality. Even writers of western-based novels outside the popular domain of "the Western" have found the mythic material unavoidable.

The Western novel has carried two themes into and through its mythic geography: heroism and regeneration. From the beginning the western hero, almost always male and often the title of the story in which he appears, has been portrayed as an individual coming out of the world of the common man yet alienated from that world by circumstance or choice. The features of character and ability that set the hero apart from others also enable the hero to be the champion of community. But the stories of heroism have also been stories of regeneration: the hero's own, the community's, and, by extension, the nation's. In the most traditional Westerns the theme of regeneration is joined to heroism through love and often marriage. This was Wister's most important contribution to the Western story, and it remains a central matter even in *Lonesome Dove,* with Gus McCrae's thoughts so frequently and affectionately drawn to Clara Allen.

The Western novel has also offered a set of consistent images of the West itself. The most obvious is the image of the West as a place where civilization and wildness collide—and therefore a testing place for both individuals and society. This image exploits the physical features of western landscapes, the often biased interpretation of Native Americans as "wild," and the sense of the West as a place rich in crime that, like the Indians, must be removed. As a result the West of the Western is a highly moral setting, where the difference between good and evil is often as clear as that between civilization and wildness, farms and badlands, snow-capped mountain peaks and rugged canyons.

The popular culture West of the Western is also a place of horses and cattle, especially the latter. One of the richest ironies of the Western is its fixation on cattle ranching and cattle drives, features of advancing civilization that rapidly brought the wild, unsettled West to an end after 1860.[44] This irony is a key to understanding a central fact about the image of the West in the Western. It is a place—and a time—that is *gone.* Even for Wister in 1902 the world of the Virginian was "a vanished world."[45] The Western has always provided a West heavier in nostalgia than any other element, even violence or heroism. The true subject of the Western is not what happened once or how things really were; rather, it is the fact of the West's passing. Even in a sophisticated novel like Wallace Stegner's *Angle of Repose,* the story is about the loss of the West and its presumed values.

The Western is loss recollected in popular imaginative terms rather than loss recorded in history. As such, the Western has served as a record of American attitudes. For the most part these are conflicting attitudes: nostalgia and progress, individualism and community, violence and love, hatred and respect for Native Americans, and action and order. As a cultural form the Western thrust simultaneously forward and backward, was both progressive and regressive, promoted the advance of civilization while celebrating a primitive past. Moreover, it was an adaptable form: once established, the Western fit the needs of different writers and different audiences. It changed over time—survived war, prosperity, depression, another world war—and still retained its basic structure. Most of all, its inner paradoxes, sometimes reconciled in oversimplified ways, meshed easily with the complex anxieties of a traditionally rural society that rapidly became urbanized and industrialized. The mythic nature of the Western lies less in any godlike quality of the hero or any legendary attributes of setting or plot than in its deep and often contradictory appeals to American readers.

Notes

1. John R. Milton, *The Novel of the American West* (Lincoln, Nebr., 1980), xiv.

2. Richard Slotkin, *Regeneration through Violence: The Mythology of the American Frontier, 1600–1860* (Middletown, Conn., 1973). The dime novel origins of the Western are noted in much of the historical attention to the genre, including E. Douglas Branch's study *The Cowboy and His Interpreters* (New York, 1926), Joe B. Franz and Julian Ernest Choate Jr.'s *The American Cowboy: The Myth and the Reality* (Norman, Okla., 1955), and Russel B. Nye's *The Unembarrassed Muse: The Popular Arts in America* (New York, 1970); the work of Daryl Jones provides a detailed study of the dime novel Western, especially *The Dime Novel Western* (Bowling Green, Ohio, 1978). It should be noted, however, that few writers of Westerns in the twentieth century, except for Zane Grey and Clarence Mulford, appear to have been avid readers of dime novels. On the matter of Cooper's influence, it is often assumed that the Leatherstocking novels gave inspiration to the twentieth-century Western. In *The Six-Gun Mystique* (Bowling Green, Ohio, 1975), a study of the Western as popular culture, John Cawelti flatly states, "The Western was created in the early nineteenth century by James Fenimore Cooper" (34). Such statements seem highly presumptuous, however, possibly reflecting the scholar's own awareness of Cooper rather than any direct influence on the

writers of Westerns. James K. Folsom, in *The American Western Novel* (New Haven, Conn., 1966), makes a reasonable case for the diffusion of Cooper's influence among the writing of western fiction in general.

3. Richard Etulain, "The Origins of the Western," *Journal of Popular Culture* 5 (Spring 1972): 803.

4. Facts about *The Virginian* and Wister's life are taken from G. Edward White, *The Eastern Establishment and the Western Experience: The West of Frederic Remington, Theodore Roosevelt, and Owen Wister* (New Haven, Conn., 1968), and from Ben Merchant Vorpahl, *"My Dear Wister": The Frederic Remington–Owen Wister Letters* (Palo Alto, Calif., 1972).

5. Owen Wister, *Owen Wister out West: His Journals and Letters*, ed. Fanny Kemble Wister (Chicago, 1958), 30, 32.

6. Vorpahl, *My Dear Wister*, 178. The development of Wister's cowboy hero in his early stories and *The Virginian* is well explained in two articles by Neal Lambert: "Owen Wister's Lin McLean: The Failure of the Vernacular Hero," *Western American Literature* 5 (Fall 1970): 219–32; and "Owen Wister's Virginian: The Genesis of a Cultural Hero," *Western American Literature* 6 (Summer 1971): 99–107.

7. Owen Wister, *The Virginian* (New York, 1979 [1902]), 4.

8. Ibid., 303.

9. The Virginian's dialectical contradictions are discussed in John Cawelti's *Adventure, Mystery, Romance: Formula Stories as Art and Popular Culture* (Chicago, 1976), 215–16.

10. Larzer Ziff, *The American 1890s: Life and Times of a Lost Generation* (New York, 1966), 347–48.

11. Biographical information on Bower is scarce, but Stanley R. Davidson's "Chip of the Flying U: The Author Was a Lady," *Montana: The Magazine of Western History* 23 (Spring 1973): 3–15, provides a sketch of her life. Also see Roy W. Meyer, "B. M. Bower: The Poor Man's Wister," *Journal of Popular Culture* 7 (Winter 1973): 667–79; and William Bloodworth, "Mulford and Bower: Myth and History in the Early Western," *Great Plains Quarterly* 1 (Spring 1981): 95–104.

12. B. M. Bower, *Chip of the Flying U* (New York, 1906), 32.

13. B. M. Bower, *Lonesome Land* (New York, 1912), 37.

14. B. M. Bower, *The Lure of the Dim Trails* (New York, 1907), 42.

15. Virtually the only available source of information about Mulford's life is an unpublished master's thesis by Joseph Perham, "Reflections on Hopalong Cassidy: A Study of Clarence E. Mulford" (University of Maine, 1966). Some biographical information drawn from Perham appears in William Bloodworth, "Mulford and Bower."

16. Clarence E. Mulford, *Hopalong Cassidy* (New York, 1910), 65.

17. Clarence E. Mulford, *Bar-20 Days* (Chicago, 1911), 157.

18. Clarence E. Mulford, *Bar 20* (New York, 1907), 74.

19. Clarence E. Mulford, *The Orphan* (New York, 1908), 6.

20. Robert Warshow, "Movie Chronicle: The Westerner," in *The Immediate Experience* (Garden City, N.Y., 1962), 153.

21. Mulford, *Hopalong Cassidy*, 1.

22. Zane Grey, *The Heritage of the Desert* (New York, 1910), 146.

23. Zane Grey, *The Rainbow Trail* (New York, 1915), 310.

24. See William Bloodworth, "Zane Grey's Western Eroticism," *South Dakota Review* 23 (Autumn 1985): 5–14.

25. William F. Nolan, *Max Brand: Western Giant* (Bowling Green, Ohio, 1986), 1–2. "New book" refers to first-time publication in book form of stories first published in magazines or, in some cases, from unpublished manuscripts.

26. Frederick Faust, *The Notebooks and Poems of "Max Brand,"* ed. John Schoolcraft (New York, 1957), 24.

27. Zane Grey, *Nevada* (New York, 1927), 135–36.

28. Ernest Haycox, *Starlight Rider* (New York, 1972), 15.

29. "Formulaic" is a term used extensively in John Cawelti's work on the Western, first in *The Six-Gun Mystique* (Bowling Green, Ohio, 1975) and then in his more inclusive *Adventure, Mystery, Romance* (Chicago, 1976). Westerns, in Cawelti's view, involve an implicit but not overly restrictive formula, as do other kinds of popular stories.

30. Quoted in S. Jean Mead, *Maverick Writers: Candid Comments by Fifty-two of the Best* (Caldwell, Idaho, 1989), 122.

31. Quoted in Mead, *Maverick Writers*, 12.

32. Louis L'Amour, *Hondo* (Greenwich, Conn., 1953), 5.

33. Ibid., 158.

34. Ibid., 159.

35. In the 1930s L'Amour wrote occasionally for the pulps, although his interest at that time was in stories of the Far East, not Westerns. From the pulps, he said in a memoir concentrating mainly on his reading, "I learned much. A pulp story had to start fast and it had to move, and above all, you had to have a story to tell" (Louis L'Amour, *Education of a Wandering Man* [New York, 1989], 125).

36. John D. Nesbitt provides an excellent comprehensive discussion of L'Amour novels in "Change of Purpose in the Novels of Louis L'Amour," *Western American Literature* 13 (Spring 1978): 65–81, pointing out how L'Amour had managed at that point to keep up with the changing tastes of the American public. The author continued to do so until his death. One of his last novels, entitled *The Last of the Breed* (1986), involves an Air Force major whose experimental aircraft is forced down by Russians in Siberia. The hero, whose ancestors are Sioux and Cheyenne, calls on ancient skills as he escapes his captors, survives the fierce Siberian weather, and eludes a Soviet Yakut as he retraces the migratory path of his ancestors from Siberia to North America.

37. L'Amour, *Education of a Wandering Man*, 136.

38. I have made this point in greater detail elsewhere. See William Bloodworth, "Literary Extensions of the Formula Western," *Western American Literature* 14 (Winter 1980): 287–96.

39. Jack Schaefer, *Shane* (New York, 1949), 101.

40. Edward Abbey, *The Brave Cowboy* (New York, 1956), 124.

41. Larry McMurtry, *Lonesome Dove* (New York, 1986), 931.

42. William S. Hart, *My Life East and West* (Boston, 1929), 174–76.

43. William W. Savage Jr., *The Cowboy Hero: His Image in American History and Culture* (Norman, Okla., 1968), xxvi.

44. It is interesting to note that a recent comic box office hit, Billy Crystal's *City Slickers* (1991), defines true manhood, once again, as taking good care of cows. In having three New Yorkers, each involved in a midlife crisis, seek regeneration by participating in a cattle drive from New Mexico to Colorado, the movie precisely recapitulates the central motif of the Western as it was expressed by Owen Wister and Zane Grey.

45. Wister stated this in his preface to the novel. See *The Virginian*, ix–x.

Suggestions for Further Reading

FICTION

Benton, Mike. *The Comic Book in America.* Dallas, 1989, 1993.

Bloodworth, William A. *Max Brand.* New York, 1993.

Bold, Christine. *Selling the Wild West: Popular Western Fiction, 1860–1960.* Bloomington, Ind., 1987.

Cawelti, John. *The Six-Gun Mystique.* Bowling Green, Ohio, 1975.

Cook, Michael L. *Dime Novel Roundup: Annotated Index, 1931–1981.* Bowling Green, Ohio, 1983.

Denning, Michael. *Mechanic Accents: Dime Novels and Working Class Culture in America.* London, 1987.

Etulain, Richard W., and Michael T. Marsden, eds. *The Popular Western: Essays toward a Definition.* Bowling Green, Ohio, 1974.

Folsom, James K. *The American Western Novel.* New Haven, Conn., 1966.

Goulart, Ron. *Cheap Thrills: An Informal History of the Pulp Magazines.* New Rochelle, N.Y., 1972.

Horn, Maurice. *Comics of the American West.* New York, 1977.

Horn, Maurice, ed. *The World Encyclopedia of Comics.* 2 vols. New York, 1976.

Jones, Daryl. *The Dime Novel Western.* Bowling Green, Ohio, 1978.

Milton, John R. *The Novel of the American West.* Lincoln, Nebr., 1980.

Slotkin, Richard. *Regeneration through Violence: The Mythology of the American Frontier, 1600–1860.* Middletown, Conn., 1973.

Smith, Henry Nash. *Virgin Land: The American West as Symbol and Myth.* Cambridge, Mass., 1950.

Tompkins, Jane. *West of Everything: The Inner Life of Westerns.* New York, 1992.

Tuska, Jon, and Vicki Piekarski. *The Frontier Experience: A Reader's Guide to the Life and Literature of the American West.* Jefferson, N.C., 1984, 1990.

Tuska, Jon, and Vicki Piekarski, eds. *Encyclopedia of Frontier and Western Fiction.* New York, 1983.

Weinberg, Robert. *The Louis L'Amour Companion.* Kansas City, 1992.

Wister, Owen. *The Virginian.* New York, 1902.

PART TWO

Live Entertainment

THREE

Thomas L. Altherr

Let 'er Rip: Popular Culture Images of the American West in Wild West Shows, Rodeos, and Rendezvous

SINCE THE LATE nineteenth century several types of historical pageantry have helped to keep alive images of the mythic West in American popular culture. Chief among these have been the Wild West, the rodeo, and in more recent decades, the rendezvous. Like many other historical celebrations, these institutionalized ceremonies have often sacrificed historical accuracy in favor of nostalgia and the satisfaction of hegemonic needs of constituencies to reinforce self-identity. Each emerged during a time of transition and offered a comfortable, if simplistic, stylized tableau of a phase of much more complicated western history. Urban populations could throng to these pageants either to escape the pressures of the present or to see theatricalized justifications of the later stages of Manifest Destiny. Males uncertain of changes in the roles and expectations of men could feast on visualizations of times when "men were *real* men." Whites who presumed they were superior to other races but were increasingly uncomfortable in a multicultural America could for the most part ignore the multiracial realities of the West or consign them to the harmless past. Not only did the Wild West, rodeo, and rendezvous preserve and demonstrate outmoded customs, skills, and derring-do to the delight of audiences that had little or no direct contact with the West, but they enabled viewers to revel in that obsolescence. Why settle for a tawdry depiction of agricultural boredom, tedious travel, and stultifying isola-

tion when an afternoon with "Buffalo Bill" Cody's troupe, an evening
at a Madison Square Garden rodeo, or a weekend at a rendezvous
could deliver what most Americans believed or wished was the real,
exciting Wild West? Far more than just commercialized forms of entertainment, the Wild West, the rodeo, and the rendezvous touched deeply on American desires for the supposedly more sharply defined cer-
tainties of American frontier expansion. In the process these historical
pageants often reflected, and sometimes helped shape, American life
and thought.

———————

Despite recent attacks on the Old West as a land of trigger-happy gunmen or reckless Anglo males who exploited the region's women, Native Americans, minorities, and resources, and regardless of the revi-
sionism associated with the "new western history," the mythic West
continues to thrive in popular imagery.[1] Recent movies and television
shows have recycled the old western myths in various forms. Country
music continues to perpetuate a version of the Old West that is one
part simple-minded nostalgia, one part lonesome roustabouterie, and
one part hillbilly hedonism. An aged president rode the range on his
Santa Barbara ranch. Cowboy colonels plotted forays into Central
America. Rambo launched into a new set of Indians, either in South-
east Asia or the Middle East; Indiana Jones dueled with similar bunch-
es. Louis L'Amour spit out literary bullets, rarely hitting any target but
fantasy. Tacky trinkets (of the sort that Europeans used to foist on Indians) litter the shelves of every western souvenir palace, jumbling decades, personages, states and territories, and mountains and plains into
an all-purpose mélange of images guaranteed to avoid any hint of reality. Western wear emporia still do a brisk business selling the apparel of
the dream. Ralph Lauren took the look, very expensively, to the national fashion market. Some men and women continue to idolize the
Marlboro Man as the epitome of masculinity. Dude ranches offer up
landlocked "fantasy cruises" for affluent dilettantes who want to sample the rigors of western life. Restaurants such as Denver's Buckhorn
Exchange serve up slices of the Old West, both figuratively and literally, offering elk medallions and buffalo steaks. The "politically incor-
rect" and historically inaccurate Old West refuses to fade away in
American popular culture.

    Similarly contributing to this lingering yearning for a Golden Age
of the West have been the numerous western-oriented spectacles and
pageants, direct descendants of the Wild West shows that flourished in
the last two decades of the nineteenth century and the first two of the

twentieth one before fading out by the 1940s. "Theme" amusement parks such as the Disney duo and the Six Flags over (fill in the blank) versions mix stereotypical western subjects with their other attractions. Western towns, such as Central City, Colorado, or Deadwood, South Dakota, that cater to the tourist trade rarely fail to include some restored relic of the town's past, such as the old jail or saloon. Outside modern-day Tucson visitors can flock to Old Tucson, a re-created extended movie set, to catch rapid glimpses of different types of Old West buildings and witness simulated showdowns several times daily. Cheyenne's Frontier Days, Calgary's Stampede, and other pageants combining some old Wild West show acts with modern rodeo still pack in the crowds. "Frontier towns" across the country in such nonwestern regions as Lake George, New York, have retailed the Old West for quick consumption by easterners. Would-be cowboys throng to the dude ranches (the West's century-old answer to the bed and breakfast) and lately can fork out big bucks to accompany an actual trail drive, as the movie *City Slickers* (1991) illustrated. Reenactor military units replay several western battles, ranging from a Civil War confrontation, Glorieta Pass in New Mexico, to the Custer battle in Montana (although the latter threatened to get tense a couple of years ago when Sioux activists suggested that, like their forebears, they might attack for real). These units spend much time trying to ensure historical accuracy, and usually their hearts are in the right place, but their larger, healthier twentieth-century bodies and maintained teeth undercut the push for verisimilitude. With its complement of restored forts, such as Fort Laramie in Wyoming and Fort Davis in Texas, as national historic sites, the National Park Service keeps the past alive, although the service has become far more sensitive to the need for balanced interpretation. In recent years, as several western states and towns have commemorated their centennials, a variety of celebrations have reenacted or dramatized some pivotal event in the state's history. Oklahomans, for example, in 1989, staged repeats of the fabled Sooner Land Rush of 1889. Covered wagon caravans wended their way over remnants of the old trails. These centennial fetes were not without controversy, however, as vocal Indian groups challenged these displays of past white imperialism. For the most part, however, onlookers ignored the complaints and lapped up the Old West scenes. On their part tribal peoples have shared in the perpetuation of western myths. Some Indian extravaganzas and powwows have gone beyond original Indian purposes and become commercialized spectacles for white audiences and native hucksters. Beyond the shores many Europeans and Japanese have gobbled up the western mythos, as Karl May's nineteenth-century novels, "spaghetti" and Japanese Western movies, and Czech Pony Express riders attest.[2] In these marketable formats, still appealing to Americans and foreigners after all these years, the Old West persists.

In particular three types of these western pageants—the Wild West show, the rodeo, and the rendezvous—deserve historical examination, because of their tremendous past and present popularity. Although each overlaps somewhat with other forms of Old West celebrations, each derived from different times and parts of the historical West and from somewhat different motivations to preserve the Old West. The Wild West show combined various aspects of the drama of western conquest, ranging from hunting, trapping, and mining to Indian warfare. Rodeo developed directly from cowboy work contests and the rather specific years of the cattle trade, from the late 1860s to the early 1890s. The more recent craze for rendezvous pays homage to the fur-trade decades, the preagricultural frontiers of the 1820s, 1830s, and 1840s. Curiously all three originated in the serious business of conquering and exploiting the lands, resources, animals, and people of the West, but all three have transmogrified into displays of play, amusement, and entertainment.

None of the three was entirely new. The human need for spectacle and pageantry goes back deep into antiquity. Ancient and medieval Europeans thrived on a variety of circuses, parades, holidays, fairs, and other frolics that the Church could barely contain. Many of these gatherings, some of which have lasted to the present in one form or another, featured remembrances of historical events, glorifications of actual or legendary heroes, and exhibits of exotic animals and peoples. Colonizing the Americas, Europeans brought with them this penchant for pageantry. Election and militia training day feasts were plentiful in the Anglo colonies; fiestas were common in the Hispanic borderlands. Renaissance Europeans were inveterate exhibitors of animals and exotic peoples, which they would transport great distances for commercial exploitation. Slaves in the colonies reenacted African ritual celebrations or fashioned modified ones in the New World. In northern cities free blacks held parades in which they mocked their white "superiors" through role reversal. No strangers to the need for entertainment themselves, native tribal populations adhered to rigorous schedules of dances, healing ceremonies, ritual humiliations, and other convocations, most of which made the tribal knowledge, norms, and history accessible to the populace in tribe, clan, or other kinship group form.

By the post–Civil War era the cultural necessity for leisure-time entertainment became, if anything, more pronounced. On one level the lyceum and Chautauqua movements sought to fill the gap, but most

Americans, middle-class and otherwise, rushed into other, more popular cultural types of amusement: such sports as baseball, boxing, and horseracing; theatrical productions, melodramas, and minstrel shows; board, card, and parlor games; dime novel, romance, and biography reading; light opera, such song tours as those of Jenny Lind, and what later generations would call "pops" concerts; picnicking, touring, and vacationing in the nearby countryside; dining at restaurants, ice cream socials, and Saturday night dances; landscape painting, limning, and for some, photography; collecting stamps, coins, knickknacks, and other collectibles; amateur bird study, botanizing, and visits to zoological gardens and natural history museums; and a host of other activities. Even political campaigns took on the aura of entertainment, as the two major parties masked their lack of ideological diversity with pomp and bombast. After the 1880s trolleys allowed the working classes more mobility to search out new types of leisure at amusement parks; department stores—"palaces of consumption"—strove to make shopping, especially by women, a form of pleasure; and the novelty of the motion picture signaled the coming trend in expanded mass culture. Cultures from the new wave of immigrants added to the national mix. And throughout this period, the circus, with its collection of animal acts, human derring-do, freak shows, magic exhibitions, and other carnival attractions, remained intensely popular. Phineas T. Barnum was only one of several effective circus organizers who succeeded in drawing massive crowds. Ringling Brothers, the Bailey organization, and later, the Sells-Floto outfit cashed in on the circus formula. Such was the entertainment milieu when William F. "Buffalo Bill" Cody, William F. "Doc" Carver, Nate Salsbury, Gordon "Pawnee Bill" Lillie, and others dreamed up the Wild West in the early 1880s.

Actually, many of the elements for the Wild West had reached audiences earlier than the 1880s. As Don Russell showed in his history of the genre, entrepreneurs had been exhibiting distinctly western phenomena in the East as early as 1843. That year P. T. Barnum apparently bought a traveling herd of buffalo in Boston and transported them to Hoboken, New Jersey, where he enthralled New Yorkers with a "Grand Buffalo Hunt." Rodeos, or perhaps more accurately, cowboy "roundups," were semiregular occasions in the Southwest by the late 1840s. Continuing the trend from colonial times, other exhibitors had organized staged Indian dances and re-creations of historical themes such as Pocahontas's "rescue" of John Smith. Circus pioneers, such as Isaac Van Amburgh, had put together the three-ring format by the 1850s, and in 1860 James "Grizzly" Adams treated New Yorkers to his touring wild animal menagerie. These trends accelerated after the Civil

War. Early rodeos at Deer Trail, Colorado, in 1869 and Cheyenne in 1872 demonstrated the potential for that crowd pleaser. "Wild Bill" Hickok joined in the merriment, participating in a "Grand Buffalo Hunt" in Niagara Falls in 1872, but his death in Deadwood in 1876 closed out what might have been a showmanship career to rival Cody's.[3] And of course, Cody himself, the subject of many dime novels, had been capitalizing on his fame on the theatrical circuit for about a decade before the Wild West crystallized. Indeed, his role in the 1876 play *The Red Right Hand; or, Buffalo Bill's First Scalp for Custer,* in which Cody fought and stabbed Yellow Hand in the climactic stage battle, had brought him further celebrity box office receipts.

Whatever the case of the exact origin of the Wild West, the extravaganza owed much to Cody and his 1882 brainstorm of organizing a Fourth of July "blowout" in his adopted hometown of North Platte, Nebraska. Hearing that townsfolk had planned nothing special for the Fourth, according to accounts that border slightly on legend, Cody himself took the bull by the horns. The center of attraction would be Cody displaying his buffalo-shooting tactics with steers and blank ammunition, but he also lined up local businesspeople to sponsor prizes for cowboy skills events. About 1,000 cowboys showed up, exceeding Cody's own hopes for 100. The shindig was apparently such a success that Cody imagined an even larger, traveling, commercial version, the Wild West show. That winter he interested Nate Salsbury and Doc Carver in a partnership. Salsbury, who actually preferred to wait a year, had in mind more of a horsemanship demonstration, but Cody and Carver were busy fleshing out the more elaborate Wild West format. After a near-fiasco of a dress rehearsal in the town that became Columbus, Nebraska, during which the mule pulling the stagecoach ran wild at the sound of gunfire, the Wild West opened in Omaha officially on May 19, 1883. The Wild West was off and running, ready to dazzle nonwestern audiences for decades to come.

Although Cody and Carver quarreled during that first tour, and Cody would reveal his own business ineptitude, the company survived the first year and regrouped for 1884 as "Buffalo Bill's Wild West— America's National Entertainment." Carver departed and paired with Captain Jack Crawford, another frontier scout, to form their own show. Despite a steamboat wreck that sank much of the entourage's equipment, forty-four days of rain, and injuries to the performers, the gala attracted 41,448 patrons in Chicago and did well in New York. For 1885 Cody and Salsbury were lucky enough to recruit Annie Oakley, whose wizardry with firearms enthralled spectators, and to re-sign the Hunkpapa Sioux chief Sitting Bull, who had become disgruntled on the 1884 tour. Fortunes began to turn upward. In 1886 the entourage enjoyed a long stand on Staten Island from June to September. Cody wrote of the profits to Jack Crawford, saying, "My success here has been the greatest ever known in the amusement business, the receipts greater, and New York is wild over the show. I am taking about $40,000 a week—something never heard of before."4 Cody returned to Staten Island again in 1888, to even larger crowds.

Confident that the Wild West would continue to capture audiences, Cody and his partners broadened their vision. They arranged for long bookings on permanent grounds, secured a run at Madison Square Garden in New York, and packed up the show for Europe. In 1887 Cody and company toured England, to the widespread applause of the English and Queen Victoria. Over the next five years the show traveled Europe often, making stops in France, Spain, Italy, Germany, Belgium, Ireland, Scotland, and, of course, London again. These European adventures served to whet the American appetite for the Wild West even more. At this time, when Americans were just coming to understand that the frontier was slipping away and that wholesale urbanization and industrialization marked the future, Wild West promoters sensed a widespread market for glorified western pageantry. Setting up across from the World's Columbian Exposition in Chicago in 1893, Cody raked in profits estimates of which range from $700,000 to $1,000,000, not bad for a depression year. The next year, however, saw a drop in earnings and other changes. With Salsbury ill and unable to keep up his end of management, the team signed a contract with James Bailey of circus fame to handle logistics. Instead of playing long stands, the show now went on the road for quick stops. In 1895 Cody's pageant performed at 131 stands in 190 days, covering over 9,000 miles. That exhausting pattern became the norm for the next six years.

As the century turned Buffalo Bill's luck dropped off dramatically. Salsbury, the organizational genius, died in December 1902, while the show was set to tour Europe. An outbreak of glanders in France forced the destruction of 200 horses, and Cody himself took a nasty spill from a horse. Financially he entered a similar tailspin, making investments that gave mediocre returns and failing to manage the troupe's expenses effectively. By 1907 he was mired in debt. Even though he streamlined the format of the show, stripping it of the more carnival-like attractions of Bailey's influence, his Wild West teetered on the brink of financial ruin. To offset this Cody merged with Pawnee Bill Lillie, whose own show Cody had helped to founder in previous years. The merger saved the enterprise, however, and in 1910 Cody cleared $400,000. That was his last good year, a burst of false hope, because the next year's receipts totaled only $125,000. Coupled with more fiscal bungling, this bad fortune tossed Cody into the position of accepting a loan from Denver *Post* publisher and Sells-Floto Circus part-owner Harry Tammen. Arguments ensued among Cody, Lillie, and Tammen, and business was disastrous in 1913. By September, with the venture in uncertain ownership status, the show went up for auction. Friends chipped in to save Cody's white horse, Isham, but the rest of the stock and equipment scattered to purchasers. Bereft of his own show now, Cody signed on with Tammen to make some "historical" motion pictures and appear in the circus. Disagreements over deceptive advertisement sent Cody packing from Tammen's circus, and in 1916 he tried one last gasp with the 101 Ranch Wild West show. After some initial success Cody succumbed to heat and exhaustion. An autumn cold worsened, and on January 10, 1917, the once-robust western entertainer died in Denver.

Famous as he was, Buffalo Bill was not the only western entrepreneur to cash in on the national and international hunger for Wild West thrills. Adam Forepaugh, Pawnee Bill Lillie, and Doc Carver were all serious competitors. In 1887 and 1888 Forepaugh, billing himself and his show as "4-paw," exhibited in Madison Square Garden. Enlarging his previous Philadelphia circus, Forepaugh added a "Progress of Civilization" pageant that featured "Custer's Last Rally." His son, a trick rider and animal handler, performed multiple-horse riding stunts and even taught a horse to walk a tightrope thirty feet high. But otherwise, as Don Russell remarked, there "was much in the Forepaugh Wild West that seems to imitate the Buffalo Bill show": "'Carazo, the Female Crack Shot of the World' was a close approximation of Annie Oakley; there was a Cowboy Brass Band, and Round-Up Bob, champion trick rider and roper of Texas."[5] The show also had Doc Carver's services for a stretch, although it is unclear whether or not Carver was a partner. The elder Forepaugh died in 1890, and afterward the show faded into the Bailey and Sells circus empire. Gordon Lillie, who had been the Pawnee interpreter for Cody's show in 1883, decided to branch out on his own after 1886. Encouraged by the European demand, Pawnee Bill put together a troupe of over eighty Indians, fifty cowboys and vaqueros, thirty trappers and frontier scouts, and 165 animals bound for Brussels, only to have the show canceled because of German emperor Wilhelm I's death. Instead Lillie toured several American cities, with fewer profits than they might have had in Europe. He apparently attempted to recruit Annie Oakley and her husband Frank Butler, although accounts are unclear as to which show the couple performed for that season. At Gloucester Beach, New Jersey, however, the show drew over 150,000 people in a five-week period. Such success may have prompted a billing war, which Cody won, because shortly after a financially bleak circuit of southern fairs, Pawnee Bill's group disbanded. Lillie himself landed on his feet as a commissioner in the Oklahoma Land Rush, and in late 1889 he regrouped his show. Pawnee Bill's Historic Wild West survived the rigors of the amusement business and was still solvent enough to bail out Buffalo Bill by merger in 1908. Relying on much the same formula as Cody did—a female sharpshooter named May Manning (Pawnee Bill's wife), trick riders and ropers such as Lillie's younger brother, Albert, frontier scouts such as "Iodine the Trapper," and Indians of Plains warfare fame such as the Pawnee Left Hand—Lillie's extravaganza ranked as one of the better ones.

Doc Carver, Cody's early partner, had branched out on his own, enlisting Captain Jack Crawford in 1883 for a two-year stint in Carver and Crawford Wild West (known briefly as Coup and Carver's Wild West in 1884). In 1887–88 Carver played for Forepaugh's show, but in 1889 he launched Dr. W. F. Carver's Wild America, which carried on to 1893. This version featured scouts Billy Garnett and Buckskin Frank McPartlin, the Sioux chief He Crow, and Indelicio Maldanado, a trick roper from Mexico. After 1893 Carver seems to have faded from the Wild West show scene, but he did stage diving horse stunts into the next century.

Those three promoters, however, faced other competitors as well. There may have been as many as eighty companies touring in the decades at the turn of the century.[6] Don Russell, in *The Wild West*, supplied a list of 116 different Wild West shows that populated the market from 1883 to 1957.[7] Many were ephemeral, lasting a season or less, and others were reshiftings of personnel and attractions from previous shows. Few could challenge Cody, Carver, Forepaugh, and Lillie's domination, but some of their names reveal the exotic flavor of the business:

Buckskin Joe's Realistic Wild West (1891)
Buck Taylor's Wild West (1894)
Col. Frederic T. Cummins Indian Congress (1898–1904)
Cole Younger and Frank James Wild West (1903, 1908)
Gabriel Brothers Champion Long-Distance Riders Wild West (1904)
Miller Brothers 101 Ranch Real Wild West (1907–16, 1925–31, 1945–46, 1949)
Tiger Bill's Wild West (1909–13)

Young Buffalo Wild West (1909–11)
California Frank's All-Star Wild West (1911)
Kit Carson's Buffalo Ranch Wild West (1911–14)
Mighty Shows and Buffalo Tom's Wild West (1912–14)
Texas Kidd's Reproductions of Frontier Days (1912–57)
Arlington & Beckman's Oklahoma Ranch Wild West (1913)
Bee Ho Gray's Wild West (no date)
Jones-Williamson All-Star Rodeo, Hippodrome, and Western
    Attractions (1935)
Ken Maynard's Diamond K Ranch Wild West and Circus (1936)
Col. Tim McCoy's Real Wild West and Rough Riders of the
    World (April 14–May 4, 1938)
Monroe's Robbins Circus with Hoot Gibson's Congress of
    Rough Riders, Indians, and Cossacks (1938)
Gene Autry's Flying A Ranch Stampede (1942)

Obviously, in many of these companies the Wild West segment was
but part of the show; some titles listed "Ten Minutes of Wild West."
Few were able to stand alone but had to attach their fortunes to circus
formats. Moreover, rodeos, such as Cheyenne's Frontier Days, began
staging Wild West acts, further blurring the boundaries between the
two types of entertainment. One thing is certain, however: although
other Wild West shows carried on after Cody's death, most Americans
have associated the phenomenon with him. As historian William
Goetzmann noted:

> Buffalo Bill maintained a rare, symbiotic relationship with other
> popular media of the day, from dime novels to illustrated news-
> papers. Feeding upon each other, as well as upon Buffalo Bill's
> imagination about Western adventure, the popular literature de-
> veloped archetypes of Western life: the rough-hewn cowboy, the
> renegade Indian, the intrepid scout. Buffalo Bill brought all these
> to life in his Wild West Show. It was unique, not only in its scope
> and ambition, but because it brought authentic figures from the
> West before the American public, blurring the distinction be-
> tween make-believe drama and reality.

Or as historian Robert Athearn phrased it succinctly: "No one packaged and sold the [Wild West] myth better."[8]
    What then was the Wild West show exactly? What acts, skits, tricks,
and panoramas did the audiences find so appealing? What additions
and deletions did the savvy showmen make to keep the mix from getting stale? What stereotypes of the Old West did the promoters rely on

and expect the patrons to recognize readily? In the main the Wild West show was a mélange of set pieces illustrating particular types of confrontations or experiences in the Anglo westward movement. With little regard for chronological accuracy or fidelity to subregion, the Wild West show mixed roping, riding, and rodeo-like stunts with reenactments of historical battles with Indians, simulated buffalo hunts, stagecoach holdups, and other contemporaneous events. Some shows settled on a set order of events, usually building up to some climactic spectacle or battle re-creation. Others fumbled around, searching for an appealing mix of attractions. Each company could rely on old favorites such as the Custer battle scenario to please throngs, but the troupes were quick to add features that referred to recent world military events, especially the Spanish-American War or occasionally Asian wars. Depending on the percentage of circus acts and nonwestern attractions, a Wild West show might or might not have seemed distinctly western in flavor. By the 1910s the shows usually contained a curious mixture of Old West nostalgia pieces and some emphasizing twentieth-century material progress or American adventurism across the seas. Stagecoaches and automobiles coursed the same arena tracks; elephants and quarter horses trampled the same dust; and Indians and cossacks or Chinese jostled in the arrangement of events. One type of spectacle, the staged hunts, did seem to diminish by the new century. Whether that was due to decreased availability of bison, the increasing antihunting or nonhunting sentiments among the audiences, or the sheer logistical problems of managing the balky ungulates is unclear, but the Grand Hunt in which Cody glorified had all but disappeared by the 1910s.

As most Wild West shows strove to emulate or outdo Buffalo Bill's version, a quick survey of the types and order of acts in his shows will suffice to illustrate the typical patterns. At his first show in 1883 Cody employed the following acts in the following order: (1) a grand introductory march; (2) a bareback pony race; (3) a Pony Express reenactment; (4) a simulated attack on the Deadwood mail coach; (5) a hundred-yard race between a mounted Indian and one on foot; (6) a shooting exhibition by Captain Adam H. Bogardus; (7) a similar event with Cody and Carver; (8) a (foot? horse?) race between cowboys; (9) some rodeo prototype events labeled "Cowboy Fun"; (10) wild Texas steer riding; (11) roping and riding buffalo; and (12) the climactic "Grand Hunt on the Plains," which also included a faked battle with Indians. By 1885 the format was evolving, as Annie Oakley and Sitting Bull joined the company. Cody trimmed the Grand Hunt to himself chasing a few bison. An event labeled "Attack on the Settler's Cabin"

closed the show, and he also added a version of his duel with Yellow
Hand. For a winter indoor engagement in 1886–87, Cody and set designers Steele Mackaye, Matt Morgan, and Nelse Waldron put together an extravaganza they advertised as "The Drama of Civilization,"
which took the onlookers through four eras of Turnerian development: "The Primeval Forest," "The Prairie," "Cattle Ranch," and
"Mining Camp." Eventually the pageant tacked on a fifth scenario,
"Custer's Last Stand," which outstripped the others in popularity. In
1887 musical accompaniment became standard, as the Cowboy Band
emerged. Questions over Indians' health threatened to change the
show in the late 1880s, and Cody himself hustled out to Dakota Territory in December 1890 to try to intervene in the Ghost Dance controversy, so Salsbury switched the emphasis to horsemanship. Corps of
German, English, and American soldiers and cossacks displayed military and riding skills in the 1891 season. By 1900 Cody was introducing a new wrinkle, the latest military excitement such as the Battle of
San Juan Hill or the Boxer Rebellion. After a few years of this trend,
however, beginning in 1907 Cody took the show back more to its
western roots, replacing the San Juan Hill piece with "The Battle of
Summit Springs" and augmenting the performance with a horseback
football game between cowboys and Indians and a simulated train
holdup. The Custer battle finale gave way to "A Holiday at TE
Ranch," based on Cody's own spread in the Big Horn Basin of Wyoming. The merger with Pawnee Bill Lillie took the show in yet another direction. The "Far East" segment and continuing sideshow elements gave the show more of a circus air than a Wild West one. Such
was the hybrid format when the show went into auction in 1913. Other contemporaneous Wild West shows and successors hewed fairly
closely to the path Cody, Carver, and Lillie blazed.

Historian Sarah Blackstone, in her book *Buckskins, Bullets, and
Business,* separates Buffalo Bill's Wild West acts into six classes: races,
shooting displays, specialty acts, military exhibitions, riding and horse
acts, and dramatic spectacles.[9] Races, whether between humans, horses and humans, or eventually, automobiles, were standard attractions
throughout the Wild West shows. Supplying plenty of action, drama,
and winners, the various races had an inherent structure that rarely
failed. Trick-shooting events were (pardon the pun) surefire crowd
pleasers. The noise may have frightened a few more timid souls at first,
but overall audiences cheered these exhibitions loudly. Sometimes the
shooting was somewhat "rigged," as the shooter would substitute very
fragile glass balls for other, harder targets, but the clientele seems to
have bought the illusion of accuracy nevertheless. Under specialty acts

Blackstone found a grab bag of events including trick-roping and ani-mal-roping stunts, the Pony Express gallop, acrobatic acts, cyclist and animal jumping contests, football on horseback, and automobile polo. This was one of the more fluid categories, as these events came and went depending on the circus emphasis of the show that season. Also somewhat changeable was the military exhibition category. From time to time the show highlighted precision marching, artillery, and lifesav-ing drills, as well as maneuvers by the Aurora Zouaves. Horse-and-rid-er acts were ever-popular ones in the Wild West lineup. "Rough Rid-er" demonstrations by cossacks, gauchos, and Mexicans eventually dropped off in time allotments, but other equestrian displays held steady. The more staid "Virginia Reel on Horseback" and rambunc-tious rodeo-type riding thrilled crowds equally. And of course, the flamboyant entry parade, with Cody himself swooping in last on his white horse and making a sweeping gesture with his hat, left indelible memories. The last category, the dramatic spectacles, demanded the most complex logistics in the show. Often panoramic in scope, the pageants hurled numbers of participants, animals, and humans at each other. Nonetheless, the choreography had to be clear enough to avoid confusing the onlookers. These spectacles ranged from the favorite Custer's Last Stand to the attack on the settler's cabin to the stagecoach attack to the charge up San Juan Hill. Usually one of these wrapped up the performance. Most customers must have left the arena seats satisfied, having witnessed a full variety of western Americana.

Blackstone might have added yet another category, that of Indian-oriented events. From 1885 onward, with the success of Sitting Bull's presence, Cody and other Wild West impresarios relied heavily on In-dian stars, either for their charisma or for their riding and stage skills (fig. 3.1). So many Sioux and other Plains Indians toured with the shows that, in the minds of many showgoers, the Plains Indian became the archetypal American Indian. Repeated scenes of Indian attacks and last stands provided riveting examples of the supposed savageness of Indians and acted as justifications for the various military, missionary, and removal campaigns whites had waged against them. Audiences sat-ed their curiosity about Indians and at the same time gained assurance of the righteousness of the doctrine of progress. In another sense, how-ever, the employment of Indians backfired. Reformers bent on con-verting the tribespeople into productive Christian citizens looked askance at the Wild West shows. As historian L. G. Moses remarked, "Almost from the beginning of Indian participation in Wild West shows, allegations of mistreatment and exploitation reached the vari-ous secretaries of the Interior and commissioners of Indian affairs,

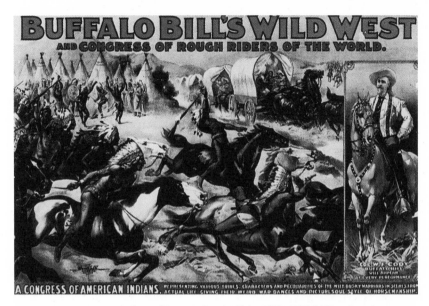

Figure 3.1. Posters such as this one for Buffalo Bill's Wild West in 1899 helped popularize romanticized images of Indians. (Library of Congress.)

causing them to be concerned about the shows' effects on assimilation-ist programs and on the image of the Indian in the popular mind."[10] Herbert Welsh's Indian Rights Association, Carlisle School's Richard Henry Pratt, and after 1911, the Society of American Indians com-plained steadily that the extravaganzas fostered nostalgia for hunting and war on the part of Indians who should have been accepting agri-culture and peaceful citizenship. Although Cody and other showmen had to answer these charges and occasionally release an Indian, the ac-cusations of exploitations were apparently overblown. So thought Commissioner of Indian Affairs Francis E. Leupp in 1910:

> I have heard the complaint made that it is degrading to an Indi-an who has taken a few steps up the path of civilization, to let him don his fanciful toggery once in a while and imitate the war-riors and hunters of his race in a past era; yet the same critics raise no protest against plays like "Samson" or "Macbeth," . . . which depict the life and manners of our own race when it was still in a semi-barbarous state. I have known a good many Indian tent ac-tors, and I have yet to meet one who is not perfectly appreciative of the difference between the old and the new, the real and the imitation, in spite of the fact that twice a day he puts on buckskin

leggings, sticks feathers in his hair, and gallops his pony around an ellipse of tanbark.

Leupp promised that the Indian Bureau had been and would continue to be scrupulous in its efforts to secure fair contracts and other protections for the Indian performers, by "the exercise of a little paternalism."[11] This debate, however, was probably moot. Promoters and patrons alike viewed the Indian as integral to the Wild West show and would have finagled some way to get "poor Lo," that national pet, into the arena.

What effects overall did the Wild West shows have on American culture? What popular culture messages did these exhibitions convey to audiences at home and abroad? The shows undoubtedly catapulted a few individuals out west to see the region firsthand. Artists Paul Frenzeny and Hermon Atkins MacNeil were probably two who saw the exhibitions and headed west for more inspiration.[12] For most, however, the shows crystallized the drama of the Anglo-American westward movement in exciting and self-congratulatory ways. Morality plays of sorts, the Wild West shows clarified the ambiguities of the Old West. Perhaps Sarah Blackstone capsulized it best: "But the show was full-blown propaganda—glorifying the process of the winning of the American West and declaring to the world that America had won a resounding victory in its efforts to subdue the wilderness. The backbreaking, bloody, and often fatal task of taming the frontier was romanticized and glorified by Cody through his Wild West until the truth was so totally mixed with the myth as to be indistinguishable."[13] Claiming to deliver only "accurate" scenes of the Old West and drawing on performers who had experienced careers in the West as scouts and hunters, the Wild West shows were long on bombast and short on introspection. Suspecting that audiences would not sit still long for recreations of the more arduous and boring aspects of westward movement—in other words, most of it—promoters chose the atypical, the flashy, and the exotic and helped to fashion them into new stereotypes. The shows served as visual confirmations for showgoers who may have had imbibed the dime novels, a hundred or so which pertained to Buffalo Bill, or seen a few woodcuts or stereoscope photographs. As Moses noted, "The many people who dreamed about the West and longed for excitement and diversion from mundaneness had few places to look for it except upon the printed page—except, that is, until the appearance of the Wild West shows."[14] So strong was this appeal that Western movies took their cues from the shows, and it was a while before the silver screen made damaging inroads on the live performances. For many Americans the Wild West show had become the true and only West.

Within the larger framework of the show, the different types of acts may have delivered other messages or drawn on other American affinities. In a chapter entitled "Messages and Meanings" Blackstone attempted a semiotic analysis of the six acts, one that is only partially successful and that may display the excesses of the semiotic approach more than its benefits.[15] Nevertheless, some of her comments and her grouping of the six types of acts are useful. Concerning the first category, nineteenth-century Americans loved races of all sorts, finding even hippodrome cycling and pedestrianism more thrilling than do modern crowds. One cardinal proposition of the gospel of progress was speed. Horse and human races particularized that doctrine, although focus on railroads and, later, automobiles would make those races seem quaint. For Americans who believed in variations of social Darwinism, races symbolized the implied societal and racial struggles. Regarding shooting acts, enough time had elapsed since the Civil War to allow onlookers to forget the more gruesome aspects of shooting and gunplay. As Blackstone conjectured, crowds liked a little bit of danger, such as in the shooting of an apple off a poodle's head.[16] Precision shooting underscored the national attachment to mechanization, streamlined systems, and efficiency, especially during the Progressive Era. And even though American soldiers had been nothing special in marksmanship circles, the Codys, Carvers, and Oakleys suggested that all Americans were "straight-shooters," a badge of cultural pride worn proudly.

Specialty acts depended on the specific nature of each for their appeal. The rodeo-type and roping stunts derived from an increased willingness to see the cowboy trade as far more glamorous than it was. The Pony Express demonstration capitalized on nostalgia for a mail system four or five decades out of date. Other more exotic acts were clearly circus-oriented and played on the crowd's tastes for the slightly freakish or distinctly foreign yet digestible bits of the world beyond America's relative isolation. Football on horseback and auto polo merged the love for modern machines and organized sports with the old frontier individualism. Military exhibitions, the fourth type, satisfied audience members who wished to believe in the efficiency of military units. Precision marching and artillery and lifesaving drills comforted the domestic citizen. Blackstone suggested that such also may have reinforced the American faith in the militia tradition.[17]

Horsemanship displays illustrated alternately the mastery over and partnership with animals that humans had attained on the frontier, premises that would work equally well for the developing rodeo. Whether they were the more rowdy Rough Rider acts or the stately equestrian ones, these attractions elevated the mundane to art form. The sixth category, the dramatic spectacle, paralleled the nineteenth-century penchant for melodramas, which established clear-cut heroes and villains and built up to an emotionally cathartic climax. They also obviously relied on patriotic identifications with various battle and campaigns, either those of the border wars with Indians of the 1860s and 1870s or later ones such as the Wounded Knee battle or Spanish-American War fighting. The pervasiveness and durability of the last-stand scenes far outran their actual numbers in the real West. Art historian Alex Nemerov commented on this tendency in his study of Western images:

> Numerous representations of last-stand fights by different writers and artists suggested not only that such fights regularly took place (how could so many people be wrong?); more crucially, these paintings and stories suggested that they occurred in virtually the exact terms in which they were represented. Each image featured heroic whites desperately fighting larger numbers of Indian adversaries. Taken together, the sameness of these images—the appearance of identical last stands in different media in the work of different artists and writers—testified to the truth of such an event as a last stand.[18]

Chiming in that chorus, of course, were the Wild West shows. The last stands also demonstrated that some audiences sublimated self-identification with the desperate bunch attempting to stave off doom. Folklorist Bruce Rosenberg declared the Custer massacre the national "epic of defeat," cultural historian Richard Slotkin saw the last-stand scenes as metaphors of industrialists warding off labor disruption, and historian Robert Wiebe argued that small towns in general felt themselves under siege by alien, immigrant-infested cities.[19] If such interpretations are correct, the Wild West show touched deep chords in the American psyche, doing much more than merely serving as entertaining, action-packed pageants of nostalgia. Viewing the Wild West show, the American middle class held up a mirror to its own values and goals: a conquest of the cultures of an indigenous race, a compression of ethnic cultures into Americanism, a championing of class dominance, and an affirmation of male prowess (fig. 3.2).

The cultural institution of rodeo has had similar appeal for American audiences. Whereas the national clamor for the Wild West show has, for all intents and purposes, faded into history, interest in rodeo has grown or held steady since its inception in the 1800s. Proudly proclaiming their sport to be the only one to have developed from work skills—although some participants in logger contests and college

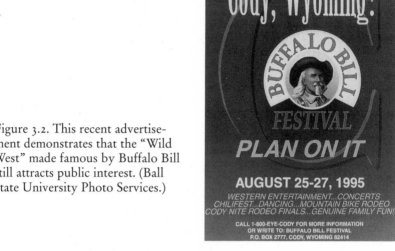

Figure 3.2. This recent advertisement demonstrates that the "Wild
West" made famous by Buffalo Bill
still attracts public interest. (Ball
State University Photo Services.)

woodsmen/woodswomen teams would challenge that claim—rodeo
enthusiasts see it as authentically American and western.[20] Just as many
Americans adopted the cowboy as a traditional symbol of American
values of individualism and hard work, so did they latch onto the cowboy's sport. Seemingly missing much of the team emphasis common in
other American sporting pastimes, rodeo has focused on the solitary
struggle of human and beast. Students of rodeo would be quick to
point out that the contestants rely heavily on their trained horses, arena clowns, and other cowboys for support and safety, but even still,
Americans have cropped out those helpers from the stock imagery of
the sport. Latter-day culture heroes, rodeo cowboys have functioned
emblematically as free frontier spirits conquering the wild forces of the
plains. No Beowulf slaying a Grendel could have more satisfied Americans hungry for mythic assurance.

There seems to be some dispute about the American origins and
development of rodeo. Historian Mary Lou LeCompte argued that
rodeo as twentieth-century Americans came to know it derived not
directly from spontaneous cowboy roundups of the cattle-trade heydays but rather from Wild West shows, Frontier Days, Roundups, and
Stampedes: "Attempts to promote rodeo as an indigenous sport rather than an outgrowth of various events such as shows, fairs, and carni-
vals produced the myth that it was a direct descendant of informal
contests among cowhands during the 1860's-1880's, and cause a signifi-

cant era of rodeo history to be ignored and forgotten."[21] Indeed, on closer inspection, the sport seems to be not Anglo-American at all but more of Hispanic birth. Moreover, the term *rodeo,* coming from the Spanish verb *rodear,* meaning "to gather or surround," referred more to the actual work of rounding up cattle. Of course, these workdays also involved many of the skills that surfaced later on in the sport. Travel writer Charles Nordhoff described such at a California rodeo in 1873: "Then were seen some really magnificent feats of horsemanship; each vaquero vied with the other in this display; and as the day grew, fresh horses were saddled, and no bull was so wild that he did not find his master."[22] More likely, modern-day rodeo developed from a different phenomenon, the *charreria.* Mexican and Hispanic cowboys, *charros,* perfected most of the rodeo style and events in the *charreria* before the arrival of Anglos in the West and continued to stage the events at fiestas and holidays even as Anglos filtered in. Modern enthusiasm for the sport in Mexico attests to its durability into this century, as Hispanic influence on the supposedly "American" sport remained strong. Turn-of-the-century Texan and Mexican vaqueros and ropers such as Antonio Esquivel, Indelicio Maldanado, and Vincente Oropeza were headliners at shows and rodeos.[23] Failures to declare these Hispanic origins may have resulted from bias against Hispanic culture, as Arnoldo DeLeon argues, or, as LeCompte thought, from an Anglo-American need to establish rodeo as an "American" sport, much in the same way that baseball propagandists created the Cooperstown myth.[24]

For some time historians assumed that the first roundup with Anglo-American cowboys on American soil happened in Santa Fe in 1847, because Captain Mayne Reid recorded seeing one. LeCompte has demonstrated that Reid really was referring to a roundup in Mexico, however, not in New Mexico.[25] It may not have been until the late 1860s that roundups coalesced into informal rodeos. Deer Trail, Colorado, was the site of one such get-together between neighboring outfits in 1869, and over the next decade similar events occurred in Cheyenne, Wyoming, and Pecos, Texas. Probably the first rodeo to offer prizes came in Prescott, Arizona, in 1888, and shortly thereafter, in 1891, Miles City, Montana, included an "official" rodeo as part of the Montana Stock Growers' Association festivities. In 1897 Cheyenne jumped in with the Frontier Days celebration, the "Daddy of 'em All," which soon grew to rival Prescott's claim of being the "Grand-daddy of 'em All." So successful were these ventures that communities across the West began staging annual or periodic rodeos as parts of fairs or pageants, such as Denver's Festival of Mountain and Plain. By the

1910s a few of these local events, such as Cheyenne's Frontier Days or the Pendleton, Oregon, Roundup, had attained great prominence. In 1912 Albertan Guy Weadick accomplished his goal of bringing rodeo up to snuff in western Canada when he organized the Calgary Stampede, which took place annually after 1923.

Following the path of the Wild West shows, rodeo promoters started taking the stampedes eastward into large arenas. Although some dyed-in-the-wool westerners guffawed about rodeo in big-city locales, the 1916 Stampede in Madison Square Garden marked a turning point for rodeo. No longer only a local or regional attraction, rodeo began to capture a more national audience. The World's Championship Rodeo, which ran from 1926 to 1959 in Madison Square Garden, became one of the premier contests, prompting imitators in Chicago, Boston, and other cities. With larger crowds came larger prize purses, standardization of event judging, and professionalization. Rodeo promoters formed the Rodeo Association of America in 1929, and seven years later, cowboy entrants responded with the Cowboys' Turtle Association, so named because of the slowness in organizing. By 1945 the Rodeo Cowboys Association replaced the CTA, and in 1975 the group added the term "Professional," a clear indication of the completion of the trend, a long way from the days of Deer Trail or Prescott.

Although the changes brought in the customers and enriched a few cowboys, some rodeo organizers missed the old atmosphere of smaller rodeos. After helping to stage the 1916 New York Stampede, Guy Weadick retreated to smaller aims with his Calgary Stampede. Anthropologist Elizabeth Lawrence, in her study of rodeo in the 1970s, found some recent cowboys lamenting the number of rodeos in indoor arenas and claiming that rodeos had "lost touch with the very essence of the West—the landscape and the sky."[26] As had the Wild West shows, rodeo had changed from its original formats, adding, subtracting, or modifying events for crowd appeal. What resulted was a dilution of the primal meaning of such stunts as bareback bronco busting and calf roping. Many a modern cowboy has some experience in the actual cattle trade, but others simply learn the techniques, striving to beat the clock or impress the judges and pick up the winner's purse. Perhaps the economic motive had always been there, as cowboys competed for cash to offset seasonal unemployment,[27] but the close connection with circuses, Wild West shows, and frontier days celebrations helped to shift the emphasis to showmanship, extravaganza, and commercialism.[28] Patrons who had little contact with the cattle industry knew no difference, and even if they had such contact, they probably preferred the structured excitement of the sport.

The fact that rodeo became a sport also contributed to its metamorphoses. As with other sports that derive from folk games, rodeo underwent standardization of events, rules, judging, and equipment. Early rodeos featured various events in no set pattern and stuck with a tone closer to the workday rhythms. By the 1920s, and especially after the accrediting organizations formed in the 1930s, rodeo shifted to a more regimented, statistics-oriented format. Luck still entered into the draw of the bronc or bull for each contestant, but increasingly standardized timing, judging, and rules were allowing comparisons on a nationwide basis. Although never totally spontaneous, rodeos at first consisted of more rudimentary stunts. Saddle bronc riding occurred in arenas or fields without chutes, elaborate fencing, or spectator stands. Riders had to ride the bronc until the judges considered it "gentled." By the 1910s these events gave way to stylized riding, one hand on the saddle horn, stirrups and spurs high, hand and hat waving, for a much briefer time, eventually established as eight seconds. The cowboys scored points for their pains, whether or not the horse was any tamer than at the start. Indeed, almost the reverse became true: a wilder bucking horse helped raise the point total and thrilled the crowd. Later on bareback bronc riding and bull riding emerged as regular events, employing much the same stylized techniques and time period. In the timed events—calf roping, steer wrestling ("bulldogging"), and steer roping—changes also came about to standardize the performances and create excitement for the crowd. Bulldogging dated from 1904 (although Hispanic roundups held some forms of steer wrestling), when the famous African American cowboy Bill Pickett astonished crowds by tackling the bull, biting its upper lip, and dragging the startled animal to the ground. Early on the livestock got a longer headstart, seventy-five or a hundred feet; that distance later diminished to thirty feet so that entrants could display their speediness even more effectively. From time to time rodeos also included barrel racing, chuck wagon racing, clown acts, and parades interspersed among the more traditional rough-stock riding and timed events. Even in these the emphasis fell on the side of showmanship, razzle-dazzle, and rehearsed spontaneity, far cries from the work skills of the cattle-drove heydays.

As rodeo progressed more into the realm of sport and commercialism, certain stars emerged. Turn-of-the-century fans enthused at the feats of Booger Red, Bill Pickett, and Yakima Canutt. By the 1920s and 1930s adulation came to rest on Ike Rude, Bob Crosby, and Freckles Brown, among others. After World War II (rodeo had continued during the war, much like professional baseball, as a morale booster), the new faces included Casey Tibbs, Bill Linderman, Harley May, and perhaps most famous, Jim Shoulders. By the mid-1960s Larry Mahan took over the reins from Shoulders's generation, winning the All-Around Cowboy title six times and capitalizing on his fame with endorsements, a line of cowboy boots, and television appearances. Since Mahan, no particular rodeo cowboy has attained his level of fame, but rising prize money continues to lure great numbers of competitors. More recently cable television sports channels such as ESPN have helped to fatten the prizes and gain a wider audience for the sport.

For the most part professional rodeo remained a white male's bastion. Campaigns by males to counter political and social feminism had failed, and the melting pot that was supposed to result in the assimilation of immigrants into white, Anglo-Saxon culture had hardly materialized, yet an audience at a rodeo could reverse the clock or cancel out present concerns. Ignoring historical realities of the cattle trade and the development of rodeo, Americans settled on Anglo stereotypes of the cowboy, and these largely carried over into the sport. Similarly, in the rough-and-tumble "man's world" of rodeo, women seemed at best irrelevant intruders. As Lawrence remarked about the space behind the chutes, "A woman is taboo here and if she gains admittance is treated as a nonperson."[29]

Nevertheless, women and non-Anglo cowboys have had some share of the fanfare. Far from being just pretty faces in the crowd, such as Miss Black Velvet Rodeo and assorted rodeo queens, women contestants tussled with the animals professionally. The Wild West shows gave women a springboard, for Annie Oakley and May Manning showed that their skills rivaled the men's. In early Frontier Days a woman occasionally appeared in the bronc-riding events, but it was probably not until Guy Weadick opened up the Calgary Stampede to a full range of women's events that women's chances improved. Helen Bonham, Bertha Blancett, Lucille Mulhall, Fannie Sperry, Tillie Baldwin, and Florence LaDue all exhibited their skills to appreciative crowds in the 1910s and 1920s. Few earned enough on the circuit to make a living, but most outearned other women of the day.[30]

Fox Hastings Wilson, Tad Barnes Lucas, and other cowgirls carried on the tradition into the 1930s, but eventually women's place in the sport diminished. In the late 1930s and early 1940s male riders marginalized female riders by keeping them out of the cowboys' "union," the CTA. Women were hurt by other changes in the rodeo business. When Gene Autry began producing rodeos in the 1940s, he spotlighted singers and other entertainers at the expense of contestants in general and females in particular. Women who used to compete against men suddenly saw their roles reduced to secondary ones as barrel racers and rodeo queens.

In the 1970s a Girls Rodeo Association was formed to provide more opportunity for females, but rodeos for women were far less common than those for men. Many rodeos trimmed the women's events to only barrel racing, and even that fell off the Cheyenne Frontier Days program in the 1980s, finally returning in 1991. Female contestants were demanding prize monies on a par with those for males.

Non-Anglo males also made some inroads. The black star Bill Pickett toured with the Miller Brothers 101 Ranch show, introduced bulldogging, and eventually died of rodeo injuries. Nollie Smith rode in the 1913 Cheyenne Frontier Days. In 1982 Charles Sampson became the first black entrant to win the bull-riding world championship. Winning the 1975 All-Around Cowboy title, Leo Camarillo rejuvenated the Hispanic rodeo connection with the Mexican ropers and *charros*. As for Indians, they have had less luck in the arena, although early stars in the Wild West shows and trick roper Will Rogers, of Cherokee heritage, testify to some Native American presence.

In the 1979 film *Heartland* Wyoming rancher Clyde Stewart mutters to his cowhand, "Rodeos are for fools who don't give a damn about their animals." This shows that rodeo has not been without its critics. Although early American animal rights luminary Henry Bergh gave his approval to the rodeo acts in Buffalo Bill's 1886 Staten Island show, other humane societies began to attack various aspects of rodeo. Some groups wished for the total abolition of acts that endanger or humiliate animals; others singled out one or two acts that they considered particularly odious. Steer roping and bulldogging drew a lot of criticism early in the century, with the result that several states and rodeos prohibited those events. Later on calf roping received similar protest, but less restriction ensued. Afraid of losing customers, rodeo managers began to cooperate with the humane societies, especially the American Humane Association. As the agendas of the animal rights movement broadened, however, compromises became fewer. By the 1960s the Society for Animal Rights, Friends of Animals, and the Humane Society of the United States lobbied the federal and state governments intensely and picketed rodeos (especially in Madison Square Garden), demanding abolition of the sport. Peter Singer and others castigated any group that collaborated with rodeo promoters. Even though contestants went a long way to minimize abuse, and some studies purported to show that rodeo actions do not significantly hurt the livestock, the issue has remained controversial.[31]

Despite the criticism rodeo has survived and shows few signs of disappearing. Attendance may be plateauing at some of the larger rodeos—Cheyenne's Frontier Days drew about as many customers in 1991 as it did in 1990—but the sport will probably always retain a certain grass-roots strength (fig. 3.3). The cowboy and rodeo Halls of Fame in Colorado Springs and Oklahoma City and the National Cowgirl Hall of Fame in Hereford, Texas, have lent the aura of immortality to the sport and its legends.[32] Even if the West loses population or grows more slowly than other sections, rodeo will elicit a fierce regional attachment. Wyoming continues to feature the bucking bronco and rider on its license plates. In its presentation of animal-human contests as authentically western ones derived directly from cattle-trade days, rodeo will continue to excite those westerners and easterners alike who place great stock in the enhanced sets of imagery. To Americans who fear conformist impulses, rodeo seems to be a breath of fresh individualism; to those who lament a drop-off in national patriotism, this pageantry provides an infusion of the so-called Old West pioneering spirit. At bottom these contests might reflect, as Lawrence suggested, an ambivalence toward taming the wilderness, a series of contradictions in which the cowboy, and by extension, the rodeo performer, exerts mastery over the animal all the while empathizing with the beast and admiring its wildness.[33] Fewer and fewer Americans tend livestock, and rodeo will never command the large television audiences that major professional sports do, but rodeo will remain an integral part of American popular culture, a ritual of national self-definition fraught with the mixed emotions of the winning of the West.

———————

Most recently in the realm of American western popular culture, the phenomenon of the "mountain man rendezvous" has reappeared. "Join in as the buckskinners, muzzle-loaders, and friends re-create the West's fur trade era. Almost everyone's in costume. What about you?" urged the June 1985 *Sunset* magazine.[34] Much like the rodeo and the Wild West show before it, the modern rendezvous, or "rondy," has emerged as a showpiece of an imagined segment of the Old West, a temporary alternative to the workaday world. According to one account, "the rendezvous provides a glorious escape from a Muzak-modulated, computer-controlled society to a time when a man could survive by his skills—or die trying."[35] Building on the assumption that the trappers of the fur-trade era lived bold, reckless lives, current devotees convene during summers in locales of historical significance to relive, as much as possible, the halcyon days of the 1820s, 1830s, and 1840s. Many buckskinners insist on authentic period-piece clothing, tools, firearms, foodstuffs, beverages, shelters, and other paraphernalia and seek to minimize intrusions of technology from later periods. Others allow a rather indiscriminate mix of "looks" from various

THE CELEBRATION OF THE WEST THAT'S ALL GO & NO WHOA.

Cheyenne Frontier Days is America's greatest western celebration. Cowboys. Indians. Country music stars. Parades. Pancake breakfasts. A carnival midway. A western art show & sale. And, of course, the nation's biggest outdoor rodeo. Call (800) 227-6336.

Figure 3.3. The public's continuing fascination with cowboys and rodeos makes the annual Cheyenne Frontier Days a major tourist attraction. (Ball State University Photo Services.)

decades and regions, and some even rename modern items to incorporate them into the rendezvous flavor. Some typical transpositions include "keys to my pony" (car or truck keys), "Jim Bridger lantern" (flashlight), "liquid char-cloth" (butane lighter), "brain-tanned whale blubber" (foam mattress pad), "gas beaver" (chainsaw), "sinew" (wax-covered nylon string), "snowbank" (cooler), "Fort AHHH" (portable latrines), "bear grease" (any lotion or oil), and "smoke signals" (phone calls).[36] The result has been a form of "street theater" wherein the participants are also the audience (although some rendezvous are open to outside tourists).

The origins of this movement remain cloudy. National forests have always housed a number of "mountain men" secretly living off the land; perhaps they held clandestine rendezvous. This modern public and visible version appears to have gathered momentum in the early 1970s. By 1972 there was the American Mountain Men organization, claiming 400 members, which met annually at Henry's Fork on the Green River in Wyoming. By 1985 *Sunset* listed forty-two of the more than fifty formal rendezvous the staff located in the West, ranging from the Western States Muzzleloaders Association's Jedediah Smith Rendezvous in Grants Pass, Oregon, to the Wind River Muzzleloaders Memorial Day Weekend Black Powder Shoot and Rendezvous. Some were drawing 2,000 participants, and occasionally 5,000, such as at the

National Association of Primitive Riflemen's Rocky Mountain National Rendezvous in Jefferson, Colorado. According to Gregory Coon, by the end of the decade, some attracted 10,000.[37] Beyond these formal rendezvous were many more smaller, unadvertised gatherings. Clearly the modern-day emulators were outnumbering the historical trappers dramatically.

What would explain this sudden upsurge in rendezvous? Few historians or cultural anthropologists have paid any attention to this trend, but some speculations may be in order. Most definitely the lure of the mythic West has given the rendezvous a magnetic appeal, similar to that of the Wild West shows and rodeos, but other factors may be at play. For some, the rendezvous is an offbeat summer vacation, replete with plenty of camaraderie, recreation, fishing, and lie swapping. For others, they are very serious offshoots of the survivalist crusade, demonstrations of primitive skills for a possible postapocalyptic society. Obviously there are distinct connections to the primitive weapons movement, for many participants are black powder musket and rifle enthusiasts and National Rifle Association members. Expectations of socially sanctioned drinking bouts, rough-and-tumble wrestling and fighting, and other boisterousness undoubtedly interest many attendees. Money-making possibilities may also rank high; most rendezvous feature trade fairs offering goods for tourist consumption or barter with other buckskinners. Ironically, the get-together might display a form of conspicuous consumption in that the "trappers" have the leisure to luxuriate in this lifestyle and the money to afford the travel and the gear. As Coon pointed out, what might appear to be "an inexpensive hobby" could cost thousands of dollars.[38] Either the absence or enforced subjugation of women may represent some long-held male fantasy to escape the supposed confines of the modern female. The fascination with the rendezvous may also bear direct relation to a rebirth of conservatism and patriotism in the Reagan years; ironically, actual historical rendezvous often coincided with Fourth of July celebrations and stimulated patriotic outbursts against non-American and nonwhite trappers. The nationwide boom in "living history" demonstrations may also account for the craze. The rondy is just the western version of the Civil War battle reenactment. Other forms of popular culture may deserve some credit. The surprise hit Robert Redford movie *Jeremiah Johnson* (1972) and other mountain man films may have prompted many "pilgrims" to search for contemporary "griz." Reasons may vary from one participant to another, but apparently the rendezvous threatens to be a strong contender in western popular culture for years to come.

For all their purported authenticity, however, the rendezvous miss some of the obvious historical truths about their fur-trade-era counterparts. Historians usually credit William Henry Ashley with having introduced the first rendezvous in July 1825 and note that the move was a calculated one to streamline the American fur-trade industry. As LeRoy Hafen remarked, "The first rendezvous was held at his direction and was so successful that it replaced the earlier method of maintaining a fort as a trading post."[39] Although the mountain men took advantage of the gathering to carouse, catch up on news, settle old scores, and maybe procure a concubine, at base these were economic institutions during which the companies and the trappers haggled over some very vital monetary transactions. By emphasizing the former aspects of the rendezvous, the modern ones downplay the latter actualities, which Goetzmann outlined in his essay on trappers as Jacksonian-era "expectant capitalists."[40] Similarly the recent rondies give little clue of just how hard most of the work and living conditions were for the average trapper. As it so often does, nostalgia seems to have trimmed away the negatives and left the play elements. Most contemporary buckskinners would shudder at having to live the full year in the mountains and run screaming for the comfortable accoutrements of the present. Moreover, the rendezvous pays little homage to the real predecessors of those Johnny-come-lately Americans, namely, the Native American, Spanish, French, Scottish, English, and Russian fur traders who established the networks well before Lewis and Clark left St. Louis in 1804. There are some forms of rendezvous east of the Mississippi, but the preponderance is in the West; unfortunately, this reinforces a misperception that the fur trade was only a western enterprise and neglects the massive role the fur and deerskin trades made in opening up colonial eastern frontiers. Last, the present festivals skirt past the manifest racism inherent in much of the early fur trade. To be sure, there was much cooperation, but there was also racial distrust and enmity.

That all three of these types of western popular culture—the Wild West show, the rodeo, and the rendezvous—claim to be authentic reflections of the Old West is hardly surprising. No Wild West show or rodeo, which are commercial ventures after all, would advertise itself as fake. Indeed, both strove to create an aura of historical legitimacy by featuring actual participants, frontier scouts or hunters or Pony Express riders for the Wild West shows and working cowboys for the rodeos. Rendezvous, which obviously by the late twentieth century could not draw on any real mountain men of the pre-1840 era, still made fierce assertions of authenticity. The degree to which audiences have swallowed these claims remains somewhat problematic. One school of thinking has maintained that popular culture by its very pervasiveness is invasive, that it molds societal values directly, and that audiences have little critical ability to separate fact from fancy. Another camp has argued that popular culture is a purposeful reinforcement of group self-identity, an establishment of hegemony over competing constituencies, a self-reflexive justification of dominance and expropriation. Yet another has suggested that viewers suspend disbelief and agree to participate in the ritual cognizant of its defective realism, aware of the historical sleights of hand. The long tradition of tall tales indicates that Americans have always relished more than a bit of hyperbole. Averring authenticity, the Wild West shows, rodeos, and rendezvous set the boundaries of acceptance of national gullibility about the real West.

These western extravaganzas have produced a collection of ambiguous effects on Americans. On one level they have functioned as relatively harmless avenues of escapism. As Athearn wrote about Western fiction, "Bored Americans, living quiet, uneventful lives in eastern villages, got away from the monotony of their security by escaping momentarily into a vicarious West, set before them in print."[41] It might be too much of a stretch to agree with literary scholar T. K. Whipple that "the story of the West is our Trojan War, our Volsunga Saga, our Arthurian Cycle, our Song of Roland," but certainly the shows, rodeos, and rendezvous have served in the Geertzian sense as "deep play." Wild Wests, rodeos, and rendezvous have each reflected self-defined American values and have been responses to cultural tensions and transitions during the decades of their emergence and peak performance. Stripping away disturbing questions of repercussion and consequence, these pageants have presented the West as an ordered experience, "visible, tangible, graspable."[42] Simultaneously reinforcing a generally shared set of cultural assumptions that the nineteenth-century conquest of the West was a positive necessity and providing a vehicle for lamenting that loss of wilderness, these presentations offered a clear-cut, calming resolution of anxiety and paradox.

And yet that is exactly why the Wild West shows, rodeo, and rendezvous fail as viable explanations of the American West. As rationalizations of Anglo-American adventurism, each covers up some untidy tableaux of western sordidness. A recent writer in *Elle* phrased this concisely: "Mythologizing what was in reality a brutal two-centuries-long land grab, we sweetened our past with nostalgia, and won the West all over again."[43] Each depicts its era as one of frolic and play, rambunctiousness and danger, and rarely gives any hint of the tedium and hard work. The fur trade, the cattle industry, Indian wars, and agricultural settlement of the West were mostly accompanied by sheer boredom, monotony, and repetition. No Wild West show included an act showing trappers slogging through a cold stream, cowboys coughing at the trail dust, cavalry patrolling the telegraph wire, or farmers methodically growing wheat. Similarly, these pageants have ignored the ephemerality of most western experiences. The fur trade did not last a long time (although *Jeremiah Johnson* would have us believe he is "up there still"), the cattle heyday spanned a short couple of decades, the Indian wars had temporal limits, and most revealing, the Pony Express lasted for little more than a year. Instead the shows implied a feeling of permanence and longevity that betrayed the facts. Perhaps novelist Larry McMurtry captured this well in *Buffalo Girls* when he had the old trapper Jim Ragg sneer about Cody's show: "'What Wild West?' he said, to a little blonde whore who stopped to tease him. 'What Wild West? If Billy Cody can make a poster about it than there ain't no Wild West.'"[44] Moreover, the heavy dose of nostalgia inherent in the festivities may harm more than charm. As historian Christopher Lasch wrote, "Nostalgia neither provides a necessary sense of continuity in a time of rapid change nor serves as unadulterated escapism. It evokes the past only to bury it alive."[45] At their worst these displays may have been instrumental in fostering the sorts of abusive western behaviors that outdoor writer Edward Abbey treated so scathingly:

This thought leads me to that contemporary phenomenon, the instant redneck. The natural redneck comes from the country, from small towns, and is generally too dumb or too stubborn to leave. The instant redneck comes from the city or the affluent suburbs, where his father has made a lot of money. Cushioned by a nice trust fund or comfortable inheritance, the instant redneck migrates west, buys himself a little hobby ranch, a pair of tight jeans, a snap-button shirt, one of those funny hats with the rolled brim like the male models wear in Marlboro ads, and a ninety-dollar pair of tooled leather boots with pointy toes. . . . Now in full cowboy costume, he buys his first pickup truck, a huge lumbering four-by-four tractorlike gas hog of a *deus machina* loaded with roll bars, mag rims, lug tires, KC road lights, gyroscopic beer can holder, CB (Cretin Broadcasting) radio, and Tampax slot. He buys a gun for the gun rack, pops the top from his first can of Coors (a sweet, green provincial brew mass-produced from reprocessed sewage water near Denver), and roars off in all directions to tear up the back country and blast away at wildlife. The instant redneck. A real man at last.[46]

The past is slippery and in certain "usable past" adaptations morally suspect. The time has come to recognize the malleable nature of popular culture, its tendencies toward the polymorphous and eclectic, its willingness to satisfy emotionally at the expense of historical accuracy. But what the hell, pardner, hand me my Colt, toss that glass target in the air, flip me that rope, help me straddle that saddle, tear me off a chunk of jerk and gimme a swig of Taos lightning, and let 'er rip!

Notes

1. The "new western history" is showcased in two recent anthologies: Patricia Nelson Limerick, Clyde A. Milner II, and Charles E. Rankin, eds., *Trails: Toward a New Western History* (Lawrence, Kans., 1991); William Cronon, George Miles, and Jay Gitlin, eds., *Under an Open Sky: Rethinking America's Western Past* (New York, 1992). The staying power of the Old West is the focus of Robert Athearn's study *The Mythic West in Twentieth-Century America* (Lawrence, Kans., 1986).

2. Nadine Frey, "Eurowest," *Elle*, September 1990, 229.

3. Don Russell, *The Wild West or, A History of the Wild West Shows, Being an Account of the Prestigious, Peregrinatory Pageants Pretentiously Presented before the Citizens of the Republic, the Crowned Heads of Europe, and Multitudes of Awe-Struck Men, Women, and Children around the Globe, Which Created a Wonderfully Imaginative and Unrealistic Image of the American West* (Fort Worth, Tex., 1970), 2–3.

4. William F. Cody to John Wallace Crawford, July 21, 1886, William F. Cody Papers, Denver Public Library; quoted in Sarah J. Blackstone, *Buckskins, Bullets, and Business: A History of Buffalo Bill's Wild West* (Westport, Conn., 1986), 18.

5. Russell, *Wild West*, 31–32.

6. Blackstone, *Buckskins, Bullets, and Business*, 8.

7. Russell, *Wild West*, 121–27.

8. Athearn, *The Mythic West*, 253.

9. Blackstone, *Buckskins, Bullets, and Business*, 105–23.

10. L. G. Moses, "Wild West Shows, Reformers, and the Image of the American Indian, 1887–1914," *South Dakota History* 14, no. 3 (1984): 193.

11. Francis E. Leupp, *The Indian and His Problem* (New York, 1910), 325.

12. See Joni Louise Kinsey's thumbnail biographies of various western artists in *The West as America: Reinterpreting Images of the Frontier, 1820–1920*, ed. William H. Truettner (Washington, D.C., 1991), 353, 359.

13. Blackstone, *Buckskins, Bullets, and Business*, 1.

14. Moses, "Wild West Shows," 195.

15. Blackstone, *Buckskins, Bullets, and Business*, 105–23.

16. Ibid., 111.

17. Ibid., 116–17.

18. Alex Nemerov, "Doing the 'Old America,'" in *The West as America*, ed. Truettner, 291.

19. Bruce Rosenberg, *Custer and the Epic of Defeat* (University Park, Pa., 1975); Richard Slotkin, *The Fatal Environment: The Myth of the Frontier in the Age of Industrialization, 1800–1890* (Middletown, Conn., 1986); Robert Wiebe, *The Search for Order* (New York, 1967).

20. See, for example, Cleo Mackey, *The Cowboy and Rodeo Evolution* (Dallas, 1979).

21. Mary Lou LeCompte, "Wild West Frontier Days, Roundups and Stampedes: Rodeo before There Was Rodeo," *Canadian Journal of Sport History* 16, no. 2 (1985): 54.

22. Charles Nordhoff, *California: For Health, Pleasure, and Residence* (New York, 1873), 240–41.

23. Mary Lou LeCompte, "The Hispanic Influence on the History of Rodeo, 1823–1922," *Journal of Sport History* 12, no. 1 (Spring 1985): 21–38.

24. Arnoldo DeLeon, *They Called Them Greasers* (Austin, Tex., 1983), ix–x, 33–35; LeCompte, "Hispanic Influence," 21.

25. Mary Lou LeCompte, "The First American Rodeo Never Happened," *Journal of Sport History* 9, no. 2 (1982): 89–96.

26. Elizabeth Atwood Lawrence, *Rodeo: An Anthropologist Looks at the Wild and the Tame* (Knoxville, Tenn., 1982), 21.

27. Kristine Fredriksson, *American Rodeo: From Buffalo Bill to Big Business* (College Station, Tex., 1985), 11.

28. LeCompte, "Wild West Frontier Days."

29. Lawrence, *Rodeo*, 14.

30. LeCompte, "Cowgirls at the Crossroads: Women in Professional Rodeo, 1885–1922," *Canadian Journal of Sport History* 20, no. 2 (1989): 27–48.

31. See Fredriksson, *American Rodeo*, chaps. 10–12.

32. Stephen O'Shea, "Cowgirl Cults," *Elle*, September 1990, 218.

33. Lawrence, *Rodeo*, 270–71.

34. "Rendezvousing with the Mountain Men," *Sunset*, June 1985, 98.

35. "Sons of Davy Crockett," *Newsweek*, July 20, 1981, 61.

36. Gregory S. Coon, "Recreating the Pre-1840 Frontier: or the Mountain Man Lives in the 21st Century," unpublished paper and demonstration delivered at the Rocky Mountain American Studies Association conference, Denver, April, 1991, 6.

37. "Rendezvousing with the Mountain Men," 92–93, 101; Coon, "Recreating the Pre-1840 Frontier," 2.

38. Coon, "Recreating the Pre-1840 Frontier," 6.

39. LeRoy R. Hafen, ed., *Mountain Men and Fur Traders of the Far West* (Lincoln, Nebr., 1982), 89.

40. William H. Goetzmann, "The Mountain Man as Jacksonian Man," *American Quarterly* 15, no. 3 (Fall 1963), 402–15.

41. Athearn, *Mythic West*, 253.

42. T. K. Whipple, quoted in Athearn, *Mythic West,* 255; Clifford Geertz, "Deep Play: Notes on the Balinese Cockfight," in *Myth, Symbol, and Culture,* ed. Geertz, 1–37 (New York, 1974), 23.

43. Ron Hansen, "Cowboy Dreams," *Elle,* September 1990, 168.

44. Larry McMurtry, *Buffalo Girls* (New York, 1990), 12.

45. Christopher Lasch, "The Politics of Nostalgia," *Harper's,* November 1984, 70.

46. Edward Abbey, *Abbey's Road* (New York, 1979), 164–65.

Suggestions for Further Reading:

LIVE ENTERTAINMENT

Athearn, Robert. *The Mythic West in Twentieth-Century America.* Lawrence, Kans., 1986.

Blackstone, Sarah J. *Buckskins, Bullets, and Business: A History of Buffalo Bill's Wild West.* Westport, Conn., 1986.

Borne, Lawrence R. *Dude Ranching: A Complete History.* Albuquerque, N.Mex., 1983.

Cody, William F. *The Life of Honorable William F. Cody, Known as Buffalo Bill.* Lincoln, Nebr., 1978 (1878).

Dary, David. *Cowboy Culture: A Saga of Five Centuries.* Lawrence, Kans., 1981.

Fredriksson, Kristine. *American Rodeo: From Buffalo Bill to Big Business.* College Station, Tex., 1985.

Hanes, Bailey C. *Bill Pickett, Bulldogger: The Biography of a Black Cowboy.* Norman, Okla., 1977.

Harris, Charles W., and Buck Rainey, eds. *The Cowboy: Six Shooters, Songs, and Sex.* Norman, Okla., 1976.

Kramer, Jane. *The Last Cowboy.* New York, 1977.

Lawrence, Elizabeth Atwood. *Rodeo: An Anthropologist Looks at the Wild and the Tame.* Knoxville, Tenn., 1982.

LeCompte, Mary Lou. *Cowgirls of the Rodeo: Pioneer Professional Athletes.* Urbana, Ill., 1993.

Martin, Russell. *Cowboy: The Enduring Myth of the Wild West.* New York, 1983.

Russell, Don. *The Wild West or, A History of the Wild West Shows, Being an Account of the Prestigious, Peregrinatory Pageants Pretentiously Presented before the Citizens of the Republic, the Crowned Heads of Europe, and Multitudes of Awe-Struck Men, Women, and Children around the Globe, Which Created a Wonderfully Imaginative and Unrealistic Image of the American West.* Fort Worth, Tex., 1970.

Sands, Kathleen M. *Charreria Mexicana: An Equestrian Folk Tradition.* Tucson, Ariz., 1993.

Savage, William W. *The Cowboy Hero: His Image in American History and Culture.* Norman, Okla., 1979.

Slatta, Richard W. *Cowboys of the Americas.* New Haven, Conn., 1990.

———. *The Cowboy Encyclopedia.* Santa Barbara, Calif., 1994.

PART THREE

Movies and Television

FOUR

John H. Lenihan

Westbound: Feature Films and the American West

THE DEPLETION OF Western movies over the past two decades contrasts markedly with the growing number of books and articles on the Western. Indeed, to write about the Western as a staple of feature film entertainment is to write about a phenomenon more distant than was the historical late nineteenth-century West to those who produced the first Western films.

Frederick Jackson Turner had delivered his famous thesis entitled "The Significance of the Frontier in American History" barely a year before Thomas Edison in 1894 began to put on film brief shots of Indians, cowboys, or western landscapes. Only four years earlier the "battle" of Wounded Knee had marked a tragic epilogue to the nearly four decades of Indian wars that would inform the plot narratives of so many Western films. Train holdups out west were still a matter of public concern when Edwin S. Porter directed *The Great Train Robbery* (1903) for the Edison Company. More than just the action vignettes that Edison and other film pioneers already had projected for curious audiences, *The Great Train Robbery* was distinguished by its better-defined, ten-minute narrative in which a gang holds up a train and is subsequently hunted down by a posse. Filmed in the wilds of New Jersey, Porter's one-reeler contained motifs that would soon become associated with the Western genre, such as outlaws conducting a robbery, fistfights, chases on horseback, and abundant gunplay. Seen today, the costumes and settings evoke images of the nineteenth-century frontier, even though at the time of its release *The Great Train Robbery* was also a contemporary crime thriller.

If *The Great Train Robbery* and the numerous Western one-reelers that sought to capitalize on its success were grounded in near-contemporary settings and situations, they also drew from an already existent imaginary West. Well before the motion picture camera was employed for entertainment purposes, the West had become as much popular myth as historical reality. In the course of the nineteenth century heroic tales of civilizing a frontier wilderness permeated captivity narratives (themselves derivative of earlier seventeenth- and eighteenth-century tales of whites kidnapped by Indians), literary fiction (most notably James Fenimore Cooper's Leatherstocking Tales), popular biographies of frontier figures, stage melodramas, Buffalo Bill Cody's Wild West extravaganzas, and hundreds of dime novels. Owen Wister's best-selling novel *The Virginian* (1902) crystallized much of the evolving idealization of America's frontier heritage in the central figure of the cowboy and was itself subject to both stage and screen adaptations. Filmmakers eager to capitalize on the success of *The Great Train Robbery* (which had originally appeared as a popular stage melodrama), as well as Wister's popular novel, would thus have at their disposal a rich vein of familiar character types, plot conventions, and stock narrative themes from an already established Western genre.

The motion picture proved ideally suited for capturing the sheer spectacle of gunfights, Indian attacks, galloping horses, and the vast expanses of unspoiled wilderness that lay just across the horizon from the occasional ranch, shantytown, or trading/army post. The capacity for visual excitement was enhanced significantly as production companies, confident of the continued popularity of Westerns, began by 1910 to shift their resources to westerly locales and especially California to benefit from authentic-looking western landscapes, perpetual sunshine, and a plentiful supply of cheap labor—including unemployed cowboys displaced by the demise of open-range ranching.

One of the first to recognize the advantages of outdoor location filming in California also became the first western star. G. M. "Bronco Billy" Anderson (formerly Max Aronson) had appeared in *The Great Train Robbery* and, in a series of films beginning with *Bronco Billy's Redemption* (1910), popularized the notion of centering a Western's story and action on a familiar character. Attired with an elaborate cowboy outfit and exhibiting an alternately good-natured and pugnacious manner, Bronco Billy frequently played the "good bad man," an outlaw who from film to film exhibits his inner decency and heroism by coming to the rescue of a woman or child.

While Anderson was establishing the screen's first notable western persona and thereby setting a precedent for innumerable B series productions that revolved around a recognizable western player, other filmmakers, such as Thomas Ince and D. W. Griffith, instilled the Western with higher production values and more dramatic scenarios. Indian-white confrontations became a particularly widespread subject, one that reflected the Western's central preoccupation with civilization's triumphant conquest of the frontier, as well as long-standing racial attitudes. Inherited from earlier decades was the ambivalent notion of the Indian as noble savage, at once a proud child of nature vanquished by advancing pioneers and soldiers and a barbaric obstacle to a more progressive culture. Thus in *Ramona* (1910) D. W. Griffith adapted Helen Hunt Jackson's tragic novel about white society's victimization of the Indian and later in his stylistically more elaborate *Battle of Elderberry Gulch* (1913) depicted Indians as marauding savages, complete with a last-minute cavalry rescue of the two "femme fatales" trapped in a cabin—a finale that Griffith would reconstruct for his masterpiece *Birth of a Nation* (1915), with the Ku Klux Klan rescuing white womanhood from marauding blacks. The ease with which Griffith could interchange Indians and blacks as threats to white civilization suggests a deep-seated racism in modern life that could be readily transposed onto screen stories of another time and place, including the late nineteenth-century frontier.

Still, it is significant that not all Westerns of the early silent period villainized the Indian. More than one film dealt with miscegenous love affairs, although with predictably fatal consequences for the Indian partner. Such was the theme of the successful stage play *The Squaw Man*, which Cecil B. DeMille brought to the screen in 1914 (and again in 1918 and 1931). Marking DeMille's debut as a screen director and among the first Hollywood feature-length films (six reels, compared to the three reels of Griffith's *Battle of Elderberry Gulch*), *The Squaw Man* told of an Englishman who buys a ranch in Wyoming and marries an Indian girl. The story ends with her tragic death, whereupon the Englishman returns to his homeland with their young son to claim an inherited estate and begin life anew with the genteel lady he had left behind.

With the success of *The Squaw Man* and the even lengthier (nine reels) film *The Spoilers* (1914), the feature Western would become a mainstay of an increasingly organized and commercially profitable American film industry. John Ford, who began his directing career at Universal cranking out short action vehicles, delivered his first feature-length Western in 1917. *Straight Shooting* was one of a series of Westerns

Ford made with Harry Carey playing the reformed outlaw Cheyenne Harry, with Harry this time switching sides in a range war to help farmers fend off a greedy rancher.

As important as John Ford would become in later decades as perhaps the supreme artist of Western films, his place at this stage of the genre's history was overshadowed by that of actor-director (and in later films producer and screenwriter) William S. Hart. Raised in the late nineteenth-century rural Midwest, Hart brought to the screen a genuine affection for America's frontier heritage, which he always avowed to depict with utmost visual authenticity. At the same time, Hart was a professional thespian (he performed roles in the stage productions of *The Squaw Man* and Owen Wister's *The Virginian*) who brought to his feature films a mannered acting style, together with a propensity for melodramatic plots and Victorian sentiment. Striving for realism in costumes and sets, Hart's films were nonetheless unabashedly moralistic. "By their fruits ye shall know them" reads the biblical inscription that concludes *The Toll Gate* (1920), as Hart (playing his favorite role as the good bad man) saves yet another community and thereby redeems himself from his criminal past. What distinguished Hart's Black Deering (*The Toll Gate*) or Blaze Tracy (*Hell's Hinges*, 1916) from the good bad man characterization of Bronco Billy Anderson or Cheyenne Harry Carey was the sheer intensity with which Hart juxtaposed his troubled, austere character with the almost apocalyptic conflict between the forces of good and evil on the frontier.

The combination of visual realism and somber moralism with which Hart's Westerns depicted the purging of communities from vice and corruption was appropriate fare for an America embarked on progressive reform at home and making the world safe for democracy on the battlefields of France. The promise of World War I as an Armageddon that would cleanse the world of its infirmities proved disillusioning, however, so that following the debacle of Versailles much of America's progressive idealism gave way to a more conservative political atmosphere and a greater cultural emphasis on individual fulfillment as opposed to a widespread social commitment to reform. When William S. Hart resisted altering his melodramatic formulas to accommodate the country's change in mood, his Westerns declined in popularity, particularly by comparison with the lighter fare Tom Mix offered from the late 1910s through the 1920s. Shedding any pretense of a serious message or characterization, Mix dazzled audiences with daredevil stunts and formulaic glitz that profoundly influenced the future course of series Westerns that revolved around a particular cowboy star (fig. 4.1).

Figure 4.1. Tom Mix drawing his six-guns in the movie *Fighting for Gold* (1919). (Library of Congress.)

Just as it is oversimplifying the decade of the twenties to play up its jazz-age antics and "lost generation" revolt against mainstream values, one tends to overlook the popularity of those Westerns that perpetuated traditional images of a glorious frontier heritage. The decade belonged as much to the small-town fundamentalism of William Jennings Bryan as it did to the urban cynicism of H. L. Mencken. And it was the folksy bravado of Charles Lindbergh that captured the decade's imagination more than did any representative of the lost generation. There is no incongruity, then, with the spirit of this multilayered decade and the fact that the film industry invested large sums in several epic-scale celebrations of America's conquest of the West.

The forerunner of this epic trend and the most expensive Western to date was Paramount's *The Covered Wagon* (1923). This adaptation of Emerson Hough's novel of the previous year dazzled critics and audiences alike with its sweeping panoramas of covered wagons fording a river or crossing vast expanses (filmed on location in Nevada and Utah) and its elaborate staging of brave pioneers fighting the hazards of weather and Indians. The film captured the 1920s' ambivalence between rural-communal values and business materialism in its scenes of the wagon train splitting up, as some headed for Oregon to build their farms while others set out for the gold fields of California. Although the plot and characterization were minimal and the pace slow, director James Cruze compensated with a pictorial grandeur unsurpassed in any previous Western.

The immense success of *The Covered Wagon* prompted producer William Fox to finance John Ford's film *The Iron Horse* (1924), an equally ambitious epic about the transcontinental railroad. More action-packed and cinematically fluid than the Paramount-Cruze wagon train opus, *The Iron Horse* nonetheless subordinated considerations of plot and character to the sheer spectacle of battling hostile Indians and other obstacles to national progress. Along with *Three Bad Men* (1926) *The Iron Horse* is considered to be director John Ford's most impressive venture into Western filmmaking prior to *Stagecoach* (1939).

A more successful integration of spectacle and narrative was William S. Hart's *Tumbleweeds* (1925). Plagued in the early 1920s by a marital breakup, an unresolved paternity suit, and a contract dispute with Paramount following the mediocre success of his last several Westerns, Hart now hoped for a successful comeback. With considerable financial backing from United Artists, *Tumbleweeds* combined the poignant theme of the passing of the cowboy frontier with the spectacle of the Oklahoma land rush. "Boys, it's the last of the West," bemoans Hart in response to the onrush of settlers that spells the end of the open-range cattle frontier. The film's melancholic mood parallels the fact that this was to be Hart's final Western. He retired from the screen following a dispute over distribution rights, returning only briefly in a touching prelude for the 1939 reissue of *Tumbleweeds.*

Paramount followed up the success of *The Covered Wagon* with three other epic Westerns: *North of 36* (1924), *The Pony Express* (1925), and *The Vanishing American* (1926). Adapted from a Zane Grey story, *The Vanishing American* was noteworthy for its sympathetic treatment of reservation Indians subjected to the exploitive abuses of a corrupt Indian agent. As was often the case with later pro-Indian films, however, *The Vanishing American* focused its indictment of white injustices on a patently evil individual (the agent played by the veteran villain-character actor, Noah Beery) and diluted its interracial romance by having the Indian protagonist (played by white star Richard Dix) die in the final reel. Moreover, in accordance with contemporary evolutionist theories, the film's prologue obviated any question of national guilt with its Spencerian reference to the Indian being subject to the struggle for survival of the fittest; implicitly, the Indian was no match for the superior white race.

Aside from these Paramount releases and an occasional epic from other studios, such as Fox's *The Iron Horse* or Universal's *The Flaming Frontier* (a 1926 Custer yarn that blamed the Indian uprising on crooked politicians), Hollywood preferred less risky medium-budgeted features such as Paramount's lucrative series of Zane Grey films. The cheaper series Western highlighting a particular cowboy film star would comprise most of Hollywood's output in the genre through the next two decades, a trend accentuated in the 1930s by the institution of the double bill, which required cheap fillers.

There was some speculation in the late 1920s that the Western was losing its appeal with a public that seemed to prefer the aerobatic exploits of Charles Lindbergh to the horse-bound movie cowboy. A more serious problem affecting the future of the genre arose from Hollywood's conversion to sound films. Anxious to profit from this technological breakthrough in movie entertainment, producers were hesitant to invest in Westerns because of the difficulty of recording sound outdoors. Then, in 1929, Fox surmounted the sound barrier with the first all-talking outdoor feature, *In Old Arizona.* More than a technological novelty, this spirited saga of the Cisco Kid captured five nominations for Academy Awards, including that for the best actor award, which was won by the film's star, Warner Baxter. Paramount's all-talking adaptation of *The Virginian* also appeared in 1929, its popularity a further indication that the genre would survive the transition to sound.

Survival rather than thriving applies to the feature Western for the next ten years. While B Westerns were cranked out in assembly-line fashion, major film production concentrated on topical social and political melodramas, gangster and horror thrillers, musicals, comedies, and a smattering of historical romances. The early 1930s nevertheless looked promising for large-scale Westerns, which included MGM's *Billy the Kid* (1930) and *The Squaw Man* (1931; Cecil B. DeMille's second remake of his 1914 Indian romance), Fox's *The Big Trail* (1930), and R.K.O.'s *Cimarron* (1931). *The Big Trail* and *Cimarron* in particular drew on the epic format of *The Covered Wagon*. For *The Big Trail* Fox employed the services of director Raoul Walsh, whose *In Old Arizona* had reaped the studio both profits and awards, and used a 70-mm wide-screen process to highlight the visual grandeur of its epic tribute "to the men and women who planted civilization in the wilderness and courage into the blood of their children." In addition to providing such spectacular scenes as the lowering of wagons, animals, and people over a huge cliff, *The Big Trail* introduced to the screen a new leading man in the person of John Wayne. Aside from including a token reference to some friendly Cheyennes and Pawnees, the film for the most part links the Indian with other hazards (ferocious rain and snow storms, raging rivers, muddy terrain). Faced with a massive attack by "savages," the wagon train leader assures his flock that "Injuns have never yet prevented our breed of men from travelin' into the settin' sun."

Although *Cimarron* was pointedly critical of white discrimination against the defeated Indian, it was just as nationalistic in heralding the coming of civilization to the raw frontier, as is clear in its stirring foreword: "A nation rising to greatness through the work of men and women . . . new country opening . . . raw land blossoming . . . crude towns growing into cities . . . territories becoming rich states." Beginning with a thrilling staging of the Oklahoma land rush of 1889, the film was based on Edna Ferber's popular novel about Yancy Cravat (Richard Dix) and his bride, Sabra (Irene Dunne), who together help to transform the raw settlement of Osage into a prosperous city. Yancy epitomizes the rugged individualist whose vision ("We're goin' into new things . . . a new empire") inspires wife and fellow pioneers to build the new civilization but whose wanderlust and distaste for society's prejudices and greed (including crooked politicians who cheat Indians out of land) drive him on two occasions to ride off to new adventures: "Sugar," he tells his perplexed wife, "if we all took root and squatted, there'd never be any new country." The final stage of progress is left to domesticated entrepreneurs and civic leaders, including Sabra, who toward the film's conclusion is elected to Congress. If civilization has spelled the loss of unfettered individualism (Yancy winds up a grizzled drifter), it also promises prosperity (there is no hint of the depression in the concluding scenes of present-day Oklahoma); a veritable ethnic melting pot (the Cravats' son marries their maid, who happens to be an Osage princess, while the local Jewish store merchant informs a boastful descendant of a signer of the Declaration of Independence that his ancestor delivered the Ten Commandments); and a new role of political leadership for women ("Now, what do you think of women in politics?" asks a wife, to which her husband replies, "Ha Ha, I give up").

As progressive as the film may appear, it does not entirely discard traditional prejudices. Sabra may be a model for the political woman, but through most of the film she is the long-suffering wife whose domestic virtues are constantly praised by the grateful Yancy. His final words as he lies dying in Sabra's arms define for the audience her most enduring quality: "Wife and mother, stainless woman. Hide me in your love." Similarly the film combines its message of tolerance with prejudicial stereotypes. This is most apparent in the depiction of Issaiah, a black youngster whose most endearing quality is his loyalty to the Cravats ("Please take me with yo, master Yancy"); when Issaiah tries to accompany the Cravats to church, much to the consternation of other parishioners, Yancy gently bribes him with the promise of a new suit to go back home, the film thus affirming the need for a kind of benevolent segregation. Still, *Cimarron* remains more racially sensitive than earlier Westerns, if only in avoiding the casual slur that was all too typical of scripts ("They may call you Black Deering, but by God you're white" [*The Toll Gate*]; a cowboy good-naturedly calling the Chinese cook a "slant-eyed muskrat" [*The Virginian*]).

Until the recent *Dances with Wolves* and *Unforgiven, Cimarron* was the only Western to have won the Academy Award for best picture, in addition to winning another two of the seven Oscars for which it was nominated. Yet the box office earnings of the latest of the Western epics were not sufficient to dissuade studios from emphasizing lower-budget B Westerns for most of the depression decade. Johnny Mack Brown and John Wayne, the promising young stars of *Billy the Kid* and *The Big Trail*, respectively, found themselves relegated mostly to B Westerns. Then, following Cecil D. DeMille's *The Plainsman* and three other Paramount-produced large-canvas Westerns from 1936 to 1938, nearly every studio from 1939 to 1941 filled the nation's screens with major productions featuring top stars, including newcomers to the genre such as Tyrone Power (*Jesse James*), Henry Fonda (*Jesse James, Return of Frank James*), James Stewart (*Destry Rides Again*), and Errol Flynn (*Dodge City, Virginia City, Santa Fe Trail, They Died with Their Boots On*).

With the notable exception of *Destry Rides Again* (1939), a boisterous spoof of the conventional lawman/town-taming motif, most of the new crop of big Westerns were pseudohistorical pageants of American progress or notorious outlaws. DeMille's *Union Pacific* (1939) thus commemorated the transcontinental railroad builders as paving the way for civilization in a lawless, Indian-infested wilderness, whereas Fox's lavishly technicolored *Jesse James* (1939) inspired a cycle of outlaw-as-social-victim sagas. Although these two types of Westerns differed in focus—one highlighted heroic pioneers of national progress, whereas the other showcased decent men driven to outlawry by social and political injustices—they shared a preoccupation with a nation plagued by corrupt capitalists and politicians. In *Union Pacific* "money-grubbing financiers" out to "sell Union stock short and buy Central" attempt to sabotage a construction feat that will not only unite the country but provide work and wages to thousands of unemployed Civil War veterans. Whereas DeMille differentiated between financial grafters and enlightened railroad builders, Nunnally Johnson's script for *Jesse James* treated railroad promoters as exploitive capitalists whose control of the courts allowed them to cheat and foreclose on struggling farmers. Much like early depression gangster films, *Jesse James* appealed to a public incensed with legal injustices and attracted to colorful individuals who defied a corrupted system. And like the gangster, the western outlaw is held to account (hence Jesse's death) to the degree that his lawlessness becomes self-serving and divorced from the public good. Warner Brothers obviously had the outlaw-gangster parallel in mind when it cast James Cagney and Humphrey Bogart as rivals in both the gangland opus *The Roaring Twenties* (1939) and the Western saga *The Oklahoma Kid* (1939). There is also a startling resemblance between *Jesse James* and the 1940 film adaptation of John Steinbeck's *Grapes of Wrath*. Both are premised on the plight of farmers being driven from the land by insensitive capitalists. Moreover, both were produced by Darryl Zanuck for Twentieth Century–Fox and scripted by Nunnally Johnson, and both included in their casts Henry Fonda (Frank James and Tom Joad) and Jane Darwell (Ma James and Ma Joad).

The fact that Westerns in the last years of the depression depicted outlaws as populist victims of capitalist exploitation and at the same time celebrated a proud national heritage is indicative of an America that continued to blame the plight of dispossessed farmers and unemployed workers on shyster politicians and greedy robber barons while exhibiting a renewed national pride and democratic idealism in response to the fascist tide sweeping Europe and Asia. As the prospect of intervention in another world war drew closer, Westerns preached the urgency of protecting democracy from demagogic tyrants (e.g., William Quantrill—fictionalized as Will Cantrell—in *The Dark Command* [1940] and John Brown in *Santa Fe Trail* [1940]), from war profiteers (*They Died with Their Boots On* [1941]), or, as the title character of MGM's *Billy the Kid* (1940) is warned, from "Napoleons, Hannibals, or Billy the Kids."

John Ford's *Stagecoach* received the most acclaim among the many first-rate Westerns in these prewar years. That it managed to win two of the five Oscars for which it was nominated (supporting actor and music score) even though it lost in the best picture category was remarkable given the unparalleled competition in 1939 from classics such as *Gone with the Wind, The Wizard of Oz, Mr. Smith Goes to Washington, Ninotchka,* and *Wuthering Heights.* Without a Western to his credit for some thirteen years, John Ford transported a talented cast headed by a B Western player (John Wayne) to Monument Valley and, at a reportedly modest cost of $250,000, directed a simply structured narrative that effectively integrated character development and social tensions with picturesque landscapes and spectacularly staged action. In the course of a hazardous stagecoach journey climaxed by an Indian attack, an assortment of social outcasts and prominents reveal their nobler selves and, except for a fraudulent banker (a stock depression villain), commit to their mutual survival. Away from the social prejudices and legal impediments of civilization, the Ringo Kid (Wayne) and Dallas (Claire Trevor) regain a lost innocence, and at the end of the film the sheriff allows them to ride free of what is sarcastically referred to as "the blessings of civilization."

However befitting the social consciousness of the depression, Ford's critical view of civilized society in *Stagecoach* softened somewhat in the early postwar years with his wistful rendering of the Wyatt Earp–Tombstone episode in *My Darling Clementine* (1946) and in his patriotic cavalry/Indian trilogy starring John Wayne (*Fort Apache* [1948], *She Wore a Yellow Ribbon* [1949], and *Rio Grande* [1950]). These films, together with *Wagonmaster* (1950) and especially *The Searchers* (1956), established Ford as the consummate screen auteur of frontier Americana.

The late 1940s and 1950s not only were the richest period for John Ford's artistry but also marked a renaissance of sorts in terms of both the quantity and quality of Western movies. Competition from television

spelled the end of the B series Western by the mid-1950s, but Hollywood more than compensated with an outpouring of feature Westerns
adorned with wider screens and more frequent use of color, greater variety and complexity of content and characterization, and big-name
casts. From 1946 to 1960 Gary Cooper, John Wayne, James Stewart,
Alan Ladd, Gregory Peck, Charlton Heston, William Holden, Robert
Mitchum, Burt Lancaster, Kirk Douglas, Robert Taylor, Rock Hudson,
Glenn Ford, Richard Widmark, Fred MacMurray, and Ronald Reagan
each starred in at least five Westerns, while Joel McCrea, Randolph
Scott, and newcomer Audie Murphy became almost exclusively Western
stars. Calling the Western "the American film *par excellence*," France's
André Bazin, along with other European and American (most notably
Robert Warshow) critics, began in the 1950s to acknowledge the myth-
ic and artistic importance of the genre, as manifested particularly in the
postwar work of director-auteurs such as John Ford, Howard Hawks,
Anthony Mann, and Budd Boetticher (fig. 4.2).

On the set of *Shane* in 1951 actress Jean Arthur praised the Western
for stressing personal fortitude: "The greed and brutality that abound
in our world exist because most of us lack the gumption to do battle."[1]
Arthur's remarks undoubtedly applied in her mind to the film in
which she costarred with Alan Ladd. *Shane* was an immensely popular Western in the classical mold of a lone gunman (a variation of the
good bad man from the silent era) coming to the aid of a pioneering
farm community threatened by a land-hungry cattleman. This very
traditional theme is played out in ritualistic fashion, the genre's familiar iconography of landscape, costume, fistfights, and shoot-outs aes-
theticized to highlight the mythic dimensions of the film's characters
and conflicts.

Shane's self-conscious evocation of the mythic West is particularly
conspicuous given the fact that many postwar Westerns were moving
in an opposite direction. Two films made in 1943, *The Outlaw* and *The
Ox-Bow Incident,* marked a significant departure from genre conventions that was to reoccur in subsequent Westerns. *The Outlaw,* followed three years later by *Duel in the Sun* (1946), highlighted the sexual and neurotic behavior of major characters, whereas *The Ox-Bow
Incident* presented an unsparingly grim indictment of an entire community given to mob hysteria. The traditional Western was not suddenly or entirely displaced thereafter, but Westerns (undoubtedly influenced by the film noir and social-realist trends in 1940s films) did
become increasingly infused with psychological and social dimensions,
which rendered problematic the conventional portrait of stalwart heroes and virtuous communities.

Figure 4.2. A good-guy reputation established in Western films helped Ronald Reagan become one of the most popular politicians in U.S. history. (Richard Aquila Collection.)

In contrast to the confident stoicism of Alan Ladd's Shane character were the many psychologically disturbed or profoundly disillusioned protagonists who were estranged from or threatening to the larger society. James Stewart epitomized the new emotionally fragile, tormented hero in the five Westerns he made with director Anthony Mann, beginning with *Winchester 73* (1950) and reaching near-hysterical proportions in *The Naked Spur* (1953). In the latter film an obsessive struggle to bring in a dangerous outlaw for bounty leaves Stewart physically and emotionally battered as he is forced to confront the reality of his own dehumanization. No less afflicted with angst were Glenn Ford and Kirk Douglas in their Western roles, while the heretofore stalwart John Wayne played unstable characters in Howard Hawks's *Red River* (1948) and John Ford's *The Searchers* (1956), as did Randolph Scott in Budd Boetticher's *Decision at Sundown* (1957).

Although some of these Westerns retain the traditional notion of a progressive society to which the hero must become reconciled (*Red River* being a prime example), others linked the hero's estrangement to failings within society itself. Thus *The Gunfighter* (1950), in which Gregory Peck's powerful performance in the title role formalized the 1950s prototype of the wearied, self-recriminating gunman, juxtaposes the protagonist's basic integrity with the banality, hypocrisy, and vicariously violent tendencies of the "respectable" townspeople. The film at once lauds the gunfighter's efforts to forsake his irresponsible ways and questions the worth of the society with which he seeks reconciliation.

One of the most widely acclaimed Westerns of the 1950s, *High Noon* (1952), was a veritable litany of social ills. Civic complacency and cowardice, conformity to public opinion, racism, opportunism, and an obsession with material security are among the unseemly traits of a town's comfortably middle-class populace that fails to support its retiring marshal (Gary Cooper in an academy award–winning performance) in a showdown with four killers. *High Noon* in effect reverses the traditional Western ideal of reconciling heroic individualism with the larger social good. The community to which the hero has committed himself is hardly worth saving.

In addition to engaging in social criticism that resembled current intellectual reservations about suburban middle-class anxieties and conformity, screenwriter Carl Foreman claims that he fashioned *High Noon* as a metaphorical attack on Hollywood's submission to congressional anticommunist investigations that threatened his own career and that of others in the late 1940s and early 1950s. Foreman in effect was blacklisted and evidently believed that, like Marshal Kane, he had been pressured by the film community to defer to rather than resist the congressional bad guys who had invaded their midst. Neither producer Stanley Kramer nor director Fred Zinnemann have voiced any such political intent for the film, however, nor does the film itself unequivocally reflect Foreman's alleged message. Supporters of the House Committee on Un-American Activities or of Senator Joseph McCarthy could just as well identify with the hero's refusal to defer to community pressures (i.e., liberal opponents) to compromise with bad guys (i.e., communists) who threatened to subvert the town. In effect, the film speaks to a concern shared by McCarthyites as well as their critics: the urgency of awakening a dangerously complacent society to that which threatened its freedom, whether that threat was defined as communist subversion or congressional witch-hunting.

Designed, as Westerns always had been, principally as entertainment, *High Noon* was nonetheless one of many Westerns of the postwar period to contain themes and perspectives that were topical, if not altogether provocative. If the anticommunist right was the intended target of *High Noon*, as it was allegedly of Nicholas Ray's bizarre attack on mob violence in *Johnny Guitar* (1954), other Westerns took the opposite stance, highlighting the urgency of rooting out subversive evils. The same year that Gary Cooper played Carl Foreman's allegorical victim of McCarthyism in *High Noon,* in *Springfield Rifle* he played an undercover agent who feigns being an Army deserter to infiltrate an espionage operation headed by a traitor high in the ranks of the military. The counterespionage premise of *Springfield Rifle* was practically interchangeable with the same studio's (Warner Brothers) anticommunist thriller of the previous year, *I Was a Communist for the FBI* (1951). For *The Man behind the Gun* (1953), a Western that starred Randolph Scott as an undercover agent exposing a separatist conspiracy in Los Angeles, publicists at Warner Brothers made sure in the film's advertisements that audiences would not miss the contemporary point: "When the Golden State was black with treason . . . this Soldier-without-a-uniform blasted it clean." Similarly, in publicizing an earlier Scott Western, *Colt .45* (1950), Warners highlighted the theme of keeping a new weapon "out of the hands of the wrong element—Indians and bandits in the Colt days, Russians and the Iron Curtain now."² The cold war link had been no less obvious in Republic's *The Fabulous Texan* (1947) when Andy Devine warned, "The land o' your birth is becomin' a Siberia."

Cold war anxieties were also reflected in cavalry-Indian scenarios that preached the urgency of firm, decisive action to contain or defeat an unregenerate aggressor. Those who discount the hero's warning against appeasement, as in *Arrowhead* (1953) and *Drum Beat* (1954), are predictably done in by the treacherous enemy. Films that depicted the Indian as a hostile menace, however, were bucking the tide of Westerns that, like some of the early silents, sympathetically portrayed the Indian as a victim of white prejudice. Particularly influential was *Broken Arrow* (1950), a Western whose message of peace and racial tolerance signaled a more liberal slant that would come to dominate the Western by the mid-1950s—coincidental with the waning of McCarthyism, the promise of "peaceful coexistence" in the cold war, and the breakthrough in civil rights prompted by the Supreme Court's ruling in *Brown v. Board of Education* (1954). However condescendingly these films portrayed the Indian as worthy of being treated like a white person (hence the casting of white stars as Indian protagonists—Jeff Chandler in *Broken Arrow,* Rock Hudson in *Taza, Son of Cochise* [1954], Burt Lancaster in *Apache* [1954], and Victor Mature in *Chief Crazy Horse* [1955]), they did increasingly suggest that prejudice was not a mere aberration confined to a few evil whiskey traders or arrogant military commanders but a widespread societal flaw that had to be confronted and turned around. Interracial sex became a potent symbol of both the ideal of racial accommodation and the miscegenous anxieties underlying white prejudice. By killing off the Indian partner of racial bonding in *Broken Arrow,* the filmmakers may well have been deferring to real-life taboos against miscegenation even as they decried such discrimination in the film itself. A similar ambivalence occurs in films such as *The Searchers* (1956), *Trooper Hook* (1957), and *The Unforgiven* (1959), which ostensibly attack racial intolerance rooted in miscegenous fears while at the same time affirming the threat of Indian savagery to white womanhood. If demeaning Indian stereotypes were slow to disappear, the trend was nevertheless toward a more critical stance regarding white discrimination at a time when Americans were experiencing the equally slow breakdown of racial segregation in the South and the beginnings of a civil rights movement that would drastically alter if not entirely rectify decades of racial inequality.

Meanwhile, Westerns of the middle and late 1950s continued in the manner of *High Noon* to address all manner of social ills, from conformity-induced identity crises (*The Fastest Gun Alive* [1956]) and civic complacency (*The 3:10 to Yuma* [1957]) to parental-youth conflicts (*Gunman's Walk* [1958]). Nicholas Ray's *The True Story of Jesse James* (1957) and Arthur Penn's *The Left-Handed Gun* (1958) offered timely depictions of Jesse James and Billy the Kid as brooding, delinquent youths; Ray had earlier directed James Dean in the popular juvenile melodrama *Rebel without a Cause* (1955), and a decade later Penn's *Bonnie and Clyde* (1967) and *Alice's Restaurant* (1969) would strike a responsive chord with America's young counterculture. Topicality extended to broaching hitherto taboo subjects, such as the intimations of homosexuality in *Warlock* (1959) or incest in *The Last Sunset* (1961). Although mild by today's standards, the forced stripping of Julie London in *Man of the West* (1958) or the rape sequence that begins *Last Train from Gun Hill* (1959) were considered daring in the 1950s.

The traditional motif of upright lawmen ridding the West of desperadoes remained alive and well in such major productions as *Gunfight at the O.K. Corral* (1957) and *Rio Bravo* (1959), the latter allegedly intended by director Howard Hawks to counter the social criticism in *High Noon.* Nevertheless, both films reflected the impact of the new trends by highlighting emotionally unstable characters (Kirk Douglas in *Gunfight* and Dean Martin in *Rio Bravo*) and omitting the kind of socially progressive or nationalistic overtones that pervaded earlier Westerns. Similarly, the one epic-scale Western of the late 1950s, *The Big Country* (1958), was less intent on heralding the pioneering spirit of its Texas setting than on deflating frontier-bred notions of honor and violent bravado.

In a decade disparaged for its unquestioning complacency regarding social problems, it is striking that a genre designed for mass appeal exhibited such a critical perspective. As popular culture, the postwar Western gives evidence of a disquieting mood and critical sensibility in the Truman-Eisenhower years that is often obscured by nostalgic and condescending hindsight. The turbulent and protest-filled Johnson-Nixon years would effect a harsher and more despairing vision of America's frontier heritage, but one that was less a radical departure from than an accentuation of characterizations and perspectives generated in the 1940s and 1950s.

The new decade that began politically with John F. Kennedy's promise of a "New Frontier" of reform and world leadership also began with several Westerns that resurrected a more positive, heroic vision of the old frontier. John Wayne, although not a Kennedy liberal, delivered his own brand of reviving the American spirit in his extravagant production of *The Alamo* (1960). Two years later, MGM marshaled an all-star cast for its epic celebration of America's westward expansion, *How the West Was Won* (1962). Owing its immense success at the box office in large part to its being a showcase for the gigantic wide-screen process of Cinerama, *How the West Was Won* failed to spark a revival of the nationalistic perspective that had once pervaded the genre. To the contrary, filmmakers through much of the 1960s and 1970s carried the revisionist trend evident in 1950s Westerns to new extremes. Such was to be expected if the feature Western was to retain credibility with an increasingly younger movie audience full of misgivings about the America they had inherited, an America that reverberated with civil rights demonstrations and urban ghetto uprisings, antiwar protests that portrayed the Vietnam War as a manifestation of U.S. imperialist aggression, and countercultural assaults on a presumably technocratic "military-industrial complex."

John Ford's vision of the West became noticeably darker in his final contributions to the genre. His *Two Rode Together* (1961) was an uncharacteristically cynical and bitter variation on the centuries-old captivity narrative in which an entire community exhibits the kind of racial hatred that Ford had depicted as an individual flaw in *The Searchers*. In *Cheyenne Autumn* (1964) Ford emphasized the tragedy of the Indian experience itself, as if to redress his own record of demeaning stereotypes as far back as *Stagecoach* or *The Iron Horse*. Still, Ford's casting of white actors in prominent Indian roles plus a last-reel suggestion that the U.S. government would reverse its unjust policies differentiated *Cheyenne Autumn* from stronger indictments of American atrocities in such films as *Soldier Blue* (1970) and *Little Big Man* (1970)—two of the more obvious manifestations of antiwar and counterculture attitudes in Westerns made during the Vietnam War.

In keeping with the changing racial climate of the 1960s, Westerns not only highlighted white America's transgressions against Indians but began to address the issue of prejudice with respect to blacks. Until the 1960s African Americans had been conspicuously absent from mainstream Westerns other than in minor roles as loyal slaves or wards (like Issaiah in *Cimarron*). There were productions, from the silent period to the 1940s, designed for black audiences with all-black casts, but these more often than not were simple imitations of standard B movie scenarios. John Ford's *Sergeant Rutledge* (1960) broke precedent by casting Woody Strode in the prominent role of a black soldier falsely accused of raping a white woman. Although its racial message was compromised somewhat by heralding black heroism against stereotypically savage Indians, *Sergeant Rutledge* did offer an uncommonly dignified portrait of blacks forced to contend with a bigoted, white-dominated society. After decades of deploring the plight of a defeated Confederacy, Hollywood addressed the injustices of slavery in *The Scalphunters* (1968), *The Skin Game* (1971), and *Buck and the Preacher* (1972). The last film was among the first and most successful of Westerns featuring a predominantly black cast. Directed by its star, Sidney Poitier, *Buck and the Preacher* projected not only a racially divided America but the promise of African Americans defeating their white oppressors (southerners trying to force freedmen heading west back to the plantations) and building a viable community of their own. In the early 1970s football celebrities Jim Brown and Fred Williamson became two of the better-known action stars in crime thrillers and Westerns that highlighted rugged, defiant black heroes. A recent attempt to resurrect the black Western is Mario Van Peebles's *Posse* (1993).

Westerns seemed less affected by the woman's movement of the 1960s. The genre had always been male-oriented by virtue of its emphasis on physical, violent conflict, with the ideal woman portrayed as a domesticating influence on the hero and, accordingly, a symbol of civilization's triumph over wilderness. The antithesis of the virtuous schoolmarm/pioneer wife/rancher's daughter is the more aggressive, erotic saloon woman (prostitute) who, even though she may exhibit affection and respect for the hero (e.g., Marlene Dietrich's Frenchie in *Destry Rides Again*), usually ends up dead or discarded because of her transgressions. Still, within the limits of this dichotomized character convention, there have emerged resourceful, assertive woman characters such as Irene Dunne's Sabra (*Cimarron*), Claire Trevor's Dallas (*Stagecoach*), and Joan Crawford's Vienna (*Johnny Guitar*). In the 1940s and 1950s Barbara Stanwyck consistently portrayed tough-minded women whose dominating presence was reflected in titles like *The Great Man's Lady* (1942), *Cattle Queen of Montana* (1954), and *The Maverick Queen* (1956). With some exceptions that include Jane Fonda in *Cat Ballou* (1965) and *Comes a Horseman* (1978), Raquel Welsh in *Hannie Caulder* (1972), Julie Christie in *McCabe and Mrs. Miller* (1971), and Conchata Ferrell in *Heartland* (1979), few Westerns offered substantive roles for women or otherwise accommodated the growing impetus for sexual equality in the 1960s and 1970s.

No Western theme has been explored with greater frequency since the early 1960s than that of the passing of the frontier. In John Ford's elegiac Western *The Man Who Shot Liberty Valance* (1962), the ostensible protagonist is a lawyer (James Stewart) who leads a wild west town into the modern era wherein the communal rule of law displaces the individualistic code of the six-gun. Nonetheless, Ford clearly mourns the loss of the frontier individualist (represented by the proud, self-reliant rancher played by John Wayne) who, as revealed late in the film, is responsible for saving the lawyer's life, thus making possible the very civilization that would render his own way of life obsolete.

Whereas Ford declined to cast the modern era in an unfavorable light, other than to regret what had been lost in the process, films set in the modern West, from *The Misfits* (1961) and *Lonely Are the Brave* (1962) to the adaptations of Larry McMurtry's *Hud* (1963) and *The Last Picture Show* (1972), invariably emphasized a hopelessly tedious and cruelly dehumanizing modernity that had encroached on the individual freedom and dignity associated with the now-defunct frontier. More typical were Westerns set near the turn of the century when cowboys, lawmen, and outlaws encountered an emerging civilization of middle-class blandness and conformity, technology (typically the automobile) that seemed more intrusive than purposeful, and often an oppressive corporate-legal establishment. Those who resisted the new order were ruthlessly eliminated, whether Indians (*Little Big Man* [1970]) or stubbornly independent outcasts (Warren Beatty's gambler-entrepreneur in *McCabe and Mrs. Miller* [1971] or Paul Newman's and Robert Redford's outlaws in *Butch Cassidy and the Sundance Kid* [1969]).

No film director in these years eulogized the passing of the frontier with greater feeling or ferocity than Sam Peckinpah. Obscuring the melancholic sensitivity of *Ride the High Country* (1962) and more comical *Ballad of Cable Hogue* (1970) was the notoriety accorded

Peckinpah for the graphic violence of *The Wild Bunch* (1969). Throughout his best work, however, was Peckinpah's affinity for the aging westerner struggling to survive changing times with dignity intact. Particularly in *The Wild Bunch* and his last Western, *Pat Garrett and Billy the Kid* (1973), Peckinpah does not gloss over the reality of disorder and violence that in part belies his characters' fond reminiscences of the Old West. But he does nevertheless posit a modern order capable of even greater violence against those who fail to conform. For all their unseemly traits, Peckinpah's wild bunch and Billy the Kid embody the only remaining semblance of freedom and spontaneity in a world that is being put under wraps.

Despite Sam Peckinpah's distinction as a Western filmmaker and the proliferation of equally somber portraits of a declining frontier, audiences tended to favor more upbeat variations of the same theme or Westerns with triumphant protagonists. While Peckinpah's *The Wild Bunch* attracted considerable press attention and a respectable audience, its popularity at the box office in 1969 paled by comparison with either *Butch Cassidy and the Sundance Kid* or *True Grit*. John Wayne's enduring popularity had much to do with the success of *True Grit,* as did Paul Newman's with *Butch Cassidy*. More important with respect to the latter film, however, was its blend of personable characters, cheeky humor, lushly photographed settings, and romantic interludes to render the revisionist doomed-outlaw theme a more viable commercial entertainment than *The Wild Bunch*.

True Grit was John Wayne's ticket to the much-coveted Oscar award and belated recognition as an actor as well as superstar. The fact that Wayne was ranked among the top ten box office stars every consecutive year from 1959 to 1974 suggests that old-fashioned heroism had not entirely gone out of style (fig. 4.3). Although Wayne consciously avoided the cynicism and despair prevalent in Westerns of the period, his films did depart from the traditional format in one respect: where the hero (including Wayne's own portrayals in earlier years) ultimately aligned himself with a progressive society, in the 1960s and 1970s he often remained apart from a society governed by bumbling/corrupt bureaucrats or, as in *True Grit,* an ineffectual justice system. Particularly in films directed by Andrew McGlaglen for Wayne's own Batjac Company, the star conveyed his conservative beliefs in a free, competitive society of self-reliant but socially responsible individualism. Whereas the New Mexico cattle baron John Chisum is symbolic of corporate encroachment in Peckinpah's *Pat Garrett and Billy the Kid,* as played by Wayne in McGlaglen's *Chisum* (1970), he is a self-made frontier patriarch whose innate sense of justice contrasts with

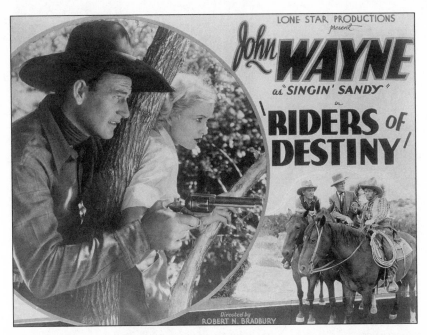

Figure 4.3. Poster for one of John Wayne's early B Westerns before he became Hollywood's premier feature-film western hero. (courtesy of the Ray White Collection.)

both a corrupt legal establishment and a youthfully impetuous Billy the Kid. At a time when generational differences informed much of the dissension in America, Wayne often assumed in his Westerns the role of the stern but caring father figure, assuring even into death in *The Cowboys* (1972) the passing of his traditionalist values to a respectful younger generation.

Quite a different screen persona of triumphant individualism emerged in three Italian Westerns (*A Fistful of Dollars, For a Few Dollars More,* and *The Good, the Bad, and the Ugly*—all released in the U.S. in 1967) directed by Sergio Leone and starring Clint Eastwood. Superior guile and efficiency with a gun are the principal attributes of Eastwood's "man with no name" as he fends off vicious rivals for bounty or buried loot, bereft of Wayne's typical moral rectitude. Previous American Westerns such as *Vera Cruz* (1954) or *The Magnificent Seven* (1960) had featured hardened, disillusioned mercenaries, but usually with the promise of regeneration through commitment to some cause such as befriending oppressed Mexicans. The Leone-Eastwood hero had no illusions to begin

with, nor was there any cause worthy of commitment other than looking out for oneself in a bleak, violent world.

More "spaghetti" Westerns followed with their ever-familiar Spanish desert landscapes, violent theatrics, and imported Hollywood play-
ers such as Lee Van Cleef alternating with international newcomers
such as Terence Hill. Also on view were German Westerns filmed in
Yugoslavia, British Westerns filmed in Spain (*Shalako* [1968], featuring
Britain's Sean Connery and France's Brigitte Bardot), and assorted in-
ternational collaborations such as *Red Sun* (1971), which assembled
America's Charles Bronson, Japan's Toshiro Mifume, and France's
Alain Delon under the direction of Britain's Terence Young. Sergio
Leone's large-scale rendition of the classic pioneer story *Once upon a
Time in the West* (1969) would be hailed a masterpiece by some genre
connoisseurs, but it was Leone's former star player, Clint Eastwood,
who would draw the big audiences after his return to Hollywood.
While retaining the squinty-eyed deadly persona and some of the stylistic peculiarities of the Leone films, Eastwood's American Westerns
lent his character a more traditional sense of purpose for his violent
behavior, such as avenging a personal or social injustice in *Hang 'Em
High* (1968), *Joe Kidd* (1972), and *High Plains Drifter* (1973). A comparison of the third film with two subsequent Westerns he directed as
well as starred in, *The Outlaw Josey Wales* (1976) and *Pale Rider*
(1985), shows a marked progression from the darkly cynical world carried over from his Italian Westerns to one that promised personal or
communal redemption (fig. 4.4).

Eastwood's portrayal in *Coogan's Bluff* (1968) of a modern-day
Arizona deputy who transports his western-style law enforcement to
the crime-ridden streets of New York City proved prophetic of not
only Eastwood's own transition from cowboy to cop hero in the immensely successful *Dirty Harry* (1971) but also the transition in audience preference from Westerns to crime thrillers. "The Western is
dead," pronounced critic Pauline Kael in 1974, adding (with Eastwood's "Saint Cop" clearly in mind) that the western hero has "moved
from the mythical purity of the wide-open spaces into the corrupt
modern cities and towns."[3] The mythic purity that Kael refers to had
already been assailed, perhaps irrevocably, in the Western itself, to the
point where the genre had lost much of its original rationale as a staple
of film entertainment. Significantly, in the same year that Kael pronounced the Western's demise, Mel Brooks's irreverent lampoon of the
genre, *Blazing Saddles* (1974), took the box office by storm to become
the highest-grossing Western to that time. Genre spoofs date back to
the silent era, but when combined with the revisionist/antihero trend
of the 1960s and 1970s, parodies like *Cat Ballou* (1965), *Support Your*

Figure 4.4. Clint Eastwood in *The Outlaw Josey Wales* (1976). (Courtesy of the Ray White Collection.)

Local Sheriff (1969), and especially *Blazing Saddles* assumed added significance as portents of the Western's losing its grasp on the popular imagination.

John Wayne made his final screen appearance, appropriately enough, in the year of America's bicentennial. In *The Shootist* (1976) Wayne plays a gunfighter dying of cancer in a turn-of-the-century town where he is regarded as a dangerous anachronism. Opening clips from earlier Wayne films, together with public knowledge of the actor's own bout with cancer, provide the film's elegiac theme an added resonance related directly to Wayne's being the sole survivor of a brand of screen heroism that had all but vanished by the mid-1970s. Indeed, by the time of Wayne's death three years later, the future of the genre he had helped to shape seemed more precarious than ever. The colossal failure of Michael Cimino's reportedly 50 million dollar epic *Heaven's Gate* (1980), followed a year later by the universal panning accorded *Legend of the Lone Ranger* (1981), further discouraged Hollywood from what by then seemed a risky investment. Anticipations in 1985 that *Silverado* and Eastwood's *Pale Rider* would spark a revival of the Western were dampened by the mediocre success of both films. *Young Guns* (1988) profitably tapped the youth market with its "brat-pack" cast reenactment of the Billy the Kid saga, although returns on the sequel *Young Guns II* (1990) proved disappointing.

Three surprise successes in recent years have given Hollywood some pause to reconsider the genre's fate. In early 1989 the CBS mini-series telecast of Larry McMurtry's Pulitzer Prize–winning *Lonesome Dove* attracted an estimated 40 million viewers for each of four nights and won seven Emmy awards. Just as eventful on the movie front were Kevin Costner's *Dances with Wolves* (1990) and Clint Eastwood's *Unforgiven* (1992). Both films drew large audiences and won multiple Oscars, including best picture. *Dances with Wolves* combines a classic romanticism with an ethnically sensitive rendering of the Indian-white conflict that owes much to *Broken Arrow* and its revisionist successors. If Costner's epic breaks little new ground with the Western, Eastwood's *Unforgiven* challenges genre conventions at every turn, none more so than that of violent heroism. Far from the coolly amoral "man with no name" of the Leone films or the wronged outlaw Josie Wales, Eastwood's William Munny is a widowed gunfighter-turned-sodbuster whose desperate quest for reward money to afford a better life for his two children plunges him into a nightmare of senseless violence. Haunted by the memory of his deceased wife, Munny is by turns ravaged by fever, nearly beaten to death, and given to inglorious acts of violence. His climactic shoot-out with a sadistic sheriff spells not heroic triumph but a tragic reversion to the rampaging beast he once was.

Without incorporating a racial theme per se, Eastwood did feature a prominent black actor (Morgan Freeman) as Munny's closest neighbor and friend who accompanies him on the fateful journey. Much more was made of Kevin Costner's proclivity for "political correctness" in *Dances with Wolves* by virtue of his avowed transcendence of Indian stereotypes, as well as the presence of a strong female character as the hero's romantic interest. But then, most Westerns have been in the context of their times politically correct, albeit less self-consciously so. William S. Hart was no less out of date in 1920 than was Kevin Costner seventy years later when in *The Toll Gate* Hart's Black Deering asks the sheriff to let him die "like a white man." American society has changed drastically since then, and the Western has seldom been far out of step.

Notes

1. *Hollywood Citizen News,* January 16, 1941, 8.
2. Production files, "Man Behind the Gun" and "Colt .45," Warner Brothers Collection, Special Collections, Doheny Library, University of Southern California, Los Angeles.
3. Pauline Kael, "The Current Cinema: The Street Western," *New Yorker,* February 25, 1974, 100.

Selected Bibliography

The following is a selection of book-length publications that are pertinent to the history of the A Western and that proved particularly useful for this essay. Omitted are works that focus on filmmakers or particular western themes.

Adams, Les, and Buck Rainey. *Shoot-Em-Ups: The Complete Reference Guide to Westerns of the Sound Era.* New Rochelle, N.Y., 1978.
Bataille, Gretchen M., and Charles L. P. Silet, eds. *The Pretend Indians: Images of Native Americans in Movies.* Ames, Iowa, 1980.
Bazin, Andre. *What Is Cinema?* Trans. Hugh Gray. Vol. 2. Berkeley, Calif., 1971.
Brownlow, Kevin. *The War, the West, and the Wilderness.* New York, 1979.
Buscombe, Edward, ed. *The BFI Companion to the Western.* New York, 1988.
Calder, Jennie. *There Must Be a Lone Ranger: The American West in Film and Reality.* New York, 1975.
Cawelti, John. *The Six-Gun Mystique.* 2d ed. Bowling Green, Ohio, 1984.
Etulain, Richard W., ed. "Western Films: A Brief History." *Journal of the West* 22 (October 1983). Special issue.
Eyles, Allen. *The Western.* New York, 1975.

Fenin, George N., and William K. Everson. *The Western: From Silents to Cinerama.* New York, 1973.

Frayling, Christopher. *Spaghetti Westerns: Cowboys and Europeans from Karl May to Sergio Leone.* London, 1981.

French, Philip. *Westerns: Aspects of a Movie Genre.* New York, 1977.

Friar, Ralph, and Natasha Friar. *The Only Good Indian . . . The Hollywood Gospel.* New York, 1972.

Garfield, Brian. *The Western: A Complete Guide.* New York, 1982.

Hardy, Phil. *The Western.* London, 1983.

Hitt, Jim. *The American West from Fiction (1823–1876) into Film (1909–1986).* Jefferson, N.C., 1990.

Kitses, Jim. *Horizons West.* Bloomington, Ind., 1969.

Lenihan, John H. *Showdown: Confronting Modern America in the Western Film.* Urbana, Illinois, 1980.

Manchel, Frank. *Film Study: An Analytical Bibliography.* Vol. 1. London, 1990.

Meyer, William R. *The Making of the Great Westerns.* New Rochelle, 1979.

Nachbar, John G., ed. *Focus on the Western.* Englewood Cliffs, N.J., 1974.

———. *Western Films: An Annotated Critical Bibliography.* New York, 1975.

Nachbar, John G., Jackie R. Donath, and Chris Foran. *Western Films Two: An Annotated Critical Bibliography from 1974 to 1987.* New York, 1988.

Parish, James Robert, and Michael R. Pitts. *The Great Western Pictures II.* Metuchen, N.J., 1988.

Pilkington, William T., and Don Graham, eds. *Western Movies.* Albuquerque, N.Mex., 1979.

Pitts, Michael R. *Western Movies.* Jefferson, N.C., 1986.

Slotkin, Richard. *Gunfighter Nation: The Myth of the Frontier in Twentieth-Century America.* New York, 1992.

Tompkins, Jane. *West of Everything: The Inner Life of Westerns.* New York, 1992.

Tuska, Jon. *The Filming of the West.* Garden City, N.Y., 1976.

Warshow, Robert. *The Immediate Experience: Movies, Comics, Theater and Other Aspects of Popular Culture.* New York, 1962.

Wright, Will. *Six Guns and Society: A Structural Study of the Western.* Berkeley, Calif., 1975.

FIVE

RAY WHITE

The Good Guys Wore White Hats:
The B Western in American Culture

ETWEEN 1930 AND 1954 Hollywood produced more than 2,000 low-budget B Western movies that millions of Americans (both juveniles and adults) enjoyed at Saturday matinees and evening showings. Costing only a few thousand dollars to make and following formula plots, the grade B Westerns usually were shot in seven days or less and featured such stars as Buck Jones, Ken Maynard, John Wayne, Gene Autry, Roy Rogers, Eddie Dean, and Lash LaRue. These and several dozen other cowboy stars working for different studios each appeared in several B Westerns annually. Because Westerns were cheaply made, they almost always turned a profit; when they ceased to do so in the 1950s, production was halted.

The B Western formula plots romanticized and glorified the American West, depicting the struggle between a hero and his sidekick and villains who stole cattle, land, and gold mines or who tried to take over valleys, towns, banks, and watering holes. The heroes always triumphed over the villains and departed the screen ready for action the following week.[1]

In the 1950s millions of Americans viewed these same films on television; thirty years later hundreds of thousands more renewed their acquaintance with the B Western or became new fans of this nostalgic genre through the medium of videotape and cable television. Videotape alone in the 1980s and 1990s made available to the public hundreds of B Westerns that had not been viewed for decades.

These films are important historical artifacts that can be used to understand mid-twentieth-century American culture. While providing entertainment for several generations of Americans, B Westerns reflected American values of the 1930s and 1940s. They mirrored attitudes toward individualism, race, and gender, as well as the hard times of the Great Depression, aspects of World War II, and even the anticommunism of the cold war period.

The B Westerns of the 1930s and 1940s were the successors of earlier silent Western films, which in turn were an outgrowth of dime and Western adventure novels or Wild West shows. Filmmakers began using western themes and scenes in short experimental productions even before the turn of the century. In 1898 the Edison Company filmed the plotless and brief *Cripple Creek Bar-room*, a movie tableau that depicted one version of a western saloon. Five years later Edwin S. Porter and the Edison Company produced *The Great Train Robbery*, the simply plotted but sophisticatedly edited ten-minute Western that established the format for many future Western movies.

Although *The Great Train Robbery* set the pattern for B Westerns, the real foundation for the genre was laid with hundreds of one- and two-reelers made by directors such as D. W. Griffith and Thomas Ince. These short films firmly established the first Western movie star, Bronco Billy Anderson, as well as the techniques, plot formulas, and standards followed by later Western film producers.[2]

By the 1920s the two-reeler Westerns had developed into feature-length dramas, becoming the bread-and-butter products of most Hollywood studios. Indeed, the popularity of Westerns soared during the decade, for their obvious moralism, action, and optimism matched the national mood. Within that milieu a host of cowboy film stars, led by William S. Hart and Tom Mix, became heroes to millions of Americans. The rapid technological and social change of the 1920s was an obvious counterpoint to the Western film hero's innocence and simple codes of justice, providing Americans with an idyllic link to the past. The Western, with its nostalgic cowboy hero, offered security to Americans and helped them to formulate both an individual and a national identity.[3]

Hollywood produced more than a thousand Westerns during the 1920s, averaging about 100 motion pictures a year. These feature films varied as to the star, budget, production values, and story.[4] Epic Westerns were the most prestigious because of their big budgets, casting, scripts, and publicity. Perhaps no more than a dozen epics were made during the decade, including *The Covered Wagon* (Famous Players–Lasky, 1923), *The Iron Horse* (Fox, 1924), *North of 36* (Paramount,

1924), and *The Pony Express* (Paramount, 1925). Shot on a grand scale by major studios, the epic Westerns celebrated the nation's frontier past. Although the epics' relationship to low-budget Westerns is slight in a technical sense, their magnitude and extensive publicity probably contributed to the public's interest in all Westerns.

Classifying non-epic silent Westerns is difficult, for they range widely in quality and often share characteristics with epics in regard to production values, scripts, and acting. The size of the budget alone cannot be used as a yardstick to classify these films, as would be the case during the later sound era, when features were made for double bills. The sharpest distinctions in 1920s Westerns appear when they are examined in relationship to their individual stars.

The major Western film dramas of the late 1920s were influenced by the earlier Westerns of William S. Hart and Tom Mix. The style of the two stars contrasted sharply: Hart made somber, grim, and gritty Westerns, whereas Mix spotlighted daredevil action, humor, and showmanship. Hart's popularity faded by the mid-1920s, leaving Mix as the nation's number-one Western film personality. His importance as a Western movie star is evidenced by the fact that his cowboy contemporaries emulated his style, dress, and demeanor. In doing so some of them equaled or surpassed the Mix films in quality.[5]

Mix's competitors, occupying a level of popularity just below his, included Buck Jones, Hoot Gibson, Ken Maynard, Harry Carey, Tim McCoy, and Fred Thompson. These actors portrayed strong, tough, and fearless Anglo-Saxon cowboys on the silent screen, and all except Thompson made the transition to sound and contributed significantly to the development of the low-budget sound Western.[6] Tom Mix also made that transition, and although his career in the sound era was limited, he, as much as any one individual, influenced the nature and style of the sound B Western. His humor, costumes, heroic style, and equestrian skills are all evident in the B Westerns of the 1930s and 1940s. Moreover, his name and image as a stereotypical movie cowboy remained in the minds of Americans long after his death in 1940.

In addition to Mix and other top-level performers, several dozen other Western actors starred in the horse operas of the 1920s. This group of performers and films can be classified according to acting, budget, production values, script, and studio. Included were such stars as Jack Hoxie, Art Acord, and Pete Morrison. These secondary stars made good action-packed films for Universal's Blue Streak Westerns series. With small budgets and less sophisticated acting and scripts, these films did not match the quality of those of the major stars. On the other hand, the fact that the films were Universal products, with solid production values and good distribution, helped Hoxie, Acord, and Morrison attain ranking near the top stars. In fact, if these three actors were judged only on the Westerns they made for studios other than Universal, their ranking would likely be in a lower category.[7]

A host of lesser Western actors starring in the productions of minor studios occupied the next level below Hoxie, Acord, and Morrison. Tom Tyler, Yakima Canutt, Bob Custer, Buffalo Bill Jr., Bob Steele, Lane Chandler, Edmund Cobb, Wally Wales, Buddy Roosevelt, Jack Perrin, and Leo Maloney, among others, made low-budget Westerns produced or released through minor companies such as FBO, Rayart, Arrow, Aywon, Syndicate, and Artclass. Despite the skimpy budgets of their films, these cowboy stars demonstrated both skill and style before the cameras and developed followings of their own. Some of these actors went on to star in low-budget Westerns during the early 1930s, but with the exceptions of Bob Steele and Tom Tyler, none ever reached the plateau of Jones, Gibson, Maynard, or McCoy. On the other hand, many of these secondary silent stars continued their careers as bit players in both Westerns and non-Westerns during the 1930s and 1940s. A few even extended their careers to the television Westerns of the 1950s and 1960s.

In addition to these secondary cowboy stars, many lesser-known actors appeared in even cheaper Westerns during the 1920s. For example, Bill Patton, Dick Hatton, Ben Wilson, and William Fairbanks worked for Prairie Productions, Sierra Pictures, H. B. Carpenter Productions, and other small companies that cranked out the cheapest Westerns of the decade. The fact that we now know little about these actors or their films suggests that the films suffered from poor production values, inadequate distribution, and perhaps even inferior scripts. Despite these shortcomings, however, the existence of these extremely inexpensive Westerns indicates the presence of a broad audience for Westerns—an audience that helped to lay the foundation for the sound B Western.

Although the secondary cowboy stars never made the big time, it is important to note that three of them—Jack Perrin, Wally Wales, and Leo Maloney—appeared in what has been classified as the first sound B Western, *Overland Bound* (Rayton Talking Pictures/Presidio, 1929). Along with acting in the film, Maloney directed and produced it.[8]

One silent star who does not fit any of the preceding categories but who had a relationship to the sound B Western was George O'Brien. He became an established Western star in 1924 when he appeared in the epic *Iron Horse*, but his appearance in non-Western films in the 1920s prevents him from being classified strictly as a Western actor. At the same time, his solid acting, powerful physique, and striking good looks all enhanced his career, eventually making him one of the most significant B Western actors of the 1930s.[9]

Both the major and minor silent Western screen stars who made the transition to talking features helped to establish a solid foundation for the sound B Western. Their success checked the cutback in Western film production ordered by fearful studio executives who thought that sound technology could not be applied to outdoor films. By the early 1930s nearly every Hollywood studio had its Western production unit. Throughout the decade these studios averaged a release of 100 Westerns annually, matching almost precisely the production rate of the previous decade.

Action characterized the B Westerns of the early 1930s, as Mix, Jones, Gibson, Maynard, McCoy, Tyler, and Steele engaged in fast-paced chases, knock-down-and-drag-out fistfights, and numerous loud and smoky shoot-outs. Each of these action stars developed his own style and screen personality along with his own following of fans. The most popular was Buck Jones, whose rugged, handsome features, trim physique, and neat western costumes complimented his strong, quiet, and gentle character. Working for Columbia Pictures, Jones starred in twenty-seven Westerns between 1930 and 1934.[10]

Making approximately the same number of Westerns for the same studio was the aloof and often austere Tim McCoy, who dressed in black and presented a military bearing. His stern, hard gaze put many a villain in his place, while his fanning technique with his six-gun often put them on the floor.[11]

Whereas McCoy was stiff and forbidding in his films, Hoot Gibson portrayed a relaxed and homely cowboy who looked like he slept in his clothes. His folksy demeanor coupled with deliberate humor proved appealing. Hoot's audience's identified with him and saw him as "just plain folk." He was the one film cowboy who often chose not to wear a gun.[12]

While Gibson was plain and common, Ken Maynard was handsome and slick. Astride his smart, bleach-white horse, Tarzan, the daredevil Maynard would try almost any trick or stunt. Maynard was not an accomplished actor, often fumbling his words and blurting out choppy sentences, but on horseback he had no equal. The action in both his silent and early sound Westerns is unsurpassed in boldness and excitement. Although equestrian work was the most important aspect of his film performance, Maynard introduced the musical Western, which changed the whole nature of the genre. Maynard incorporated music and song into several of his Universal Westerns in 1929 and 1930. He was a self-taught musician who played at least four instruments, and in 1930 he recorded several western songs with Columbia Records (fig. 5.1).[13]

Figure 5.1. Ken Maynard, complete with white hat, white-handled six-gun, and a trusty steed (named Tarzan), typified the B Western hero. (Courtesy of the Ray White Collection.)

Less exciting but a better actor was Tom Tyler, a world champion weightlifter who made an impressive appearance on the screen. His piercing dark eyes—he wilted many a villain with his cold, menacing stare—and unusually throaty voice became his trademarks. Although Tyler never reached the peak of cowboy stardom achieved by Jones, Maynard, and Gibson, he nevertheless starred regularly in the productions of several small independent studios.[14]

Bob Steele, with his compact build, determined features, and boyish curly hair, was the physical opposite of the muscular Tom Tyler. His nickname, "Battling Bob," resulted from his numerous cinematic fistfights in which he waded into screen heavies twice his size with arms swinging and fists hitting like a trip-hammer. His father, Robert North Bradbury, directed him in many films, and Steele's ego was such that he never hesitated to take minor roles in both Western and non-Western features. Steele's action roles, good looks, and youthfulness contributed to his success in silent films, as well as in later sound West-

erns. Following Ken Maynard's lead, Steele also became an early singing cowboy star in *Oklahoma Cyclone* (Tiffany, 1930).[15]

George O'Brien was another screen star who easily made the transition to sound, becoming one of the best B Western actors of the 1930s.
His Fox Westerns of the early 1930s possessed superior scripts, direction, and production values, and his good acting, warmth, and humor
added to the quality of these films. In the late 1930s O'Brien signed a
lucrative contract with RKO for up to $21,000 a picture, making him at
one point the highest-paid B Western star of the period. O'Brien continued making Westerns for RKO until he entered the armed services in
1941.[16]

Although the performances of these silent stars enabled them to
make the transition to the sound era, a new generation of cowboy stars
began to make its appearance in sound Westerns of the early 1930s.
The most important newcomer was John Wayne, who after several bit
parts in the late 1920s gained a starring role in *The Big Trail* (Fox,
1930). The big-budget Western flopped at the box office, but it established a western persona for Wayne that continued throughout his career. In 1931 and 1932 he appeared with Buck Jones and Tim McCoy
in three Columbia Westerns, and within a year he signed a contract
with Warner Brothers to star in a series of five remakes of Ken Maynard's silent First National features. Wayne became an established B
Western star with sixteen films for Monogram Pictures between 1933
and 1935. These Monogram Westerns enabled Wayne to perfect his
acting and develop a trademark style. Wayne also contributed to the
realism of screen fistfights when he, stunt man Yakima Canutt, and
director Robert North Bradbury developed the "pass system." This
method of filming involved the precise placement of cameras to make
near misses appear to be actual punches.[17]

John Wayne has been erroneously credited with being the first singing film cowboy because of his appearance as "Singing Sandy" in the
Monogram feature *Riders of Destiny* (1933). Actually his voice was
dubbed (the singer was probably Bob Steele's twin brother, William
Bradbury), as it was in a few other Monogram and Republic pictures.[18]
Wayne detested playing the role of a singing cowboy, especially when
he went on tour and his fans would ask him to sing.

About the time that John Wayne became an established Western star,
an important development occurred that significantly affected the
growth of the B Western. In 1935 Herbert J. Yates merged his film-
processing company, Consolidated Film Industries, with two small independent studios, Monogram Pictures and Mascot Pictures, to form Republic Pictures. Republic immediately became the number-one producer

of B Western films and serials, a position it maintained for the next two decades. Republic built its reputation on quality and put together a stable of Western stars who regularly ranked high in popularity and money-making. Two Republic stars, Gene Autry and Roy Rogers, dominated the top spot of the *Motion Picture Herald*'s list of top money-making Western stars every year except one between 1936 and 1954.[19]

The creativity of Yates and Republic's executives revealed itself in the mid-1930s when Republic took two initiatives—"musical Westerns" and "trio Westerns"—that became important trends in the evolution of the B Western.

Although Ken Maynard had already sung a few songs in his Westerns, it was Gene Autry who proved instrumental in the development and popularity of the musical Western. In the early 1930s Autry was a popular "hillbilly" recording artist who starred on *National Barn Dance*, a Chicago radio program. Autry's established reputation as a country singer prompted Nat Levine, owner of Mascot Pictures, to offer the singer a movie contract. In fact, Autry had already made his first singing appearance in one of Ken Maynard's Mascot pictures, *In Old Santa Fe* (1934); he also had a small part in a Maynard serial entitled *Mystery Mountain* (1934). Maynard's drinking and obstreperous behavior during the making of this serial so alienated him from Mascot's owner that at the conclusion of the filming the star quit the studio. Imperturbed, Levine starred Gene Autry in another serial, *Phantom Empire* (1935), originally scheduled for Maynard (fig. 5.2).[20]

When Autry's contract was transferred to Republic as part of the Mascot merger, the new studio's executives cast him in a series of musical Westerns that quickly established him as a major star. In little more than a year, Gene Autry topped the *Motion Picture Herald*'s poll of major money-making Western film stars, a position he maintained until 1942, when he entered the armed services during World War II.[21]

Autry's instant popularity and the success of Republic's musical Western prompted other studios quickly to produce films featuring singing cowboys. Within two months of Autry's first Republic release, Warner Brothers had singer Dick Foran on the screen singing western ballads.[22] Bob Baker, after beating out a young singer named Leonard Slye (Roy Rogers), warbled for Universal Studios in a series of Westerns. Monogram Studio tried to match Autry's success with Jack Randall, a handsome young actor and singer, but poor production values doomed the series to failure. Independent producers promoted former opera singer Fred Scott in a series of Westerns released through Spectrum Pictures.[23]

Figure 5.2. Gene Autry and his horse Champion. (Courtesy of Gary Yoggy.)

Although these cowboy singers tried to copy Autry, they were not his equal in either style or appeal. The one country singer who did offer the Republic star some competition was Tex Ritter. In 1936 Ritter came to Hollywood from New York, signing a contract with independent producer Edward Finney for twelve Westerns to be released through Grand National Pictures. A native Texan who possessed a deep interest in authentic cowboy songs, Ritter had gained radio and acting experience in New York. Although he was not the recording star that Autry was, he nevertheless had a large repertory of genuine western songs that he and his directors incorporated into the story lines of his films.[24]

Whereas Ritter offered Autry competition from a rival studio, Roy Rogers presented a challenge from within. Indeed, Herbert Yates used Rogers as a lever to control his top star. When Autry demanded more money for his performances, Yates simply brought in Leonard Slye, changed his name to Roy Rogers, and starred him in Westerns designated for Autry. Autry eventually got what he wanted, but in the meantime Rogers became a popular Western star in his own right. He played second fiddle to Autry at Republic until Autry left for the armed services in 1942; at that point the studio boosted the budgets of the Rogers films and began promoting him as "King of the Cowboys."[25]

At the same time that Republic was promoting singing cowboys, it also initiated a series of Westerns featuring three heroes—a "trigger trio" known as the Three Mesquiteers. Based on characters developed by Western novelist William Colt McDonald, the Mesquiteer series included fifty-two features produced over a seven-year period (1936–43). Twelve different actors formed nine different trios during the life of the series. The most popular and successful of these trios was the one comprising Robert Livingston, Ray Corrigan, and Max Terhune. They made fourteen features and developed a spirit and cohesion unmatched by other trios. The popularity of the Mesquiteers was instantaneous. The new, fresh idea of three heroes teaming up to bring law, order, and justice to the frontier possessed much appeal. The idea of three heroes cooperating seemed to fit the New Deal spirit of the 1930s, when the nation pulled together to overcome the depression. World War II intensified and emphasized this need for teamwork and may have helped to maintain the series' popularity. Strong casting also gave the series appeal. Box office returns put the Three Mesquiteers in the top money-maker category for Western stars for five straight years.[26]

The success of the trio format prompted other Hollywood studios to copy it. One of the most successful clones was Monogram's Range Busters (1940), which starred former Mesquiteers Ray Corrigan and Max Terhune, along with John King. Before the series ended Dave Sharpe and Dennis Moore replaced or substituted for Corrigan and King. By 1943, when the series concluded, Monogram had produced twenty-four Range Busters features. In 1941 Monogram started a second trio series, the Rough Riders, featuring former silent stars Buck Jones, Tim McCoy, and Raymond Hatton. Only eight features were made in this series, as a result of McCoy's entering the armed service and Jones's death in Boston's Coconut Grove nightclub fire. The successful use of established Western stars in the Rough Riders prompted Monogram to develop the Trail Blazers series, starring Ken Maynard, Hoot Gibson, and singing cowboy Bob Baker. Bob Steele soon replaced Baker in the series. Maynard quit shortly thereafter, complaining about low pay and dissatisfaction with Steele. The series then continued for a brief time with Chief Thundercloud as Maynard's replacement. The Producers Releasing Corporation (PRC) copied the other studios when it initiated the Texas Rangers series in 1942, starring Dave O'Brien, James Newill, and Guy Wilkerson. Tex Ritter eventually replaced Newill, and the series ended in 1945 with twenty-two features.[27]

Some film historians place another series in the trigger trio category—the Hopalong Cassidy series, which was released through Paramount Pictures. The film hero Cassidy, a character based on the Western novels of Clarence E. Mulford, usually had two sidekicks, one a young, hot-tempered, romantic cowboy and the other a crusty old codger. Despite the fact that the screenplays emphasized three lead personalities, the Hoppy character dominated the stories and action, thus putting the series in a slightly different class than the typical trios. Producer Harry Sherman, after buying screen rights to Mulford's Cassidy novels, brought the series to the screen in 1935. Sherman selected William Boyd, a matinee screen idol of the silent era, to play the title role. The series was an instant success as Boyd took the original grizzly Hopalong character and turned him into a gallant, genteel, and fatherly cowboy. Boyd may well have been the best actor of all the B Western screen stars. He also had the foresight to purchase the television rights to his sixty-six features made between 1935 and 1948, which when released for television in the 1950s made him a millionaire.[28]

Other B Western stars of the 1930s and 1940s were Tom Keene, Charles Starrett, Johnny Mack Brown, Wild Bill Elliott, Tim Holt, Buster Crabbe, Russell Hayden, Allan "Rocky" Lane, and Don "Red" Barry. In the late 1940s a new set of film heroes appeared, including Sunset Carson, Eddie Dean, Jimmy Wakely, Lash LaRue, Whip Wilson, Monte Hale, and Rex Allen. As was true of these actors' predecessors, this new generation included both action and singing cowboys. But, although they made solid and interesting Westerns, their careers, beginning in the closing days of the B Western era, never allowed them to reach the level of popularity attained by some of their predecessors.

The coming of television both helped and hurt the B Western. When television emerged as a major entertainment force in the late 1940s and 1950s, it recycled the B Westerns for home audiences. At the same time television enabled viewers to watch B-grade Westerns at home, killing the genre for theater distribution. Higher production costs, along with money being channeled to television Westerns, also contributed to the demise of film B Westerns. By the early 1950s Hollywood slowed its production of low-budget Westerns, and in 1954 Allied Artists produced the last of the genre, *Two Guns and a Badge*, starring Wayne Morris and Beverly Garland.

For a generation audiences cheered B Western heroes, developing strong loyalties to particular stars and their brand of Western, either action or musical. Regardless of preference, the Saturday-front-row kids left the movie houses to relive and reenact the story in their own backyards. Using cap pistols and stick horses, they played the roles of their favorite cowboy stars and filled their minds with myths, values, and images of nonaging cowboy heroes who could overcome any odds, solve any problem, and win any fight (fig. 5.3).

B Westerns were packed with values and fictional stories that reflected events, attitudes, and thinking in the 1930s and 1940s. The simplicity of the plots, with their emphasis on the certain triumph of good over evil, revealed an optimistic frame of mind that Americans generally exhibited about life. Of course, the Hays morality code that governed the content of Hollywood movies ensured that screen villains would always pay for their sins with either death or imprisonment.[29] Despite this industry requirement, these films presented a spirit of optimism and hope that was deeply ingrained in Americans, a spirit that appealed to audiences especially in the dreary days of the Great Depression and World War II. In that sense the B Westerns were fantasy and escapist entertainment. Perhaps one could not change his or her immediate economic or employment status or do much about the horrors of World War II, but in the darkness of the local theater, society's problems could be solved in about one hour.

The speed with which the B Western hero outsmarted and dispatched the villains also expressed the American appreciation for action. These fast-paced horse operas fit what most Americans conceived to be the proper method of problem solving: do something, and do it quickly. If one solution does not work, try something else, be pragmatic. Although specific problems may have changed as Americans moved from the rigors and dangers of early frontier life to the urbanized and industrialized world of the twentieth century, Americans retained their restlessness, nervous energy, and desire to solve problems quickly and pragmatically. They never hesitated to take action to change and perfect their new society in such reform efforts as the progressive movement and the New Deal. Nor did they hesitate to protect America from foreign enemies in two world wars. Despite all the changes of the twentieth century, or perhaps because of them, Americans maintained a strong nostalgia about their frontier past. These attitudes were tapped by scriptwriters of the 1930s and 1940s who incorporated the alleged frontier traits of action and pragmatism into B Western film plots.

Closely related to this American affinity for action is an admiration for individualism, and the B Western hero was the ideal expression of that quality. He was usually a strong, determined Anglo-Saxon who dominated the action in each film plot. He was quick on the draw, handy with his fists, respectful of women, and disdainful of liquor, and

Figure 5.3. These two young guns from Buffalo, New York, ca. 1952, were typical of many youngsters who emulated their favorite Western stars by playing cowboys and Indians. (Richard Aquila Collection.)

no problem was too big for him to solve in one hour. Although he often had a sidekick or, as in the trigger trios, two buddies, the hero usually acted alone, often against great odds. American film audiences liked this individualistic and independent hero and identified with him. Only two series of Westerns had non-Anglo-Saxons as heroes: the Cisco Kid series featured a Mexican hero, and the Herb Jeffries series featured a black hero. Since black and brown cowboys actually numbered in the thousands in the real American West, the fact that B Western cowboy heroes were almost always white Anglo-Saxon Protestants reflects the era's prevailing attitudes of white superiority.

B Western fans identified with the hero because they knew that he would succeed in making society safe, law abiding, and orderly. Law and order was a general theme that permeated every B Western plot. The villains, usually saloon owners, gamblers, businessmen, bankers, or ranchers, violated the laws of society and infringed on the rights of individuals and communities in their greedy pursuit of wealth and power. In order to obtain land, water, cattle, horses, or precious minerals, the villains often committed murder or other crimes. On occasion the villains controlled the sheriff and his deputies or the local judge. As a threat to law and order these worthless varmints had to be brought to justice, a feat always accomplished by the hero. It is interesting to note, however, that the hero, in his zeal and determination to ensure the triumph of right over wrong or to bring the villains to justice, sometimes winked at the law and occasionally violated it outright, with no explanation for his action. These transgressions on the part of the hero and some other respectable characters seem to have been accepted because they were done to right an obvious wrong or to trick a criminal. For instance, in *Wild Horse Rustlers* (PRC, 1943) hero Bob Livingston steals from a mortuary the body of a man killed by the villain. He takes the corpse to the villain's hideout at night, props it against a window, and pretends that the dead man is talking. The object is to make the villain think that the man is still alive so that he will shoot him again, thus exposing the outlaw for what he is. The villain does indeed shoot the corpse, confirming that he is the killer. Strangely enough, however, the hero does not act on the evidence. Instead, he drops the body and leaves it for the villain to return to the mortuary. Snatching a body from the mortuary and using it in this way does not fit the law-abiding image of the B Western hero, but in this particular film the illegal action is presented as a perfectly acceptable means to expose the real criminal.

In the *Sombrero Kid* (Republic, 1942) the hero (played by Don "Red" Barry) gets into a fistfight in a saloon with a villain who delib-

erately provoked the fight. The knock-down-and-drag-out brawl concludes with the villain dying after hitting his head on the bar's foot rail.
After Barry is arrested, tried, and found guilty of murder, the judge,
recognizing that Barry is the good guy, slips the hero a coat with a
concealed weapon. Barry discovers the gun in the pocket and uses it to
escape. He then joins the local gang of outlaws, engages in robberies,
and even destroys federal mail before getting the goods on the bad
guys. No stated rationale is ever made for the hero's illegal actions, but
in the overall context of the picture his actions seem justified.

In *Colorado Sundown* (Republic, 1952) the hero (played by Rex
Allen) tries to convince the sheriff to break into a villain's sawmill
office to look for some poison. When the lawman explains that their
actions would constitute "breaking and entering," Allen's character
responds by kicking in the door of the office, insisting that they had to
do it to prevent the villain from destroying the evidence.

Although most B Western heroes did not wink at or violate the law,
these and numerous other examples of "heroic" law violations can be
found in B Western movies. Their prevalence raises several questions.
Why were the illegal actions of the heroes accepted when the stories
themselves were depicted in such simple contrasts of right and wrong?
What do these films reflect about attitudes toward law, order, and justice in mid-twentieth-century America? These movies seem to suggest
that Americans believe that under the right conditions it is acceptable
to violate the law to achieve justice. The most important thing in B
Westerns was that good should conquer evil, even if liberties had to be
taken with the law. In taking such questionable action, the heroes
maintained their "good guy" status because they were operating not
for selfish or personal motives but rather for the good of society. In
that context the illegal actions of the hero were rationalized as benefi-
cial. For the B Western, the ends justified the means.

The emphasis on the hero in the B Western gave the stories a male
orientation. B Western heroines generally were passive and submissive,
and in many of the stories almost nonexistent. Some plots even possessed an antifeminist bent, keeping women subordinate to men. For
example, in Gene Autry's first feature film, *Tumbling Tumbleweeds* (Republic, 1935), the hero tells the heroine he does not know whether to
kiss or spank her. In *Arizona Terror* (Tiffany, 1931) the villain beats his
girlfriend (off camera) for flirting with hero Ken Maynard. This manly
orientation of the B Western fit the generally accepted pattern of male
domination in the 1930s and 1940s. Of course, there were exceptions. In
1939 singer and radio personality Dorothy Page assumed the hero's role,
carrying a six-gun without surrendering her traditional femininity in a

series of Westerns produced by Grand National Pictures.[30] During the 1940s a number of B Westerns featured smart, strong, and forceful feminine villains. Jenifer Holt's performance as a ruthless leader of an outlaw gang in *Hawk of Powder River* (PRC, 1948) exemplifies this alternative female role. June Vincent portrayed one of the most vicious and interesting villains found in any B Western; her character and attendant henchmen poisoned and shot both humans and animals in *Colorado Sundown* (Republic, 1952).

Perhaps the most significant variation of the heroine's persona came with the characters played by Dale Evans, Jane Frazee, and Penny Edwards in the Roy Rogers Westerns made during and after World War II (fig. 5.4). The war required women to alter traditional social roles as they assumed jobs vacated by the men in uniform. Evans, Frazee, and Edwards, while appropriately feminine in their roles, reflected the changing times. For example, in *Susanna Pass* (Republic, 1949) Dale Evans played the role of a scientist who holds a Ph.D. and is a former Marine. The three actresses appeared in a variety of other nontraditional roles: ranch owner, nightclub singer, newspaper reporter, tugboat captain, airline owner, rocket scientist, and deputy sheriff. Unlike traditional western heroines, who were passive and helpless, the characters played by Evans, Frazee, and Edwards were smart, independent, and outspoken. They always had a central role, often working in tandem with hero Roy Rogers to solve the community's problems. Although the screenwriters for these films did not completely abandon the conventional feminine qualities of the heroine, they scripted roles that fit the new expectations for women of the 1940s.

B Westerns also stereotyped African Americans, Hispanics, Indians, and Asians. African Americans usually had minor roles that portrayed them in the stereotypical fashion of most 1930s movies, speaking in dialect and being subservient to white people. Fred Toones, an accomplished black actor who appeared in numerous B Westerns in the 1930s and 1940s, usually played this subservient role, occasionally spicing it with humor. Blue Washington, the skilled actor who played John Wayne's sidekick in *Haunted Gold* (Warner Brothers, 1932), portrayed a superstitious and fearful Negro who would shudder and shake whenever he thought ghosts were around. Etta McDaniel played the stereotypical strong, sensible southern mammie in a later John Wayne film, *The Lonely Trail* (Republic, 1936). The only black actor to portray a B Western hero was Herb Jeffries, a pop vocalist and band singer who made four all-black-cast Westerns in the late 1930s.[31] These features, generally made for black audiences and scripted by black writers, were directed and produced by whites. The initial production,

Figure 5.4. Dale Evans with Roy Rogers and the Sons of the Pioneers. Pat Brady, second from left, later joined Roy and Dale on their weekly TV show. (Courtesy of the Ray White Collection.)

Harlem on the Prairie (Associated Features, 1937), played in first-run theaters, including the Rialto on Broadway in New York, and was reviewed in *Time* magazine. Black Westerns followed the conventional B Western pattern and plot and even used the same racial stereotypes. The limited and stereotypical roles of blacks in B Westerns contributed to the myth that African Americans played small roles in the history of the American West.

Hispanics had more prominent roles in B Westerns, playing a variety of parts including bandits, sidekicks, ranch owners, heroes, and heroines. Female roles varied from the upper-class woman of unquestioned purity to the lower-class, hot-blooded "Mexican" spitfire. Regardless of the role the Hispanic actor was usually stereotyped by his or her accent, clothes, or station in life. In the Ken Maynard feature *The Arizona Terror* (Tiffany, 1931) Michael Visaroff portrayed Vasquez, the quintessential Hollywood Mexican bandit, complete with a humorous but sinister personality. Nena Quartero appeared as his girlfriend, a seductive senorita who lusted for Maynard's character. Hispanics in B Westerns often appeared cruel, whether they were villains or heroes. For instance, in *Western Justice* (Supreme/William Steiner,

1935) Julian Rivero's character hangs and skins a despicable villain, while two other heroes, both Anglos, look on in silent horror. Occasionally Hispanic heroes provided more positive images. Duncan Renaldo played heroic roles in both the Three Mesquiteer and the Cisco Kid series; in these films he was smart, polished, and suave. Some Roy Rogers films of the 1940s also portrayed Hispanics in a positive light. The 1947 feature *The Gay Ranchero* (Republic) depicted Tito Guizar as Roy's trustworthy friend and the even-tempered sweetheart of fiery Estelita Rodriguez. Several B Westerns that starred Anglo cowboys Buck Jones and Tim McCoy as Hispanic heroes also advanced the film image of Hispanics.

Though less visible than Hispanics, American Indians usually were portrayed more favorably in B Westerns. Although stereotyping did occur and Indians were treated paternalistically in the films, Indians were often friends of the hero, who helped them deal with an antagonistic white society. This theme was evident in the Gene Autry feature *The Cowboy and the Indians* (Columbia, 1949), in which Autry and a female doctor foil the efforts of a crooked Indian agent who tries to take advantage of some reservation Indians. A more unusual plot occurs in *Texas Terror* (Republic, 1935), when hero John Wayne's character calls on his Indian friends to help round up the villains. One of the few B Westerns to portray Indians negatively was the Three Mesquiteers feature *Riders of the Whistling Skull* (Republic, 1937). While accompanying archaeologists searching for a lost Indian city, the Mesquiteers encounter a torture cult of savage and ruthless natives. These Indians display few redeeming qualities as they attempt to capture and murder the members of the expedition.

Like Indians, Asians played an important role in western American history, but one would never know it from B Western movies, where they appeared mostly as houseboys, cooks, and occasionally, sinister villains. In the Range Busters feature *Saddle Mountain Roundup* (Monogram, 1941) Willie Fung plays a Chinese ranch cook who dresses in Chinese clothing and speaks broken English; the Anglo characters in the film treat Fung paternalistically. Another film in the same series, *Texas to Bataan* (Monogram, 1942), features an Asian ranch cook who turns out to be a Japanese spy; he is depicted in more sinister terms than Fung, with stereotyping also evident. An interesting twist on Asian characters in B Westerns sometimes occurred when the hero disguised himself. For example, in *Six Gun Trail* (Victory, 1938) Tim McCoy played a "Charlie Chan" type character who solved a mystery. Although McCoy's Asian character was shrewd and intelligent, stereotyping was nevertheless evident. The B Westerns' treatment of racial minorities generally reflected American attitudes of the 1930s and 1940s that characterized those minorities as inferior to whites.

B Westerns not only expressed American values; they also reflected events of their period. Some made in the 1930s focused on the depression. *Wyoming Outlaw* (1939), a Three Mesquiteers film starring John Wayne, Ray Corrigan, and Raymond Hatton, mixed cowboy heroics with the hard times of the depression. The film—based on a true incident involving an outlaw in Wyoming—had Wayne and his two sidekicks befriending an unemployed dust bowl cowpoke who steals and kills one of their cows to feed his hungry family.[32] After learning that the poacher's father has lost his job as a road gang foreman because he had no money to pay off a corrupt political boss, Wayne goes to the state capitol to talk to the politicians about eliminating corruption. Although the Mesquiteers are not able to save the young cowboy from resuming his life of crime, their fists and guns do help the state government to put a stop to the corrupt local political boss. The film emphasizes that Americans were often unemployed due to circumstances beyond their control. Moreover, it makes a positive statement about government's ability to protect the interests of the people. *Wyoming Outlaw* and other similar B Westerns comforted millions of destitute Americans who looked to the government for help. At the same time economic or political themes never overshadowed the action and cowboy heroics that made B Westerns exciting, escapist entertainment for depression era audiences.

World War II was another subject for B Westerns. Like dozens of Hollywood films of the war era, B Westerns sometimes tried to contribute to the war effort. For example, in *The Night Riders* (Republic, 1939) the Three Mesquiteers had to deal with a dictatorial villain who was using his storm trooper private army to establish a land empire in California. The heroes compare the villain's land-grabbing activity to that of a dictator, a thinly veiled allusion to Hitler, Mussolini, and Tojo. The plot enables John Wayne to make perhaps his first patriotic comment on screen. When one of the Mesquiteers, played by Ray Corrigan, tells him, "Used to be a time when being an American meant something," John Wayne's character, Stony, replies, "Still does. [It] stands for freedom and fair play." The third Mesquiteer, played by Max Terhune, then points out, "This madman is grabbing off everything in sight. He's become a dictator." Stony concludes, "All the more reason why we've got to fight. Men who opened up this country didn't sit around crying for help. They did something."

Other B Westerns also focused on World War II subjects. In *Wild Horse Rustlers* (PRC, 1943), Bob Livingston and Al "Fuzzy" St. John encounter and bring to justice Nazi saboteurs trying to poison horses earmarked for the U.S. Cavalry. The fact that few horses were used during World War II did not stand in the way of the scriptwriter's attempt to produce a patriotic film backing the American war effort. As the heroes of *Wild Horse Rustlers* chased the foreign agents, they referred to other aspects of the home front—rationing, conservation, and hoarding sugar—that were important to Americans. The film director had the Nazi agents dressed in cowboy garb, giving raised arm salutes, shouting "Heil Hitler," and praising the Third Reich. As implausible as *Wild Horse Rustlers* now appears, it seemed natural and right in the 1940s, especially to juvenile audiences at Saturday matinees. In *From Texas to Bataan* (Monogram, 1943) the Range Busters trigger trio had to chase down a Japanese espionage ring and deliver a herd of horses to American troops in the Philippines. In *Raiders of Sunset Pass* (Republic, 1943) a wartime labor shortage on the western range prompted a local cowgirl to organize the Women's Army of the Plains (WAPS) to help fight local rustlers.[33]

After 1945 some B Westerns focused on spies, traitors, rockets, and atomic technology, reflecting Americans' preoccupation with the cold war. For example, in *Bells of Coronado* (Republic, 1950) Roy Rogers worked undercover with a federal agent to prevent outlaws from smuggling uranium out of the country. In *Spoilers of the Plains* (Republic, 1951) Rogers prevented a foreign agent from stealing the guidance mechanism of an American rocket, causing the hero to comment in McCarthyesque terms that one can never be sure about a person's loyalty, even a neighbor's. Although the number of B Westerns with cold war plots was small, the ones that were made reflected both attitudes and events of the period.

The B Western offers much to both the scholar and the film buff. As a successful popular culture form, it has entertained several generations of Americans. In the process B Westerns became important cultural artifacts, reflecting and sometimes shaping American attitudes, actions, and events. As historical documents B Westerns serve as a window to the nation's past, providing glimpses of fantasies and myths that contributed to the development of the national character. These nostalgic and mythic images included the Westerns' exotic locales, strong Anglo heroes, delicate heroines, and morality-play plots. Action, gunplay, and fistfights were depicted as everyday occurrences in the West. Packed with values, the films stereotyped males, females, and minorities, and they reflected both attitudes and events of the 1930s, 1940s, and 1950s. They simplified American life and provided escape and fantasy for

Americans in troubled times. Although B Westerns still provide entertainment and excitement for fans, they also constitute a valuable source
for scholars interested in recent American society and culture.

Notes

1. No scholarly history of the B Western exists, but the best and most in-
formative survey is Don Miller, *Hollywood Corral* (New York, 1976); for general information on the studios that produced B Westerns see Miller's *B Movies* (New York 1987 [1973]). Les Adams and Buck Rainey's *Shoot-Em-Ups:
The Complete Guide to Westerns of the Sound Era* (New Rochelle, N.Y., 1978)
and Rainey's sequel, *The Shoot-Em-Ups Ride Again* (Metuchen, N.J., 1990),
provide a survey history of the B Western plus the most complete listing of
Western films and credits available. Michael R. Pitts's *Western Movies: A TV
and Video Guide to 4200 Genre Films* (Jefferson, N.C., 1986) provides credits and a comment or opinion on each Western listed plus an extraordinary
index that gives recognition to the supporting actors of B Westerns in a way
that no other author or researcher has. Jon Tuska's *The Filming of the West*
(Garden City, N.Y., 1976) is an important and opinionated history of Western
film that has good chapters on the development of the B Western and its major stars. An excellent short history of the B Western is Gary Kramer, "The B
Western: A Brief History," published as an introduction to a syllabus for a
history course on the B Western taught at Ball State University, Muncie, Indiana. The most complete biographical dictionary of B Western actors is Ted
Holland, *B Western Actors Encyclopedia: Facts, Photos, and Filmographies for
more than 250 Familiar Faces* (Jefferson, N.C., 1989). David Rothel has produced several books important to the history of the B Western, including *An
Ambush of Ghosts, A Personal Guide to Favorite Western Film Locations*
(Madison, N.C., 1990); *The Singing Cowboys* (New York, 1978); and *Those
Great Cowboy Sidekicks* (Waynesville, N.C., 1984). Some initial ideas for this
essay on the significance of the B Western were originally published in Ray
White, "Cowboys in the Classroom: The B Western Movie as a Teaching Re-
source," *Indiana Media Journal* 5, no. 3 (Spring 1983): 16–26.

2. George N. Fenin and William K. Everson, *The Western from Silents to
the Seventies*, rev. ed. (New York, 1973), 46–56; Tuska, *Filming of the West*, 6;
Adams and Rainey, *Shoot-Em-Ups*, 21.

3. For a penetrating analysis of the mythic and nostalgic West see Gerald
D. Nash, *Creating the West: Historical Interpretations* (Albuquerque,
N.Mex., 1991), especially chap. 5, "The West as Utopia and Myth," 197–257.
Nash points out that Americans in the generation from 1890 to 1920 experienced a "profound sense of loss, a feeling of loss for the disappearance of
a world they had cherished" (198). Western films were an expression of that
nostalgia.

4. *The American Film Institute Catalog of Motion Pictures Produced in the United States, 1921–1930*, 2 vols. (New York, 1971).

5. Information on William S. Hart and Tom Mix is available in a variety of sources. For a brief and general analysis of their careers see Tuska, *Filming of the West*, 28–34, 51–59, 81–86, 115–22, 143–47, 150. For Hart's assessment of his own life and career see his autobiography, *My Life East and West* (Boston, 1929); an analysis of Hart's career that maintains that his films were extensions of himself and his family life is Diane Kaiser Korsarski, *The Complete Films of William S. Hart* (New York, 1980); an encyclopedic work on Tom Mix is M. G. Norris, *The Tom Mix Book* (Waynesville, N.C., 1989), which provides biographical information, photographs, and filmography; just as comprehensive is Richard F. Seiverling, *Tom Mix, Portrait of a Superstar: A Pictorial and Documentary Anthology* (Hershey, Pa., 1991). See also John H. Nicholas, *Tom Mix Riding up to Glory* (Oklahoma City, 1980); and Olive Stokes Mix, *The Fabulous Tom Mix* (Englewood Cliffs, N.J., 1957).

6. Fred Thompson died of tetanus at the peak of his career in 1928. An excellent biography of Thompson is Edgar M. Wyatt, *More Than a Cowboy: The Life and Times of Fred Thompson and Silver King* (Raleigh, N.C., 1988). A brief biography and filmography can be found in Buck Rainey, *Saddle Aces of the Cinema* (New York, 1980), 260–67.

7. Jon Tuska briefly reviews the silent film careers of these cowboy stars in *Filming of the West*, 105–11, 136–37; biographical information on some of these lower-echelon silent era cowboy stars can also be found in Kalton C. Lahue, *Winners of the West: The Sagebrush Heroes of the Silent Screen* (South Brunswick, N.J., 1970). Information on the credits and plots of most of the silent Westerns and their stars can be found in *The American Film Institute Catalog*.

8. Adams and Rainey, *Shoot-Em-Ups*, 43.

9. Tuska, *Filming of the West*, 100, 102, 174, 347–52.

10. Buck Rainey has written more on Buck Jones than any other film historian has. His *The Saga of Buck Jones* (Nashville, 1975) provides biographical information and an analysis of Jones's films. His recent *The Life and Films of Buck Jones: The Silent Era* (Waynesville, N.C., 1988) and *The Life and Films of Buck Jones: The Sound Era* (Waynesville, N.C., 1991) include annotated filmographies of Jones's silent and sound films.

11. Tim McCoy and Ronald McCoy, *Tim McCoy Remembers the West: An Autobiography* (Garden City, N.Y., 1977).

12. Little research has been done on Hoot Gibson's film career. The best analysis is Jon Tuska, *Filming of the West*, 71–77, 104–6, 109–11, 114–15, 171–86, 422–24. See also Buck Rainey, "Hoot Gibson, Cowboy 1882–1960," *Films in Review* 29 (October 1978): 471–83. For a brief biography and filmography see Bobby J. Copeland, "The Hooter," *Under Western Skies* 35 (1989): 4–23.

13. For the most detailed information on Ken Maynard, see Jon Tuska's three-part "In Retrospective: Ken Maynard": part 1, *Views & Reviews*, 1, no. 1 (Summer 1969): 6–13; part 2, *Views & Reviews*, 1, no. 2 (Fall 1969): 23–35; part 3, *Views & Reviews*, 1, no. 3 (Winter 1970): 22–43. These essays became

the basis for more than two chapters on Maynard in *Filming of the West,* 159–67, 262–78, 291–300, 397–99, 422–24, 472–74. Tuska also deals with Maynard in *The Vanishing Legion: History of Mascot Pictures, 1927–1935* (Jefferson, N.C., 1982). A brief analysis of Maynard's career is Raymond E. White, "Ken Maynard: Daredevil on Horseback," in *Shooting Stars: Heroes and Heroines of Western Film,* ed. Archie P. McDonald, 20–41 (Bloomington, Ind., 1987).

14. For both biographical information and a filmography see "Tom Tyler," *Wild West Stars* 18 (circa December 1973): 2–26; Miller, *Hollywood Corral,* 48–51.

15. Miller, *Hollywood Corral,* 43–48; Stormy Weathers, "The Kid," *Under Western Skies* 28 (August 1984): 5–21, provides a review of Steele's career; Buck Rainey, "Bob Steele: The Whirlwind Kid," *Heroes of the Range: Yester-year's Saturday Matinee Movie Cowboys,* 41–70 (Waynesville, N.C., 1987), includes a brief biography and complete filmography. Bob Nareau's *The "Real" Bob Steele and a Man Called Brad,* ed. Ed. Berger (Mesa, Ariz., 1991), provides biographical detail on his career and family, especially on his father, B Western director Robert North Bradbury.

16. Tuska, *Filming of the West,* 347–57; Adams and Rainey, *Shoot-Em-Ups,* 179; Buck Rainey, *Heroes of the Range,* 25–40; *1958 International Motion Picture Almanac* (New York, 1957), 657.

17. Much has been written about John Wayne, with most of it focusing on his career after 1940. Information on his B Western years can be found in a variety of sources. Maurice Zolotow's sympathetic biography *Shooting Star: A Biography of John Wayne* (New York, 1974) has much interesting and personal information. Miller, *Hollywood Corral,* 63–71, provides an excellent short analysis of Wayne's early Western film career. Richard E. McGhee, *John Wayne Actor, Artist, Hero* (Jefferson, N.C., 1990), does something that few if any authors have done: analyze Wayne's 1930s B Westerns as a reflection of American society during the depression; see 3–13, 57–73. See also Emanuel Levy, *John Wayne: Prophet of the American Way of Life* (Metuchen, N.J., 1988). A survey and filmography of John Wayne's Monogram Lone Star Westerns is John A. Rutherford, "Lone Star Cowboy," *Under Western Skies* 40 (1991): 4–18. For an account of Yakima Canutt's stunt work with John Wayne see Yakima Canutt with Oliver Drake, *Stunt Man: The Autobiography of Yakima Canutt* (New York, 1979), 88–93.

18. Paul Malvern, the producer of John Wayne's Lone Star Monogram series, says that Bob Steele's twin brother, William Bradbury, dubbed Wayne's voice in *Riders of Destiny* (telephone interview with Paul Malvern, October 1985).

19. The only history of Republic Studios is Richard Maurice Hurst, *Republic Studios: Between Poverty Row and the Majors* (Metuchen, N.J., 1979); *1958 Motion Picture Almanac,* 657.

20. The best assessment of Autry's influence as a singing movie cowboy is Douglas B. Green, "The Singing Cowboy: An American Dream," *Journal of Country Music* 7 (May 1978): 4–62. Green theorizes on the positive impact that Autry's Western movie musicals had on the popularity of country and

western music in *Stars of Country Music,* ed. Bill C. Malone and Judith Mc-Culloh (Urbana, Ill., 1975), 155–71. Autry's autobiography with Mickey Herskowitz, *Back in the Saddle Again* (Garden City, N.Y., 1978), provides a personal view of the star's career.

21. Hurst, *Republic Studios,* 35–146; *1958 Motion Picture Almanac,* 657.

22. Adams and Rainey, *Shoot-Em-Ups,* 125–26; Autry's *Tumbling Tumbleweeds* was released September 5, 1935, and Foran's *Moonlight on the Prairie* came out on November 1, 1935.

23. Miller, *Hollywood Corral,* 127–36.

24. The best biography of Tex Ritter is Johnny Bond, *The Tex Ritter Story* (New York, 1976). See also Miller, *Hollywood Corral,* 131–33; and Tuska, *Filming of the West,* 427–28.

25. For Rogers's own account of his professional career, see Roy Rogers and Dale Evans with Jane Stern and Michael Stern, *Happy Trails: Our Life Story* (New York, 1994); Rogers and Evans also produced, with Carlton Stowers, *Happy Trails* (Waco, Tex., 1979). See also Tuska, *Filming of the West,* 461–68; and Miller, *Hollywood Corral,* 111–24. The most detailed and encyclopedic work on Roy Rogers is Robert W. Phillip's *Roy Rogers* (Jefferson, N.C., 1995)

26. *1958 Motion Picture Almanac,* 657.

27. Little work has been done on the "trigger trios," but Don Miller in *Hollywood Corral* provides information on them; see 157–65, 210, 217–22. Even better is Stormy Weathers's article "Western Trios," *Under Western Skies* 24 (July 1983): 35–51, which suggests some series that are not ordinarily included with the obvious trigger trios. For individual listing and credits of the trios see Adams and Rainey, *Shoot-Em-Ups,* chaps. 3–5.

28. The most important work on the Hopalong Cassidy series is that of Francis M. Nevins, *The Films of Hopalong Cassidy* (Waynesville, N.C., 1988); Nevins offers an analysis and comparison of the Clarence Mulford novels and films in *Hopalong vs. Hoppy,* special issue, *The Films of Yesteryear* 6 (1981).

29. The morality code for Hollywood motion pictures was established in 1934 and brought the films under the close scrutiny of the Motion Picture Producers and Distributors of America directed by Will Hays. For firsthand information on the establishment of this code see Will H. Hays, *The Memoirs of Will Hays* (New York, 1955), 448–51. A reprint and analysis of the code can be found in Gerald Mast, *The Movies in Our Midst: Documents in the Cultural History of Film in America* (Chicago, 1982), 321–33.

30. *Ride 'Em Cowgirl* (Grand National, 1939) is probably the best of the three Westerns Dorothy Page made; the two others are *Water Rustlers* (Grand National, 1939) and *The Singing Cowgirl* (Grand National, 1939).

31. Jeffries's films included *Harlem on the Prairie* (Associated Features, 1937), *Two Gun Man from Harlem* (Hollywood Productions, 1938), *Harlem Rides the Range* (Hollywood Pictures, 1939), and *The Bronze Buckaroo* (Sack Amusement Co., 1939). The first of these films was reviewed in *Time,* December 13, 1937, 24, an unusual occurrence for a low-budget Western, maybe the only B Western ever reviewed by the magazine. Biographical information on

Jeffries can be found in Lawrence Toppman, "He Brought Black Cowboy to All-White Westerns," *Charlotte [N.C.] News,* July 15, 1982; see also "The Dark Horse Operas: A Film Article," *Negro History Bulletin* 36 (January 1973): 13–14; Roger D. Kinkle, *The Complete Encyclopedia of Popular Music and Jazz, 1900–1950,* 4 vols. (New Rochelle, N.Y., 1974), 2:1170.

32. An account of the real Wyoming outlaw can be found in George Morrill, "The West's Most Incredible Outlaw," *American History Illustrated,* December 1983, 40–45.

33. Raymond E. White, "Hollywood Cowboys Go to War: The B Western Movie during World War II," *Under Western Skies* 25 (September 1983): 23–66.

SIX

GARY A. YOGGY

Prime-Time Bonanza!
The Western on Television

TWO OF THE FIRST heroes ever to appear on the television screen were Hopalong Cassidy and the Lone Ranger. In the years that followed Hoppy's debut in 1948, well over 150 "oaters" rode into countless millions of American living rooms. No television program genre, not even the situation comedy, ever became so dominant at any given moment in time as the Western during the late 1950s and early 1960s. And no format produced more movie stars, from Clint Eastwood (*Rawhide*), Steve McQueen (*Wanted Dead or Alive*), and James Garner (*Maverick*) to Burt Reynolds (*Gunsmoke*) and Roger Moore (*Maverick*).

Eighteen new Westerns appeared on the home tube in 1958, when twelve of the top twenty-five Nielsen-rated shows were Westerns, including a phenomenal seven of the top ten.[1] The following season Westerns reached their peak with forty-seven broadcast nationally each week during prime time.[2] There were so many popular and well-made Westerns that in 1959 the industry gave the genre its own Emmy, placing it on an equal footing with comedies and dramas (ABC's *Maverick* won).[3] The history of TV Westerns parallels American history in the post–World War II era. TV Westerns reflected and affected the nation's cold war mentality, as well as other important historical and cultural trends.

Early television Westerns were usually made with a juvenile audience in mind. Postwar baby boomers were taught lessons in patriotism, tolerance, fairness, and other traditional values designed to protect them from communism and juvenile delinquency in an era of rapid change. The plots were simple and to the point. Good always triumphed over evil, crime did not pay, and the hero was invariably brave, just, kind, smart, and tough. Television shows modeled after the old B Western movies that were such an integral part of those Saturday matinees of the 1940s became a television sensation in the 1950s. Gene Autry and Roy Rogers joined Hoppy and the Ranger as "good guys" who never shot first and rarely killed the "bad guys." They simply incapacitated them by expertly shooting their pistols out of their hands before turning them over to the law for punishment.

The first *Hopalong Cassidy* TV shows were simply condensed versions of the earlier feature-length films based on the character of Cassidy. The response was so great that William Boyd, the actor who played Cassidy in the films, made a new series of shows especially for the new medium.

Within two years of his debut on television Hoppy was a national hero. In 1950 he was President Truman's guest of honor for "I Am an American Day." He drew the largest circus crowd in history at the Chicago stadium and headlined Macy's Thanksgiving Day parade. Boyd became a millionaire through the sale of school lunchboxes, gun and holster sets, cowboy outfits, and dozens of other items emblazoned with the Hoppy logo. To further promote the Cassidy image, Boyd founded a club called "Hoppy's Troopers," which briefly rivaled the Boy Scouts in memberships. Its code of conduct emphasized loyalty, honesty, ambition, kindness, and other virtues (fig. 6.1).[4]

The Lone Ranger joined Hoppy on the home screen in 1949. Originally developed in 1933 by George W. Trendle and Fran Striker as a program for Trendle's Detroit radio station, WXYZ, *The Lone Ranger* was later broadcast nationally over the Mutual Radio Network. By 1939 over 20 million people were listening to the three-times-a-week show. It became so popular that it spawned movie serials, feature films, comic strips, books, and eventually the TV show.

The Lone Ranger was ABC's first big hit. Clayton Moore played the masked man in 195 of the 221 episodes filmed between 1949 and 1957 (John Hart filled in for 26 episodes in 1952). Jay Silverheels appeared as the Ranger's faithful Indian companion, Tonto, in all the programs. Children liked the show because there was plenty of action, while parents approved of the Ranger's high moral code (he never smoked, swore, or drank alcohol; he used precise speech, without slang; and he never shot to kill, in accordance with a strict writer's guide established by Trendle).[5]

Figure 6.1. William Boyd starred as Hopalong Cassidy in one of TV's earliest and most successful Westerns aimed at youngsters. (Courtesy of the Ray White Collection.)

Both Gene Autry and Roy Rogers were established radio and film stars when they made their first appearances on the new medium. A year after *The Gene Autry Show*'s debut (July 23, 1950) Autry launched his own Hollywood production company, Flying A Productions. In addition to being responsible for Autry's show, the company produced *The Range Rider*, which starred former stunt man Jock Mahoney; *Buffalo Bill, Jr.*, featuring Dick Jones; *Annie Oakley*, with TV's first western heroine, played by Gail Davis; and *The Adventures of Champion*, which displayed the talents of Autry's "wonder horse."

The season after Autry took the plunge into television, Roy Rogers, "The King of the Cowboys," did the same, bringing along his wife, Dale Evans, his horse, Trigger ("the smartest horse in the movies"), and his German shepherd, Bullet. Pat Brady was Roy's humorous sidekick, who usually drove around in Nellybelle, his cantankerous jeep. Within a few years of Rogers's TV debut, merchandise bearing his name or likeness was earning manufacturers millions of dollars.

Other successful juvenile shows included *The Cisco Kid* (one of the first syndicated shows to be filmed in color), featuring Duncan Renaldo as O'Henry's "Robin Hood of the Old West" with Leo Carrillo as Pancho, his faithful comedy sidekick; *Sky King,* which centered on a sophisticated contemporary western hero (portrayed by Kirby Grant) who used a twin-engine Cessna called the Songbird in lieu of a horse to hunt down evildoers; *Wild Bill Hickok,* about a U.S. marshal who brought law and order to the Old West with his sidekick Jingles (played, respectively, by Guy Madison and Andy Devine, who had created the characters on radio); and *The Adventures of Kit Carson,* purporting to depict the escapades of the legendary frontiersman and Indian scout on the western frontier of the 1880s (with Bill Williams in the title role).

Two additional Westerns for children featured animal heroes: *Rin Tin Tin*, set in the Old West, starred a German shepherd who, along with his youthful companion Rusty (Lee Aaker), assisted the 101st Cavalry of Fort Apache in its never-ending struggle against rampaging Indians; and *Fury,* the award-winning series that related the adventures of a tough orphan (Bobby Diamond), his guardian (Peter Graves), and a magnificent black mustang. Each episode dramatized a simple lesson about civil defense, bicycle safety, wildlife preservation, freedom of the press, family responsibilities, or fire prevention.[6]

Throughout the 1950s Westerns became the most popular genre of juvenile television programs, especially among boys.[7] This popularity can be attributed to a close adherence to the formula that had been established during years of B Westerns and several dozen kid-oriented shows from the golden age of radio. The formula included the brave, infallible hero to uphold the mythical "code of the West," the comic sidekick to break the "monotony" of nonstop action with a few laughs, children in supporting roles to give young viewers a sense of involvement in the stories, and a noble and trusted steed to carry the hero out of harm's way.[8]

Women rarely appeared as continuing characters in juvenile Westerns (notable exceptions were the title character of *Annie Oakley* and Dale Evans in *The Roy Rogers Show*) When female characters did appear, they were usually in trouble and needed assistance from the hero. They were in stories to be rescued, but rarely kissed. The women in TV Westerns—like their counterparts in real life—were dependent on males for leadership and protection. As women in postwar America were assigned exclusive roles as wives, mothers, and homemakers, TV Westerns reinforced those soon-to-be outdated stereotypes.

The hero's code was the key to understanding children's Westerns. The code was spelled out in Gene Autry's "Cowboy Commandments." According to Autry, Herb Yates at Republic Studios had designed the "Ten Commandments of the Cowboy" to communicate Autry's positive image to young viewers. The code listed the attributes of the perfect cowboy: "1) He must not take unfair advantage of an enemy; 2) He must never go back on his word; 3) He must always tell the truth; 4) He must be gentle with children, elderly people, and animals; 5) He must not possess racially or religiously intolerant ideas; 6) He must help people in distress; 7) He must be a good worker; 8) He must respect women, parents, and his nation's laws; 9) He must neither drink nor smoke; and 10) He must be a patriot." Author Ralph Brauer maintains that the cowboy hero exemplified "values which Americans believe are typically theirs and theirs alone. The hero was clean living and clean thinking—clean in thought, word and deed . . . and each week the essential goodness (of the hero) was demonstrated by the downfall of the villain, who was, in every way, the antithesis of the hero."[9]

The western hero as portrayed in these children's Westerns in many ways resembled a medieval knight. He was a champion of the oppressed, the weak, the less fortunate, and those in need of help, such as widows, orphans, and the elderly. He brought law, order, and justice to the frontier. He was a model of honesty, integrity, fairness, courage, hard work, mental alertness, mercy, tolerance, and patriotism, and he attempted to instill these qualities in his young viewers.[10]

Walt Disney's entrance into the genre in the mid-1950s changed the course of the television Western. His version of the life of Davy

Crockett premiered on three hour-long episodes of the popular *Disneyland* program: "Davy Crockett, Indian Fighter" (Dec. 15, 1954), "Davy Crockett Goes to Congress" (Jan. 26, 1955), and "Davy Crockett at the Alamo" (Feb. 23, 1955). The series was a ratings blockbuster and led to an unprecedented commercial craze for a myriad of items produced in Crockett's name or image. The fad abated only when, according to sociologist Paul Lazarsfeld, "almost every child had his cap, rifle, powderhorn, book and record."[11] Disney's phenomenal success, along with the earlier merchandising successes of Hopalong Cassidy, Gene Autry, and Roy Rogers, made advertisers aware of the financial rewards awaiting those who successfully tapped into the baby boomer market.

At the insistence of ABC, Disney continued to feature western heroes on his *Disneyland* series, including Andy Burnett, Texas John Slaughter, Elfego Baca, Zorro, and Daniel Boone, as well as airing further exploits of Davy Crockett. Although they were all well received by viewers, none precipitated the public reaction that the first Crockett series had launched.

Television historian J. Fred MacDonald calls the Davy Crockett programs "transitional" in the history of the television Western, pointing out that although they were designed for children, they depicted adult values and relatively mature emotions.[12] Crockett's world included characteristically juvenile elements, such as a trusty sidekick (Georgie Russell), a rifle named "Old Betsy," and a set of moral values that dealt only in "black-and-white" issues. On the other hand, Davy possessed several "grown-up" qualities. The death of his wife produced grief and gave Crockett an air of vulnerability. Furthermore, Davy was both a patriot and a political philosopher. Finally, no television Western to date had depicted death and violence to such an extent, nor had the hero of any previous juvenile Western been allowed to die.

Whereas Disney's Westerns were aimed primarily at children, other programs were being developed that were designed for the prime-time adult viewer. With the coming of *The Life and Legend of Wyatt Earp* and *Gunsmoke* in the fall of 1955, the Western craze began. Many factors added momentum to this trend. President Eisenhower's fondness for Western novels stimulated interest in the historic West. Westerns offered an escape from the confusing, complex problems of the present to a simpler time when the good guys always won and the bad guys always lost. Cold war America was searching for heroes.

Westerns reflected the average American's conception of the East-West struggle. Westerns "were social allegories in which honest, hard-working American folk were threatened, without good reason, by evil forces," writes J. Fred MacDonald. "The honest folk never asked for trouble, never did anything to precipitate it. But it was now upon them, and it called for heroic intervention by a brave soul."[13]

David Shea Teeple, writing in *The American Mercury* in 1958, argued that American diplomats could benefit greatly from viewing TV Westerns. According to Teeple, the popularity of these programs proved that "the American public . . . wants to abandon the grey philosophies of fuzzy minds and return to the days when things were either black or white—right or wrong." To prove his point Teeple summoned an array of TV's western heroes:

> Would a Wyatt Earp stop at the 38th Parallel, Korea, when the rustlers were escaping with his herd? Ridiculous! Would a Marshal Dillon refuse to allow his deputies to use shotguns for their own defense because of the terrible nature of the weapon itself? Ha! Would the Lone Ranger *under any circumstance* allow himself to be bullied and threatened by those who sought to destroy the principles by which he lives? Would Jim Hardy of *Wells Fargo* attempt to *buy* friends who would fight for the right? Can you imagine Paladin of *Have Gun Will Travel* standing aside, while women and children were being massacred? Can you imagine Cheyenne living in a perpetual state of jitters because he feared the next move of some gunslinger? Would Judge Roy Bean release a murderer on some technicality devised by a slick lawyer? Would Wild Bill Hickok sell guns to the bad men?[14]

By the mid-1950s the assumption that Westerns were "just for kids" began to change as theatrical films such as *High Noon* (1952) and *Shane* (1953) placed more serious plots in Western settings. These films, which were both critical and commercial successes, became known as "adult Westerns." In its waning years radio drama also had experimented with Western stories aimed at a mature audience, and although all the shows but *Gunsmoke* were short-lived, most critics agreed that several were among the best dramatic programs ever broadcast.

It is difficult to define the adult Western as a genre. Ralph Brauer concludes that the networks' idea of "adultness" simply meant that the shows must have more violence.[15] Whereas Roy Rogers merely shot the gun out of the villain's hand, the adult Western hero would usually kill him or at least beat him senseless. According to J. Fred MacDonald, the components of the adult Western included a certain type of sponsor ("expensive, obviously adult products" like automobiles, beer, cigarettes, and soap products), "characters that broke old stereotypes" (if they made mistakes, "they were compelled to suffer the consequences"), "attractive young men in starring roles" (e.g., James Garner, James Arness, Hugh O'Brien, Steve McQueen, and Clint Walker), and trained and talented personnel behind the scenes (e.g., Charles Marquis Warren, Sam Fuller, Budd Boetticher, and Toy Garnett); in total, the genre blended "dramatic conflict, human insight, outdoor beauty, and subtle moralizing" without eliminating action.[16]

The genre was defined during the "golden age of television Westerns" by *Time* magazine:

> The new horse operas are generically known as adult Westerns, a term first used to describe the shambling, down-to-biscuits-realism of *Gunsmoke*, but there are numerous subspecies. First came the psychological Western, which populated the arroyos with schizophrenic half-breeds, paranoid bluecoats, and amnesic prospectors. Then there was the Civil Rights Western and all the persecuted Paiutes, molested Mexicans, downtrodden Jewish drummers and tormented Chinese laundrymen had their day. Scriptwriters are now riding farther from the train, rustling plots from De Maupassant, Stevenson, even Aristophanes, introducing foreigners and dabbling in rape, incest, miscegenation, and cannibalism.[17]

Obviously the characters in the adult Western had more substance than the stereotypical B Western variety. Here one found a hero who was more human and consequently more believable than the one-dimensional stars of the kiddie Westerns—a complex mixture of good and evil, strength and weakness. The hero of the adult Western could have doubts, make mistakes, and have misgivings about what he had to do.[18]

The villains in adult Westerns also were a different breed. Not a totally evil and cowardly character motivated solely by greed or a lust for power, as was so often the case in juvenile Westerns, the villain could be the victim of circumstances beyond his or her control. Psychological problems and social conditions frequently motivated evildoers in adult Westerns, at least in part.

In addition, it was not unusual to find the controversial themes that had been so scrupulously avoided in juvenile Westerns. Excessive violence and stories dealing with sex, religion, and racial discrimination—especially toward Native Americans—appeared in most successful adult Westerns. There was also a much greater attempt at historical accuracy in these programs, although literary license was employed liberally when producers did not find truth to be more exciting than fiction.

Most television historians cite 1955 as the year when the adult Western made its initial appearance on the home screen. *Death Valley Days,* however, which had thrived on radio for some fifteen years (1930–45), preceded the landmark *Gunsmoke* and *Wyatt Earp* by over three years. The series presented an anthology of stories based in fact and focused on the legends and lore of California's Death Valley, an area that over the years had attracted numerous pioneers, prospectors, and bandits.

In terms of stories *Death Valley Days* was clearly the first adult Western. Most of the stories were of the human-interest variety, with the emphasis on gentle comedy and drama rather than violence and action. Hundreds of actors appeared in the series, most of them not big names. Although some of them went on to greater fame and fortune (e.g., Vic Morrow, Doug McClure, Robert Blake, Clint Eastwood, Deforrest Kelley, Gavin MacLeod, Carroll O'Connor, and Dabney Coleman), the emphasis in *Death Valley Days* was clearly on the plots. The only regular was the host and narrator (Stanley Andrews was "The Old Ranger" for the first thirteen seasons, followed by Ronald Reagan, Robert Taylor, Dale Robertson, and Merle Haggard in short stints). Nearly 600 episodes were filmed, most of them on location in Death Valley.

In September 1955 the networks launched four prime-time adult Westerns to join the syndicated *Death Valley Days*: *Gunsmoke* on CBS; *Cheyenne* and *The Life and Legend of Wyatt Earp* on ABC; and *Frontier* on NBC. Only the last failed to achieve long-term ratings success.

Premiering four days ahead of *Gunsmoke, Wyatt Earp* at first glance appeared to be cast in the mold of most juvenile Westerns. Hugh O'Brien looked nothing like the legendary hero, and critics claimed that the show whitewashed Earp. Still, it presented the man's life much more accurately than, say, the earlier *Wild Bill Hickok* series did for its eponymous hero, for other than using Hickok's name, the show had nothing to do with either the life or personality of that historic figure.

Most of the *Wyatt Earp* episodes were based on historical events in the life of the West's most famous lawman. The conflict between a previously lawless town and an effective, dedicated lawman provided a strong basis for the weekly stories, and according to television critics Harry Castleman and Walter J. Podrazik, "the program was well executed and avoided obvious Western film cliches even within the obligatory fights, chases and shootouts."[19]

Every effort was made to create sets and costumes that were accurate, even to the make of Earp's gun, the Buntline Special. The scripts followed Earp from his arrival in Ellsworth City, Kansas, through his career in Dodge City and Tombstone, Arizona, concluding with a five-part dramatization of the famous gunfight at the O.K. Corral. The show propelled O'Brien from obscurity to overnight fame. Taking the role seriously, he did extensive research into Earp's character and developed a genuine empathy for him.

The pattern established on the *Wyatt Earp* show was later followed (albeit with varying degrees of success) by Gene Barry in *Bat Masterson*, Scott Forbes in *Jim Bowie*, Barry Sullivan as Pat Garrett in *The Tall Man*, Jock Mahoney in *Yancy Derringer*, Fess Parker in *Daniel Boone*, and Jeffrey Hunter in *Temple Houston.*

Immediately preceding *Wyatt Earp* on ABC's Tuesday evening schedule was *Warner Brothers Presents*, a dramatic trilogy that included *Casablanca* (a program about international intrigue loosely based on the Bogart film); *King's Row* (a medical series based on a popular film); and *Cheyenne,* a Western starring an unknown actor named Clint Walker, based on a little-known B movie.

All three shows were lavishly produced by Warner Brothers, but the main reason that *Cheyenne* succeeded while the others failed was Walker. Over six feet, five inches tall, he had broad shoulders and a magnificent physique. Furthermore, unlike most other adult Westerns, the series stressed plot and action rather than dialogue and character development. Each episode depicted the exploits of frontier scout Cheyenne Bodie, a white man raised by Indians and learned in the ways of both the whites and the Cheyennes. Drifting from job to job, he encountered beautiful women, bad guys, and gunslingers. One week he might be a ranch foreman, another an army scout, and yet another a lawman.[20]

Writer Douglas Brode sees *Cheyenne* as "a composite of the American westerner in all his possible roles" and as such serving "as the prototype for TV's roving adult Western hero—a wanderer without ties or attachments or even a single constant companion."[21] Other less successful variations on this theme included *Bronco* (Ty Hardin), *The Rebel* (Nick Adams), *The Restless Gun* (John Payne), *The Texan* (Rory Calhoun), *The Westerner* (Brian Keith), *The Loner* (Lloyd Bridges), *A Man Called Shenandoah* (Robert Horton), *Hondo* (Ralph Taeger), *Destry* (John Gavin), and *Shane* (David Carradine).

The most successful adult Western in history, *Gunsmoke,* was introduced to the television audience by John Wayne on September 10, 1955. Many viewers were already familiar with the show because it had been created for CBS radio by producer Norman MacDonnell and writer John Meston in the spring of 1952. The creators' original intent had been to transfer the radio cast (including William Conrad as the resolute and determined marshal, Matt Dillon) to television, but the

TV series director, Charles Marquis Warren, felt that the stocky Conrad did not project the proper physical presence for the visual medium.

John Wayne, after turning down the role himself, had recommended James Arness, a young, relatively unknown actor friend. Although Arness had limited film experience, his imposing stature made him ideal for the job. At six feet, seven inches, he was even bigger than Wayne and proved to be perfect as the heroic marshal.

In *Gunsmoke* viewers found something unique: a western hero who was not invincible and a western story that was not predictable. Dillon got his man not because he was always faster or stronger or even braver but because he was smarter. People were intrigued. Dillon was clearly a hero, but he did not perform heroic acts in the conventional way. He seemed genuinely disturbed when he had to kill a man. In the words of a British journalist, "he appeared more trigger sorry than trigger happy."[22]

Each week more people tuned in to see this Western that broke all the traditional rules of the genre. There were few chases and even fewer barroom brawls. The hero did not go around warbling songs to beautiful damsels in distress. He did not even ride a white steed that could fly like the wind and rescue his master when evildoers had gotten the best of him.

Gunsmoke also took the western heroine down from her pedestal and brought her into the real world in the person of saloon "hostess" Kitty Russell (played to perfection by Amanda Blake), who could be both tough and tender with equal conviction. There was even a hint of a more serious off-screen relationship between Matt and Kitty.

Dillon differed in other ways from television's more conventional western heroes. He drank occasionally in the Long Branch saloon, though never to excess. Most unorthodox of all, Dillon frequently violated the unwritten "code of the West" that had governed the actions of virtually all previous cowboy heroes: he did not always let his adversaries draw first. Sometimes he shot them from ambush or even in the back if it was necessary.

Still, Dillon was not a violent man by nature, and he sometimes wondered whether he was the right man to fill a marshal's job. Most other lawmen took a simple view of their work. They represented "good," whereas all lawbreakers represented "bad." For them there was nothing in-between. To Matt Dillon, however, there was an in-between, and it was a sizable one. Just a few men were totally bad, and not many were wholly good. Bad men occasionally got off to bad starts, but most were not basically vicious. Good men were reasonably honest and kept their word most of the time. If they made a mistake once in a while, they should be forgiven. Thus was the moral side of Matt Dillon's world filled not with black and white but with various shades of gray. In sum, he was more thoughtful and introspective than most western men of action.

The series passed through three different stages all built on the simple premise of a U.S. marshal trying to maintain law and order in Dodge City, Kansas, during the 1870s. The first six years of thirty-minute programs were based primarily on the radio scripts of John Meston. These were followed by the early hour-long episodes, which permitted considerably more character development. Finally the anthology format was adopted, which focused more on the roles played by weekly guest stars (fig. 6.2).

By modifying its emphasis *Gunsmoke* survived longer than any other dramatic series on television. Former *Gunsmoke* production assistant Kristine Fredricksson points out that watching the 640 episodes of the series, a total of 521.5 hours of film, "would take twenty-three days of around-the-clock viewing or translated to prime-time programming, five years of daily three-hour sessions."[23]

As a Saturday-night television institution, *Gunsmoke* ranked in Nielsen's top twenty shows from 1956 until 1965, reaching number one from 1957 through 1961. After moving to Monday evenings in 1967, the series returned to the top twenty and remained there until its final season on the air (1974–75).

Gunsmoke ranks as the number-one dramatic television series of all time by a wide margin. Douglas Brode calls the show "a true archetype of Western drama for television" and claims that "the appeal of an archetype is as immediate and lasting on TV as in any other medium of communication." Over its twenty-year run *Gunsmoke* reflected changing values and issues of national concern such as gender roles and violence in the media. For example, the evolution of Miss Kitty's character paralleled gains made by women in the postwar decades. She evolved from one of the prostitutes employed by the Long Branch saloon during the program's early years to a self-assured entrepreneur running her own saloon during the show's later seasons. (Amanda Blake actually left the show one year before it was canceled.) When the surgeon general came out with a statement that "there was a causal relationship between television violence and antisocial behavior," CBS quickly developed new guidelines for *Gunsmoke*: "Teaser openings were to be banned and victims of violence were not to be shown at the time of impact. Weaponry was to be kept to a minimum and trailers promoting upcoming episodes would have to keep violence in the proper context."[24]

Figure 6.2. The original cast of *Gunsmoke* included (from left to right) Milburn Stone as Dr. Galen (Doc) Adams, Dennis Weaver as Chester Goode, Amanda Blake as Kitty Russell, and James Arness as Marshal Matt Dillon. (Courtesy of Gary Yoggy.)

Imitations of *Gunsmoke* came and went (*Lawman, Wichita Town, Tombstone Territory, Cimarron City, Cimarron Strip*), but there were other successful variations that made some lasting impact on the genre. Two Westerns that debuted in the fall of 1957 broke the mold of the traditional cowboy hero by introducing central characters who were guided more by self-interest than by any mythical "code of the West." The two brothers on *Maverick*, who would rather run than fight, were professional con artists and gamblers. Paladin, whose business cards read "Have Gun Will Travel" (the phrase was also the show's title), was a professional gunfighter who usually sold his services to the highest bidder. Joining them at the top of the Nielsen ratings one season later was bounty hunter Josh Randall, who in *Wanted: Dead or Alive* seemed to be less interested in upholding the law than in collecting a sizable reward for his efforts.

Maverick, a western term, means one who does not conform to the practices of his group. It was probably coined after Samuel Maverick, a Texan who did not brand his cattle. Brothers Bret and Bart Maverick supported their expensive tastes and habits with clever schemes and con games. Their one concession to morality was to save their most outlandish exploits for overblown figures of authority, usually in defense of hopeless causes and mistreated underdogs. The brothers occasionally worked as a team but usually went their separate ways in search of high stakes and beautiful women (fig. 6.3).

The viewer could be certain that when it came time for a showdown, the Mavericks would try to talk things over and, failing in that, would slip quietly out of town. Bret was fond of quoting advice given him by his "Pappy" in such homilies as "He who fights and runs away, lives to run away another day" and "a coward dies a thousand deaths, a brave man only once. A thousand to one's a pretty good advantage."

Maverick's producer, Roy Huggins, explained during the series' second season, "What we set out to do was create a character that deliberately broke all the rules of the traditional Western hero. He's a little bit of a coward, he's not solemn, he's greedy, and not above cheating a little. He's indifferent to the problems of other people. He's something of a gentle grafter."[25]

Cast in the lead (as Bret) of the first Western series not to take itself too seriously was an actor who did not take himself too seriously. James Garner, veteran of several "heavy" roles on *Cheyenne*, proclaimed, "Bret Maverick is lazy. I'm lazy. And I *like* being lazy!"[26] Jack Kelly was added to the cast (as Bart) about two months into the series to keep the show from straying too far from the traditional Western mold.

Figure 6.3. Westerns dominated prime-time television in the late 1950s and early 1960s. The Warner Brothers stable included (from left to right) Wayde Preston (*Colt .45*), Ty Hardin (*Bronco*), Jack Kelly (*Maverick*), John Russell (*The Lawman*), James Garner (*Maverick*), Peter Brown (*The Lawman*), and Will Hutchins (*Sugarfoot*). (Richard Aquila Collection.)

Paladin, like Maverick, rode onto television screens in the fall of 1957. Like Maverick, he was part hero, part antihero. Unlike *Maverick,* however, there was very little humor in *Have Gun Will Travel.* Defying Western custom, Paladin was a good guy who dressed all in black. A professional gunman, Paladin was a mercenary who sold his services to almost anyone who could afford them, but he was far from your average illiterate, unrefined gunslinger. A soldier of fortune who got paid for many of his good deeds, he was also a gentleman of culture, refinement, and impeccable taste who resided in elegance in a fine San Francisco hotel. He preferred gourmet food to chuck wagon grub and frequently quoted the classics rather than homespun homilies. Moreover, he was college educated, having attended West Point in pursuit of a military career.

The story of Paladin begins with a nameless former army officer losing more money than he can afford in a poker game with a wealthy land baron. To pay off his debt, he agrees to kill an outlaw named Smoke who has been plaguing the baron. On completing the task the former officer adopts Smoke's disguise—a black outfit and the symbol of the paladin (a white chess knight fastened to his holster)—as well as Smoke's policy of hiring out his guns and expertise to those who are unable to protect themselves.

Paladin's famous calling card read, "Have Gun Will Travel. Wire Paladin, San Francisco." He quickly became television's most appealing nonconformist. Nobody "owned" him. In fact, he often displayed open contempt for the invariably rich people who hired him and on occasion was known to turn against them if they were on the wrong side of fairness and justice.

CBS selected the rugged six-foot, two-inch Richard Boone to play the title role. Boone, a distant nephew of Daniel, was a former ordnance officer in the U.S. Navy who was right at home working with Paladin's belt derringer, six-shooter, saddle rifle, and homemade machine gun. Endowed with action and interesting plots by such distinguished writers as Sam Peckinpah, *Have Gun Will Travel* was an immediate hit and ran five seasons.

Josh Randall, the central character in *Wanted: Dead or Alive,* which debuted in the fall of 1958, appeared at first glance to be the most superficial of television's western antiheroes. Randall was a bounty hunter who checked wanted posters, tracked down and captured the culprit, and returned to claim the reward. As played by Steve McQueen, he showed little emotion and was a man of few words, more adept at using his gun, a "Mare's Leg" (a unique cross between a handgun and a rifle), than talking his way out of tight situations. Still, Randall could be as soft-hearted as any other western hero.

Since bounty hunters were common in the West during the last half of the nineteenth century, the stories seemed plausible; moreover, the opportunity for violence was great, since criminals could be captured dead or alive. The potential excitement coupled with the charisma of the rugged, unflappable McQueen proved to be a winning formula.

Another successful adult series, *Wagon Train,* was not a conventional Western at all but a dramatic anthology that happened to be set in the nineteenth-century American West. *Wagon Train* combined guest stars with a cast of regulars to relate the stories of various members of the caravan and how and why they were heading west. The show focused on the week's guest rather than the wagonmaster (first Major Seth Adams, played by Ward Bond, and later Chris Hale, played by John McIntyre) or his crew (which featured scout Flint McCullough, played by the handsome Robert Horton). The wagonmaster and crew served mainly as commentators on the action or as continuity devices.

Inspired by John Ford's epic film *Wagonmaster* (1950) and given authenticity by the supervision of Western historian and novelist

Dwight B. Newton, this series had a simple, loose formula. The regulars acted as protectors and counselors to the traveling party as they fought outlaws, hostile Indians, and the extremes of nature, often stepping aside and allowing the traumas and complications affecting the passengers to carry the episodes. This permitted scriptwriters a wide range of plots dealing with character development and kept the program consistently sophisticated and engrossing.

Produced at the then staggering cost of $100,000 per episode, the list of guest stars who appeared on the series included Ernest Borgnine, Bette Davis, Mickey Rooney, and Mercedes McCambridge. This format managed to keep *Wagon Train* rolling for eight seasons and provided a pattern that was later successfully adopted by two other Western blockbusters, *Rawhide* and *The Virginian*.

Rawhide was the closest television came to an authentic "sweat and blood" Western. The series, which premiered in January 1959 as a mid-season replacement, was the creation of veteran Hollywood writer-director Charles Marquis Warren. Warren, who had been instrumental in developing the TV version of *Gunsmoke,* based the series on the great cattle drives of the 1870s, when drovers moved herds from Texas to railheads in Kansas and Missouri.

Seeking to depict the "working West" of the cattle kingdom and the men and women who inhabited it, Warren based much of his story details on a diary written by George Duffield, who had served as a drover on a cattle drive from San Antonio to Sedalia, Missouri, in 1866. From Duffield's diary came the unique terminology that gave the series much of its realism (e.g., *beeves, trail boss, ramrod, drag,* and *point*).[27] The lead characters were trail boss Gil Favor (superbly played by Eric Fleming), a tough man of action who possessed good judgment, compassion, and an iron will, and his ramrod, Rowdy Yates, a handsome young cowpoke who often let his emotions get him into trouble, especially when pretty girls were involved (the role that launched the career of superstar Clint Eastwood). With its gritty realism *Rawhide* was exceeded in longevity on the home tube only by *Gunsmoke, Bonanza,* and *The Virginian.*

The late 1950s and early 1960s saw the emergence of a new breed of adult Western, the "domestic" or "family" Western. Several of these series were quite successful: *The Rifleman* (the first of this format); *Bonanza* (longest running); *The Virginian* (TV's first ninety-minute Western); *The Big Valley* (featuring a matriarchal family); *The High Chaparral* (a modified version of *Bonanza*; see fig. 6.4); and *Lancer* (although it only ran two seasons). It could be argued that domestic Westerns struck a responsive chord during the cold war era, which

Figure 6.4. *The High Chaparral* was one of the more successful Westerns of the late 1960s and early 1970s. Unlike most TV Westerns, it featured strong female and Hispanic characters. The cast included the following actors: top row, Leif Erickson (as Big John Cannon); middle row, Cameron Mitchell (as Buck Cannon), Linda Cristal (as Victoria Montoya Cannon), and Henry Darrow (as Manolito Montoya): and bottom row, Mark Slade (as Billy Blue Cannon). (Richard Aquila Collection.)

witnessed the idealization of the family, but other factors might explain the rise of this genre. As historian Rita Parks has pointed out, dramatic programs that focus on family life have always been "a staple in mass media story telling."[28] Successful domestic situation comedies, from *Bachelor Father* to *My Three Sons,* may have also influenced producers of television Westerns.

As if to emphasize the rigors of life in the Old West, each of the TV Western families was headed by a widower (or in the case of *The Big Valley,* a widow). Several of these patriarchs had been widowed more than once. In fact, Ben Cartwright (*Bonanza*) had suffered the loss of three wives. Only Big John Cannon (*The High Chaparral*) was married at the time the stories took place (although his first wife was killed off in the series' opener).

The Rifleman, premiering in 1958, focused on the warm relationship between Lucas McCain, a New Mexico homesteader struggling to make a living off his ranch, and Mark, his young son. The series took its name from the trick rifle that Lucas always carried, a modified Winchester with a large ring that cocked the weapon as he twirled it. The shooting, however, was played down, and Lucas's attempts to make a man of Mark gave the hero more credibility than those of most other television Westerns enjoyed. In every episode of *The Rifleman* Mark learned something about life on his own or from his father, thus giving the series genuine family appeal. Chuck Connors, a six-foot, five-inch former major league baseball and basketball player, endowed Lucas McCain with strength and sincerity, while young Johnny Crawford projected just the proper amount of innocence as Mark.

Whereas the McCains represented middle-class homesteaders struggling to eke out a living from the land, the Cartwrights were representatives of the upper class struggling to defend their vast property holdings. Set in the vicinity of Virginia City, Nevada, during the Civil War era soon after the discovery of the fabulous Comstock silver lode, *Bonanza* was the story of Ben Cartwright (portrayed by the silver-haired, Canadian-born Lorne Greene) and his three sons (each by a different wife): the serious, thoughtful, mature Adam (Pernell Roberts); the gentle, sensitive giant Hoss (Dan Blocker); and the impulsive and romantic Little Joe (Michael Landon). *Bonanza* emphasized the bonds of affection among four strong men, as well as their affinity for the land. Although family differences were frequent, these were always put aside when the family's honor or property was threatened by corrupt and thieving outsiders.

In addition to emphasizing male bonding and family love, *Bonanza* had another distinction that helped to ensure its success: it was the first network Western to be televised in color. The great expanse of gorgeous outdoor scenery displayed in the show was probably the most significant factor in stimulating the early sale of color television sets. It also helped to keep *Bonanza* at or near the top of the Nielsen ratings during its early years. In the long run, however, it was believable and likable characters coupled with interesting stories that kept the series on NBC's schedule for nearly fourteen seasons.

On initial viewing *The Big Valley*, which focused on the trials and tribulations of a single-parent family, the Barkleys, as they strove to manage a 30,000–acre ranch in California's San Joaquin Valley, appeared to be just a slightly more elaborate version of *Bonanza*. There were, however, several significant differences. The Barkley holdings, while not nearly as large as the Cartwright's, were more diversified. Furthermore, the house itself was markedly more sophisticated, resembling a white pillared antebellum southern mansion with Victorian furnishings and the best in wine, books, and china. It should be noted that at the time *The Big Valley* was being telecast (1965–69) women were still being treated as domestic consumers who were vital members of the viewing audience. Most important, the show's family was a matriarchy headed by the recently widowed Victoria Barkley. Successful TV Westerns like *Wagon*

Train, Rawhide, Bonanza, and *The Virginian* all had featured female guest stars on a regular basis for some time. What was unique about Victoria Barkley was the strength and dominance of her character. Mrs. Barkley was to the TV Western what Betty Friedan, Bella Abzug, and Shirley Chisholm were to the era's politics. Most of the women in earlier television Westerns had appeared in secondary roles as barmaids, farmers' wives, or simply damsels in distress. Although Victoria Barkley was a heroine with feminine characteristics, she also had an inner strength that equaled that of any man, including Ben Cartwright.

Adding credibility to the role was veteran actress Barbara Stanwyck, who gave some of her finest screen performances in Westerns. Stanwyck expressed great pride that *The Big Valley* was the first and only adult Western to feature a female lead. She explained in the *New York Times,* "some producers think women did nothing in those days except keep house and have children. But if you read your history they did a lot more than that. They were *in* cattle drives. They were *there.*"[29]

Stories on *The Big Valley* were built around the widowed matriarch, her four adult children (three after the youngest son returned to college), and their continual struggle against the lawless elements of the Old West. Jarrod (Richard Long), Nick (Peter Brock), Audra (Linda Evans), and Eugene (Charles Briles) were Victoria Barkley's children. Although Victoria treated Heath (Lee Majors) as if he were her own son, he was the result of an illicit liaison between her husband and an Indian woman. Populated with such evil characters as murderers, bank robbers, Mexican revolutionaries, and con artists, the action-packed programs also used major guest stars in featured roles.

By the mid-1960s Westerns were declining in popularity on the home screen, so the networks tried covering the traditional terrain with some new approaches. The only new TV Westerns with any staying power were *The Wild, Wild West,* a unique combination of espionage thriller and Western, and *Little House on the Prairie,* which shifted attention from the cowboy to the farmer.

The Wild, Wild West, which ran on CBS from 1965 to 1969, was the creation of Michael Garrison, who was obviously influenced as much by the popular James Bond films and their TV clone, *The Man from U.N.C.L.E.,* as he was by earlier television Westerns. Two U.S. government agents, James T. West and Artemus Gordon (played with wit and charm by Robert Conrad and Ross Martin), were sent to the western frontier by President Ulysses S. Grant to thwart radical, revolutionary, or criminal groups attempting to take over the country. Armed with the latest scientific gadgets, West and Gordon traveled in a special three-car train. West was handsome, athletic, and expert at all forms of self-defense and weaponry. Gordon was a master of disguises and dialects. Although criticized for its excessive violence, the series, by gently spoofing both the Western and espionage genres, developed especially offbeat and intriguing story lines.

Only one series with a western setting was successful in attracting substantial numbers of viewers during the Vietnam era. By some standards that program, *Little House on the Prairie,* would not even be considered a Western. Although set in the American West during the 1870s, it did not have the usual trappings associated with Westerns. There were few cowboys and even fewer Indians in the stories, and the town of Walnut Grove, Minnesota, where the stories took place, did not even have a saloon.

The series, based on Laura Ingalls Wilder's Little House on the Prairie stories, owed as much to *The Waltons* as it did to television Westerns. Presenting a sentimental view of the trials and tribulations of a homesteader family struggling to make a living on a small farm on the frontier, episodes presented character studies of individual family members and their friends in times of crisis. Usually told from the perspective of the second-oldest daughter, Laura (sweetly portrayed by Melissa Gilbert), the plots dealt with the Ingalls family's constant struggle against natural disasters and ruined crops, as well as dealings with other members of their little community.

The program played down violence, presenting it as the exceptional rather than the commonplace experience of family life in the Old West. The series was the inspiration of Michael Landon, who had won a large following as Little Joe in *Bonanza.* Landon not only produced, directed, and wrote many of the episodes, but he also played the lead role of Charles Ingalls, the young father and struggling homesteader loved by his family and respected by his friends and neighbors.

The popularity of this type of Western in the mid-1970s was a clear indication that the cowboy hero was being replaced in our national consciousness. "A decade and a half earlier, farmers were relegated to secondary roles in westerns as the unromantic hardworking characters a roaming cowboy hero must help out of a jam," writes Douglas Brode. "Now, our national vision and collective sensibility had shifted drastically enough that the routine existence of farmers could touch us in a way that an idealized image of cowboys as rugged individualists could not."[30]

To understand the reasons for the demise of the traditional television Western one needs to reexamine the factors that led to their initial popularity. In 1959 ABC's program director, Thomas W. Moore, explained to *Time* magazine that "the western is just the neatest and quickest type of escape entertainment, that's all."[31] Other theorizers made a more convincing case. *Time* reported in 1959 that

> the western helps people to get away from the complexities of modern life and back to the "restful absolutes" of the past. . . . In the cowboy's world, justice is the result of direct action, not of elaborate legality. A man's fate depends on his own choices and capacities, not on the vast impersonal forces of society or science. . . . The western is really the American morality play in which Good and Evil, Spirit and Nature, Christian and Pagan fight to the finish on the vast stage of the unbroken prairie. The hero is a Galahad with a six-gun, a Perseus of the purple sage. In his saddlebags he carries a new mythology, an American Odyssey that is waiting for its Homer. And the theme of the epic, hidden beneath the circus glitter of the perennial Wild West show, is the immortal theme of every hero myth: Man's endless search for the meaning of his life.[32]

Writing over thirty years later Pulitzer Prize–winning critic William A. Henry III agreed, adding,

> the public was attracted to the heroic dimensions of those earlier and simpler times, to the pioneer values on which the nation had been built (and to which, politicians kept proclaiming, a wayward land should revert) and to that era's seeming moral clarity. By the western's conventions after all the good guys in white hats could be distinguished at a glance from the bad guys in black. In a modern world that sensed itself obligated to a cold war of perplexing tolerance rather than a hot war of righteous obliteration, this older world seemed seductively straightforward.[33]

Henry further explained that "within this myth of simplicity and purity lay not only the roots of the western's rise but the seeds of its decline. Many of the things that made the western so right for 1959 made it wrong for the sixties and painfully out of sync with the seventies, when the format virtually disappeared from the small screen."[34]

The political turbulence of the 1960s, with the explosion of the civil rights movement and the rise of the feminist movement, coupled with growing opposition to the war in Vietnam and an increasing revulsion toward violence in general resulting from a sickening series of assassinations, made the Western less and less relevant. Americans were rejecting rugged individualism in favor of collective action. According to Henry:

As blacks and other minorities grew more assertive of their rights, they grew less tolerant of entertainments, no matter how accurate historically, that showed them being put down. At the same time, the nation as a whole slipped from jingoistic pride in wars of conquest against American Indian tribes to a distinct sense of shame.... [Furthermore], the women's movement changed the consciousness of the nation's wives and mothers, and of their husbands and sons. As a result of the new value placed on male sensitivity rather than stoicism, the nation's male archetype shifted from John Wayne to Alan Alda.[35]

There were, of course, significant changes in American foreign affairs as well. The cold war was replaced by detente, which more recently gave way to *glasnost,* followed by the eventual end of the cold war. There were also trends within the television industry that worked against the Western. The shows were becoming more expensive to make, for they required at least some on-location shooting. Wages were rising, and unions were making other costly demands. Moreover, all this was occurring in a genre that by the 1970s appealed primarily to children, senior citizens, and poor, unsophisticated rural viewers—widely regarded by advertisers as the least susceptible to pitches for impulse purchase of consumer goods.

In addition there had been too many Westerns on the air with too many gimmicks trying too hard to be all things to all viewers. Too many plots seemed too familiar. Too few young stars were interested in gambling their careers on a dying genre. So the networks simply stopped producing Westerns.

According to J. Fred MacDonald, in his widely acclaimed *Who Shot the Sheriff?* the TV Western is dead. With various aspects of the genre "co-opted by space adventures, urban police dramas, seductive prime-time soap operas and even situation comedies," MacDonald sees little reason to expect its resurrection. In fact he predicts "the possibility of its extinction by the twenty-first century."[36]

Is MacDonald right? Is there no viable future for the Western on television? It is true that recent series have not fared well: *Wildside* (1985) lasted only six weeks on ABC (scheduled opposite such blockbuster hits as NBC's *Cosby Show* and CBS's *Magnum, p.i.*); *Outlaws* (1987) lasted only half a season on CBS (but it was more a fantasy detective show than a Western); *Paradise* (*Guns of Paradise* during its last season) lasted two and a half seasons (1988–91) but was canceled by CBS when its rating dropped to sixty-eighth; and although *The Young Riders,* launched in 1989, was renewed by ABC for a third season, it ranked a dismal eightieth.

By the early 1990s, however, there were some indications that the TV Western was far from dead. The most encouraging sign that devotees of the Western could find was the critical, as well as popular, success of two CBS miniseries, *Lonesome Dove* (1989) and *Return to Lonesome Dove* (1993).

Many TV Westerns of the 1990s bore the imprint of the new revisionist school of western history popularized by historians such as Richard White, Donald Worster, and Patricia Nelson Limerick. Whereas traditionalists of the Turner school saw the West as a rough-hewn egalitarian democracy, where every man had a piece of land and the promise of prosperity, revisionists claim that the West became quickly dominated by big-money interests and big government. Instead of being a place of success, happiness, and progress, the region became rife with tragedy, conflict, destruction, and failure. New western historians contend that in "winning the West" pioneers were motivated by economic greed, resulting in the plunder of the environment, dislocation of Native Americans, and exploitation of women and minorities. These historians see the legacy of the West as depleted natural resources, fragmented families, racial strife, and vast disparities between the rich and poor.

Dr. Quinn, Medicine Woman, which debuted on CBS in January 1993 and focused on a woman in a role traditionally performed by a man, was unquestionably the most revisionist Western yet to be broadcast. Accused by some critics as being too politically correct, Dr. Quinn defended the environment against plunder, practically endorsed gun control, personified sexual equality, and tirelessly preached tolerance toward immigrants, blacks, Indians, and ladies of ill repute. More important, *Dr. Quinn* was a huge Saturday night ratings success.

Even *Walker, Texas Ranger,* which premiered on CBS in April 1993 and was a more traditional Western set in the contemporary West, paid some deference to modern trends. Walker's uncle was a Cherokee, his partner was a college-educated black from an urban ghetto, and his sometime romantic interest was a liberated feminist prosecuting attorney. Of all the recent TV Westerns, *The Adventures of Brisco County, Jr.,* which debuted on the fledgling Fox Network in 1993, was perhaps the most free of revisionist influence. Although the program costarred a black actor as one of its bounty hunters, it was basically a cross between a cliffhanger B Western and *The Wild, Wild West* of an earlier era.

TV Westerns, like other television drama, are products of their times. Television Westerns have reflected historical forces, social concerns, and cultural values from the cold war era, when Hoppy, Gene, and Roy rode across the video range fighting for truth, justice, and the American way, through the tumultuous 1960s and early 1970s, when good guys like Matt Dillon had to balance their deeds against the increasing violence in American society and the Vietnam War, and into the 1980s and 1990s, when Dr. Quinn and other new-breed western heroes have become spokespeople for contemporary concerns.

Without a doubt Westerns have made a significant contribution to television's past; whether Westerns have a major role to play in television's future is less clear. Lovers of the genre can only hope that there is still a significant place on the home screen for that unique American literary creation, the Western.

Notes

1. Tim Brooks and Earle Marsh, *The Complete Directory to Prime Time Network TV Shows, 1946–Present,* 5th ed. (New York, 1992), 1097.

2. Buck Rainey, *The Shoot-Em-Ups-Ride Again* (Metuchen, N.J., 1990), 225.

3. William A. Henry III, "They Went Thataway!" *Memories,* Dec. 1989/Jan. 1990, 77.

4. Mario de Marco, *Hopalong Cassidy: Knight of the West* (privately printed, 1983), 100.

5. David Rothel, *Who Was That Masked Man? The Story of the Lone Ranger* (New York, 1976), 86; Gary H. Grossman, *Saturday Morning TV* (New York, 1981), 400.

6. Gary H. Grossman, *Saturday Morning TV,* 186–92, 321.

7. Wilbur Schramm, Jack Lyle, and Edwin B. Parker, *Television in the Lives of Our Children* (Stanford, Calif., 1961), 230.

8. Gary A. Yoggy, "When Television Wore Six-Guns: Cowboy Heroes on TV," in *Shooting Stars: Heroes and Heroines of Western Film,* ed. Archie P. McDonald (Indianapolis, 1987), 229.

9. Information about Autry's "Cowboy Commandments" can be found in the Berkeley Pop Culture Project's *Whole Pop Catalog* (New York, 1991), 588, and David Rothel, *The Singing Cowboys* (New York, 1978), 17. During the 1950s kids in the Roy Rogers Riders Club agreed to obey the following rules, which are very similar to Autry's "Cowboy Commandments": (1) be neat and clean; (2) be courteous and polite; (3) always obey your parents; (4) protect the weak and help them; (5) be brave but never take chances; (6) study hard and learn all you can; (7) be kind to animals and care for them; (8) eat all your food and never waste any; (9) love God and go to Sunday School regularly; and (10) always respect our flag and our country. Ralph Brauer's comment is taken from Brauer, *The Horse, the Gun and the Piece of Property: Changing Images of the TV Western* (Bowling Green, Ohio, 1975), 42.

10. Gary A. Yoggy, *Riding the Video Range: The Rise and Fall of the Western on Television* (Jefferson, N.C., 1995), 6.

11. Quoted in J. Fred MacDonald, *Who Shot the Sheriff?* (New York, 1987), 40.

12. Ibid., 41

13. J. Fred MacDonald, *Television and the Red Menace: The Video Road to Vietnam* (New York, 1985), 140.

14. David Shea Teeple, "TV Westerns Tell a Story," *The American Mercury*, April 1958, 116.

15. Brauer, *The Horse*, 55.

16. MacDonald, *Who Shot the Sheriff?* 47–50.

17. "The Six-Gun Galahad," *Time*, March 30, 1959, 52–53.

18. Yoggy, *Riding the Video Range*, 78.

19. Harry Castleman and Walter J. Podrazik, *Watching TV: Four Decades of American Television* (New York, 1982), 104.

20. Brooks and Marsh, *Complete Directory*, 161.

21. Douglas Brode, "They Went Thataway," *Television Quarterly* (Summer 1982): 34.

22. Quoted in Robert de Roos, "Private Life of 'Gunsmoke' Star," *Saturday Evening Post*, April 12, 1958, 110.

23. Kristine Fredricksson, "Gunsmoke: Twenty-Year Videography, Part I," *The Journal of Popular Film and Television* 12, no. 1 (Spring 1984): 16.

24. Brooks and Marsh, *Complete Directory*, 1111; Brode, "They Went Thataway," 35; Suzanne and Gabor Barabas, *Gunsmoke, a Complete History* (Jefferson, N.C., 1990), 151.

25. Quoted in Castleman and Podrazik, *Watching TV*, 116.

26. Quoted in Yoggy, "When TV Wore Six-Guns," 241.

27. Richard K. Tharp, "Rawhide, Part 1," *Reruns: The Magazine of Television History*, April 1982, 7.

28. Rita Parks, *The Western Hero in Film and Television* (Ann Arbor, Mich., 1982), 139.

29. Quoted in Jerry Vermilye, *Barbara Stanwyck* (New York, 1975), 135.

30. Brode, "They Went Thataway," 40.

31. Quoted in "The Six-Gun Galahad," *Time*, March 30, 1959, 53.

32. Ibid., 53.

33. Henry, "They Went Thataway!" 78.

34. Ibid., 81.

35. Ibid., 83.

36. MacDonald, *Who Shot the Sheriff?* 134.

Suggestions for Further Reading

MOVIES AND TELEVISION

Brauer, Ralph. *The Horse, the Gun, and the Piece of Property: Changing Images of the TV Western.* Bowling Green, Ohio, 1975.

Calder, Jennie. *There Must Be a Lone Ranger: The American West in Film and Reality.* New York, 1975.

Cary, Diana Serra. *The Hollywood Posse: The Story of a Gallant Band of Horsemen Who Made Movie History.* Boston, 1975.

Cawelti, John. *The Six-Gun Mystique.* 2d ed. Bowling Green, Ohio, 1984.

Dunning, John. *Tune in Yesterday: The Ultimate Encyclopedia of Old-Time Radio.* Englewood Cliffs, N.J., 1976.

Everson, William K. *The Hollywood Western.* New York, 1969, 1992.

Fenin, George N., and William K. Everson. *The Western: From Silents to Cinerama.* New York, 1973.

French, Philip. *Westerns: Aspects of a Movie Genre.* New York, 1977.

Garfield, Brian. *Western Films: A Complete Guide.* New York, 1982.

Hadley-Garcia, George. *Hispanic Hollywood: The Latins in Motion Pictures.* New York, 1990.

Hitt, Jim. *The American West from Fiction (1823–1876) into Film (1909–1986).* Jefferson, N.C., 1990.

Holland, Ted. *B Western Actors Encyclopedia.* Jefferson, N.C., 1989.

Johnstone, Iain. *Clint Eastwood: The Man with No Name.* New York, 1981; 2d ed., 1988.

Kitses, Jim. *Horizons West.* Bloomington, Ind., 1969.

Lenihan, John H. *Showdown: Confronting Modern America in the Western Film.* Urbana, Ill., 1980.

MacDonald, J. Fred. *Who Shot the Sheriff?* New York, 1987.

McDonald, Archie P., ed. *Shooting Stars: Heroes and Heroines of Western Film.* Indianapolis, 1987.

Miller, Don. *Hollywood Corral.* New York, 1976.

Miller, Leo O. *The Great Cowboy Stars of Movies and Television.* Westport, Conn., 1979.

Nachbar, Jack, ed. *Focus on the Western.* Englewood Cliffs, N.J., 1974.

Null, Gary. *Black Hollywood: The Negro in Motion Pictures.* New York, 1975; 2d ed., 1990.

Place, J. A. *The Western Films of John Ford.* Secaucus, N.J., 1974.

Rainey, Buck. *The Shoot-Em-Ups Ride Again.* Metuchen, N.J., 1990.

Rollins, Peter C. *Hollywood as Historian: American Film in a Cultural Context.* Lexington, Ky., 1983.

Rothel, David. *The Great Cowboy Sidekicks.* Metuchen, N.J., 1984.

———. *The Roy Rogers Book.* Madison, N.C., 1987.

———. *The Singing Cowboys*. South Brunswick, N.J., 1978.

Thomas, Tony. *The West That Never Was*. New York, 1989.

Tompkins, Jane. *West of Everything: The Inner Life of Westerns*. New York, 1992.

Tuska, Jon. *The American West in Film: Critical Approaches to the Western*. Westport, Conn., 1985.

———. *The Filming of the West*. Garden City, N.Y. 1976.

Wright, Will. *Six Guns and Society: A Structural Study of the Western*. Berkeley, Calif., 1975.

Yoggy, Gary A. *Riding the Video Range: The Rise and Fall of the Western on Television*. Jefferson, N.C, 1995.

PART FOUR

Music

SEVEN

Richard Aquila

A Blaze of Glory: The Mythic West in Pop and Rock Music

POPULAR MUSIC HAS enjoyed a long and profitable relationship with the American West dating back to at least the late 1800s. The West has inspired numerous hit records, from early pop songs such as Billy Murray's "San Antonio (Cowboy Song)" (1907) to later hits like Jon Bon Jovi's rock classic "A Blaze of Glory (Theme from *Young Guns II*)" (1990) or Garth Brooks's country recording "The Cowboy Song" (1993).

Western images in popular music often reflected, and sometimes helped shape, historical forces and events. They demonstrate how various generations have used the mythic West in a variety of ways to define cultural identities and to cope with social change. They also suggest that popular music was offering its audience a revisionist approach to the mythic West for almost two decades before the "new western historians" arrived on the scene.

The American West became a staple of popular music during the 1800s and early 1900s. By that time audiences were already well acquainted with the mythic West of popular culture. Sensational dime novels of the mid-1800s recounting the action-packed heroics of historical figures like Buffalo Bill Cody and Kit Carson, as well as fictional characters such as Deadwood Dick or Seth Jones, were loosely based on western themes first introduced in the early 1800s by James Fenimore Cooper's Leatherstocking Tales. Later Western fiction such as Owen Wister's novel *The Virginian* (1902) and Andy Adams's quasi-historical *Log of a Cowboy* (1903) added even more depth and realism to mythic images of cowboys and the West, as did outdoor entertainment such as Buffalo Bill's Wild West show, popular Western films beginning with *The Great Train Robbery* (1903), and the paintings and sketches of popular artists such as Frederic Remington and Charles Russell.

Folk ballads served as prototypes for pop songs about the American West. After they were collected and published in books such as N. Howard "Jack" Thorp's *Songs of the Cowboys* (1908) and John Avery Lomax's *Cowboy Songs and other Frontier Ballads* (1910), or magazine articles such as Sharlot M. Hall's "Songs of the Old Cattle Trail," which appeared in the March 1908 issue of *Out West*, western folk ballads became part of the pop music mainstream, further reinforcing public notions of the mythic West.[1]

Like other forms of popular culture, folk songs usually depicted the West as a land of exotic beauty, opportunity, romance, and excitement or recounted exciting exploits of colorful western characters. For example, folk songs such as "Home, Home on the Range" and "I Ride an Old Paint" dealt with the West's potential for beauty and freedom. "Texas Rangers," which was widely distributed as a broadside by a New York printer in 1891, portrayed exciting gunfights between cowboys and Indians. Nineteenth-century ballads such as "The Yellow Rose of Texas," "The Girl I Left behind Me," and "Red River Valley" pictured cowboys as tragic, romantic figures who were often the victims of unrequited love. Other popular songs, such as "My Love Is a Rider," made it clear that cowboys were too restless to settle down with one woman.[2]

Numerous songs added to the cowboy's image as a colorful, rugged individual, a western knight astride his trusty steed jousting against the twin perils of the Wild West and civilization. "Whoopee Ti Yi Yo, Git along Little Dogies" described the dashing, cavalier cowboy with his hat "throwed back" and spurs "a-jinglin'." "The Old Chisholm Trail" depicted cowboys as lone riders, facing the dangers and hardships of cattle drives. "Rye Whiskey" applauded the cowboy's love of alcohol, gambling, and freedom. Ballads like "Jesse James," "Sam Bass," and "Billy the Kid" spotlighted wild gunfighters and outlaws.[3]

Although most folk songs glorified the mythic West, a few took a more realistic approach. "The Cowboy's Lament" (more commonly known as "The Streets of Laredo") told the tragic story of a young, naïve cowpuncher who fell prey to the cowboy myth: "It was once in the saddle I used to go dashing. . . . Got shot in the breast and I'm dying today." The popular ballad "Bury Me Not on the Lone Prairie" also illustrated the harshness of life and death in the American West. The song tells of the last request of a dying young cowboy: "O bury me not on the lone prairie, where the coyotes howl and the wind blows free." It ends on a somber note. His friends "took no heed to his dying prayer. In a narrow grave, just six by three, they buried him there on the lone prairie."[4] Folk songs containing negative images of the American West were the exception rather than the rule, however, and most Americans by the turn of the century were more in tune with positive images of the mythic West.

Pop musicians of the early 1900s found great success singing about the same mythic West made famous in folk music and popular culture. For example, Billy Murray's "San Antonio" capitalized on the cowboy's sudden popularity following the publication of Owen Wister's best-selling western novel *The Virginian,* while romanticized Indians—similar to those found in other areas of popular culture—became the subjects of hits such as Dan Quinn's "Hiawatha" (1903) or Paul Whiteman's "Indian Love Call" (1928). Elsie Baker's "Trail of the Lonesome Pine" (1913), Irving Kaufman's "California and You" (1914), and Al Jolson's "California, Here I Come" (1924) reminded listeners that happiness and exotic western landscapes went hand in hand.[5]

The public's fascination with the mythic West in music and other areas of popular culture may be linked to several developments. The late nineteenth and early twentieth centuries witnessed the transformation of America from a rural, agrarian nation into an urbanized, industrial one. The mythic West provided a clear national identity during rapidly changing times. It assured middle-class Americans of the Progressive Era that government reforms to regulate robber barons, political bosses, and "New Immigrants" were not going to dramatically alter the American character. When the United States entered World War I, the mythic West became the perfect symbol of American patriotism. As historian Robert Athearn explained, "At a time when America was off on the great adventure in Europe, bent upon making the world safe for America's conception of democracy, the link between frontier values and patriotism became increasingly evident."[6]

Following the war the traditional values associated with the mythic West offered comfort to those Americans who were concerned about the rising materialism and rapid social change of the 1920s. The mythic West reminded white, native-born Americans about their roots, and in a time of rising nativism, it provided a means to distinguish them from minorities and New Immigrants. Ironically, the mythic West also gave immigrants the opportunity to learn about their new country's heritage. The mythic West's epic tales of survival and conquest set in the splendor of majestic mountains, raging rivers, and wild frontiers provided bearings for those adrift in changing times. Its legendary heroes and villains gave meaning to national purpose, and its setting somewhere in the past met the nostalgic needs of those who found it difficult to cope with the present.

The mythic West served as a psychological safety valve, offering idyllic, rural settings and vicarious thrills for those working and living in urban areas. The new technologies that gave birth to modern popular music, as well as the print media and the motion picture industry, provided an inexpensive means of escape to an exciting locale—an exotic West of the imagination populated by colorful cowboys, Indians, gunslingers, and desperadoes.

By the turn of the century Americans were becoming increasingly more aware of the passing of the frontier. As novelists such as Owen Wister and Emerson Hough wrote wistfully about the Old West, the historian Frederick Jackson Turner was explaining "the significance of the frontier in American history" before a meeting of historians in Chicago in 1893. Other Americans mourned the passing of the West by turning to pop culture for memories. Although the actual frontier may have ended in the early 1890s, the mythic West could still be explored through popular music and other forms of popular culture.

The 1930s and 1940s witnessed the triumph of the mythic West in popular music, as performers from a variety of backgrounds made extensive use of western themes first introduced in the late nineteenth and early twentieth centuries. Although there were always exceptions, such as Woody Guthrie's bleak *Dust Bowl Ballads,* most popular songs of this era continued to glorify the mythic West. Following the lead of earlier pop music, hit records such as Ben Selvin's "When It's Springtime in the Rockies" (1930), the Sons of the Pioneers' "Tumbling Tumbleweeds" (1934), and Bing Crosby's "Deep in the Heart of Texas" (1942) portrayed the West as an exotic land where one could find happiness or freedom.[7]

Popular music of the 1930s and 1940s also continued to paint romanticized pictures of mythic western figures. The cowboy's romances and alleged rugged individualism were depicted in songs such as Patsy Montana's "I Wanna Be a Cowboy's Sweetheart" (1936) and Bing Crosby's "Riders in the Sky (a Cowboy Legend)" (1949). There were also songs about Indians (Charlie Barnet and his orchestra's "Cherokee" [1939]), muleskinners (Frankie Laine's "Mule Train" [1949]), pioneers (Bing Crosby's "Along the Santa Fe Trail" [1941]), and exciting historical events (the Mills Brothers' "Across the Alley from the Alamo" [1947]).[8]

The tremendous popularity of western-influenced music was evident throughout American culture in the 1930s and 1940s. Print collections of cowboy songs, such as Margaret Larkin's *Singing Cowboy* (1931), went through numerous editions, while radio programs such as Chicago's WLS *Barn Dance* or Nashville's WSM *Grand Ole Opry* were showcases for the western stylings of country performers such as Jimmie Rodgers, Bob Wills and his Texas Playboys, and Hank Williams.

Hollywood also spotlighted songs about the mythic West. The romance to be found out west set the stage for a 1936 hit by Nelson Eddy and Jeanette MacDonald, "Indian Love Call," from the film version of *Rose Marie*. Another movie, *The Paleface*, featured "Buttons and Bows," which became a hit for six different pop singers in 1948.

The West was given a major boost in popularity by the advent of "singing cowboy" movie stars in the 1930s and 1940s. Two in particular became extremely popular. B Western film star Gene Autry galloped onto the pop charts with songs such as "The Last Round-Up" (1933), "Tumbling Tumbleweeds" (1935), and "(Spurs That) Jingle, Jangle, Jingle" (1942), which glorified the cowboy and the American West. Roy Rogers enjoyed similar success with western hits such as "Hi-Yo Silver" (1938) and "Blue Shadows on the Trail" (1948). The "King of the Cowboys" even received an Oscar nomination for "Dust," a song from his 1938 film *Under Western Stars*.

Broadway added to the growing fame of the American West. Margaret Larkin, a collector of cowboy songs, joined forces with playwright Lynn Riggs and produced *Green Grow the Lilacs* in 1931. The Broadway play, which highlighted folklore and traditional folk ballads, provided the basis for the later Rodgers and Hammerstein musical *Oklahoma*, which enjoyed a record-setting run on Broadway between 1943 and 1948. Its success led to other Broadway shows, including Irving Berlin's *Annie, Get Your Gun* and Lerner and Loewe's *Paint Your Wagon*, as well as western-influenced ballets such as Aaron Copland's *Rodeo* (1938) and *Billy the Kid* (1942).

Throughout the 1930s and 1940s songs about the American West were among the most successful in American pop music. In 1932 President-elect Franklin D. Roosevelt declared that his favorite song was "Home, Home on the Range," a safe political choice since it was probably the most-played song on the radio. In 1947 the Kansas legislature adopted it as the state's official song.[9]

Americans of the 1930s and 1940s had ample reasons for wanting songs about the mythic West. The mythic West's vision of the United States as a pastoral, idyllic nation that promoted opportunity, freedom, and justice for all continued to appeal to Americans experiencing the urbanization, industrialization, and alienation of modern times. In addition, the mythic West may have had a special attraction for Americans troubled by the Great Depression and World War II. Formulaic pop culture Westerns, like old friends, offered audiences continuity and stability in rapidly changing times. They also provided audiences with vicarious thrills and temporary escape from the problems of the real world.

Nevertheless, the mythic West was not just a means of escape to a simpler, more romantic time. It also showed Americans how to cope with contemporary problems. By tapping into shared memories of the alleged western experience, the mythic West provided solutions that might be applied to social problems, as well as wartime enemies. It reminded Americans about their rugged individualism, their sense of mission, the need for action, and their just cause. Political and economic crises of the 1930s and 1940s demanded cooperation from the American people, and the mythic West provided the vehicle to mobilize public unity and patriotism. The myth had always portrayed life in simple terms, a struggle between good and evil that American good guys always won. It assured Americans that they were on the right track. All they had to do was remember who they were. Americans could conquer all economic and military problems if only they stuck to their guns and to the traditional values that had won the West.

If the West of the imagination provided the perfect myth for a time that demanded consensus, it also offered the necessary antidote to the collectivism of the era. Though Americans had to join together to combat the Great Depression and the Axis powers, they could do so realizing that the basic American character was not being altered. The mythic West, stressing individualism, freedom, regeneration, action, and opportunity, was a constant reminder of traditional American values and dreams.

Popular music continued to make use of traditional images of the mythic West in the years immediately following World War II. Numerous pop songs, including Tennessee Ernie Ford's "Cry of the Wild Goose" (1950) and Mitch Miller's "Yellow Rose of Texas" (1955), followed the well-established formula of portraying the West as an exotic land where one could find happiness and freedom. Other hit records continued to showcase colorful western characters. Rugged cowboys or gunslingers were featured in hits such as Frankie Laine's "High Noon" (1952) and Dinah Shore's "Cattle Call" (1957), and romanticized Indians appeared in Slim Whitman's "Indian Love Call" (1952) and Hank Williams's "Kaw-Liga" (1953).[10]

Even early rock and roll—generally considered a music of rebel-lion—often relied on traditional images of the mythic West. Marty Robbins reached the number-one spot on the rock charts with "El Paso" (1959), a rambling, romantic western ballad about dance-hall girls, desperadoes, and gunfights. Gunslingers appeared in many oth-er songs, including Johnny Cash's "Don't Take Your Guns to Town" (1959) and Marty Robbins's "Big Iron" (1960). One of the Old West's most enduring legends was recalled in "The Ballad of the Alamo," which became a hit in 1960 for both Marty Robbins and Bud and Travis. The gold rush provided the setting for Johnny Horton's "North to Alaska" (1960).[11]

The era's stereotypes of Native Americans were also common in early rock and roll. Indians were depicted comically in two number-one hits in 1960: Johnny Preston's "Running Bear," which featured tom-toms and stereotypical Indian chants, told the story of a lovesick warrior who drowned while attempting to swim to his sweetheart; Larry Verne's "Please Mr. Custer (I Don't Want to Go)" presented a humorous account of a cowardly soldier terrified of Indians. It includ-ed references to scalping and warriors "running around like a bunch of wild Indians."[12]

Like other pop music, rock and roll viewed the West as a Garden of Eden. In 1962 a California group called the Beach Boys wrote and re-corded "Surfin' Safari." The song dealt with surfing, the California sun, and western hedonism.[13] By accident or design the Beach Boys tapped into an image already well established in the American mind. Their song about California echoed the theme of the mythic West as a Garden of Eden.

The Beach Boys epitomized the California surfing sound. After their initial success they strung together a series of hit records, includ-ing "Surfin' U.S.A." (1963) and "Surfer Girl" (1963), which reinforced California's image as paradise.[14] Their phenomenal success inspired Jan and Dean, the Surfaris, the Rivieras, and other 1960s rockers to sing about California's fun and sun.[15] Their lyrical message was always the same: the Golden State was the place to be. There, one could find hap-piness through surfing, sunshine, and romance. These performers were tapping the myth of the West in its simplest form, the Garden of Eden as typified in California.

Rock music's preoccupation with California reflected America's. By the 1950s and early 1960s hundreds of thousands of Americans were flocking to that state in pursuit of health, wealth, and happiness. If adults had California fever, rock music was spreading it to the kids.

Rock and roll's treatment of California is not surprising. Of all the areas of the West, California has most frequently been viewed as a paradise. The name itself has connotations of Eden; California was named after a mythical island in a popular romantic novel published in the early sixteenth century. According to the story, California was a worldly paradise ruled by an Amazonlike class of beautiful women.[16]

By the nineteenth century California was well established as a western utopia. Walt Whitman praised the Golden State's salubrious climate, fertile lands, and rich ores. One modern scholar, Kevin Starr, notes that "geographically and psychologically" California was the "ultimate frontier." Starr points out that California's gold rush "was linked imaginatively with the most compelling of American myths, the pursuit of happiness." Moreover, California's natural setting promised "beauty, life, health, abundance, and perhaps most important of all, a challenging correlative to inner inspiration."[17] California came to epitomize all the American West had to offer. It is therefore not surprising that rock and roll—like earlier forms of popular music—turned to California as the site of a western Garden of Eden.

The mythic West remained an important subject for popular music during the 1950s and early 1960s for several reasons. In many cases performers were simply trying to capitalize on the public's continuing fascination with the American West. Ever since the late nineteenth century audiences had repeatedly shown that they were willing to pay for books, movies, songs, or any other pop culture products that dealt with the mythic West. Westerns grew even more popular in the 1950s and early 1960s. Novelists such as Louis L'Amour cranked out novel after novel of western thrills. Television shows aimed at children popularized western heroes such as Hopalong Cassidy, the Lone Ranger, and Wild Bill Hickok. Adult Westerns on television featured more complicated good guys such as Matt Dillon, Paladin, and Maverick. And major motion pictures such as *The Searchers, Gunfight at the O.K. Corral,* and *Jubal* brought the West to the big screen. The mythic West's proven marketability made it a natural subject for singers and songwriters of the era.

At the same time the mythic West had a particular appeal for Americans of the 1950s and early 1960s. Lessons gleaned from the western experience seemed ideally suited to many of the era's problems. For example, the myth of the West offered clear strategies for defeating cold war enemies. Just like Indians or outlaws, communists could be contained if hardworking, individualistic Americans would join together to stop the threat. The mythic West often demonstrated that action and pragmatic solutions would ensure the triumph of good over evil. Even the United States' rise to globalism in the post–World War II era could be viewed as the logical extension of Manifest Destiny. The myth of the West made it clear that America's sense of mission and just cause demanded no retreat and no surrender.

The mythic West reflected and reinforced the public's wish for consensus and conformity in the cold war era. It espoused traditional values, such as patriotism and rugged individualism, and endorsed America's traditional patriarchal, white, Anglo-Saxon, Protestant culture. It also provided a safe topic for popular artists working in the shadows of McCarthyism. Even John F. Kennedy saw fit to cloak his domestic program in the western guise of the "New Frontier."

If the mythic West gave some Americans a blueprint for solving the era's problems, it offered others the means to avoid modern crises. For many the myth of the West served the same function as always: it provided vicarious thrills and escape from troubled times while representing continuity with the nation's alleged "Golden Age." By identifying with the mythic West Americans could rest assured that the American character had not changed, despite increased urbanization, industrialization, technology, and militarism. Americans could conform more easily to the consensus behavior of the 1950s and early 1960s knowing that the mythic West guaranteed their individualism. Songs and other pop culture products about the mythic West were welcome reminders that despite all the changes that the United States had gone through since World War II, the American character was still the same.

After the mid-1960s rock and pop music continued to make extensive use of images of the American West. The biggest change, however, was the emergence of a new duality in portrayals of the West. To be sure, the more traditional images of the mythic West were still there. Pop and rock continued to deal with exotic western landscapes, cowboys, Indians, and other romantic western characters, and the West was still portrayed as a source of happiness, freedom, and opportunity. Nonetheless, traditional western songs were joined by newer songs that either challenged the mythic West or used traditional western images in new ways to critique American society and culture.

The first category—songs that continued to glorify the mythic West—remained extremely popular after 1965. Following the lead of earlier pop music, numerous songs from this era praised the geographic West as a source of happiness. California remained for many the primary source of the myth. The Beach Boys' formula California sound produced hit records such as "Do It Again" (1968), "California Saga (On My Way to Sunny Californ-i-a)" (1973), and *Endless Summer* (1974), an album that included all their greatest hits about California's sun and fun. The Mamas and the Papas' million-seller "California Dreamin'" (1966) reinforced the notion that California was the land of milk and honey. Noting the dreary skies and cold winters of the East, the lead singer concludes wistfully, "I'd be safe and warm if I was in L.A."[18]

The rise of the counterculture in the mid-1960s provided a more sophisticated and alternative image of California as a Garden of Eden. Extending the traditional search for the mythic West, the Haight-Ashbury district of San Francisco became a hippie paradise drawing thousands of youths westward in search of opportunity, peace, love, freedom, and spiritual salvation. The hippies' back-to-basics philosophy might even be interpreted as a conservative return to the life-styles and freedoms associated with the western ideal. Although the hippie movement may have been as much a generational or temporal phenomenon as a regional or spatial one, and although pockets of the counterculture existed throughout the United States, the spiritual center of the movement remained California, especially San Francisco.[19]

The belief that California was a Garden of Eden was implicit in much of the music produced on the West Coast during these years. Scott McKenzie's 1967 hit "San Francisco" described the peace and love that could be found on the West Coast and reminded listeners that if they were going to attend a "love-in" scheduled for San Francisco in the summer, they should wear flowers in their hair. Such songs not only reflected listeners' dreams but sometimes motivated action. Throughout 1967 many young people, inspired by rock lyrics about the West Coast nirvana, traveled to Haight-Ashbury from all over the country, eager to participate in the Summer of Love.[20]

Pop and rock music explored other areas besides California in search of the mythic West. There were songs about Colorado, Texas, Nebraska, Arizona, Oregon, Wyoming, and other areas of the trans-Mississippi West.[21] Colorado in particular frequently served as the new El Dorado. The high priest of the new Colorado utopia was a young man named Henry J. Deutschendorf Jr. Taking his stage name from the place he sang about, he gained fame as John Denver.

In 1972 Denver's song "Rocky Mountain High" helped to establish Colorado's image as a new Garden of Eden. Denver's lyrics conveyed spiritual regeneration as he sang exuberantly but reverently about Colorado's sky, mountains, and natural beauty: "It's a Colorado Rocky Mountain high, I've seen it rainin' fire in the sky." Tinged with a country and western flavor, the song had an upbeat melody, crisp tone, and clear vocal, all of which evoked the simplicity and beauty of a benign, if not benevolent, natural western environment.[22] This western utopia, unspoiled by humans, boasted green forests, bubbling brooks, and clean air. It was the perfect environment for Americans who had just recently discovered ecology as the antidote for industrial pollution.

The tremendous popularity of songs about Colorado and the West suggests that by the 1970s many Americans were beginning to sense that California might not be the answer to their problems after all. But, if the California Dream was over, the dream of finding happiness elsewhere in the West continued. Like prospectors from the previous century, Americans of the 1970s and 1980s turned away from California in search of new opportunities in the Rockies, the Sun Belt, or other more rural areas of the West. These changing perceptions translated into new migration patterns that saw relatively more Americans moving to Arizona, Utah, and Colorado instead of California.

Whereas some rock and pop songs of this era focused on the geographic West, others spotlighted colorful western characters or images. Numerous songs conveyed stereotypical images of the Wild West, gunfighters, prospectors, and noble "Red Men."[23] The cowboy, in particular, remained a popular subject for hits on the pop charts. James Taylor used the cowboy's romantic image quite effectively on "Sweet Baby James" (1970), a plaintive ballad about a lonesome young cowboy tending his herd. Glen Campbell tapped listeners' collective memory of cowboys and rodeos with his million-seller "Rhinestone Cowboy" (1975). Bon Jovi's heavy metal classic "Wanted Dead or Alive" (1987) used the traditional cowboy/gunslinger image to explore the loneliness of rock and roll singers on the road. Even the original singing cowboy, Gene Autry, returned to the top of the pop charts in 1993 with "Back in the Saddle Again," from the soundtrack of the movie *Sleepless in Seattle.*[24]

Bob Dylan, the poet laureate of the rock world, was another popular artist who frequently turned to mythic western figures for inspiration. Dylan's 1968 album *John Wesley Harding* used the legendary gunman/outlaw to symbolize western individualism and justice. In 1975 Dylan released "Lily, Rosemary, and the Jack of Hearts," an intriguing musical mystery about a murder that occurs during a bank robbery in a typical western town. Dylan used familiar images of saloons, gamblers, romance, shoot-outs, and getaways so effectively that some Hollywood producers considered making the song into a movie.[25] Dylan returned again to western images in 1992 when he recorded "Diamond Joe," a traditional folk song about cowboys and the Old West.

Groups with western-influenced names also kept alive images of the mythic West: there were the Outlaws, the Cowboy Junkies, Cochise, the James Gang, Pure Prairie League, Kansas, the New Riders of the Purple Sage, Crazy Horse, the Eagles, Cymarron, and Rick Nelson and the Stone Canyon Band, to name just a few (fig. 7.1).

The existence of such groups and songs glorifying the mythic West is not surprising, since that tradition goes back to the nineteenth century. What is surprising is the number of pop and rock songs after 1965 that ran counter to traditional images of the American West.

By the late 1960s and early 1970s some rock artists and rock music fans were beginning to question the reputation of California and the West as a Garden of Eden. Many young Americans, disheartened by American politics, the Vietnam War, the shootings at Kent State, and the fading of the counterculture, grew more cynical and decided that the "greening of America" was not going to occur—not even in the West. Their disenchantment with the promises of the mythical West was reflected in various songs. Dion's 1971 hit "Sanctuary" mirrored the changing times: "Well I got to Haight, I was a little late, it was an ended dream I found." Albert Hammond's 1972 recording "It Never Rains in Southern California" also expressed disbelief in the mythic West. The lyrics told of a young man who headed for California, believing it was the land of eternal sunshine and happiness. One disappointment after another forces him to conclude, "It never rains in California . . . it pours, man, it pours."[26]

The most significant rejection of California as the focal point of the mythic West can be found in *Hotel California*, the Eagles' award-winning album of 1976. Its title song alluded first to the Garden of Eden myth: "Plenty of room at the Hotel California / Any time of year, you can find it here." It ended with an indictment of the California Dream. The Eagles' dissatisfaction with California and its life-styles was evident as they sang, "We are all just prisoners here of our own device."[27]

The *Hotel California* album expressed the hopelessness and anomie many youths felt during the mid-1970s. Young Americans had every reason to feel betrayed. The assassinations of John and Robert Kennedy and Martin Luther King Jr. shattered their naïveté. The Vietnam War killed off their friends and heightened generational conflict. The Johnson and Nixon presidencies persecuted them. Watergate disillusioned them. The OPEC oil embargo threatened their consumerism and America's affluent society. Throughout all those crises, however, the illusory West had promised hope and happiness. Consequently, the Eagles' despair on learning that even California was a lie was hardly surprising.

The Eagles reflected the nether side of the California Dream—a countertheme that has long existed in the American mind. One of the

Figure 7.1. Western influences are common in rock music. By the early 1970s, even former teen idol Rick Nelson was wearing fringed leather jackets and cowboys boots, while leading a country rock group called the Stone Canyon Band. (Richard Aquila Collection.)

dangers of the California Dream, according to scholar Kevin Starr, always has been its "obsession with self-fulfillment." California's image as the land of opportunity, health, and happiness created unrealistic expectations and ultimately despair for many Californians. The Eagles' bitterness with the California Dream, as reflected in *Hotel California*, is not a new phenomenon. The sad realization that California was not the land of milk and honey was evident at least a century earlier. As Kevin Starr points out, the protagonist in Walt Whitman's "Facing West from California's Shores" looks out across the Pacific, where westward movement had begun generations before. The earth had been circled, but still no one had found utopia, leading Whitman's sad and lonely figure to ask, "But where is what I started for so long ago . . . and why is it yet unfound?"[28] For Whitman, then, and the Eagles in 1976, California had no answer.

Later songs showed similar dissatisfaction with lands of the mythic West. Bruce Springsteen used the bleakness of the western landscape to establish a hopeless mood on recordings such as "Badlands" (1978) and "Nebraska" (1982). The Eagles' "Tequila Sunrise" (1973) placed broken dreams and loneliness in a western setting, and the Bodeans' "Red River" (1989) provided a new twist to the traditional "Red River Valley" tale. In the Bodeans' dark version the narrator not only loses his love but witnesses her drowning suicide.[29]

Along with rejecting alleged locations of the mythic West, pop and rock music after the mid-1960s often used traditional western images in new ways to critique contemporary American society and culture. Neil Young's "After the Gold Rush" (1970) and "Heart of Gold" (1972) employed well-known images of prospectors and miners to comment on the failure of the American Dream. "Desperado," a 1974 hit for the Eagles, questioned the "rugged individualism" of cowboys, desperadoes, and other western folk heroes. The Eagles' "Last Resort" (1976) told the sweeping story of America's westward movement, alluding to settlers, Indians, the frontier, and Manifest Destiny. Between the lines we hear a scathing attack on America's contempt for the environment and minorities, as well as the Eagles' dissatisfaction with the American Dream. Even western heroes were not immune to reinterpretation: in Bruce Cockburn's "Kit Carson" (1992) the erstwhile frontier hero was a murderer who exploited the West's native people and resources.[30]

Revised images of Indians also began appearing in rock and popular music after the mid-1960s. The music industry enabled Native Americans to go on record with their versions of the settlement of the West. Buffy Sainte-Marie—a Cree—found success in the mid-1960s and early 1970s with "Now That the Buffalo's Gone" and "My Country 'Tis of Thy People You're Dying," songs that described the atrocities American Indians experienced at the hands of whites. Floyd Westerman, a Sioux, also attracted public attention in the early 1970s with his album *Custer Died for Your Sins,* which like Vine DeLoria's best-selling book of the same name, condemned Anglo-Americans for their mistreatment of Native Americans.

Several rock hits further developed the theme of Native Americans as victims of injustice and oppression. Michael Murphey's "Geronimo's Cadillac" (1975) used a historical anecdote about the famous Apache war chief to question America's treatment of minority groups. Murphey noted with a twist of irony: "We stole their land and we won't give it back, [but] we sent Geronimo a Cadillac." Murphey's downtrodden Indian—a far cry from the comic Indian in Larry Verne's 1960 recording "Mr. Custer"—demonstrated how much American attitudes toward Indians had changed over a fifteen-year period.[31]

After the mid-1960s pop and rock songs also revised images of women in the West. No longer were women treated as passive, secondary figures. Instead, they became more individualistic in songs such as Neil Young's "Cowgirl in the Sand" (1970) or more assertive and sexually liberated on hits such as Appolonia 6's "Sex Shooter" (1984), from Prince's movie *Purple Rain.*

Perhaps most surprising is that even country music—the long-time keeper of the flame for the mythic West—often critiqued the western myth after the mid-1960s.

"Progressive country"—associated with performers such as Tompall Glaser and Kris Kristofferson—was the first country style to find success on the pop charts after the mid-1960s. Country music became even more mainstream following the success of movies such as *Electric Horseman* (1979) and *Urban Cowboy* (1980), leading to the rise of a new generation of country singers including Garth Brooks, George Strait, Clint Black, Dwight Yoakam, Emmylou Harris, and Sweethearts of the Rodeo, who performed in cowboy hats, boots, and other western garb. Riders in the Sky, a comedy singing group that performed in full cowboy regalia, became so popular in the 1990s that they got their own syndicated radio show, as well as a Saturday morning cartoon program.

Significantly the country music recorded by all these performers sent out mixed messages about the mythic West. In most cases the western imagery remained quite traditional. Many country artists found success on the pop charts with songs that glorified various areas of the West. For example, Waylon Jennings made the top forty in 1977 with "Luckenbach, Texas," which applauded the simple, down-home life-styles of rural Texas. Two years later, Jennings's close friend, Willie Nelson, wrote and recorded "Denver," celebrating the Mile High City's western heritage. Nelson compared the "bright lights of Denver" to "ten thousand jewels in the sky" and explained that a man could find a new life there, where he would be judged only by the "look in [his] eye."[32]

Country songs on the pop charts also made use of traditional western stereotypes involving desperadoes, gamblers, gunslingers, and of course, cowboys.[33] Willie Nelson's best-selling album *Red Headed Stranger* (1976) strung together fifteen related songs telling the story of a Montana drifter. The rambling plot was set against a backdrop of western skies, wide-open spaces, romance, honky-tonks, and horses. In 1990 Michael Martin Murphey achieved popular and critical success with *Cowboy Songs,* an album that included familiar ballads such as "Tumbling Tumbleweeds," "Red River Valley," "Home on the Range," and "O Bury Me Not on the Lone Prairie." In addition the phenomenal success on the pop charts of Garth Brooks, Clint Black, and other "hat acts" kept the cowboy image alive into the 1990s.

At the same time country music contained many nontraditional images of the American West. One example can be found in the music of Waylon Jennings, Willie Nelson, and other members of country music's so-called "Outlaw" movement. These country artists were dubbed outlaws in the 1970s because their long hair, clothing, appearances, and musical stylings borrowed heavily from rock and roll.

On one level the Outlaws can be viewed as modern-day social bandits, continuing the outlaw/antihero tradition of legendary bad men like Billy the Kid and Jesse James. On another level, however, the Outlaws must be seen as critics of the mythic West. The performers' appearances and demeanor seemed to question traditional values and images associated with the mythic West, while their music and styles reflected the ambiguous morality and cynicism of an audience that had experienced the divisive Vietnam War, urban unrest, college protests, and Watergate. Some Outlaw songs openly challenged popular western myths. Willie and Waylon joined forces on the 1978 hit "Mammas Don't Let Your Babies Grow up to Be Cowboys," which refuted the romantic image of the cowboy.

More mainstream country artists also recorded nontraditional western songs. The mythic cowboy came under further attack on several hits, including Heather Miles's "Rum and Rodeo" (1992), which suggested that some men destroyed their lives trying to be modern-day cowboys, or Garth Brooks's "The Cowboy Song" (1993), which described the harsh reality of the cowboy's life.

Rugged individualism also was questioned. The Pirates of the Mississippi's 1992 hit "A Streetman Named Desire" criticized the president of the United States for not doing more to help America's homeless, who were poor through no fault of their own. Garth Brooks's "Wolves" (1992) explained how western farmers and ranchers could lose out to nature despite all their hard work and effort.

Even the notion of the mythic West as the bastion of white, male supremacy came under attack. Garth Brooks's music video "The Thunder Rolls" (1990) used common western imagery to explore male infidelity and wife beating. Another Brooks's song, "We Shall Be Free" (1992), argued for racial tolerance; unlike most country music, his recording included a black choir.

Images of western women also began to change in country music after the mid-1960s. Independent individuals such as Emmylou Harris, Rosanne Cash, Sweethearts of the Rodeo, Suzy Bogguss, and other western-influenced female artists replaced the passive ladies found on earlier country and western songs or in B Westerns. Specific songs also depicted women as more independent. Dan Seals's "Everything That Glitters (Is Not Gold)" (1986) focused on one woman whose quest for independence and success made her too self-centered. Rodney Crowell's music video "Even Cowgirls Get the Blues" (1993) presented a more positive image of modern western women, depicting the ability and strength of female rodeo stars.

In short, country music—like other forms of contemporary popular music—now includes a real duality of western images. The nether side of the mythic West has always been present in popular music, but the dark side is now more prominent than ever before.

The mixed messages contained in contemporary popular music suggest several possible conclusions. First, the traditional images of the mythic West found in contemporary pop and rock music reflect continuity in American society and culture. They plug into our collective memory, demonstrating that the mythic West is still very much alive in modern America. Americans cling to the myth for the same reasons they always have. The mythic West not only provides excitement and escape from contemporary social and political change, but it offers advice on how to cope with modern problems. It suggests that if modern-day Americans remain true to rugged individualism and other traditional values associated with the Old West, they, too, can succeed. Pop and rock songs featuring cowboys, Indians, and other traditional images from the pop culture West continue to provide the perfect soundtrack for Americans desperate for a glorious past (fig. 7.2).

Figure 7.2. Jon Bon Jovi, leader of the hard rock band Bon Jovi, assumes a western pose in 1989 to promote his number-one hit, "Blaze of Glory," from the Western film *Young Guns II*. (Photograph by Timothy White from *Rolling Stone*, February 9, 1989. By straight Arrow Publishers, Inc. 1989. All Rights Reserved. Reprinted by permission.)

At the same time the existence of nontraditional images of the American West in popular music reflects change and conflict in modern America. The new, alternative images of the West signal the end of consensus behavior in the post–World War II era. They suggest that many Americans are now in a state of flux, no longer certain of their own identity or future. The new revisionist images are powerful critiques of traditional American myths and values and often reflect concerns about America's foreign and domestic policies.

The new images mirror the emergence of a more pluralistic society and culture after the mid-1960s. Popular music—like all types of popular culture—is an important battleground for cultural politics. Songs are an important means by which various segments of the audience express their identities and agendas. Consequently, it is not surprising that recent pop songs about the American West reflect current public interests in the roles played by women, minorities, and other "outsiders" in American history and culture.

Although the "new" images of the West found in popular music since the mid-1960s resulted from the same historical forces that produced the "new western history," focusing on race, ethnicity, gender, and what historian Patricia Nelson Limerick has called the West's "Legacy of Conquest,"[34] it is significant to note that popular music's critique of the mythic West antedates that of the new western historians. Pop music began offering its audience a revisionist approach to the American West nearly twenty years before the "new western history" raised its voice.

Ever since the late nineteenth century popular musicians have made extensive use of images of the mythic West. In most cases popular music has portrayed the West as a romantic promised land of social, political, and economic opportunity. At the same time, however, the music has always expressed the darker side of the American West, suggesting the false hopes and dashed dreams lurking in the shadows of the mythic West. From the late nineteenth century until the mid-1960s traditional images glorifying the West predominated in popular music, but more recently, these traditional images have had to share the pop music stage with alternative visions that portray the West as a land of violence, oppression, broken promises, and false dreams.

Although the message may have changed over the years, the messenger has remained the same. From the 1800s until the present the American West has been a constant subject in popular music, indicating the powerful grip the mythic West has on the American imagination. Obviously not all Americans have shared equally in the western myth. In fact, it is striking how few African Americans, Hispanics, or other racial or ethnic minorities have recorded songs about the mythic West. What is not certain is whether this indicates that minority groups have been excluded from the myth or merely from participating in its expression.

The changing images of the American West in popular music over the past 150 years demonstrate the malleability and significance of the mythic West in American culture. Each generation has used this shared myth for its own purpose, to define itself and the problems of the nation. Like the inkblots in a Rorschach test, the mythic West has appeared in various shapes and outlines in different eras, yet it remains indelibly printed on America's national psyche.

Notes

1. One of the major sources of American folk music had been the American West. Numerous folk songs originated in cowboy ballads or frontier settings. For examples, see Haines Guy Logsdon, "The Cowboy's Bawdy Music," in *The Cowboy: Six Shooters, Songs, and Sex*, ed. Charles W. Harris and Buck Rainey, 127–38 (Norman, Okla., 1976); John A. Lomax and Alan Lomax, *Cowboy Songs and Other Frontier Ballads* (New York, 1910); and Irwin Silber, ed., *Songs of the Great American West* (New York, 1967).

2. Jim Bob Tinsley, *He Was Singin' This Song: A Collection of Forty-eight Traditional Songs of the American Cowboy, with Words, Music, Pictures, and Stories* (Orlando, Fla., 1981), 212, 126, 12, 184.

3. Tinsley, *He Was Singin' This Song*, 40, 22, 152, 153, 168, 174, 180.

4. Tinsley, *He Was Singin' This Song*, 76, 80. Other songs also captured the gritty realism of the cowboy's life, for example, "The Cowboy's Life (A Dreary, Dreary Life)," "Night Herding Song," "Blood on the Saddle," and "When the Work's All Done in the Fall," found in Tinsley, *He Was Singin' This Song*, 16, 72, 96.

5. Other hits of the early 1900s also focused on colorful western figures. Public demand for cowboy songs guaranteed the success of Charles Siringo's book *The Song Companion of a Lone Star Cowboy* (1919). Western heroism provided the perfect backdrop for Isham Jones's "On the Alamo" (1922). Idealized pioneers were recalled in the Peerless Quartet's "San Francisco Bound" (1913) and Ted Weems's "Covered Wagon Days" (1924). Romanticized Indians appeared in Harry MacDonough's "Navajo" (1904), Billy Murray's "Navajo" (1904), and the American Quartet's "Oh That Navajo Rag" (1912).

6. Robert G. Athearn, *The Mythic West in Twentieth-Century America* (Lawrence, Kans., 1986), 57.

7. Information on Woody Guthrie can be found in his autobiography, *Bound for Glory* (New York, 1943). A solid introduction to his music is provided by Jerome Rodnitzky's *Minstrels of the Dawn: The Folk-Protest Singer as a Cultural Hero* (Chicago, 1976), 43–62. The West as an exotic place where one could find happiness was the premise of songs such as Jimmie Rodgers's "Waitin' for a Train" (1929), Guy Lombardo's "Under a Texas Moon" (1930), Lawrence Welk's "Colorado Sunset" (1938), "Deep in the Heart of Texas," which became a hit record for both Bing Crosby and Alvino Rey and his or-

chestra in 1942, and Bob Wills and his Texas Playboys' "Home in San Antone" (1943). Other songs, such as "Tumbling Tumbleweeds," which became a hit record for the Sons of the Pioneers in 1934 and Gene Autry in 1935, focused on the freedom to be found on the open ranges of the mythic West. Two songs recorded during the 1930s and 1940s by the Sons of the Pioneers—"Cool Water" and "Cowboy Camp Meeting"—described the West as a source of personal and spiritual salvation.

8. Pop songs used a variety of images from the mythic West, for example, romantic images of cowboys: Tommy Dorsey's "Take Me back to My Boots and Saddle" (1935), Gene Olson's "The Last Round-Up" (1933), Art Kassel's "Back in the Saddle Again" (1940), Glen Miller's "Cowboy Serenade" (1941), Freddie Slack's "Cow Cow Boogie" (1942), from the film *Ride 'Em Cowboy*, the Ink Spots and Ella Fitzgerald's "Cow Cow Boogie (Cuma-Ti-Yi-Yi-Ay)" (1944), and Eddy Howard's "Ragtime Cowboy Joe" (1947). The cowboys' wild life-style was frequently in the spotlight. Red Ingle and the Natural Seven enjoyed success singing about the cowboy's weakness for the items mentioned in the title of "Cigarettes, Whuskey, and Wild Wild Women" (1948). Even more popular was the bizarre "Riders in the Sky (a Cowboy Legend)," which used satanic ghosts of cowboys and cattle as a warning to cowboys that they had better abandon their wild ways. It was recorded by numerous performers, becoming a hit for Bing Crosby, Burl Ives, and Peggy Lee in 1949. Gunfights and shoot-outs became the subject of songs such as Al Dexter and his Troopers' comedic "Pistol Packin' Mama" (1943). The Alamo was the subject of the Mills Brothers' "Across the Alley from the Alamo" (1947). Legendary pioneers or their routes inspired Ford and Glen's "Utah Trail" (1929), Bing Crosby's "Lone Star Trail" (1941), Bing Crosby and the Andrews Sisters' "Along the Navajo Trail" (1945), Eddy Howard's "On the Old Spanish Trail" (1947), Frankie Laine's "Mule Train" (1949), Vaughn Monroe and the Sons of the Pioneers' "Mule Train" (1949), and the Sons of the Pioneers' "Wagons West." Western romance was the focus of Bob Wills and his Texas Cowboys' "San Antonio Rose" (1939), the Dinning Sisters' "Buttons and Bows" (a 1948 hit from the film *Paleface*), and Eddy Arnold's "Texarkana Baby" (1948). Finally, popular stereotypes of American Indians can be found on Tommy Dorsey's "Indian Summer" (1939) or Charlie Barnet's "Cherokee" (1939) and "Redskin Rhumba" (1940).

9. Tinsley, *He Was Singin' This Song*, 214, 215.

10. Other hit records about the happiness or freedom to be found in the geographic West include Hank Snow and the Rainbow Ranch Boys' "I'm Movin' On" (1950), Hugo Winterhalter's "Across the Wide Missouri" (1951), and "Tumbling Tumbleweeds," performed by Roger Williams in 1956 and Billy Vaughn in 1958. Songs about colorful western characters also abounded. Gunfighters and cowboys became the subjects of Marty Robbins's popular album of the early 1960s *Gunfighter Ballads and Trail Songs*, while colorful historical events set the stage for the Norman Petty Trio's "On the Alamo" (1954) and Bill Hayes's "Wringle Wrangle," a 1957 hit from the film *Westward Ho the Wagons*.

11. Other examples of rock songs about cowboys include Link Wray and the Raymen's "Raw-Hide" (1959), the Ramrods' "Ghost Riders in the Sky" (1961), the Chipmunks' "Ragtime Cowboy Joe" (1959), and Murray Kellum's "Long Tall Texan" (1963). Several hits alluded to screen Westerns. The Olympics found success in 1958 with "(My Baby Loves) Western Movies," which used gunshots to accent musical beats. In 1962 Gene Pitney had a top-ten hit with "The Man Who Shot Liberty Valance," based on the John Wayne film of the same name. And one of the most famous western heroes on television served as the model for "The Lone Teen Ranger" (1963), recorded by Jerry Landis (who later gained fame under his real name, Paul Simon). The rock audience of the late 1950s and early 1960s listened to numerous other records about the mythic West, including albums such as Bo Diddley's *Bo Diddley Is a Gunslinger* and Marty Robbins's *Gunfighter Ballads and Trail Songs,* and singles such as Johnny Horton's "Commanche" (1960), which told the story of the only survivor of Custer's cavalry, a horse.

12. Larry Verne, "Please Mr. Custer (I Don't Want to Go)" (1960). Other songs also dealt with Indians; for example, attitudes toward mixed bloods became the subject of Marvin Rainwater's "Half-Breed" (1959). The warrior image informed Jorgen Ingmann's "Apache" (1961). Anglo attitudes toward reservation Indians were described on Rex Allen's "Don't Go Near the Indians" (1962).

13. B. Wilson and M. Love, "Surfin' Safari" (Guild Music, 1962).

14. Beach Boys, "Surfin' U.S.A." (1963); B. Wilson, "Surfer Girl" (Guild Music, 1963); B. Wilson, "Warmth of the Sun" (Irving Music, 1964); B. Wilson, "All Summer Long" (Irving Music, 1964); B. Wilson, "Girls on the Beach" (Irving Music, 1964); B. Wilson, "California Girls" (Irving Music, 1965).

15. J. Berry and B. Wilson, "Surf City" (Screen Gems/Columbia Music Co., 1963); R. Berryhill, P. Connally, J. Fuller, and R. R. Wilson, "Wipe Out" (Miraleste and Robin Hood Music, 1963); R. Wilson, "Surfer Joe" (Miraleste and Robin Hood Music, 1963); M. Levy and H. Glover, "California Sun" (Lloyd and Logan, Inc./Norm Music, Inc., 1961).

16. Frank Bergon and Zeese Papanikolas, eds., *Looking Far West: The Search for the American West in History, Myth, and Literature* (New York, 1978), 4, 76, 77; see also Garci Rodríguez Ordonez de Montalvo, *Las Sergas de Esplandián,* trans. E. Hale, "The Queen of California," *Atlantic Monthly,* March, 1864, 266–67.

17. Kevin Starr, *Americans and the California Dream, 1850–1915* (New York, 1973), 417, vii, 13, 25, 46, 68, 418.

18. J. Phillips and M. Gilliam, "California Dreamin'" (Trousdale Music, 1966).

19. For more information about the counterculture and its link to California, see Godfrey Hodson, *America in Our Time* (New York, 1976), especially part 3; Todd Gitlin, *The Sixties: Years of Hope, Days of Rage* (New York, 1987); W. J. Rorabaugh, *Berkeley at War* (New York, 1989); and Theodore Roszak, *The Making of a Counter Culture* (New York, 1969).

20. J. Phillips, "San Francisco" (Wingate Music Corp., 1967). Other records conveyed other aspects of the mythic West. The Sir Douglas Quintet sang about fun and happiness in "Mendocino." Eric Burdon and the Animals captured the feel of the counterculture, mystic rebirth, and the opportunity that was available on the West Coast in two hit records in 1967, "San Francisco Nights" and "Monterey." In 1968 Johnny Rivers achieved success with his *Realization* album, which included "Goin' Back to Big Sur," a mystical recording about the natural beauty and regenerative influence of the California coast.

21. Some performers noted that the West in general offered hope, for example, Del Shannon, "Keep Searchin' (We'll Follow the Sun)" (1965), or Rick Nelson, "Easy to Be Free" (1969). Others looked to specific geographical areas of the West for hope or escape, for example, Texas (Dean Martin, "Houston" [1965]; Glen Campbell "Galveston" [1969]); Nebraska (Moby Grape, "Omaha" [1967]); the Southwest (Glen Campbell, "By the Time I Get to Phoenix" [1967]; the Eagles, "Peaceful Easy Feeling" [1973]); Wyoming (Neil Young, "The Emperor of Wyoming" [1969]); Oregon (the New Riders of the Purple Sage, "Portland Woman" [1971]); Colorado (Johnny Rivers, "Summer Rain" [1967]; James Hendricks "Summer Rain" [1967] and *The Songs of James Hendricks* [1968]).

22. J. Denver and M. Taylor, "Rocky Mountain High" (1972). Other examples of the Colorado sound include Mary Travers, "I Guess He'd Rather Be in Colorado" (1971); James Hendricks, "Summer Rain" (1967) and *Songs of James Hendricks* (1968); the Flying Burrito Brothers, "Colorado"; and the country rock of groups like Firefall and Toby Beau. A good example of a mainstream rock and roll song that dealt with Colorado is Joe Walsh's "Rocky Mountain Way" (1973).

23. The excitement of the West set the stage for Elton John's million-selling album of 1971, *Tumbleweed Connection,* as well as the Escape Club's number-one hit of 1988, "Wild Wild West" and Kool Moe Dee's rap song "Wild Wild West" (1988). The gunfighter image was behind Cher's "Bang Bang (My Baby Shot Me Down)" (1966), Andy Kim's "Shoot 'Em Up, Baby" (1968), and Bon Jovi's "Blaze of Glory" (1990). The search for gold in the American West provided the setting for the New Riders of the Purple Sage's "Sutter's Mill" (1974) and John Stewart's "Gold" (1979). Romanticized Indians were recalled in the Yardbirds' "Ten Little Indians" (1967), Elton John's "Indian Sunset" (1971), the Sugarhill Gang's rap song "Apache" (1982), Dan Fogelberg's "Spirit Trail" (1990), and the Cult's heavy metal hit "Wild Hearted Sun (Where Do You Want Me to Run)" (1992). Wild horses provided traditional western imagery for the Rolling Stones' "Wild Horses" (1971), Michael Murphey's "Wild Fire" (1975), and Poco's "Legend" (1978). Images straight out of B Westerns informed the Standells' "Sometimes Good Guys Don't Wear White" (1966), the Electric Indians' "Keem-O-Sabe" (1969), Jim Croce's "Don't Mess around with Jim" (1972), War's "Cisco Kid" (1973), Oscar Brown Jr.'s "Lone Ranger" (1974), and the Marshall Tucker Band's "Last of the Singing Cowboys" (1979). One of the last real singing cowboys—

Roy Rogers—found some success on the rock and pop charts with "Hoppy, Gene, and Me" (1974), a nostalgic song about old-time screen cowboys that struck a responsive chord in the collective memory of aging baby boomers.

24. Traditional images of cowboys could be found on other records, for example, the Byrds, *Sweetheart of the Rodeo* (1968); James Taylor, "Sweet Baby James" (1970); Sonny and Cher, "A Cowboy's Work Is Never Done" (1972); John Denver, "I'd Rather Be a Cowboy" (1973); the Marshall Tucker Band, "This Ol' Cowboy" (1974); Paul Davis, "Ride 'Em Cowboy" (1974); the New Riders of the Purple Sage, *Gypsy Cowboy* (1972); the Amazing Rhythm Aces, "The End Is Not in Sight (the Cowboy Tune)" (1976); Aerosmith, "Back in the Saddle" (1977); Linda Ronstadt, "I Ride an Old Paint" (1979); John Denver, "The Cowboy and the Lady" (1981); Dan Seals, "God Must Be a Cowboy" (1984); and Boys Don't Cry, "I Wanna Be a Cowboy" (1986). The Baja Marimba Band found success with a remake of "Ghost Riders in the Sky" (1966), as did the Outlaws in 1980—whose name itself echoed themes of the West.

25. Bob Dylan, "Lily, Rosemary, and the Jack of Hearts" (Rams Horn Music, 1974). In 1973 Dylan composed the musical score for Sam Peckinpah's film *Pat Garrett and Billy the Kid*.

26. D. Holler, "Sanctuary" (1971); Albert Hammond, "It Never Rains in Southern California" (1972).

27. D. Felder, D. Henley, G. Frey, "Hotel California" (Long Run Music, 1976).

28. Starr, *Americans and the California Dream*, 438, 442, 443.

29. The New Riders of the Purple Sage used traditional western settings on songs such as "Garden of Eden" (1971) and "Last Lonely Eagle" (1971) to condemn the destruction of the environment and lament lost dreams. Other songs also questioned whether happiness could be found in the American West, for example, Dave Loggins, "Please Come to Boston" (1974), and Neil Young, "El Dorado" (1989).

30. Neil Young, "After the Gold Rush" (Broken Arrow Music Publishing/ Cotillion Music, Inc., 1970) and "Heart of Gold" (1972); D. Henley, G. Frey, "Desperado" (W. B. Music/Kicking Bear Music, ASCAP, 1976) and "The Last Resort" (W. B. Music/Long Run Music/Fingers Music, 1976). Other songs also used traditional western images in new ways to comment on modern society. For example, Eric Clapton's version of "I Shot the Sheriff" (1974) treated sheriffs, who previously were viewed as defenders of justice in the Old West, as forces of oppression. Bob Seger's "Against the Wind" (1980) used the cowboy as a metaphor to describe loneliness, despair, and aging. And Don McLean's "Broncho Bill's Lament" (1972) used the B Western as a counterpoint to comment on the emptiness of the mythic West.

31. Michael Murphey, "Geronimo's Cadillac" (Mystery Music, BMI, 1975). For other examples of songs depicting Indians as victims of white oppression, see Europe, "Cherokee" (1987); Robbie Robertson, "Showdown at Big Sky" (1989); Paul Revere and the Raiders, "Indian Reservation (The Lament of the Cherokee Reservation Indian)" (1971); Elton John, "Indian Sun-

set" (1971); Cher, "Half-Breed" (1973); and Neil Young, "Cortez the Killer" (1975).

32. C. Moman and B. Emmons, "Luckenbach, Texas" (1977); Willie Nelson, "Denver" (W. Nelson Music, 1975). Numerous other country songs focused on places in the American West where one could find happiness, for example, Waylon Jennings's "Oklahoma Sunshine" (1974); Eddie Rabbitt's "Rocky Mountain Music" (1976); Dan Seals and Marie Osmond's duet "Meet Me in Montana" (1985); the Bellamy Brothers' "Santa Fe" (1988); Restless Heart's "Bluest Eyes in Texas" (1988); and Little Texas's "God Blessed Texas" (1993).

33. Traditional, romanticized images of mythic western figures were depicted in numerous country songs that gained a wide popular audience, for example, gamblers (Kenny Rogers, "The Gambler" [1979]); cowboys (Larry Dalton and the Dalton Gang, "Cowboy" [1981]; Waylon Jennings, *Honky Tonk Heroes* [1973]; Willie Nelson, "My Heroes Have Always Been Cowboys" [1980]; Garth Brooks, "Wild Horses" [1990]; Toby Keith, "Should Have Been a Cowboy" [1993]; Boy Howdy, "A Cowboy's Born with a Broken Heart" [199]); desperadoes (Willie Nelson, Waylon Jennings, Johnny Cash, and Kris Kristofferson, "Highwaymen" [1988]; Charlie Daniels Band, "Billy the Kid" [1977]; Waylon Jennings, "Ladies Love Outlaws" [1972]). Also, when country purists denounced Waylon Jennings, Willie Nelson, Tompall Glaser, and other members of country music's "Outlaw" movement for incorporating rock styles into their music, rock and pop fans cheered them as rebels in the tradition of Billy the Kid, Jesse James, and other traditional western outlaws/antiheroes.

34. For an introduction to the "new western history" see "Western History: Why the Past May Be Changing," *Montana: The Magazine of Western History,* Summer 1990, 60–76; William Cronon, George Miles, and Jay Gitlin, eds., *Under an Open Sky: Rethinking America's Western Past* (New York, 1992); and Patricia Nelson Limerick, Clyde A. Milner II, and Charles E. Rankin, eds., *Trails: Toward a New Western History* (Lawrence, Kans., 1991).

EIGHT

KENNETH J. BINDAS

Cool Water, Rye Whiskey, and Cowboys: Images of the West in Country Music

GARTH BROOKS'S RECENT song "In Lonesome Dove" (1991) underscores the close connection between country music and western imagery. It is a rambling tale about love, violence, and tragedy in the Old West. The song begins with a pioneer woman being rescued in a rainstorm by a Texas Ranger, whom she later marries. After the lawman is gunned down by desperadoes, the woman raises their son alone. The boy grows up to be a ranger like his father, and at the end of the song he seeks to avenge his father's death in a showdown with the bad guys. When the smoke clears the desperadoes are dead. Although no one is quite sure, the folks of Lonesome Dove suspect that the mother is responsible for shooting the villains to avenge her husband and save the life of her boy.

The song perfectly illustrates the link between the American West and country music. It contrasts the romantic and mythic West with the violent and real one. And though the song's story line may differ somewhat from those of earlier western songs, its tone and imagery are throwbacks to the music and style of the singing cowboys of the 1930s and 1940s. There is a direct lineage between country and western musical pioneers such as Gene Autry, Tex Ritter, or Roy Rogers and current western artists like Brooks, George Strait, Clint Black, and Reba McEntire. Even the appearances of early country and western stars and current "hat acts" are remarkably similar. Pictures of Gene Autry and Garth Brooks show them both wearing oversized hats, flashy western shirts, and boots and employing the same backdrops and props. An evening watching the Nashville channel or the dance show "Whitehorse Cafe" makes obvious the connection between the West and country music.

The West has played a vital role in commercial country music, from its earliest days through the present. Significantly the image of the region presented by country artists, from early stars like Vernon Dalhart to later ones such as Waylon Jennings or Garth Brooks, has often been contradictory. The diverse images of the American West found in country music since the 1920s can be used to examine social forces at work in the United States. Country music's use of the West has reflected and sometimes shaped the historical forces of its times, as well as complex issues of gender, race, ethnicity, and class. Long before the movement toward a "new western history" took place, many country performers were challenging the mythic West and painting a much more diverse and colorful portrait of the region—one perhaps that is more fitting of the grandeur that is the West.

Those who have written about the early history of country music have noted its ties to the early frontier. Bill C. Malone's *Country Music, U.S.A.*—the standard history of country music—explains that hillbilly music evolved out of folk tunes brought by Anglo-Celtic immigrants, albeit with some African American influence, into a viable commercial product for industrial America. To Malone, this frontier experience took place not in the land west of the Mississippi River but east and south. Moreover, the archetypal country performer was not a cowboy singer but a male, Protestant, rural, folk, southern hillbilly musician.[1]

Despite the music's roots on the southern frontier, however, the West has played a significant role in its popularization, acceptance, and longevity. According to a study done by Richard A. Peterson and Marcus V. Gowan, of the 458 country groups whose names appeared in the *Country Song Roundup* in December 1950, roughly half referred to a geographic place in their names, and of those names 60 percent referred to lands west of the Mississippi. Other bands named themselves for an occupation (29 percent), selecting ranching and cowboys by more than three to one.[2] Although Malone believes that the "cowboy contributed nothing to American music," Roy Rogers maintains that the cowboy imbued the music with family and religious values. An interview with Gene Autry supports Rogers's position. Autry explained what he called the "Cowboy Commandments": the cowboy is always kind to children and animals; he never shoots anyone in the back; he is always patriotic, open, truthful, and virtuous; he promotes good will; and he does not drink or smoke. Country music cowboys have generally followed Autry's commandments, departing from them only with regard to the last two.[3]

Previous to the commercial development of what was called hillbilly music in the mid-1920s, cowboy songs and imagery had already captured the imagination of many Americans. Novels by Owen Wister and Zane Grey, silent films such as *The Great Train Robbery* (1903), and song collections from N. Howard Thorp and John A. Lomax helped to make the cowboy and the range he rode a fixture of American culture. As commercial hillbilly music developed, cowboy singers were among the first to record. In 1925 Carl Sprague recorded an authentic cowboy song, "When the Work's All Done This Fall," which proved highly successful. Other cowboy singers, usually singing traditional folk songs of the West and South, also began recording. Performers like Jules Verne Allen, Vernon Dalhart, Goebel Reeves, and Adelyne Hood sang the songs of the cowboy and the range. Some, like Otto Gray and his Oklahoma Cowboys, were recruited right off the ranch and advertised as authentic cowboys who could sing and fiddle. Gray said he tried to bring "back to the present generation the music and songs of the early days of the West."[4] These cowboy singers presented an interesting alternative to down-home hillbilly performers like the Carter Family and Gid Tanner and the Skillet Lickers. Although the latter performers emphasized, at least in the popular mind, a backwoods lack of sophistication, the former symbolized American values threatened by urbanization and industrialization.

As historian Gerald D. Nash has pointed out, the American West had great appeal for Americans of the late nineteenth and early twentieth centuries, who in the midst of great social change and political and economic crises became nostalgic for America's lost "Golden Age" in the West. Between 1890 and 1920, as the United States tried to cope with more rapid industrialization, urbanization, and immigration, as well as World War I, historians, artists, writers, and others involved in the production of popular culture invented a mythic West with agrarian values and a commonsense ideology. From the 1920s through 1945, when the nation faced the trauma associated with the Great Depression and World War II, the image of the West as savior of American values was strengthened, as writers, artists, and others used the romantic image of the West to reinforce American nationalism, individualism, and destiny. Country music and film were especially influential during this period, as the imaginary West gave way to celluloid images and romantic singing cowboy heroes.[5]

Jimmie Rodgers's arrival on the country music scene reinforced western imagery in country music. Rodgers loved to sing and talk about the cowboys and roughnecks who settled Texas. Moreover, his recordings, many of which referred directly to the West, identify one of the principal characteristics of the mythic West in country music: wanderlust. Rodgers, using images of both the West and the railroad on songs such as "Never No Mo' Blues" (1929) and "Waiting for a Train" (1929), established a place in country music for the individual who could not fit into modern society and had to wander in search of the past. This image of the roaming cowboy or hobo would become a constant in commercial country music from the early 1930s until the present.[6]

The rise of radio helped to popularize western-influenced country music. In 1922 Fiddlin' John Carson performed on Atlanta's WSB in what is regarded as the first country broadcast, and within eight years several large-market stations began regularly featuring hillbilly music. Chicago's WLS initiated the *National Barn Dance* in 1924, and by 1930 it had become one of the most successful programs on the station. Sending its signal throughout the Midwest on Saturday nights, it featured old-time music, fiddling, and cowboy tunes and introduced the country to aspiring western singers such as Gene Autry. Nashville's WSM instituted its own version of the barn dance in 1925: the *Grand Ole Opry*. All performers on the live, down-home show dressed in hillbilly costumes and adopted old-time names. Broadcast throughout the South, the *Opry* became a mainstay of country and western music. Other powerful radio stations located in Mexico along the Texas border (called "X" stations) beamed their signals across the Southwest. These also featured cowboy singers and songs. By the time that Jimmie Rodgers became the first true star of country music, a complex radio network covered most of America with hillbilly and western songs.[7]

The stage was set for a breakthrough country performer. That person was Gene Autry. He combined the visual with the aural, firmly connecting early country music to the West. Although Rodgers had introduced the idea of the roaming cowboy, Autry became its embodiment. After establishing himself as a singing radio star on WLS, in 1934 he joined the cast of cowboy actor Ken Maynard's *Old Santa Fe*. The studio had decided on a new twist—the singing cowboy—to check sagging attendance at Western movies. Autry quickly surpassed Maynard's popularity and later in 1935 starred in *Tumbling Tumbleweeds,* which set his career on track. Not only did he become the most popular cowboy star, but by 1940 he was one of the top ten box office attractions in Hollywood. Cowboy and western music now had an image to go along with the sound.[8]

The singing movie cowboy sparked a tremendous demand for cowboy singers and stars. Numerous musicians donned western garb and went to Hollywood to try their luck. The most famous, of course, was

Len Slye, better known as Roy Rogers. An original member of the
Sons of the Pioneers who had worked with Autry, Rogers filled in for
the star during a contract dispute in 1937. Rogers and another singing
cowboy, Tex Ritter, soon became Autry's chief rivals. Their success,
along with that of numerous other minor western movie and recording
stars, gave hillbilly music new credibility. Country music was now
firmly linked to one of America's most revered symbols, the cowboy.[9]

As a result many performers who were not western in any way were
soon adopting the western image. Cowboy hats, boots, vests, and
shirts became the requisite costume for many aspiring country performers, as did western-sounding names like Slim, Tex, or Hank. For
example, Ruby Blevins of Hope, Arkansas, an aspiring guitarist and
fiddler trying to crack the hillbilly music scene, used "Patsy Montana"
as her stage name and achieved success with the classic "I Wanna Be a
Cowboy's Sweetheart" (1935). She was followed by other cowgirl
singers such as Louise Massey, Texas Ruby, and Dale Evans. The western connection proved so successful that it eventually replaced the
somewhat unmarketable hillbilly stereotype. Archie Green has written
that the arrival of the cowboy to hillbilly music gave the musicians a
"ready-made uniform, and, more importantly, an heroic and dramatic
mythology." This new symbol was independent, resolute, intelligent
and the master of his own destiny, good or bad. The cowboy's image
had special relevance for the times. During the depression and World
War II Americans faced back-to-back identity crises. Throughout the
1930s the American people wrestled with the issue of individuality in
the face of the increasing organization of collective government programs. The economic crisis eventually called forth individual responses to the hardships, and although people worked together, it was their
belief in the American Dream that helped them to survive. On the
heels of this crisis World War II asked Americans to sacrifice further, as
the nation launched a crusade against fascism. The war, like the depression, forced Americans to consider notions of individual liberty in relation to societal need. The symbolic cowboy spoke directly to the issue, reminding Americans of who they were and what they stood for.
Whereas classic movies such as *The Petrified Forest* (1936), *Mr. Smith
Goes to Washington* (1939), or even *Gone with the Wind* (1939) reflected the uneasiness of many Americans, the rise of singing cowboys re-
affirmed their belief in rugged individualism and the traditional liberties associated with the mythic West. These values remain part of the
country mystique to this day.[10]

Although many performers adopted the image of the cowboy, few
recorded authentic-sounding western music. As Douglas Green has

written, "western music just didn't seem to sell on record." There were a few exceptions. Along with Autry, Rogers, and Ritter, two groups—the Sons of the Pioneers and Bob Wills and the Texas Playboys—were able to sell western songs. The Sons of the Pioneers had hit records with "Tumbling Tumbleweeds" (1934) and "Cool Water" (1948), and Wills's "San Antonio Rose" (1938) became a classic throughout popular music. The groups used the West differently: the Sons of the Pioneers emphasized the natural beauty of the region, whereas Wills tapped the festive atmosphere of house parties on the southwestern prairies.[11]

Wills's sound and style had more lasting effect than the Pioneers'. By the end of the 1940s Wills's house-party style dominated the country charts, along with another western-influenced style know as "honky-tonk," named after the bars in which it was performed. Although many honky-tonk artists favored western costumes and adopted the cowboy or western image, few sang about the mythic West. Ernest Tubb, Hank Snow, the Willis Brothers, Pee Wee King, and others aimed their music at the migrants who moved out of the South during and after World War II or listeners now working in factories rather than on farms. Despite the presence of Texas honky-tonk performers like Lefty Frizzel, Ted Daffan, and Floyd Tillman, the genre dealt more with truck drivers and barroom scenes than with cattle drives and desert vistas.[12]

The performer most identifiable with honky-tonk was just beginning to make his presence known at about the time that *Billboard* was in the process of relabeling hillbilly to country and western in the late 1940s. Hank Williams, born and raised in Alabama, rarely sang about things western but focused on broken loves, hard living, and infidelity. Nevertheless, he and his group, the Drifting Cowboys, saw themselves as modern cowboys, moving from place to place, trying to eke out an existence in a world that was changing too quickly for them to adapt. When Williams was in his teens he even ran away to Texas to become a cowboy. Although the attempt resulted in a back injury, his admiration for the West remained with him throughout his life. He owned a silver-inlaid saddle, matching Colt .45s, Stetson hats, boots, and elaborately designed and colored fringed suits.

Cowboy suits in particular came to epitomize the post-1945 image of the cowboy. Designed by Nudie Cohen of North Hollywood, California, the sparkling costumes featured sequined vests, pants, and shoes. As a tailor who catered to cowboy actors and later to many country performers, Nudie Cohen helped to shape the image of the cowboy, and perhaps the West, during this time. The flashy excess of his designer cowboy suits somehow seemed to fit the affluence and anxieties of post–World War II America. Just as the mythic West had appeal for Americans of the 1930s and 1940s, it became a patriotic symbol for Americans locked in a struggle against communism in the cold war era. The cowboy suit symbolized the advantages of the American way of life. Through film and later television, the image of the cowboy was bought and sold as an expression of patriotism. Country performers, no less than any other group, eagerly displayed their loyalty. The suits suggested the wealth and opportunity of the free West (taken in two ways), detailed the battles one had to fight for what was right, and served as a uniform in the struggle for containment.[13]

By the mid-1960s many performers within country music began to rebel against this excessive yet impotent cowboy image that was more farce than reality. Proponents of a new Nashville sound sought to distance their music from flamboyant and unsophisticated cowboys and hillbillies in hopes of expanding the country music market. Country had made significant commercial gains since World War II, with many of its largest markets in northern cities. During the 1960s Nashville music producers hoped to secure these burgeoning markets through marketable country songs that would focus more on traditional pop subjects like love, courtship, work, and America and less on truck driving, bar fights, and cheating in love. As a result the glitzy honkytonk cowboy fell on tough times during this period. Although the Bakersfield sound, led by Buck Owens, was making its presence felt in country at the same time, "uptown" country tried to purge itself of its more rustic image.[14]

The cowboy's image suffered in other ways during the tumultuous 1960s. The older, simple stereotype of the cowboy who always wore a white hat and flashy suit while obeying Autry's Cowboy Commandments seemed anachronistic in an era marked by cynicism, anti–Vietnam War demonstrations, urban unrest, and college protests. Instead of being seen as champions of justice, cowboys were more often viewed as the perpetrators of violence, exploitation, and wholesale lawlessness. Many people criticized the cowboy for contributing to the destruction of American Indian cultures, the environment, and the relative harmony that existed between the two in the West. To a nation involved in many social convulsions, the illusion of the righteous cowboy seemed to personify a country that was more interested in how it appeared than how it really was.[15]

The changing image of the cowboy was reflected in country music. By the late 1960s a new type of cowboy emerged, the outlaw. This new antihero often wore a black hat and scruffy jeans and was a heavy-

drinking, dirty, [obscured] This new outlaw was
tough, macho, a[obscured] more
likely to be the [obscured] on of
the singing cow[obscured] ess fit
perfectly the Ar[obscured] when
it seemed unsur[obscured] Vietnam, civil rights[obscured] te, in-
flation, unempl[obscured] estion
the validity of [obscured] veyor
of this destiny, [obscured] ing or
whether his jou[obscured] on and
co-optation of [obscured] led to
relaxed sexual r[obscured] a fashion industry fu[obscured] rsonal
improvement i[obscured] s. The
country was or[obscured]

By the mid-[obscured] sic, led
by the likes of [obscured] r, Kris
Kristofferson, and the Mysterious Rhinestone Cowboy, David Allen
Coe. Although the Outlaw movement was on the rise in country music, however, it never triumphed over more traditional cowboy images. The tremendous popularity of the movie *Urban Cowboy* (1980)
helped to reestablish flashy clothes and white hats. By the 1980s a new
wave of "hat acts," led by George Strait, Garth Brooks, Dwight
Yoakam, Clint Black, Emmylou Harris, Reba McEntire, Carlene Carter, John Michael Montgomery, and many others, used western clothing
and, occasionally, western songs to achieve stardom (see fig. 8.1).
George Strait, who had as much to do with the revival of hat acts in
Nashville as anyone, still promotes himself as a direct descendant of
the real cowboy, working a ranch in Texas and practicing roping steers.
The recent success of Garth Brooks—who always dresses in a cowboy
hat and shirt—is an indication that the mythic West and traditional
images of the cowboy are still profitable in country music.[17]

Thus far I have examined the history of country music to determine
how country and western music came together. Next I selectively examine how the West has been portrayed in some of country music's
classic songs. Country music's history is marked by individual performers, both male and female, who have relied extensively on cowboy
imagery in performances, costumes, and songs. For example, Rosie
Flores recently incorporated the cowboy yodel—"yippie yi oh-ki-
ay"—into her 1993 hit "Honkey Tonk Moon," which described her
desire to kick up her heels under the beauty of the western sky.

Figure 8.1. John Michael Montgomery, one of country music's
most popular "hat acts" of the
mid-1990s. (Courtesy of Atlantic
records.)

The cowboy is the most common western image found in country
music, because his individualism, appearance, and values fit audience
needs. When George H. Lewis asked country music writers what basic guidelines they followed, they agreed that simple and straightforward lyrics had to be the focus of the song. Therefore, most country
songs tend to be ballads, where the narrator tells a story. This format
favors individual performers, such as the cowboy singer, for songs
come to be identified with a particular balladeer. Country music invariably depicts the cowboy as strong yet sensitive. Cowboy heroes
and heroines have the ability to right wrongs and succeed where others fail. Significantly they do not have to be working cowboys. They
must, however, live up to the cowboy aesthetic or attitude, demonstrating rugged individualism, mobility, and a belief in some higher
authority, sometimes called a "code." The cowboy's wanderlust is truly a quest, and whether it is done on horseback, in a tractor-trailer, or
on a dance floor, only the strong survive.[18]

When country was still in its hillbilly stage, most performers tended to utilize cowboy or western images that were generally familiar to
the audience. The songs usually were written by men employed as
cowboys and did little to romanticize either the West or the cowpoke.
Songs such as Carl Sprague's successful "When the Work's All Done
This Fall" (1925) detailed the hard life on the drive and the fear of
death that haunted many workers. Songs recorded by Sprague, Goebel
Reeves, and others reflected an image of the cowboy and the West that
folklorist Richard Dorson has suggested helped to develop the "Code

of the West." These hardworking men liked to drink when their work was done, but they also held strict and respectful attitudes toward God and proper women and saw in their dreary task something meaningful and good that only a few choice men could accomplish.[19]

The strength of this cowboy code of ethics has led some scholars to describe the cowboy in terms more appropriate to the medieval knight. Certainly the visual imagery provided by B Western movies tended to emphasize this symbol over any other, but the knight does not play an active part in country music. Perhaps because country singers have to sell songs to people who are subject to human frailties, to use the image of the knight saving the day, like Roy Rogers, was too difficult to imagine. Even Rogers himself shied away from such songs and tended more toward songs about the open ranges and love. And although Billy Joe Shaver might have wanted to resurrect the cowboy to save the world in "We Are the Cowboys" (1978), very few other country performers saw the cowboy as a knight.

Although most country performers probably agree with the sentiment of Willie Nelson's "My Heroes Have Always Been Cowboys" (1980), they realized that cowboys have human traits subject to the same pressures as other people. The main difference is that the cowboy's natural life had rejuvenating potential. Lost souls could redeem life's meaning if only they could get back to the cowboy's West. Jimmie Rodgers considered Texas his home, although his music took him all over the country. In "Land of My Boyhood Dreams" (1929) he moans over the alienation of the city and wishes he could return to the West and the campfires. In "Yodeling Cowboy" (1929) Rodgers longs for the cowboy's life, where he could be free and the land would impose no law on his person. Another 1930s era song, Tex Owens's "Cattle Call," describes the hardships of a cattle drive yet paints a picture of a happy, free individual in the cowboy. Others songs, such as Leonard Whitcup's "Take Me Back to My Boots and Saddle" (1935), Gene Autry's "Back in the Saddle Again" (1939), and Patsy Montana's "I Want to Be a Cowboy's Sweetheart" (1936), invoke images of the healing powers of the West and the life-style of the cowboy. Out West a person is judged only by his or her ability to survive, and intrusions from the past rarely occur. In Montana's case the song is less about wanting human romance and more about wanting a western romance—she wants to be part of that cowboy West, too.[20]

This trend was not isolated to the 1930s, where romance for the West perhaps could be linked to the depression and a longing for the more secure past. Stuart Hamblen wrote "Texas Plains" in the early 1960s, and he used the same imagery that the depression era singers utilized. He wanted to go back West, away from the city and its progress, to horses, cows, campfire-cooked food, beautiful nights and mornings, and a sense of independence and individuality. Perhaps the most famous use of the West as redeemer of values and ideals came in 1975 when Willie Nelson released his album *Red Headed Stranger* (fig. 8.2). The album tells the story of a young ranch hand in turn-of-the-century Montana who murders his wife and her lover and then flees throughout the region in an attempt to come to grips with his actions. Eventually, through the cleansing powers of the natural environment, loneliness, and the help of God, he rectifies his guilt and is freed from the past.

Although Nelson's character might have liberated himself, he was still considered an outlaw. He does, after all, murder two people. This raises another variation on the cowboy theme: the protagonist in country music is not always on the side of the law, nor is his life always one of acceptance and worship. Often he is an outsider who chooses the lonely life of the open ranges to the company of other people. For example, Tex Ritter's "Rye Whiskey" (1948) warned mothers that a cowboy's life was a hard one and more boys were lost to drink and gambling than saved by any mystical attachment to God. The same theme can be found three decades later in Waylon Jennings and Willie Nelson's classic "Mammas Don't Let Your Babies Grow up to Be Cowboys" (1978). The two country outlaws warned listeners that the life of a cowboy—even a modern one—is full of heartbreak, loneliness, and escape. Ironically, even though the cowboy could rarely stay long in one place, he still attracted women. His wild ways and cocky self-assurance ensured that he would have few companionless nights in town. Lee Clayton's "Ladies Love Outlaws" (1972) told listeners not even to bother trying to explain why women were attracted to outlaws: ladies just could not help themselves.

One of the most prevailing images in country music is the desire to escape, usually from responsibilities, a job, a marriage, or even just the town or city. Peter Thorpe has shown that country artists commonly use several avenues of escape, including drinking, prison, religion, and nostalgia for childhood. But the "simplest and easiest is to flee."[21] The cowboy and the West offered perfect vehicles to escape, either to a nostalgic past or from the drudgery of modern society.

The West, with its open spaces and scenic landscape, was the ideal haven for those on the run. Bob Nolan of the Sons of the Pioneers relished this feature of the West and celebrated it in numerous songs. The natural beauty of the West made it seem that there would always be something better over the next hill. To Nolan and other country sing-

Figure 8.2. Western influences are clearly evident on the cover of Willie Nelson's 1975 album *Red Headed Stranger*. (Ball State University Photo Services.)

ers, this vast cornucopia equaled almost unbridled freedom. What better place to flee from responsibility than out West, where a man's past does not follow him? It may seem that this desire to wander and flee would make the cowboy depressed, but the mood tended to be much more optimistic, as the wanderers viewed themselves in almost religious terms, searching for truth in the West.[22]

One of the most popular of this type of western song is Nolan's "Tumbling Tumbleweeds." Used to launch Gene Autry's career in 1935, the song has become a classic to country musicians and fans alike. It tells the story of a wanderer who leaves his past behind to follow the wind, planting no roots and feeling little for the loss. As a cowboy he is content to follow the sun and the wind, where every day a new world is born. Four decades later Waylon Jennings recorded "Luckenbach, Texas" (1977) with a similar idea in mind, namely, leaving the trappings of the material world behind to be free in the West. Even oft-recorded "Me and Bobby McGee," written by Kris Kristofferson, uses the West as a symbolic place of freedom—the place where Bobby and the narrator part company, each searching for freedom.

The code of free-moving, outlaw-type cowboys included a respect for the West's natural beauty. In Bob Nolan's "Way Out There" the lone wanderer, tossed off a railroad car by detectives, quietly watches the beauty of the western desert where he is abandoned. He is not afraid that perhaps he will meet his death there but is at peace with the stillness he observes in nature. Even Jimmie Rodgers, in "Waiting for a Train" (1929), an otherwise depressing song about the homeless wanderings that occurred in the 1930s, sings that being put off a train in Texas was not all bad because of the surrounding beauty.

The freedom that country performers saw in the West hinged on the natural and unspoiled environment, whether real or imagined. In most cases the vastness of the area tended to dwarf human accomplishments as it celebrated an unnamed, and among the cowboys, an unworshiped God. It is not surprising that these westerners found solace not in churches constructed by men but in nature itself—the beauty of God's creation. In country music there is a heavy reliance on Christian imagery and God, and in the western realm this influence is just as strong. Consider the Sons of the Pioneers' biggest hit, "Cool Water" (1948), and the religious imagery of the green tree that awaits all those who search for truth. This symbol of the eternal satisfies the thirst of the rider and his horse, who ignore the devil's trickery and stay true to the Christian path.[23]

In most of the country songs that apotheosize the natural West, the good-versus-bad dichotomy that is so easily discernible in Nolan's composition is absent. Most tend to paint the West as a natural utopia, where the wind blows free, to paraphrase Carson Robison's often-recorded "Carry Me back to the Lone Prairie," and where one is closer to God than anywhere else on Earth. Nat Vincent's "When the Bloom Is on the Sage" (1930) invokes a similar image of a free and natural West. This rover longs to return to Texas, where he believes this utopia exists, but one senses from the song that he cannot return and therefore is destined simply to pine for the West. More recently, on Michael Murphey's *Cosmic Cowboy* album in the early 1970s, songs such as "Rolling Hills" and "South Canadian River Song" celebrated the natural beauty and pristine qualities of the West. Murphey, like

Nolan before him, saw something benevolent in the nature of the West, something early country singer Jack Guthrie also understood. Guthrie's "Oklahoma Hills" (1945) tells the sad tale of a man who wanders far from his Oklahoma home and longs to return to that special western place where man and nature coexisted. For Gail Davies's "Unwed Fathers" (1985), this free and isolated place was the perfect metaphor for those males fleeing the responsibilities of fatherhood.

This nature sometimes conjured up images of potential wealth or long-lost love. Jack Guthrie, in "Oklahoma Hills," longs for the oil wells and the cotton fields as much as he does for his pristine environment. Johnny Horton's "North to Alaska" (1960) tells of two prospectors in the Klondike gold rush of the early 1890s. The song mentions the beauty of the mountains and streams where the gold is found, but the focus is more on what comes out of them and the lack of fulfillment the gold provides. We do not learn whether the protagonist ever forsakes gold for his love, but odds are that if he was taking out chunks, he stayed while pining away for her in the local saloons. At the same time, the natural West is often used to rediscover love. This seems especially true of Texas, which has had more than its share of love songs. The often-recorded "Deep in the Heart of Texas" tells of beautiful stars and landscape, all of which remind the narrator of the one he loves. Even Bob Wills's classic "San Antonio Rose" uses the natural beauty of the Texas environment to express angst over the loss of a love.

Perhaps the loss of love only underscores the delusion that many country performers saw as their West. Kevin Starr, Roderick Nash, and others have pointed out that the western mystique has blurred the reality of urbanization, pollution, and exploitation, both human and environmental. The unrealistic nature of the mythic West found in America's popular culture has set the region and most of its people up for a fall, for the West can never live up to its myth.[24] Country music rarely dealt with the real West in the period before the 1960s, favoring the mythic version popularized by the singing cowboys of the 1930s. When negative portrayals of the West surfaced, they were usually cowboy oriented and dealt with either a gunfight or occupational hazards. Marty Robbins's "El Paso" (1959) tells the story of a man who kills for his love and then dies for one last look. Still, Robbins's cowboy is depicted as noble, while the violence, which makes up a part of the West, is dismissed as just part of the romance. The same is true of Johnny Cash's "Don't Take Your Guns to Town" (1959), only this time it is a mother warning her son not to try to be the mythic cowboy. Of course, he does not listen. As he lies dying, all he can say is that he should have obeyed his mother. Once again, the story details senseless murder, but the heartstrings are pulled not for his death but for his eternal love for his mother. In the end the young cowboy seems destined to be sacrificed for the romantic, western dream. Consider within this scenario Al Dexter's "humorous" song "Pistol Packin' Mama" (1944), which details a double murder by a scorned woman. No comment on the violence or the reasons for the murderess's actions is offered, only the observation that one more honky-tonking man is dead in the mythic West.

This tendency to accept the romanticized violence of the mythic West changed dramatically in the 1960s, as many performers became disillusioned with the West, especially California. There had been some earlier attempts to depict a truer image of the West, most notably on some of Tex Ritter's songs, especially "Blood on the Saddle" (1936). This bloody song depicts what happens when a bronco falls on a young wrangler's head. He's dead. No romance, no great cause, just blood all around. Another noteworthy country songwriter who spoke of a less romantic West was Woody Guthrie. Depression era songs like "Do Ri Me," "Talking Dust Bowl Blues," "Pastures of Plenty," and "I Ain't Got No Home in This World Anymore" reflected Guthrie's belief that much of the mythic West was an illusion designed to distract people from the realities of American society. In a way "This Land Is Your Land" is Guthrie's statement of what he believed the West, and by extension the entire country, should be like.

Those in the 1960s and 1970s who saw the West in less glorious terms were following the disillusioned Guthrie model. Like Guthrie before them, they came to realize that the mythic West was just an illusion. George Jones and Tammy Wynette exposed the harsh reality of the California Dream on their song "Southern California" (1977), demonstrating that fortunes are not easily made and that many people wait their entire lives for a break that never comes. A similar theme is expressed in Mickey Newbury's "San Francisco Mabel Joy" (1969), where a young man of fifteen leaves Georgia for the West, only to wind up cold and hungry. He is saved by a prostitute from Los Angeles, another castoff, and the two begin a love that is destined to fail. He ends up in jail and then dies, while she wanders back to Georgia in search of him.

Some songs focused on the harshness of the western landscape, but others questioned the new breed of western settlers. Merle Haggard's "Okie from Muskogee" (1969) praised traditional westerners and their fondness for patriotism, alcohol, and leather while condemning San Francisco hippies who used drugs, wore their hair long, and questioned authority. For Haggard, the West of his youth, made up of Roy

Rogers, the Lone Ranger, and a host of others, was being destroyed by these new western hippies. Like the mythic cowboy he so desperately admired, Haggard stepped forward to save his western community, and by extension, the whole country.

In the 1970s, stimulated by the Austin music scene and the mixing of rock and country in the late 1960s, a new cowboy rode into country's imagination. While Willie Nelson and Waylon Jennings presented the outlaw image, others like Michael Murphey, Emmylou Harris, Guy Clark, Jerry Jeff Walker, and the New Riders of the Purple Sage produced a modern cowboy that Murphey half-jokingly labeled the "Cosmic Cowboy." This new version of the standard country image was no longer self-assured and happy about his life of wandering and flight. This modern cowboy, mirroring the lack of American confidence at the time, was filled with self-doubt, questioned his fear of responsibility, and saw in his past the reminder of what was disappearing, or worse, what might have never been. "Lonesome LA Cowboy" (1973), by the New Riders of the Purple Sage, depicts an urban cowboy at odds with his own image and living a life that seems devoid of any mythic quest or heroic deeds. Later this theme would help to rejuvenate the cowboy image in popular music as a result of the John Travolta movie *Urban Cowboy* (1980). Nevertheless, the New Riders' and Travolta's cowboy was a far cry from earlier ones and seemed desperate to retain his image of the mythic West in the face of life's realities. The same is true of the westerner who appears on "Desperadoes" (1973), a Guy Clark song recorded by Jerry Jeff Walker. The narrator relates a tale about his grandfather, an original westerner who recalls stories of days gone by and of the disappointment of the present. There is no glory in death for this aged oil rigger, for he must close his eyes and imagine the past to die peacefully. The same theme is present in Cindy Walker's "Dusty Skies" (1970), which uses the time-tested image of the cowboy rancher to describe the environmental hardships of ranching. The story tells of a cattle rancher who is forced to move his cattle because the water and the grass are gone, never to return. The song ends with the cowboy bidding farewell to the blue skies that once made up the West.

As country music moved through the 1980s, the cowboy image came full circle. Newer acts, like George Strait, Randy Travis, Clint Black, and Garth Brooks, seemed to revive the mythic cowboy, albeit in an updated form. This modern cowboy works at a regular job all day but at night kicks up his heels and enjoys a freewheeling life.

For millions of Americans, the image of the cowboy became fashionable in the 1980s—not the rough-and-tumble look of Willie Nelson and his outlaw crowd but a cleaner look more like Strait, Black, and

Brooks. Gerald A. Schorin and Bruce G. Vanden Bergh examined American advertising in the late 1970s and early 1980s to determine its role in this western revival. Although their study revealed that ads neither set nor followed the trend, it also demonstrated that American consumers and fashion designers, like Ralph Lauren, saw in the image of the cowboy—jeans, boots, cotton shirt, hat, and shortish hair—a distinct American fashion. As one retailer reported, the western look, stressing individualism and independence, was a "very proud look."[25]

The image of the West, personified by the image of the cowboy, once again became rife with myth. These modern cowboys ride in Broncos, Blazers, or pickup trucks and purchase all the cowboy accouterments worn by their favorite country singers. Many performers, such as Strait and Chris LeDoux, are still cowboys who rope cattle, but in a modern way, at the rodeo. Garth Brooks's recent hit "Rodeo" (1991) details this rough, yet intrinsically valuable, lifestyle. And although LeDoux paints a true picture of the hardships of being a modern cowboy in the song "So You Want to Be a Cowboy" (1991), he admits that he's still "Hooked on an 8 Second Ride" (1992). Will Wright has argued that the western myth, because of its popular acceptance, must "appeal to or reinforce the individuals who view it by communicating a symbolic meaning to them." The revival of the cowboy image during the 1980s and early 1990s reflects in many ways the conservative resurgence that took place during this time period. Historian Richard White argues that the rise of Ronald Reagan and the New Right in the 1980s can be viewed, at least in part, as a reaction to the political and social convulsions of the 1960s. The New Right appealed to troubled Americans by advocating a return to rugged individualism and other traditional values associated with the West.[26] The same argument might also help to explain the newfound popularity of country music in the 1980s. Country music cowboys—like New Right politicians—promoted individualism and traditional western values as solutions to personal and societal problems.

Country music not only presented conflicting images of the West; it also mirrored Americans' ambivalent attitudes toward gender, race, ethnicity, and class. Country music's treatment of women has changed the most in recent years, perhaps reflecting corresponding changes in the role of women in American society since 1945. Prior to 1945 the role of women in country music was limited to mother/sister, sweetheart, or buddy. Women who contributed to country usually conformed to traditional country standards, which dictated that a woman's status was derived from her ability to catch and hold onto a man. Dale Evans personified this image of the western woman most clearly. As Roy Rogers' wife and costar she played a role limited to that of helpmate, fixer, and comforter to the star. Her identity was merged with that of her man. At the same time there were always some exceptions of women who were more independent. For example, in Adelyne Hood and Vernon Dahlhart's skit "Alaskan Ann and Yukon Steve," Hood portrays a woman equal to any man, as does Patsy Montana in the song "I Wanna Be a Western Cowgirl" (1939).

After World War II, perhaps reflecting gains women made during the war and in direct contrast to the renewed domestication of women in the 1950s, even more female country singers began to adopt a critical view of their role in American society, especially as it referred to their sexuality. Kitty Wells's "It Wasn't God Who Made Honky Tonk Angels" (1952) sounded the alarm for women in country to begin to challenge their subordinate status and take on a more independent, western outlook. These newer women took responsibility for their actions, found satisfaction in their less traditional roles, and found no ambiguity with the love-'em-and-leave-'em stereotype of the "fallen" woman. Those who followed Wells, like Rose Maddox, Patsy Cline, Norma Jean, and Loretta Lynn, offered new, more liberated images of women in country music, providing an alternative approach to Wanda Jackson's "Right or Wrong" (1961) or Tammy Wynette's "Stand by Your Man" (1968), both of which maintained that regardless of the man's mistakes, the woman's place was by his side.[27]

"Anytime a woman has success," notes Emmylou Harris, "it's going to open more room for other women." The commercial success of independent women in country music of the 1950s and 1960s, and the rise of the women's liberation movement in the 1970s, led to even more liberated women in country music. Many of them used western themes to display their newfound assertiveness. For example, Harris's "To Daddy" (1978) told the story of a woman who left her husband after raising the children to search for her own happiness. The album cover itself invoked the West by picturing a quarter moon shining over what appeared to be the desert. The new role of women in country did not come easy or without resistance, however. For one thing, many female consumers, who made up nearly 80 percent of the market in the 1970s, still favored traditional, male cowboy performers. As a result most record companies were reluctant to contract more than a handful of women. As recently as 1992 only 30 percent of the country acts on the major labels were women. The lack of opportunity also applied to other aspects of the industry, including engineering, production, and promotion.[28]

Now, however, with newer performers such as Harris, K. T. Oslin, Pam Tillis, Mary Chapin Carpenter, Suzy Bogguss, or Reba McEntire (who used to ride in rodeos and adopted the western image early in her career), the faux traditional stereotype of the early country woman finally seems to be on the wane. The new country women have adopted the same western attitude that men always had, focusing on control, independence, and freedom. Mary Chapin Carpenter does not sit home and wait for her man but in "I'm Goin' out Tonight" (1991) sets out to find a man who can give her what she needs. Suzy Bogguss is another woman who regularly uses western imagery and ideology in her songs. Her 1989 debut album, *Somewhere Between,* produced by Wendy Waldman, who previously worked with Linda Ronstadt and Emmylou Harris, featured a remake of and tribute to Patsy Montana's "I Wanna Be a Cowboy's Sweetheart." On other releases she dresses in western garb and sings about rodeo riders, love, and independence. Others such as Kelley Willis, the Judds, and Sweethearts of the Rodeo regularly use both western imagery and themes in their music; more and more of country's women are appropriating the cowboy look for their own.

Traditional images of women are still common in country music, however, reflecting ambivalent attitudes toward women in contemporary America. Although more women are now recording country music, Karen Saucier reminds us in her sample study of 1981 top-forty country song lyrics that the portrayal of women has changed little since the 1950s. Few lyrics discuss women's careers, and the lyrics usually refer to women only in terms of dependent relationships. According to Saucier, country music lyrics continue to reinforce the notion that a woman's best way to raise her status is through a man. Moreover, even though the percentage of gold and platinum records is higher for women than for men, males still make up two-thirds of the recording companies' rosters.[29]

What makes the rise of women in recent country music all the more interesting is that country music has usually tended to reflect and accept conservative values and attitudes. This can be seen in a number of areas, including the music's staunch patriotism, its continuing view of women as lovers, vixens, or mothers, and particularly its appeal to "average" working Americans. Country music, since its very beginning, has been identified with the working classes. Its increase in popularity after World War II came as a result of southern and rural migrants moving to urban areas of the North and West in search of employment. Although country music has expanded its market since the 1960s to include a geographically and an economically more diverse consumer, it has retained its fundamental blue-collar identity.

Country music has tended to appeal to urban and rural whites between the ages of twenty-five and forty-nine who work in crafts or as skilled and unskilled laborers. These consumers often seek in their music a reaffirmation of beliefs in God, country, and their sense of individual worth and value. As John Buckley convincingly argues, country music does not sway its listeners but rather offers them a "symbolic world" with which they can identify.[30]

The world of commercial country music, adds Melton A. McLaurin, is made up of "working-class whites, whether farmers or factory hands." The West plays a central role in this class identity, for the cowboy's life and attitude always revolved around the transient nature of his job. The romantic wandering cowboy of country music had his grounding in true economic instability, and this theme has remained constant in the genre's lyrics, even though the job has changed. The same attitudes that the cowboy expressed toward his life and work are now found throughout country music. For example, in the late 1960s Merle Haggard became a spokesman for working-class country music with songs such as "Working Man's Blues." Brooks and Dunn's 1991 hit "Boot Skootin' Boogie" tells of a workingman's desire to get through his workday so that he can put on his cowboy clothes and go dancing. The cowboy often did his job without love or malice, and for many who now labor in America's factories, offices, or trucks and who choose to view themselves in this same manner, country music has provided an escape.[31]

Country music has also maintained traditional attitudes toward minorities and ethnic groups. The music's white, Anglo-Celtic roots and formula have changed little over the years, and its treatment of ethnics and African Americans, although not hostile, has usually bordered on benign neglect. Few ethnic or minority acts have been successful on the country charts, and although the names of Charley Pride and Freddie Fender regularly make the rounds as examples of country music's diversity, the lack of minority performers beyond those two suggests that the music is either not attractive to minorities or that non-Anglo performers do not appeal to typical country consumers.

Ever since country music's inception, the West and its people have played a fundamental role in the music's popularity and ideology. In every period of its history, performers have shaped the West to fit their needs and used the music to comment on the tensions, fears, and values of American society and culture. Country music has always appealed to a distinct set of people, reflecting particular attitudes, mores, and beliefs. As a result the music provides a window through which cultural historians can view specific groups in America's recent past. Changing images of the West mirror the changing times and various historical forces, as well as complex issues involving gender, race, ethnicity, and class. Significantly country music questioned the mythic West long before the "new western history" ever did. Nonetheless, consumers of the music have repeatedly demonstrated their preference for the mythic cowboy and West, even in the face of evidence that demonstrates that the West was made up of more than cool water, rye whiskey, and cowboys. To this day many country music consumers cling to the mythic West as the last refuge for American individualism.

Notes

I wish to thank the following individuals, who helped to define the limits of this essay or who commented on early drafts: Kenneth Noe, Karen Saucier Lundy, and Richard Aquila. A special thanks to Molly Mason, a student who loaned me her coveted Garth Brooks albums.

1. Bill C. Malone, *Country Music, U.S.A.,* rev. ed. (Austin, Tex., 1985), 1–28.

2. Richard A. Peterson and Marcus V. Gowan, "What's in a Country Music Band Name," *Journal of Country Music* 2 (1971): 1–9.

3. Malone, *Country Music, U.S.A.,* 152 (of course, Malone does credit the people west of the Mississippi River with their contribution to country music, yet his title for another work examining country belies that concession: *Southern Music American Music* [Lexington, Ky., 1979]); Michael Bane, "20 Questions with Roy Rogers," *Country Music,* April/March 1992, 32–33. The Cowboy Commandments are taken from David Rothel, *The Singing Cowboys* (New York, 1978), 17.

4. For a comprehensive discussion of the rise of the singing cowboy, see Douglas B. Green, *Country Roots: The Origins of Country Music* (New York, 1976), 87–108; Malone, *Country Music, U.S.A.,* 139–75; Douglas B. Green, "The Singing Cowboy: An American Dream," *Journal of Country Music* 7 (May 1978): 4–61; Stephen Ray Tucker, "The Western Image in Country Music," master's thesis, Southern Methodist University, 15–45.

5. Gerald D. Nash, *Creating the West: Historical Interpretations, 1890–1990* (Albuquerque, N.Mex., 1991), 197–257.

6. D. K. Wilgus, "Country-Western Music and the Urban Hillbilly," *Journal of American Folklore* 83 (1970): 164–66; Malone, *Country Music, U.S.A.,* 140–43; Tucker, "The Western Image," 40–44; Nolan Porterfield, *Jimmie Rodgers* (Urbana, Ill., 1979).

7. Richard P. Stockdell, "The Evolution of the Country Radio Format," *Journal of Popular Culture* 16 (1983): 144–51; Malone, *Country Music, U.S.A.,* 100; George O. Carney, "Country Music and the Radio," in *The Sounds of People and Places: Readings in the Geography of Music* (Washington D.C., 1978), 136–37.

8. Robert Shelton and Burt Goldblatt, *The Country Music Story: A Picture History of Country and Western Music* (Secaucus, N.J., 1966), 157–60.

9. David Rothel, *Singing Cowboys,* 159–80; Tim McCarthy and Charles Flynn, eds., *Kings of the B's* (New York, 1975), 318–20; Green, *Country Roots,*

87–88; *Country: The Music and the Musicians* (New York, 1988), 492–93; Shelton and Goldblatt, *The Country Music Story,* 161–66.

10. Robert K. Oermann and Mary Bufwack, "Patsy Montana and the Development of the Cowgirl Image," *Journal of Country Music* 8 (1981): 18–32; Malone, *Country Music, U.S.A.,* 145; Green, *Country Roots,* 105; Archie Green quoted in Tucker, "The Western Image," 70–71; Excellent introductions to how Americans responded to the Great Depression and world war include Lawrence W. Levine, "American Culture and the Great Depression," *The Unpredictable Past: Explorations in American Cultural History,* 206–30 (New York, 1993); Richard H. Pells, *Radical Visions and American Dreams: Culture and Thought in the Depression Years* (Middletown, Conn., 1973); Studs Terkel, *Hard Times: An Oral History of the Great Depression* (New York, 1970); Donald Worster, *Dust Bowl: The Southern Plains in the 1930s* (New York, 1979); and Allan M. Winkler, *Home Front USA: Americans during World War II* (Arlington Heights, Ill., 1986).

11. Kenneth J. Bindas, "Western Mystic: Bob Nolan and His Songs," *Western Historical Quarterly* 17 (October 1986): 439–56; Malone, *Country Music, U.S.A.,* 147–49; Green, *Country Roots,* 102–5, 131–36.

12. Tucker, "The Western Image," 85–110; Malone, *Southern Music American Music,* 88–95.

13. Green, *Country Roots,* 4; Tucker, "The Western Image," 103–13; Malone, *Country Music, U.S.A.,* 154–55; *Country,* 494–96; For information about the cold war era, see Stephen J. Whitfield, *The Culture of the Cold War* (Baltimore, Md., 1991), especially 53–100; and Douglas T. Miller and Marion Nowak, *The Fifties: The Way We Really Were* (Garden City, N.Y., 1975), especially 105–78.

14. Tucker, "The Western Image," 113–16; Malone, *Country Music, U.S.A.,* 270–92.

15. Allen J. Matusow, *The Unraveling of America: A History of Liberalism in the 1960s* (New York, 1984), 275–440; Melton A. McLaurin, "Proud to Be an American: Patriotism in Country Music," in *America's Musical Pulse: Popular Music in Twentieth Century American Society,* ed. Kenneth J. Bindas, 23–32 (Westport, Conn., 1992); Godfrey Hodgson, *America in Our Time* (Garden City, N.Y., 1976), 263–400; and Timothy Miller, *The Hippies and American Values* (Knoxville, Tenn., 1991), which in its analysis paints the hippie as a modern-day free individual. With different clothes, this hippie would be the cowboy.

16. Edward Wilz, *Democracy Challenged: The United States since World War II* (New York, 1990), 318–21; Theodore H. White, *America in Search of Itself: The Making of the President, 1956–1980* (New York, 1982), 99–228. For interesting contemporary analysis see Charles A. Reich, *The Greening of America* (New York, 1970), especially 265–348; and Christopher Lasch, *The Culture of Narcissism: American Life in an Age of Diminishing Expectations* (New York, 1979), especially 28–70.

17. Michael Bane's *The Outlaws: Revolution in Country Music* (New York, 1978) is the best single source on the Outlaw phenomenon. See also *Country,* 519–61; Tucker, "The Western Image," 155–165; Tommy Goldsmith,

"Honky-Tonk Heritage," *Country America,* July/August 1991, 34–40; Gerry Wood, "Strait from the Heart," *Country America,* July/August 1991, 29–32.

18. George H. Lewis, "Country Music Lyrics," *Journal of Communication* 26 (1976): 37–40; William W. Savage Jr., *The Cowboy Hero: His Image in American History and Culture* (Norman, Okla., 1979), 79–95; Bindas, "Western Mystic," 452–53.

19. Richard M. Dorson, *American Folklore and the Historian* (Chicago, 1971), 67–69. For a good example of actual cowboy verse, see Katie Lee, *Ten Thousand Goddam Cattle: A History of the American Cowboy in Song, Story, and Verse* (Flagstaff, Ariz., 1976); or John I. White, *Git along Little Dogies: Songs and Songmakers of the American West* (Urbana, Ill., 1975).

20. Oermann and Bufwack, "Patsy Montana," 25–27.

21. Peter Thorpe, "I'm Movin' On: The Escape Theme in Country and Western Music," *Western Humanities Review* 24 (1970): 307–18.

22. John G. Cawelti, *The Six-Gun Mystique* (Bowling Green, Ohio, 1971), 39–65; Roderick Nash, *Wilderness and the American Mind* (New Haven, Conn., 1967), 8–22, 228–36; Patricia Nelson Limerick, *Desert Passages: Encounters with the American Deserts* (Albuquerque, N.Mex., 1985), 9–11; Bindas, "Western Mystic," 445–55.

23. For a good example of this, see Austin Fife and Alta Fife, *Heaven on Horseback: Revivalist Songs and Verse in the Cowboy Idiom* (Logan, Utah, 1970), 25–36; Cawelti, *Six-Gun Mystique,* 39–41; Bindas, "Western Mystic," 450–51.

24. Kevin Starr, *Americans and the California Dream, 1850–1915* (New York, 1973), especially 418–43; Nash, *Creating the West;* and Patricia Nelson Limerick, *Legacy of Conquest: The Unbroken Past of the American West* (New York, 1987).

25. Gerald A. Schorin and Bruce G. Vanden Bergh, "Advertising's Role in the Diffusion of Country-Western Trend in the U.S.," *Journalism Quarterly* 62 (1985): 515–22; on the country image projected throughout the 1980s, see Edward Morris, "Dittos, Duplicates, and Deja Vu: Imitation in Country Music," *Journal of Country Music* 13 (1990): 48–49.

26. For the nostalgia for the mythic cowboy, see Neil Pond, "Roy Rogers: King of the Cowboys," *Country America,* February 1992, 36–38; Jim Mueller, "The Cowboy Crooners of Yesteryear," *Country America,* February 1992, 41–42; and Michael Bane, "Twenty Questions with Ranger Doug [of the Western group Riders in the Sky]," *Country Music,* January/February 1992, 70–71. For an interesting study of the Western, see Will Wright, *Six Guns and Society: A Structural Study of the Western* (Berkeley, Calif., 1975), 2. White's comments came from Richard White, *"It's Your Misfortune and None of My Own": A New History of the American West* (Norman, Okla., 1991), 601–11.

27. Karen Saucier Lundy, "Women and Country Music," in *America's Musical Pulse,* ed. Bindas, 313–18; Robert K. Oermann, "Mother, Sister, Sweetheart, Pal: Women in Old-Time Country Music," *The Southern Quarterly* 22 (Spring 1984): 125–35; Karen A. Saucier, "Healers and Heartbreakers: Images of Women and Men in Country Music," *Journal of Popular Culture* 20

(1986): 147–66; Mary Bufwack, "The Feminist Sensibility in Post-War Country Music," *The Southern Quarterly* 22 (Spring 1984): 136–44; Sue Simmons McGinty, "Honky Tonk Angels," in *Legendary Ladies of Texas,* ed. Francis Edward Abernathy, 203–10 (Dallas, 1981).

28. Paul Kingsbury, "Women Walk the Line," *Journal of Country Music* 15 (1992): 24–26, 33.

29. Jimmie N. Rogers, *The Country Music Message: Revised* (Fayetteville, Ark., 1989); Blake Allmendinger, *The Cowboy: Representations of Labor in an American Work Culture* (New York, 1992), 7–14; Melton A. McLaurin, "Proud to Be an American," in *America's Musical Pulse,* ed. Bindas, 29; James E. Akenson, "Social and Geographic Characteristics of Country Music," in *America's Musical Pulse,* ed. Bindas, 45–51.

30. Frederick E. Danker, "Country Music," *The Yale Review* 63 (March 1974): 392–404; Karen Saucier Lundy, "Women and Country Music," in *America's Musical Pulse,* ed. Bindas, 213–19; Jimmie N. Rogers, *The Country Music Message: All about Lovin' and Livin'* (Englewood Cliffs, N.J., 1983), 152–55; Melton A. McLaurin, "Proud to Be an American," 23–32; and John Buckley, "Country Music and American Values," *Popular Music and Society* 6 (1979): 293–301.

31. Saucier, "Healers and Heartbreakers," 150, 156; Kingsbury, "Women Walk the Line," 24–26.

Suggestions for Further Reading

MUSIC

Aquila, Richard. *That Old Time Rock and Roll: A Chronicle of an Era, 1954–64*. New York, 1989.

Bane, Michael. *The Outlaws: Revolution in Country Music*. New York, 1978.

Bindas, Kenneth J., ed. *America's Musical Pulse: Popular Music in Twentieth Century American Society*. Westport, Conn., 1992.

Collins, William, Douglas P. Green, and Frederick LaBour. *Riders in the Sky*. Salt Lake City, 1992.

Green, Douglas. *Country Roots: The Origins of Country Music*. New York, 1976.

Lewis, George H., ed. *All That Glitters: Country Music in America*. Bowling Green, Ohio, 1993.

Malone, Bill. *Country Music, U.S.A.* Austin, Tex., 1985.

———. *Singing Cowboys and Musical Mountaineers: Southern Culture and the Roots of Country Music*. Athens, Ga., 1993.

Murphey, Michael Martin, comp. *Cowboy Songs*. Secaucus, N.J., 1991.

Reid, Jan. *The Improbable Rise of Redneck Rock*. New York, 1974.

Richards, Tad, and Melvin B. Shestack. *The New Country Music Encyclopedia*. New York, 1993.

Rothel, David. *The Singing Cowboys*. New York, 1978.

Silber, Irwin, ed. *Songs of the Great American West*. New York, 1967.

Tichi, Cecelia. *High Lonesome: The American Culture of Country Music*. Chapel Hill, N.C., 1994.

Tinsley, Jim Bob. *He Was Singin' This Song*. Orlando, Fla., 1981.

Ward, Ed, Geoffrey Stokes, and Ken Tucker. *Rock of Ages: The Rolling Stone History of Rock and Roll*. New York, 1986.

White, John I. *Git along Little Dogies: Songs and Songmakers of the American West*. Urbana, Ill., 1975.

PART FIVE

Popular and Commercial Art

NINE

JONI L. KINSEY

Viewing the West: The Popular Culture of American Western Painting

IN SOME WAYS ALL American western art is popular and has been since the first paintings of the region were exhibited in the 1830s. Landscapes of open plains and looming mountains or dramatic encounters of Native Americans, indigenous animals, and conquering whites seem perpetually intriguing and inspiring to a large percentage of Americans for a host of reasons. Many people respond to the directness of the images, their straightforwardness and intelligibly. Other viewers are nostalgic for a frontier that promised opportunities not readily available today, such as the chance to encounter, explore, and claim virgin territory. For still other people, the images depict a place uniquely and characteristically American, one that has fostered, among other things, some of the clearest examples of our national ideals of individualism, freedom, and courage.

Far from being a simple matter of an engaging subject and a receptive audience, western art and its appeal are bound up in a highly complex relationship that challenges the definition and implications of artistic popularity, draws attention to the role of art in the United States, and reveals much about the development of American culture and the importance of mythology in conceiving social identity.

The mere fact that western art is popular makes it historically distinctive and in some ways problematic. Few other subjects or artistic genres can claim the approval or interest of such a vast and diverse

population, and this in itself qualifies it as "popular"; that is, it is populist. The very characteristics, however, that make western art appealing to a broad public have tended to marginalize it in the history of art.
Until recently the significance of a work of art was seen as dependent
on its ability to elevate viewers' sensibilities, to separate them from the
mundane through lofty themes that were often complex or obscure in
their references. Such qualities were required for a work to be taken
seriously as art. As a result most western imagery, with its anecdotes
about the lives of common people and its dependence on histrionics (as
in dramatic cowboy-and-Indian scenes or overly spectacular landscapes), was dismissed by many art historians as lacking significant intellectual content. The fact that many western artists were also illustrators and that their work appeared in a variety of popular media such as
prints, periodicals, and dime novels did not help; such widespread
availability furthered the notion that western art could appeal only to
those without refined taste and understanding.

Although such distinctions are today often criticized for their elit-
ism and narrowmindedness, the issue of western art's popularity and
the characteristics that contribute to it remain at the core of the genre's
emergence as a legitimate scholarly subject. Art historians increasingly are recognizing the significance of popular culture and finally are
acknowledging that western art often displays real artistic achievement,
that it indeed has the power to inspire passion in viewers and prompt
them to contemplate ideas that transcend immediate circumstances.
Fundamental to this transcendent interaction is an identification with
the mythic dimension of the West itself, a dimension essential to understanding the history of western art and its endurance as a popular
genre.

Although many people had, from the earliest encounters, recognized the West's potential for mythic status in American culture,
perhaps none characterized this issue as evocatively and concisely as
historian Frederick Jackson Turner, who proclaimed in 1893 that, according to the 1890 census, the "frontier" no longer existed and that
this was highly significant because until then the existence of "an area
of free land, its continuous recession, and the advance of American settlement westward" had been the defining feature of national development.[1] Turner attributed a set of American characteristics to the frontier: "its striking acuteness and inquisitiveness; that practical inventive
turn of mind, quick to find expedients; that masterful grasp of material things, . . . that restless, nervous energy; that dominant individualism, working for good and for evil, and withal that buoyancy and ex-
uberance which comes with freedom—these are the traits of the

frontier, or traits called out elsewhere because of the existence of the frontier."[2] In a remarkably short essay Turner effectively proposed a sweeping rationale for American historical development and linked identity—both individual and national—to a single issue, the frontier. Although as a historical paradigm his theory has proved more problematic than clarifying, his recognition of Americans' psychological connection to the frontier was astute; the appeal of the West is centered in the mythic imagination. It is through this dimension that western art and its popularity may be most clearly understood.[3]

Although Turner's insights into the relationship between the frontier and the American psyche have proved to be the most influential, Turner was describing a phenomenon that had been developing since at least the 1830s and that others, including many artists, had recognized. Implied throughout his thesis is the claim that the West's hold on the American imagination lies in its distance from us, its closure. It is, in a sense, unattainable and always has been. By placing the frontier era in the past, Turner and others who followed his reasoning, such as the artist Frederic Remington and his friends Owen Wister and Theodore Roosevelt, who popularized the region in similar ways at about the same time, recognized the West's nostalgic and romantic power.[4] Nostalgia relies on the viewer being removed from the object of contemplation, either in time or in space, and the power of the West as an idea is a consequence of this distancing. Whereas twentieth-century Americans are temporally removed from the mythic frontier, the nineteenth-century artists' public, mostly easterners, was spatially separated, enjoying blood-curdling Indian battles and poignant visions of pioneering from comfortable parlors, or scenic Rocky Mountain vistas in galleries and through windows in plush Pullman railcars that effectively "framed" the views, rendering them an aesthetic rather than an arduous experience.[5] Although different in circumstance, experience, and point of view, viewers from both eras are the same in responding to the West conceptually as much as geographically.

The romantic notions that were used to rationalize much of the exploration, settlement, and development of the West are thematic staples of western art. Progress, the rallying cry intrinsic to the concept of Manifest Destiny that pervaded nineteenth-century federal policy, is evident in everything from Currier and Ives prints to Emanuel Leutze's monumental mural *Westward the Course of Empire Takes Its Way* (1862) in the U.S. Capitol. Conquest, a closely related issue, is no less visible in the sculpture of James Earle Fraser or Albert Bierstadt's *Last of the Buffalo* (1888) than it was at Wounded Knee or on the skeleton-scattered plains. Masculine or heroic action is pervasive and just as compelling in Frederic Remington's or Charles Schrevogel's canvases as it might have seemed for Kit Carson, Jim Bridger, or many other intrepid individuals who made their fame with exploits of invincibility and courage. Just as imagery has influenced our retrospective view of western history, it was itself influenced by national events, political ideologies, economic trends, and social relationships. Each work of art, when studied closely in conjunction with these issues, can provide insight into its own time, place, and circumstances, and seen as a whole, western art parallels larger historical trends in the United States. This is not to say, however, that there is always, or even usually, a one-to-one relationship between events and images; more often the art elaborates on the essential issues or circumstances and becomes highly fictitious. Art is not simply a visual record of history, even though it has important historical components and references.

Although the art of the West is somewhat more definable than the subject to which it refers, it is no less vast and varied. Art historians usually consider the work of Native Americans separately from that of European Americans because of the different cultural and aesthetic foundations. This chapter focuses on the European tradition because it was through this art that the American West became most popularly understood. Apart from this division, however, are several variables critical to making further relevant distinctions: the circumstances of the work's creation, the audience for which it was intended, and the work's position within the hierarchy of the visual arts (usually an issue of media but sometimes connected to the artist's level of expertise). Documentary fieldwork usually differs quite markedly from studio productions in both form and credibility, especially if the artist of the latter had never actually visited the West. "Grand Manner" paintings or sculptures are quite different from modest illustrations, although their popularity might be seen as comparable. The former were created as "high art" and were frequently shown in major exhibitions drawing thousands of spectators. They often sold for fabulous sums and sometimes became famous for this and through reproductions and critical reviews. By contrast, woodcut and lithographic prints were often produced by less well known artists and were considered less significant artistically, but they were seen by equally impressive numbers through their appearance on the walls of domestic interiors and in popular periodicals and tourist guidebooks. As a result these images had a profound effect, informing a wide audience about the West and helping to shape it as an idea in the popular imagination.

Intriguing about western art is the amount of crossover among these divisions. Many artists did both "high" and "low" work, appealing to different audiences through different styles, subject matter, or media. Thomas Moran, for example, a major landscape painter in the late nineteenth century, created huge oil paintings of areas that we now know as the national parks, selling them for thousands of dollars, but he made his regular income for many years through wood engravings produced for popular periodicals such as *Scribner's Monthly, Harper's Monthly,* and *Century Magazine.*[6] He saw no conflict in the two activities, saying that commercial commissions posed "no hindrance" to his art: "The real artist will express himself anyway."[7] Neither did he and many others limit themselves exclusively to western subject matter, although they regarded it as an important means to assert their identity as American artists.

This last issue is significant for understanding what artists believed to be the West's potential for visual imagery. As Henry Tuckerman pointed out in 1867, "There is nothing in the life of our cities which may be deemed original. . . . It is in our border life alone that we can find the materials for national development, as far as literature and art are concerned."[8] Life in the West and the region's varied terrain were considered uniquely American and, when portrayed by artists, could compensate for what long had been perceived as a lack of cultural achievement in the United States.[9] The "Americanness" of western art became a common point of admiration and has continued as such. It is intriguing, however, that these nationalistic claims are often directed at work created by foreign, foreign-born, or foreign-trained artists, sometimes for patrons from other countries. In other instances art was produced for U.S. government agencies or for corporate patrons that may have had agendas different from those of the artists. Our cherished self-perception is a very mediated commodity.

The earliest western art was produced by artists Samuel Seymour and Titian Peale, who accompanied Major Stephen Long's expedition to the Rockies in 1819.[10] Even though President Thomas Jefferson had asked Meriwether Lewis and William Clark to bring back nearly everything they encountered that would tell about their exploration of the Louisiana Purchase in 1804–6, he did not think to include the services of an artist, a fact that Lewis more than once lamented.[11] After 1819, however, few federal expeditions went without them, and although the abilities of the artists varied, their work helped to convey something of the land and its people to the government, which was seeking information that would facilitate settlement and development in the new territories.[12]

Field drawings were transformed into wood engravings and lithographs and published in the official expedition reports. Some survey

leaders also shared illustrations with magazine publishers in exchange
for free publicity and with guidebook authors who needed information about unfamiliar locations. As a result far more people saw the
images than would have otherwise, and the government got extra mile-
age out of its initial investment.[13] Other instances of federal cooperation with commercial enterprise included the massive Pacific Railroad
Surveys in 1853, which sought the best course for a transcontinental
line along four different routes and employed eleven artists to illustrate
the final twelve-volume report.[14]

Government art patronage extended as well to military reconnais-
sance missions and army outposts. Seth Eastman, for example, had
been a drawing instructor at the academy at West Point, but while sta-
tioned at Fort Snelling, Minnesota, in the 1830s and 1840s he learned
the Santee Sioux language and painted many pictures of the customs
and activities of the Native Americans who frequented the post.[15] This
experience informed his later illustrations for Henry Schoolcraft's
multivolume *Indian Tribes of the United States,* produced between
1851 and 1857 under the auspices of the Bureau of Indian Affairs,
which for many years remained a definitive text on the subject.[16]

The most intensive federal investigation of the West in visual form,
however, came after the Civil War with the so-called Great Surveys,
which systematically mapped much of the region from 1867 to 1879.[17]
Each of the four expeditions included photographers, cartographers,
and sometimes fine artists who, with their high levels of expertise and
increased technical ability resulting from developments in photographic processes and, in some cases, from education at foreign academies,
were able to elevate what had been largely a documentary art form
to heights usually associated only with eastern or European art.[18]
Through this achievement, and coupled with the attention of a growing popular press that publicized their work, these artists brought new
recognition to western imagery. In addition to appearing in survey reports, their photographs and paintings won awards in major exhibitions such as the Centennial Exposition in 1876. They also contributed to Congress's commitment to a national park system and were used
by industry, especially the railroads, for the commercial promotion of
the West, especially to tourists.[19] Furthermore, the evocative photographs of William Henry Jackson, Timothy O'Sullivan, Carleton Wat-
kins, and others had a profound effect on twentieth-century art, especially the nature photography of Ansel Adams, Edward Weston, and
Eliot Porter.

The appeal of the survey photographs lay in their ability to convey
an undeniable reality about the West's exotic landscapes. Unlike drawn

or painted images that were always suspect as to their "truth to nature," photography had an implicit veracity that made it seem a reliable witness to viewers far removed from the places and subjects portrayed. In 1871, for example, Yellowstone was so little known and so unlike anything most people had ever encountered that Jackson's photographs were employed to convince easterners that it was indeed a real place and a site worth special consideration.[20] Jackson's images were shown to congressmen who shortly thereafter established the region as the first national park, and millions of average Americans viewed the spectacular scenery of Yellowstone and many other sites throughout the West in stereographs, which became a popular form of parlor entertainment. Indeed, it could be said that it was principally through photography that Americans came to know the national parks and that the medium is still one of the most important means by which we enjoy them today.

At the same time, however, nineteenth-century photography lacked a key characteristic that would convey both the physical grandeur and the mythic potential of the West's scenery: color. Painters were needed for this, and on many of the Great Survey expeditions these artists worked closely with photographers, each augmenting the other's strengths and weaknesses to provide a comprehensive visual portrayal of the places they encountered.

Private excursions also fostered the development of early western art and helped to popularize the region and its mythic imagery. These journeys were sometimes the solitary crusade of a single individual, such as George Catlin or John Mix Stanley (who also participated in military expeditions and the Pacific Railroad Survey). Other times they were led by foreign visitors who hired artists to produce souvenirs of their adventures and experiences.[21] In either instance the resulting art, especially that produced in the 1830s and 1840s, was often displayed as public curiosities.

Catlin and Stanley, who focused on ethnographic and anecdotal scenes of Native Americans, compiled their work into "Indian Galleries," which were advertised widely and displayed for profit throughout the eastern United States and, in Catlin's case, in Europe, accompanied by actual Indians dancing in full regalia. Both men hoped to sell their collections to the Smithsonian Institution in Washington, but Congress refused to appropriate funds, an outcome ultimately filled with irony for the artists. Stanley optimistically left his collection on extended loan at the museum, where it was almost completely destroyed by fire in 1865, and he was never compensated for its loss. Catlin was forced to sell most of his work to creditors, and he lived out his last days in poverty *in* the

Smithsonian, a guest of the sympathetic secretary, Joseph Henry. After the artist's death much of his Indian Gallery was given to the institution, where it remains today.[22]

Congress's disinterest in the Indian pictures might be attributed to nineteenth-century hostilities toward Native Americans, as well as the tendency to ignore or refute anyone who did not regard them as impediments to "civilizing" the American continent. Both Catlin and Stanley—like other artists who had lived among the tribes—recognized the tragedy inherent in the demise of native cultures. Catlin was especially eloquent on the subject; he saw his artistic career as an effort to "become their historian." In addition to painting thousands of portraits of individual Indians and pictures of their ceremonies, hunting expeditions, and villages, Catlin wrote extensively of his experiences and understandings, most notably in his two-volume *Letters and Notes on the Manners, Customs, and Condition of the North American Indians* (1841).[23]

The most famous of the foreign private excursions that included artists were the journeys of the Swiss painter Karl Bodmer and Prussian prince Maximilian of Wied, who traveled in 1832–34 through the upper Missouri River region, and that of Baltimorean Alfred Jacob Miller and Scottish nobleman Sir William Drummond Stewart, who extended their 1837 wanderings up the Oregon Trail as far as Wyoming. Stewart was launching his fourth annual trip to the mountain men's rendezvous in the Wind River Mountains, purely for pleasure, and Miller was invited along to make mementos. The opportunity provided the artist with his first experience with the Far West and the foundation for the rest of his career. Miller produced dozens of romantic paintings of the expedition, which he exhibited in the East, and later traveled to Scotland, at Stewart's request, to decorate the family castle and hunting lodge with pictures and assorted artifacts. Stewart had shipped some buffalo from the West with the intention of starting a herd, and when two of them died during the artist's visit, Miller incorporated their horns and hooves into two magnificent chairs. These "buffalo chairs" have recently been acquired by the Gene Autry Museum of Western Heritage and Art in Los Angeles. Their "return" to the West after over a century and a half is intriguing in its implications about the popularity of such curiosities.

Maximilian's expedition was far more ambitious than Stewart's. The Prussian prince, inspired by the German naturalist Alexander von Humboldt to experience "virgin" territory firsthand, published his account with Bodmer's illustrations on his return. Karl Bodmer's paintings include some of the most eloquent and evocative images in American western art.[24] He was one of the most accomplished artists to portray the region before the 1850s, and although his subjects do not greatly differ from Catlin's, Bodmer's delicate watercolors contain nuances of tone, color, and sensitivity that render their aesthetic appeal equal to their ethnographic importance. As with Catlin's contribution, however, this latter significance should not be underestimated. The two artists were the only documenters of the Mandan Indians before their culture was wiped out by smallpox in 1837, and as a result their depictions of the tribe have been of inestimable value to anthropologists. Although perhaps the most dramatic instance of art's impact on our understanding of the West before it was irrevocably altered by white encroachment, this is just one of many ways that visual imagery has contributed to Americans' perceptions of the place. For example, the romantic paintings of Bodmer, Catlin, Miller, and other early artists became the basis for illustrations found in nineteenth-century histories, almanacs, and other books about the West. No less significant is the tremendous influence such pictures have had on the film industry. Whether moviegoers realize it or not, they have been watching Hollywood versions of Catlin, Bodmer, Remington, and Russell paintings for years, and these interpretations, which vary greatly in accuracy and point of view, have profoundly affected perceptions of the region, reinforcing American notions of a mythic West.[25]

The nineteenth century had its own version of the motion picture that was no less popular than major film releases today. Moving panoramas were all the rage in the 1850s, and among the favorite themes was the American West. The giant painted scrolls (measuring thousands of feet long) were slowly unrolled in front of theater audiences, complete with musical accompaniment, dramatic stage lighting, and narrative embellishment. Little information survives about the content of most of the panoramas because nearly all were worn out from extended use, but they were well suited to portraying the epic sweep of western scenery, a key issue in the region's appeal.[26] Just as with the giant-screen cinema, the very size and mobility of these panoramas enabled the notions of "bigness" and "westward movement" to be physically emphasized and conveyed to viewing audiences.[27]

Most panorama artists were essentially theatrical set designers and have remained little known, but some, such as Stanley or St. Louisan Carl Wimar, did pursue artistic careers more seriously. After an apprenticeship with Leon Pomarede painting a Mississippi panorama entitled *Portrait of the Father of the Waters,* Wimar went on to study

with Emanuel Leutze (of *Washington Crossing the Delaware* fame) in
Düsseldorf, Germany, in the early 1850s.[28] Düsseldorf was an important center for American artists, attracting such notable western painters as Albert Bierstadt, Worthington Whittredge, George Caleb Bingham, and Leutze himself, a German-American who painted the
monumental mural *Westward the Course of Empire Takes Its Way
(Westward Ho)* in the United States Capitol in 1861–62.[29] Although
Wimar was German by birth, his dark hair and western experience in
the frontier town of St. Louis earned him the title "Indian Painter."
While in Düsseldorf he capitalized on this image by importing buckskin clothing and artifacts that he wore and used in his paintings. On
his return to the United States Wimar continued to deal with western
subjects, painting Indian themes and buffalo hunts and, in the final
years of his short life, decorating the St. Louis courthouse rotunda
with murals of westward migration.[30]

Other prominent Missouri painters at about the same time included George Caleb Bingham and the lesser-known Charles Deas.[31] These
artists represent a different aspect of the popularizing of western imagery, primarily because of the methods they employed to distribute
their art. Although Bingham sometimes arranged for reproductions of
his paintings himself, one of the principal means by which he, Deas,
and others made their pictures available was through the American Art
Union, a midcentury organization that promoted the work of American artists to a wide spectrum of the public. An ingenious system, the
union and other similar institutions sold memberships at the modest
rate of five dollars per year, for which the members received fine art
prints on a regular basis. These prints were made from original paintings that the union purchased directly from artists. At the end of each
year in a gala celebration, the originals were raffled off to lucky members, who were automatically entered into the drawing with their sub-
scriptions. Although such lotteries were outlawed in 1852 (they were
considered gambling), for the thirteen years of their existence they
funded the work of dozens of American artists and provided pictures
for the homes of thousands of average citizens.[32]

Of the many artists who participated in the American Art Union,
Bingham and Deas were among the most popular for their scenes of
western life that capitalized on the growing popularity of frontier literature such as Washington Irving's *Astoria* (1836) and *A Tour on the
Prairies* (1835), James Fenimore Cooper's Leatherstocking Tales (1823–
41), or journals such as the *Western Review*. The artists' scenes of fur
trappers and mountain men, riverboat men, Indians engaged in all
manner of activities, and country electioneering conjoined the midcen-

tury Americans' appreciation for visual representations of everyday life with their fascination with the exotic West.[33]

Bingham, Deas, and others' success in the art unions demonstrated an obvious demand for mass-produced frontier imagery, and in the early 1850s a number of entrepreneurs stepped in to fill the void left by the institutions' demise, the most famous being the lithographic firm Currier and Ives.[34] Although the company did employ a few artists on a full-time basis, including a woman named Fanny Palmer, who did some of the firm's most memorable compositions, it generally commissioned original work from freelance artists or bought reproduction rights of existing paintings.[35] Besides Palmer, two of their most prolific western artists were Arthur Fitzwilliam Tait, who produced over forty Currier and Ives designs (often working from prints by Catlin and Bodmer, since he never visited the West), and William Ranney, a veteran of Texas's war for independence.[36]

The standard technique for this sort of printmaking was usually simple one-color (black) lithography, although hand tinting was a popular option for a slightly higher price. A more sophisticated technique, chromolithography, which required that each hue of a color image be separately drawn and printed, was also used, especially by firms such as Julius Bien of Philadelphia or Louis Prang of Boston.[37] The process was an arduous manual version of today's standard photographic printing method (four-color offset lithography), although with many more colors (sometimes upward of twenty), and the results were so faithful to the original paintings that the prints became highly sought after as affordable fine art reproductions. Of these none surpassed the deluxe set of "chromos" taken from Thomas Moran's watercolors of Yellowstone and other western areas, which Louis Prang issued in 1876.[38]

The brilliance and detail of these works were highly praised and demonstrated the medium's potential, but more often the process was used for more ordinary purposes such as calendars, broadsides, and advertising. Chromolithographs became so popular and widespread that when *The Nation* published a moralizing editorial in 1874 describing the decadence and tawdriness of contemporary society, it summarized the problem as "chromo-civilization," a designation that for many years was synonymous with popular culture.[39]

The rise of lithographic and engraving firms in the 1850s paralleled other developments in visual reproduction technology that brought about a tremendous boom in the publishing industry. Journals and weeklies proliferated, the most successful being the illustrated periodicals such as *Harper's Weekly, Harper's Monthly, Scribner's Monthly,* and *Frank Leslie's Illustrated Weekly*. These publications often featured western subject matter prominently, and many artists made a reliable income by supplying images to accompany stories. Photographic reproduction in printing was not perfected until nearly the end of the century, and for the most part the illustrations of this period were almost exclusively wood engravings, much less sophisticated than the prints of fine art presses or the more subtle lithography or steel engraving, and none used color. Nevertheless, just as with popular magazines and newspapers today, these publications had a sizable reading public, and their focus on the West's development and its visual appeal brought the region to the attention of millions of Americans. Artists such as Frederic Remington got their start in the publishing industry in the later nineteenth century, and in the early twentieth N. C. Wyeth, Howard Pyle, and countless other illustrators gave an entire generation their first view of cowboys and Indians in the pages of dime novels and adventure magazines.

The demand for illustration contributed to another type of publication that played an important role in the popularization of the American West: the guidebook. The transcontinental railroad's completion in 1869 offered all sorts of new business opportunities, and dozens of writers immediately took advantage of the availability of inexpensive visual imagery to produce illustrated guidebooks for travelers. They obtained information and material in various ways, sometimes firsthand and other times through friends in government surveys, railroad offices, or publishing houses that were commissioning illustrations. Before long their work became an important industry, forming the foundation for this century's extensive genre of travel literature.

In 1872 one particularly inventive guidebook publisher, George Croffutt, commissioned lithographer John Gast to design and print a signature image that he could include in his *Transcontinental Tourist's Guide*. The resulting picture, which Gast first painted in oil and reproduced in chromolithography and Croffutt later printed in woodcut (taking credit for the composition), was entitled *American Progress* (fig. 9.1) and is considered one of the quintessential reflections of popular sentiment about the West in the nineteenth century. Everything in the sweeping landscape is moving westward: beginning at New York harbor on the far right edge, trains course across the plains, led by stagecoaches, a Pony Express rider, farmers with plows, miners with pickaxes, and covered wagons, and these all push fleeing buffalo and Indians off the picture's left edge into murky darkness. Above the entire scene is an enormous allegorical figure of Liberty, or Progress, whom Croffutt described as a "beautiful and charming female . . .

Figure 9.1. John Gast, *American Progress*, 1872. (Courtesy of the Gene Autry Museum of Western Heritage and Art, Los Angeles, California.)

floating westward through the air, bearing on her forehead the 'Star of Empire.' . . . In her right hand she carries a book—common school—the emblem of education and a testimonial to our national enlightenment, while with the left hand she unfolds and stretches the slender wires of the telegraph, that are to flash intelligence throughout the land."[40] Such embodiments of Manifest Destiny, with their implications of potential, opportunity, and cultural preeminence, were highly influential, impressing on an entire generation that settling and visiting the West was safer, easier, and more patriotic than ever before.[41]

Tourism became especially fashionable after the early 1880s with the development of established tourist attractions and other accommodations. The most notable and enduringly popular of these are the national parks, and artists have been of critical importance in promoting interest in these sites since their beginning. The 1871 watercolors and photographs of Yellowstone by Thomas Moran and William Henry Jackson, for example, were used by railroad lobbyists to convince Congress to designate the area as the first national park in 1872, and Moran's monumental canvases of the region and of the Grand Canyon in Arizona were purchased soon afterward to hang in the U.S. Capitol, where they commemorated the incorporation of these sites into the national culture.[42] Similar images of the West's spectacles were also readily available in photographic stereographs, and wood-engraved versions were reproduced widely in guidebooks, in parlor-table publications such as *Picturesque America* (1874), and in advertisements that enticed tourists to see "Nature's Wonderland" for themselves.[43]

One of the principal effects of landscape imagery of the post–Civil War period was that it brought the West to the viewers, giving them a sense of being there. The monumental canvases of Yosemite by Albert Bierstadt, Thomas Hill, William Keith, and William Hahn, for example, utilized the conventions of "view making," which had a long European history, to frame scenic vistas for gallery visitors.[44] These paintings became so influential that when tourists visited the site, they would search out those same viewpoints, considering them the paradigmatic "pictures" of the park. This tendency has persisted today, facilitated by the National Park Service's convenient "scenic overlook" designations and ubiquitous postcards, snapshots, and videos.

Although the most frequent accolades given to such landscape paintings was for their "indisputable" accuracy, these pictures were more often highly contrived constructions that romanticize their subjects through spectacular lighting, coloration, manipulation of spatial relationships, or overblown theatricality.[45] This paradoxical mixture of reality and fantasy solidified the mythic associations the West was taking on in the closing years of the nineteenth century and was nowhere more apparent than in the art of Frederic Remington or Charles Schreyvogel, who routinely based their raucous compositions of cavalry stampedes, Indian skirmishes, or cowboys on the range on models they posed on barrels in their east coast studios.[46] Although such artifice was hardly new and would not on its own negate the "authenticity" of such scenes, Remington's relationship to his subjects was especially compromised and renders the reading of his work an intricate maneuvering of perceptions and politics, assertions and oppositions. Although Remington encouraged the many stories attesting to his rugged youth in the West and to the absolute truthfulness of his art, he actually grew up in relative affluence in upstate New York, attended Yale, and, other than a brief stint on a sheep ranch in Kansas, limited his trips west to brief excursions during which he usually wore yellow jodphurs, tall European riding boots, and a derby hat or safari helmet.[47]

Remington did fill his New Rochelle studio with artifacts acquired on western jaunts and painstakingly rendered them in his paintings and sculptures, and he relied frequently on photographs that he took himself or borrowed from friends such as Montanan Laton Alton Huffman.[48] He especially prided himself on his knowledge of anatomy, particularly that of horses. This pride is justified by his numerous, accurate, and exciting renditions of equine action, but as Remington scholar Peter Hassrick has pointed out, the claim that the artist correctly drew the complicated movement of horses' feet before the photographic motion studies of Eadweard Muybridge in the late 1870s is false and was a myth fostered, if not originated, by Remington himself.[49]

Remington's great facility at conveying compelling narratives through careful details, convincing portraits, emotional physical encounters, and striking color made him one of the most popular artists of his own time and of our own. For all his devotion to conveying his notion of truth in the West, however, his view of the region was wholeheartedly nostalgic, romantic, and increasingly fatalistic as he sought to heroicize what he believed to be its spirit, the glory of masculine action—what he called "men with the bark on." As he expressed it, "I saw men swarming into the land. I knew the wild riders and vacant land were about to vanish forever, and the more I considered the subject the bigger Forever loomed."[50] At the same time as he seemed to admire the American Indian subjects of his pictures, glorifying them as "noble savages" or at least as worthy combatants, he made little secret of his personal opinions: "Jews—InJuns—Chinamen—Italians—Huns, the rubbish of the earth I hate."[51]

Most of Remington's contemporaries were less overtly bigoted but no less consistent in their fabrication of a mythic West. Some artists, like George de Forest Brush, made no pretense of accuracy, preferring to focus on the lyrical associations of noble primitives: "In choosing Indians as subjects for art, I do not paint from the historian's or the antiquary's point of view. . . . I hesitate to attempt to add any interest to my pictures by supplying historical facts. If I were required to resort to this in order to bring out the poetry, I would drop the subject at once."[52] Whether they admitted it or not, and regardless of their degree of western experience, by the time of Turner's frontier thesis artists were inventing their notions of the region's glory or pathos nearly wholesale. Even Charles Russell, who was himself a working cowboy and lived out his life in Montana, relied more on his imagination in his paintings than actual experience. "Sinch your saddle on romance," he advised a writer friend in a letter filled with charming sketches and consistently poor spelling, "Hes a high headed hoss with plenty of blemishes but keep him moovin and theres fiew that can call the leg he limps on and most folks like prancers."[53] Russell's art indeed prances, unabashed in its enthusiastic, sentimental portrayal of a western life that, if it ever existed as he portrayed it, had mostly passed into history by the time it appeared on his canvases (fig. 9.2). Younger than Remington, Russell was still in his teens when Remington's illustrations filled the pages of *Harper's, Century, Colliers,* and *Cosmopolitan,* and he did not begin painting seriously until the mid-1890s. His best work vies with that of the elder artist in its vivid visual anecdotes of ranch life, buffalo hunts, and Indian skirmishes, but it is less consistent stylistically. Russell also used more dashing brush strokes that lend an added sense of liveliness to his art and often was more liberal in his choice of color, giving his paintings a unique expressiveness and adding to their mythic dimension.

For all their fabrications, it is the art of Russell and especially Remington, as well as that of their colleagues, Henry Farny, Walter Shirlaw, Charles Schreyvogel, and others, that has become in the twentieth century the archetypal representation of the "Wild West" and is considered the "classic" phase of American western imagery. This observation is borne out by the continuing adherence to these artists' formulas by countless "western realists" today, especially the increasingly numerous members of the Cowboy Artists of America association.[54]

By the 1910s Native Americans were so thoroughly subdued on reservations that even official government policy could romanticize their "noble" past. In 1913 the U.S. Mint eulogized both the Indian and the buffalo on a nickel coin, having already put an "Indian head" penny into circulation. Over one billion of the nickels were produced over a twenty-five-year period, and the public's reaction was "extremely positive," an outcome filled with irony in several ways.[55] By the turn of the century it was already widely recognized that the vast millions of buffalo had been hunted to virtual extinction, and the sculptor who created the design modeled his bison from "Old Diamond," a resident of the Bronx Zoo.[56] Whether the implication was intentional or not, the traditional phase *e pluribus unum,* "out of the many, one," appears on the buffalo side of the coin, and the word *liberty* is on the Indian's, just in front of the man's closed eyes.

James Earle Fraser, the sculptor of the buffalo/Indian nickel, sympathized with the plight of Native Americans and returned to the theme a number of times in his art. He had grown up in Dakota Territory knowing reservation Sioux personally, and on hearing a comment that "the Injuns will be driven into the Pacific Ocean," he was inspired to sculpt what would become his most famous monumental work, *The End of the Trail.*[57] The piece won a prize and the admiration of the preeminent American sculptor Augustus Saint-Gaudens when it was exhibited in Paris in 1898, but it got its most widespread acclaim when

Figure 9.2. Charles M. Russell's glorification of the cowboy is evident in this painting from 1909, *In without Knocking*. (Courtesy of Amon Carter Museum, Fort Worth, Texas.)

Fraser enlarged it to colossal proportions for the 1915 Panama Pacific Exposition in San Francisco, where it became the signature image of the fair and won a gold medal.[58] The sculpture's placement in the Court of Palms was no less ironic than the nickel's symbolism; palm fronds are the traditional designation of martyrs in Christian iconography, an apt association for the downcast, defeated Indian on his weatherbeaten horse.

Fraser was to go on to sculpt many other notable commissions, but through multiple versions and casts, as well as the popularity it engendered in 1915 at the fair and in hundreds of photographs, *The End of the Trail* remains his most famous work.[59] After the fair the sculpture was moved to an outdoor park in Visalia, California, where it remains today, fulfilling the early prophecy in its proximity to the Pacific ocean (fig. 9.3).[60]

Throughout the twentieth century, at least until recently, Americans' relationship with the West and its art has been largely uncritical, emphasizing adventure, beauty, and romance over its difficult implications.[61] Although innovative in other ways, artists such as the Taos school of painters or even the eloquent Georgia O'Keeffe, who explored western themes in modernist styles, have done little to challenge

Figure 9.3. James Earl Fraser's *The End of the Trail* is now displayed at the National Cowboy Hall of Fame, Oklahoma City, Oklahoma. (Ball State University Photo Services.)

this trend.[62] Curiously one of the most insightful commentaries from the early part of the century may have come from popular illustrator Norman Rockwell, who portrayed Gary Cooper, dressed for his part in *The Texan*, squatting ignobly on his saddle as he receives the finishing touches on his lipstick from a bandy-legged, cigar-smoking make-up man. More recently other artists, including Native Americans who combine their dual heritage of being Indian in a predominately white culture into a "new western art," are continuing this incisive portrayal of the ironies, curiosities, and sometimes tragedies of the contemporary West.[63] On the other hand, a sizable and very successful group of artists, the Cowboy Artists Association, has reverted to, or at least revived, the more predictable style and thematic focus of Frederic Remington, Charles Russell, and Charles Schreyvogel. This all-male group perpetuates the great western myth in all its anachronistic glory.[64]

Hollywood movies, television Westerns, country and pop music, advertising, and people's reluctance or inability to reevaluate their pasts honestly have facilitated the notion of the West as a place of untarnished truth and its formative years as an inviolable Golden Age. Such romanticism may have provided a useful antidote to the profound changes and traumas of the twentieth century. The rapid rise of mechanization, urbanization, and industrialization; the stresses brought about by massive immigration; and the real threat of social annihilation from economic depression, two world wars, and nuclear catastrophe all have intensified the need for mythologies that offer both escape and reassurance. The very clear paradigm offered by most western art—triumph over adversity—answered this longing to such a degree and became so ingrained in the popular imagination that when the National Museum of American Art in Washington suggested in the 1991 exhibition *The West as America* that there were other ways of understanding western art, ones that challenged these archetypes, the result bordered on national outrage.[65]

At first glance the show was more extensive and varied in its images and artists than most western art exhibits are, but none of the images or juxtapositions were overtly offensive. On close inspection, however, the label copy and wall texts asked viewers to reexamine the content of the paintings and their own preconceptions about the subject matter, especially in connection to issues such as myth, conquest, industrialism, power relationships, persecution of native and immigrant cultures, and destruction of indigenous animals and the environment.

As the curators themselves have admitted, the written material was direct and sometimes even confrontational. As they have also pointed out, however, although this approach and the ideology that informed the exhibition's content may have been unfamiliar to many museum visitors, they incorporated ideas that were hardly new and furthermore had been presented and published widely, not only in the ivory-tower world of academe (always considered suspect by the public) but also with great success by comparable institutions such as history museums.[66] The ideas, in keeping with the revisionist perspectives of the "new western history," questioned traditional histories of the West, particularly their reliance on a narrowly defined point of view (specifically, that of the white male) and the insistence on a notion of truth rather than the recognition of myth, with all its attendant contrivance and culturally specific ideology.[67] Although the revisionist approach still raises eyebrows and at times tempers among historians, the new western history has altered historical debate substantially. The result is a more constructive understanding of complex issues.

Regardless of the positions taken in response to *The West as America,* the controversy surrounding it ultimately validated the principal premise of the exhibition, that western art, just as with any "great" art, can, should, and does have layers of meanings that offer richness, nuance, intrigue, and insight to the viewer's experience and understanding. This content does not always reveal itself easily, however, and when discovered, it is not always pleasant or reassuring in its implications. Comments people wrote as they concluded their visit to the galleries indicate that although many rejected the interpretations that challenged traditional assumptions, they recognized, even if uneasily, that the art and its historical context were more complex than they had originally believed.[68]

As we approach a new century, our relationship to the West, its history, and mythology will undoubtedly continue to evolve. And though our understanding of western art may diversify and ultimately be transformed, the images themselves will endure unchanged (fig. 9.4). The visions of nineteenth-century artists will still testify to the pristine sublimities of unsettled territory, even as we understand that the views

Figure 9.4. Over 200,000 copies of Otto Becker's lithograph of Cassily Adams's *Custer's Last Fight* (1896) were distributed by the Anheuser Busch Brewing Company. Displayed in barrooms and homes across the country, the picture helped popularize gruesome yet heroic images of Custer's Last Stand. (Courtesy of Amon Carter Museum, Fort Worth, Texas.)

might have been constructed of a series of perspectives, with the deletion of mining debris or squatters' shacks. The anecdotal canvases of George Caleb Bingham will continue to amuse and delight, recalling a time that was like childhood, at once simpler and more difficult, for even as we understand that they tell us something of life on the river, we know that they ignore other things, such as slave trading on the Mississippi. The allegories and narratives of John Gast and William Hahn will still recall the tremendous rush to claim land and the early temerities of those who would travel simply to see it. In the post-Turnerian period of Remington and Roosevelt, canvases of stampeding cavalry will continue their campaigns, even when they are called rampages and massacres. Although the emotions they evoke may not be nostalgia and the national identity they foster not a unified one, they will, it seems certain, still compel viewers to pause and consider their relationship to a past and a place that so powerfully speaks to people. Through a sullied history, from exploration through settlement, industrialization, economic crises, and multiculturalism, the West and its art are linked to the longings of the American psyche, a need for identity, both individual and popular, that, through all its changes, will never change.

Notes

1. Frederick Jackson Turner, "The Significance of the Frontier in American History," *American Historical Association Annual Report* (New York, 1963 [Washington, D.C., 1894]), 199–227 (originally read before the ninth annual meeting of the American Historical Association at Chicago).

2. Turner, "Significance of the Frontier," 57 (emphasis added).

3. Prominent voices in the discussion of Turner's idea include Patricia Nelson Limerick, *The Legacy of Conquest: The Unbroken Past of the American West* (New York, 1987); Vernon E. Mattson and William E. Marion, *Frederick Jackson Turner: A Reference Guide* (Boston, 1985); William Cronon, "Revisiting the Vanishing Frontier: The Legacy of Frederick Jackson Turner," *Western Historical Quarterly* 27 (April, 1987): 157–76; Brian W. Dippie, "American Wests: Historiographical Perspectives," *American Studies International* 27 (October 1989): 3–25; and Michael P. Malone, "Beyond the Last Frontier: Toward a New Approach to Western American History," *Western Historical Quarterly* 20 (November 1989): 409–27.

4. See, for example, *Frederic Remington: The Masterworks,* ed. Michael Edward Shapiro and Peter H. Hassrick (St. Louis, 1988); Owen Wister, *The Virginian* (New York, 1902); and Theodore Roosevelt, *The Winning of the West,* 4 vols. (New York, 1889–96).

5. See Anne Farrar Hyde, *An American Vision: Far Western Landscape and National Culture, 1820–1920* (New York, 1990); and J. Valerie Fifer, *American Progress: The Growth of the Transport, Tourist, and Information Industries in the Nineteenth-Century West* (Chester, Conn., 1988).

6. For more on Moran's publishing career see Anne Morand and Nancy Friese, with essays by T. Victoria Hansen and Linda C. Hults, *The Prints of Thomas Moran in the Thomas Gilcrease Institute of American History and Art, Tulsa, Oklahoma* (Tulsa, 1986); and Joni L. Kinsey, *Thomas Moran and the Surveying of the American West* (Washington, D.C., 1992).

7. Thomas Moran, interview, *Pasadena Star-News*, March 11, 1916, 6; cited in Thurman Wilkins, *Thomas Moran: Artist of the Mountains* (Norman, Okla., 1966), 152.

8. Henry Tuckerman, *Book of the Artists* (New York, 1967 [1867]), 424.

9. See, for example, Thomas Cole, "Essay on American Scenery," *American Monthly Magazine*, n.s., 1 (Jan. 1835): 1–12; and Asher B. Durand, "Letters on Landscape Painting," *The Crayon* 1 (1855): 34–35. Cole and Durand quoted in *American Art 1700–1960: Sources and Documents*, ed. John McCoubrey (Englewood Cliffs, N.J., 1975), 98–110, 112.

10. For a review of this expedition see Patricia Trenton and Peter H. Hassrick, *The Rocky Mountains: A Vision for Artists in the Nineteenth Century* (Norman, Okla., 1983), 22–30.

11. See, for example, *Original Journals of the Lewis and Clark Expedition, 1804–1806*, ed. Reuben Gold Thwaites, 8 vols. (New York, 1969), 2:149–50.

12. There has been no single, comprehensive treatment of federal expedition artists, but good overviews include William H. Goetzmann, *Exploration and Empire: The Explorer and the Scientist in the Winning of the American West* (New York, 1966); Trenton and Hassrick, *The Rocky Mountains;* and Robert Taft, *Artists and Illustrators of the Old West, 1850–1900* (Princeton, N.J., 1953). For some statistics on the number of illustrations in government reports, see Martha A. Sandweiss, "The Public Life of Western Art," in Jules David Prown, et al., *Discovered Lands, Invented Pasts: Transforming Visions of the American West,* 117–33 (New Haven, Conn., 1992).

13. I explore some of these relationships in detail in my chapters "The Publishing Industry," "Popularizing the Grand Canyon," and "The Popularizing of Colorado," in Kinsey, *Thomas Moran*, 79–92, 125–37, 161–73.

14. *Reports of Explorations and Surveys to Ascertain the Most Practicable and Economical Route for a Railroad from the Mississippi River to the Pacific Ocean*, 12 vols. (Washington, D.C., 1855–60). See also Trenton and Hassrick, *The Rocky Mountains*, 67–95; and David J. Weber, *Richard H. Kern: Expeditionary Artist in the Far Southwest, 1848–1853* (Albuquerque, N.Mex., 1985).

15. Ron Tyler, Carol Clark, Linda Ayers, Warder H. Cadbury, Herman J. Viola, and Bernard Reilly Jr., *American Frontier Life: Early Western Painting and Prints* (Fort Worth, Tex., 1987), 15–55; and John Francis McDermott, *Seth Eastman: A Pictorial Historian of the Indian* (Norman, Okla., 1961).

16. Henry R. Schoolcraft, *Historical and Statistical Information Respecting the History, Condition, and Prospects of the Indian Tribes of the United States*

(Washington, D.C., 1851–57). Late in his life Eastman also decorated the meeting room of the House Committee on Indian Affairs in the U.S. Capitol.

17. See Richard Bartlett, *Great Surveys of the American West* (Norman, Okla., 1962).

18. General sources on these artists include Weston J. Naef and James N. Wood, *Era of Exploration: The Rise of Landscape Photography in the American West, 1860–1885* (Boston, 1975); and Trenton and Hassrick, *The Rocky Mountains,* 156–77. For extended studies of some major Great Survey artists, see Peter B. Hales, *William Henry Jackson and the Transformation of the American Landscape* (Philadelphia, 1988); Don W. Fowler, *The Western Photographs of John K. Hillers: Myself in the Water* (Washington, D.C., 1989); Kinsey, *Thomas Moran;* Clifford Nelson, "William Henry Holmes: Beginning a Career in Art and Science," *Records of the Columbia Historical Society* 50 (1985): 252–78; and Joel Snyder, *American Frontiers: The Photographs of Timothy H. O'Sullivan, 1867–1874* (Millerton, N.Y., 1981).

19. Although there are many instances of railroad usage of a survey artist's work for promoting tourism, the most notable example was William Henry Jackson's relationship with the industry. See Hales, *William Henry Jackson,* 141–85.

20. See Hales, *William Henry Jackson,* 67–139.

21. For Catlin, see William H. Truettner, *The Natural Man Observed: A Study of Catlin's Indian Gallery* (Washington, D.C., 1979). On Stanley, see Tyler et al., *American Frontier Life,* 137–43; and Julie Ann Schimmel, "John Mix Stanley and Imagery of the West in Nineteenth-Century American Art," Ph.D. diss., New York University, 1983.

22. The fate of Catlin and his Indian Gallery are recounted in detail in Truettner, *Natural Man Observed,* 53–59.

23. A recent examination of the treatment of the Indian in western art is Julie Ann Schimmel, "Inventing the Indian," in *The West as America: Reinterpreting Images of the Frontier,* ed. William Truettner, 149–89 (Washington, D.C., 1991).

24. For more on Bodmer, see David Hunt, Marsha Gallagher, and William J. Orr, *Karl Bodmer's America* (Lincoln, Nebr., 1984).

25. For an example of how one painter has influenced Western movies, see Edward Buscombe, "Painting the Legend: Frederic Remington and the Western," *Cinema Journal* 23 (Summer 1984): 12–27.

26. Few of these panoramas survive. The Saint Louis Art Museum does have a rare example that is virtually complete and in relatively good condition, although it is never exhibited and almost never unrolled because of its fragility. See Angela Miller, "The Soil of an Unknown America: New World Empires and the Debate over Cultural Origins," *American Art* 8 (Summer/Fall 1994): 9–27; and John F. McDermott, *The Lost Panoramas of the Mississippi* (Chicago, 1958).

27. For more on this see John L. Marsh, "Drama and Spectacle by the Yard: The Panorama in America," *Journal of Popular Culture* 10 (Winter 1976): 581–90; and Henry M. Sayre, "Surveying the Vast Profound: The Pan-

oramic Landscape in American Consciousness," *Massachusetts Review* 24 (Winter 1983): 723–42.

28. Rick Stewart, Joseph D. Ketner II, and Angela L. Miller, *Carl Wimar: Chronicler of the Missouri River Frontier* (Fort Worth, Tex., 1991), 33.

29. For more on the important career of Leutze, see Barbara Groseclose, *Emanuel Leutze, 1816–1868: Freedom Is the Only King* (Washington, D.C., 1975).

30. Angela Miller, "A Muralist of Civic Ambitions," in Stewart, Ketner, and Miller, *Carl Wimar*, 188–226.

31. The literature on Bingham is extensive. A recent study that includes a sizable bibliography is Michael Edward Shapiro, Barbara Groseclose, Elizabeth Johns, Paul C. Nagle, and John Wilmerding, *George Caleb Bingham* (St. Louis, 1990). For Deas see Carol Clark, "Charles Deas," in Ron Tyler, et al., *American Frontier Life*, 51–77.

32. Although the American Art Union in New York was the most prominent, there were a number of other such institutions in major cities. See Maybell Mann, *The American Art Union* (Washington, 1977); and Jay Cantor, "Prints and the American Art-Union," in *Prints in and of America to 1850*, ed. John D. Morse, 297–326 (Charlottesville, Va., 1970).

33. See Elizabeth Johns, *American Genre Painting: The Politics of Everyday Life* (New Haven, Conn., 1991), 60–99.

34. For an overview of the midcentury publishing of frontier images, see Bernard Reilly Jr., "The Prints of Life in the West, 1840–60," in Tyler, et al., *American Frontier Life*, 167–92. For Currier and Ives, see Media Projects, Inc., *Currier and Ives, A Catalogue Raisonne*, 2 vols. (Detroit, 1983).

35. Charlotte Steifer Rubenstein, "The Early Career of Frances Flora Bond Palmer (1812–1876)," *American Art Journal* 17 (Autumn 1985): 71–88.

36. Warder H. Cadbury and Henry R. Marsh, *Arthur Fitzwilliam Tait, Artist in the Adirondacks: An Account of His Career [and] a Checklist of His Works* (Newark, N.J., 1986). For Ranney, see Francis S. Grubar, *William Ranney: Painter of the Early West* (Washington, D.C., 1962).

37. See Peter Marzio, *Chromolithography, 1840–1900: The Democratic Art: Pictures for the Nineteenth Century.* (Boston, 1979).

38. Published as a book and in sheet form: Ferdinand V. Hayden, *The Yellowstone National Park, and the Mountain Regions of Portions of Idaho, Nevada, Colorado and Utah* (Boston, 1876).

39. E. L. Godkin, *The Nation*, September 24, 1874. For commentary, see Marzio, *Chromolithography*, 1.

40. George Croffutt, *New Overland Tourist and Pacific Coast Guide* (Chicago, 1878–79), frontispiece.

41. For more on the visualization of "Progress," see Patricia Hills, "Picturing Progress in the Era of Westward Expansion," in *The West as America*, ed. Truettner, 97–147; and Brian W. Dippie, "The Moving Finger Writes: Western Art and the Dynamics of Change," in Prown, et al., *Discovered Lands*, 89–115.

42. See my chapters on Yellowstone and the Grand Canyon in Kinsey, *Thomas Moran*, 43–137.

43. William Cullen Bryant, ed., *Picturesque America; or The Land We Live In,* 2 vols. (New York, 1874). For more on railroad advertisement, see Alfred Runte, *Trains of Discovery: Western Railroads and the National Parks* (Flagstaff, Ariz., 1984; rev. ed., 1990).

44. See Nancy K. Anderson, "The Kiss of Enterprise: The Western Landscape as Symbol and Resource," in *The West as America,* ed. Truettner, 237–83.

45. For more on this aspect of Bierstadt's career, see Nancy Anderson and Linda Ferber, *Albert Bierstadt: Art and Enterprise* (New York, 1990).

46. Schreyvogel spent considerable time in the West and researched the details of his paintings with great care; see James D. Horan, *The Life and Art of Charles Schreyvogel: Painter-Historian of the Indian-Fighting Army of the American West* (New York, 1969). Photos of Remington painting from models can be found in Shapiro and Hassrick, *Frederic Remington.*

47. Brian W. Dippie, "Frederic Remington's West: Where History Meets Myth," in Chris Bruce, Brian W. Dippie, Paul Fees, Mark Klett, and Kathleen Murphy, *Myth of the West* (Seattle, 1990), 111–38.

48. Remington's studio artifacts are preserved at the Buffalo Bill Historical Center in Cody, Wyoming. For his use of photographs, see Shapiro and Hassrick, *Frederic Remington,* 92–101.

49. Shapiro and Hassrick, *Frederic Remington,* 97. The pattern of equine motion was a subject of great debate in the late nineteenth century, and Muybridge initiated his ground-breaking photographic experiments at the instigation of a former governor of California, Leland Stanford, who bet his friend Frederick MacCrellish $25,000 that at full gallop all four horse's feet simultaneously leave the ground. Muybridge proved Stanford correct.

50. Harold Samuels and Peggy Samuels, eds., *The Collected Writings of Frederic Remington* (Garden City, N.Y., 1975), 551.

51. Letter to Poultney Bigelow, the editor of *Outing* magazine. Quoted by David McCullough, "Remington the Man," in *Frederic Remington,* ed. Shapiro and Hassrick, 29.

52. George de Forest Brush, "An Artist among the Indians," *Century* 30 (May 1885): 55; cited in Alex Nemerov, "Doing the Old America: The Image of the American West, 1880–1920," in *The West as America,* ed. Truettner, 323.

53. C. M. Russell to Frank B. Linderman, January 18, 1919; cited in Brian Dippie, *Looking at Russell* (Fort Worth, Tex., 1987), 6.

54. This point is explored more fully in a recent insightful article: J. Gray Sweeney, "Racism, Nationalism, and Nostalgia in Cowboy Art," *Oxford Art Journal* 15, no. 1 (1992): 67–80.

55. Alfred T. Collette and Donald M. Lantzy, *James Earle Fraser: The American Heritage in Sculpture* (Syracuse, N.Y., 1985), 41.

56. Ibid.

57. Ibid., 8.

58. Fraser was only eighteen years old when he won the Wanamaker Prize for *The End of the Trail* in 1898. His acquaintance with Saint-Gaudens resulted in his assisting on the master's *Sherman Memorial,* which remains today at the corner of New York's Fifth Avenue and Fifty-Ninth Street, adjacent to

Central Park and the Plaza Hotel. See Collette and Lantzy, *James Earle Fraser*, 18–19.

59. Fraser's other work includes, among many other items, the pediments of the National Archives and the Department of Commerce buildings and the monumental figures *The Authority of Law and Contemplation of Justice*, which flank the entrance to the Supreme Court Building, all in Washington, D.C. For more on *The End of the Trail*, see Dean Krakel, *End of the Trail: The Odyssey of a Statue* (Norman, Okla., 1973).

60. The 1915 version in San Francisco was actually made of stucco, and although it survived outdoors in Visalia until the late 1960s, it was replaced with a bronze version at that time. The original has been transferred to the National Cowboy Hall of Fame in Oklahoma City.

61. This phenomenon is examined in Robert G. Athearn, *The Mythic West in Twentieth-Century America* (Lawrence, Kans., 1986).

62. On the Taos school, see Charles Eldredge, Julie Schimmel, and William Truettner, *Art in New Mexico, 1900–1945: Paths to Taos and Santa Fe* (New York, 1986).

63. See, for example, *Art Journal* 51 (Fall 1992), which is entirely devoted to recent Native American Art.

64. J. Gray Sweeney, "Racism, Nationalism, and Nostalgia."

65. The response to the exhibition, which included comments from U.S. senators and the librarian of Congress, as well as from the general public and newspaper and magazine reviewers, is becoming legendary. For a perceptive review of the event, see Bryan J. Wolf, "How the West Was Hung, Or, *When I Hear the Word Culture I Take out My Checkbook*," *American Quarterly* 44 (September 1992): 418–38. The National Museum of American Art has retained a comprehensive file of the reviews of the show, as well as the comment books that chronicled public opinion.

66. See the sizable, if not always thoroughly labeled, clipping file of reviews and articles about the exhibition at the library of the National Museum of American Art, especially Elizabeth Broun, "The Story behind the Story of *The West as America*," *Museum News* (September/October 1991); William Truettner, "The West and the Heroic Ideal: Using Images to Interpret History," *Chronicle of Higher Education* 38 (November 20, 1991): 2:1–3; Truettner, "Reinterpreting Images of Westward Expansion, 1820–1920," *Antiques* 139 (March 1991): 539–55; Truettner and Alex Nemerov, "What You See Is Not Necessarily What You Get: New Meaning in Images of the Old West," *Montana: The Magazine of Western History* 42, no. 3 (Summer 1992): 70–76.

67. See, for example, Patricia Nelson Limerick, Clyde A. Milner II, and Charles E. Rankin, eds., *Trails: Toward a New Western History* (Lawrence, Kans., 1991).

68. For a sampling of these comments, see "Showdown at 'The West as America' Exhibition," *American Art* 5 (Summer 1991): 2–11. The comment books themselves are available in the National Museum of American Art.

TEN

Elliott West

Selling the Myth: Western Images in Advertising

"ADVERTISING IS THE rhetoric of democracy." So writes Daniel Boorstin, and he makes a good case.[1] Advertising is the most highly developed of our persuasive arts, made so from the continuous struggle among businesses for the favor of American consumers as they vote, economically speaking, for their toothpastes, automobiles, and breakfast cereals. Ads speak to us through the folk culture—from tall tales and hyperbole to horror fantasies and patriotic gas—that is the true common tongue of our disparate nation. This rhetoric shows the weaknesses and excesses of democracy noted by commentators from Alexis de Tocqueville to George Will. "You must write your advertisements to catch damn fools—not college professors," advised George P. Rowell, a nineteenth-century entrepreneur of the business. If you do, he added, "you'll catch just as many college professors as you will of any other sort."[2]

Advertising is most democratic in its ubiquity. An American is exposed on average to 1,500 advertising appeals every day. A typical consumer pays attention to only 76 ads out of that barrage.[3] So we walk through our days engaging in a largely unconscious conversation with hundreds of would-be persuaders. They pitch; we filter and choose. Here is an ongoing campaign with thousands of candidates, and it requires successful advertisers to understand the American mass mind even better than those office-seekers who operate in the comparatively simple marketplace of political democracy.

Small wonder, then, that advertisers have drawn heavily and often on the western myth. If no medium has been in closer communion with the mass mind than advertising, no popular tradition is more deeply entrenched in American culture than the western. Brought together, they have been a real love match. By the early 1900s portraits of buffalo and broncos were being used to sell liquor and prunes. Today, as a new century nears, western images can be seen in ads for everything from cigarettes to station wagons.

Modern advertising and the Western have had a common, interactive history. During the first third of the present century, the advertising business changed dramatically in its goals and techniques. Its earlier ideal was simply to describe the goods and services offered. In a competitive age, Horace Greeley wrote in 1850, every sensible businessman must let the public know what he is selling. But in this work, he advised, "leave clowns' jests to the circus, and let sober men speak as they act, with directness and decision."[4] By the 1920s, however, manufacturers were making their products more alluring by manipulating the consumer's aspirations and anxieties. They were moving toward the strategy later summed up by Charles Revson: "In the factory we make cosmetics. In the store we sell hope."[5] Meanwhile the circulation of periodicals was expanding at an extraordinary clip. As ad executives reached out to that mass market, it became part of their job to gauge the current American mood and to appeal to customers through their most deeply rooted values.

One of the best expressions of those values, the Western, made its appearance during the same years. The generation that saw advertising transformed also read the first modern Western novels, watched the flourish and decline of Wild West shows, and saw the earliest Western films and movie stars. Ads for Buffalo whiskey and Mohawk tires tapped the same popular fascination that brought success and fortune to Owen Wister and Bronco Billy Anderson. From then until now advertising and the western myth have been an enduring combination.

Indeed, the combination has been both enduring and revealing, for western ads can tell us a lot about ourselves. Like all varieties of the western myth, of course, they make for appallingly bad history. They gloss over the complex forces that produced the modern West, and they ignore most actors in the story. One can look through thousands of these images, for instance, without seeing a single Hispanic or Asian face, and although Indians appear occasionally, they are almost always played for laughs.[6] Nor do these ads speak equally about all parts of American society. The western myth always has appealed far more to white, middle-class men than to the poor, the black and brown, and the female.

Nonetheless, these historically botched pictures still are full of lessons. The Marlboro Man, as much as John Wayne and the Beach Boys, can teach us something about what many Americans have thought and believed—if, that is, we know what to look for.

Some ads, for instance, have drawn only superficially on western themes by using stock characters, words, and phrases drawn from popular Westerns. "You've got me corralled, Handsome," says a smiling woman of the 1940s as she chucks a cowboy under a chin shaved smooth with Barbasol. In an ad for B. F. Goodrich another woman on horseback jokes with a man changing a flat: "What's wrong, Cowboy . . . car go lame?"[7] The possibilities are as rich as the slang allows, with makers of vise grips telling customers to "Unholster your 'Hardware,' Men!" and an electronics firm, showing a repairman atop a bucking television, reminding us that "it takes a heap of Know-How to ride herd on 36,000,000 TV Sets."[8] These ads get chummy with their public through icons, symbols, and the vernacular of playgrounds, pulp paperbacks, and B movies.

Another type expresses the myth at a deeper level. In such an ad the overall impression—its details and how they are put together—invokes some basic theme of the West of popular culture. A magazine advertisement cannot tell a story in the same way that a novel or song can, since it is an unmoving visual image with minimal text. But by placing certain figures in particular situations and settings—a cowboy riding alone in the desert, perhaps, or a woman at the door of a rough cabin at the base of a rugged mountain—the flat page summons up responses. The frozen scene is from an instantly recognizable context, the mythic West.

But just what is the imagined West, that country of Louis L'Amour and Coors beer ads? It is, first, a place. Its topographical features are from west of the Missouri River: the jagged peaks of the Rockies and Sierra Nevada, the yawning canyons and vast deserts of the Southwest, and the sweeping grasslands of the Great Plains. Nonetheless, this West is not really on any map. An actual region has been idealized into a setting of unalloyed beauty. This beautiful place is also wild. Its wildness, in fact, sets it apart from wondrous landscapes of the Old World, for unlike the Swiss Alps or Scandinavian fjords, it is beyond the full grasp of civilization; its grandeur is untamed and largely untrod, at least by the shoes of clerks and bureaucrats. Because *wild* also means "undeveloped," this West is also brimming with opportunities waiting to be recognized and acted on.

The mythic West is, second, a story. In this grand drama the untrammeled, savage West—a place of terrible beasts, a great emptiness that can swallow the unwary, native peoples who proudly live by their own rules—is a testing ground for intruders. These "pioneers" (a term appropriately drawn from the Old French word for "foot soldier") come to "settle" the country, to tame it, develop its possibilities, and establish order and civilized values. They do these deeds through their fortitude, ingenuity, determination, individualism, vision, and other virtues celebrated as distinctively American.

The imaginary West as place and as story combine to make the Western. Like all myths, it appears simple. Certainly its elements and plots are predictable, and its detractors enjoy poking fun at its stark dualities and moral rigidities. Within its many forms and seemingly endless variations, however, are surprising complexities.

The Western also has a problem. Although not apparent at first glance, this problem sits at the heart of the Western. It is, in fact, as much a defining characteristic as the hero's virtues and the land's beauty. The problem appears when the place and the story come together. The West as place is pristine. Its beautiful wildness is its distinctively American quality; its untamed, undeveloped nature poses the challenge facing the pioneers. When the story unfolds and the challenge is met, however, the place is changed irrevocably. It is settled, not wild; civilized, not savage. The place, in other words, is vulnerable to the story. That story is one of people who are transformed into heroes through grappling with great challenges. When the pioneers win—and in classic Westerns they always do—those challenges vanish. The land is tamed, and the opportunities are realized. At that point the heroes have destroyed the very conditions that have brought out their best, that have made them American. The story, in short, is vulnerable to its inevitable outcome.

The place and the story, then, are interdependent and mutually destructive. When the story is over, the place is gone, and without the place there can be no story. As long as the Western is merely entertainment, this contradiction poses no difficulty. It is a good yarn that a lot of people can read and watch over and over. But the Western as myth is another matter. If this is how we have chosen to express what we believe and who we are, then the Western's problem is our own. Our beliefs and identity are as contradictory, confused, and ambiguous as the myth.

In particular the Western's problem suggests a conflict that has caught the eye of many observers. Americans seem both fascinated with progress and infatuated with a glorified past, always reaching toward the new while heroizing the folk and lifeways of a vanished age. This jumble of impulses is as old as the republic. When Walter Lippmann commented that ours is the only nation that was born perfect and is constantly working on improvements, he was thinking of that same odd blend that led Alexis de Toqueville, more than a century earlier, to call the typical American a "venturous conservative." This basic tension between old and new, progress and nostalgia, has deepened in the present century, with its sweeping, rapid changes promising wondrous innovations that will wrench us from the past.

The western myth has been an ideal medium for expressing that pull and tug of interests and loyalties. Its story of pioneers renewed through heroic accomplishment speaks to Americans' obsessive reach toward anything newer and better; its Edenic images and characters larger than life recall glory days now behind us. Western-based advertisements have drawn on this mythic tradition and have given it their own twists. As such, they are one more expression of a complicated and conflicted national character.

Western-related ads have one characteristic all their own. Unlike a film or dime novel, an ad is supposed to encourage the reader to *do* something. It cannot just tell a good story set in a pretty place. For an ad to justify its existence, customers must look at it and see or feel some immediate, motivating connection between it and the immediate world in which they act (or more precisely, in which they buy). As I will show, that poses peculiar creative challenges, especially in the light of the contradictions that always nag at the western myth in all its forms.

As they have tried to sell their goods, most western ads have fallen into one of three categories, each with its own kind of appeal. The first type, like the first component of the western myth, has concentrated on the West as a place. These ads have played on impressions of the West as a magnificent, mythic setting and, just as much, on the American fascination with movement into that place, with picking up and heading westward toward particular destinations and toward peculiarly western experiences.

The most obvious examples have been ads appealing to potential tourists. For at least eighty years periodicals have featured invitations to one and all to visit western states and cities and, with them, famous landmarks and landscapes. Readers were told to "Rest or Romance in

Albuquerque" in the 1920s and were enticed with photographs of Carlsbad Caverns in the 1940s and the wonders of Oklahoma in the 1960s. An ad for western Canada in the 1980s was glossier, but its message was no different from the others: "Alberta. Wish *you* were here."[9]

If nothing else, these ads have shown something about contemporary Americans' distinctive approach to travel. Unlike upper-class European travelers of the nineteenth century, who left home in hopes of adventures and unforeseen experiences, the modern middle-class American vacationer launches off with precise goals and a choreographed itinerary. A proper vacation, to be sure, includes the unusual—things grand, exotic, or historically blessed. Yet American tourists insist on knowing what the unusual will be. On their voyages of exploration, families sail off in their cars or planes to find places they already can describe in great detail—the Washington Monument, Old Faithful, Mount Rushmore—and if a destination differs from its familiar images, these discoverers are disappointed. In short, American vacationers usually travel to find the predictably unusual, to "discover" the expected.[10]

That fact has helped to make the West America's prime vacationland. Reared on the many manifestations of its myth, most Americans believe that they know what the West is like. Its extraordinary landscapes have been sketched, painted, photographed, and filmed so often that the images are etched indelibly into the popular consciousness. Its peoples' supposedly unique appearance and habits are staples of our mass culture.

The job of advertisers has been to entice the public with vivid assurances that to the west the exotic is guaranteed and the remarkable is marked on the map. Tourist ads not only have promised a country of topographical magnificence, they also have drawn on romantic, regenerative themes. As a place the West was not only beautiful but magically healing. Southwestern cities such as Albuquerque and Phoenix promised turquoise skies and blazing sunsets, colorful Indian and Hispanic villages, and "tissue mending sunshine." The Rockies were "a-tingle with vital forces," so "if your mind is sluggish, if your ideas come slow," a trip to Colorado was the answer. Particulars varied with the audience. A higher-brow periodical like *Atlantic Monthly* offered copy that was more consciously literary—in San Diego "stars . . . venture out tentatively, like hesitant children"—and was clearly aimed at the globe-trotting reader. Tucson was compared to Egypt, and Phoenix resorts were described as being full of "travel-wise oldsters and youngsters from the four corners of the earth." An ad in *Time*, by contrast, suggested a visitor to Albuquerque might run into a Rotarian from his hometown.[11] But the general messages were the same. To the west were geographical grandeur, exotic humanity, and nature's balms.

Most early tourists headed west by train. Railway companies, locked in a brutal struggle in a highly competitive market, were even more aggressive advertisers than western towns. The Northern Pacific, Great Northern, Rock Island, and other networks stressed many of the same themes: spectacular scenery, sun worshiping, and relaxation. Like western cities, railroads also promised the peculiarly western experience of drawing close to uncorrupted realms of nature. "Pack up your duds, dudes," ordered the Northern Pacific, which went on to reserve each customer his or her own horse at a resort "far from city civilization and . . . modern times." Other companies offered guides to dude ranches, enterprises that trafficked in the reenactment of pioneer fantasies: riding along primitive trails, singing around campfires, chatting with wranglers, and drawing close to the wild things.[12]

The most elaborate campaign was that of the Atchison, Topeka, and Santa Fe. Besides running periodical advertisements, the company hired dozens of photographers and artists to create images that were then distributed on tens of thousands of calendars and brochures. Canyons and buttes were part of a colorful desertscape unmarred by civilization. Southwestern Indians, when not giving welcoming smiles, practiced ancient rituals and lifeways that suggested a romantic union with nature. White pioneer types, such as cowboys and prospectors, worked at their tasks as if unaware of reports that the frontier had ended.[13]

These advertisements might seem simple and straightforward, but on closer look they were troubled by the central problem of the Western. Looking westward American travelers expected a mythic country that was rugged, pristine, and far from "civilization." The ads promised all that. But in the same lines they promised easy access. The railroads' offer of a rapid ride to Montana and Arizona, after all, was a boast that distance had been mastered, that the once-remote West had been brought close to the settled East. Implied here was a conquered land that incidentally had dependable amenities and hosts to anticipate the customers' needs. Glacier Park "is still the Old West," the Great Northern said in 1930, but fifteen years earlier the company had pledged that the park "offered every modern convenience."[14] Judging from these ads, the vacationer's West was savage and safe, rugged and comfortable, grandly remote and easy to reach and leave.

It was natural for a tourist to prefer a hot bath after a day of mountain gawking. But these ads also spoke of an ambivalent, even schizophrenic attitude toward the West as a physical environment. The wilderness was our national birthright, and it was our historical adversary. Its touch inspired our greatness of character; conquering it was the source of our profoundest pride. Published lures from western cities and railroads expressed that ambivalence. Come and see the wild country, they said, and be revived and healed by its isolated splendor, even as they celebrated victory in the struggle to control the West and bring it close. The advertising of tourism shows Americans' complex, garbled feelings of surrender and mastery toward a mythic landscape.

The vacationer's fantasy involved not only the land itself. Just as important was the act of going there. Packing bags and heading west to see the Grand Canyon or Yellowstone had overtones of the pioneering experience, a historical episode with many complicated connotations. In the popular mind earlier Americans who headed for the frontier were choosing opportunity over security and asserting their independence from undue restraints, cultural limitations, and perhaps even the law. Modern fantasies of heading west, therefore, were heavy with implications of individual liberation, of breaking away toward some physical and spiritual freedom. The ads discussed so far did not emphasize these themes, however. Rail travel was not well suited for escapist images; customers went where the rails ran and when the schedules dictated.

Automobiles were different, however. The advent of the car promised an unprecedented freedom of movement. For the price of a modest sedan and tank of gas, an American could indulge all sorts of free-ranging fantasies that meshed beautifully with mythic themes of escape toward the setting sun. Consequently, from the 1920s until today images of pioneering and of the wild west have been an integral part of selling not only cars but virtually all products associated with the industry—gasoline, oil, and accessories, even automobile financing plans and asphalt and concrete used in highways.[15]

"Westward Ho!" an ad for Mohawk Tires trumpeted in 1926. Under a picture of a man in a convertible cruising past a saguaro cactus, the text invited readers to "luxuriously repeat those great migrations of the ancients that implanted an eternal wanderlust in the hearts of men!"[16] Like this one, some ads have referred to using automobiles specifically to travel westward, and as such they have been basically offshoots of appeals to tourists. In a major campaign in the early 1970s Chevrolet described its various models as "A Better Way to See the U.S.A." The western portion of the United States apparently was the part most worth seeing, since most ads showed families parked in such places as Arizona's Oak Creek Canyon and Taos Pueblo.[17]

Most auto ads, however, usually have been vaguer than that. The association with the West is maintained, but the connection is strikingly unspecific. The West of these ads—and the relation of the product to that West—is far more abstract. Customers, that is, are not invited to go to a particular western place; they are encouraged merely to go anywhere. The 1927 Jordan, displayed beneath a drawing of a cowboy on a bucking horse, was described as "a nimble, fleet-footed bundle of energy—quick, responsive, unrestrained."[18] The imagery is western, while the destination is left open to the driver's fantasies.

Western themes, with allusions to restless power, have been a staple of auto ads for sixty years, but during the last quarter-century they have become far more common. This may reflect new engineering and the growing popularity of four-wheel-drive vehicles; the ability to leave the pavement and crash through brush and over small trees may feed fantasies of liberation and mastering the land that are pictured best in a western setting. But something more basic also is afoot. One of the most prominent antimodern themes in recent popular culture is the conviction that the individual has been more and more restricted by large, faceless institutions. This view—that vast corporations and sprawling government bureaucracies are bent on standardizing behavior, smothering eccentricity, and constricting individual freedoms—has surfaced in several forms: "antihero" Western films that pit likable bandits against mindless, suffocating authority, for instance, and the "outlaw" phenomenon in country and western music. In typically nostalgic fashion, those who feel chafed and confined by modern American life have turned to the imagined frontier, in particular, to its freewheeling images of breaking free of whatever would hold them back.

The automobile's promise of liberating movement is beautifully suited to expressing this discontent. Western names given to cars suggest this new emphasis. Earlier ones were taken from explorers who were loyal agents of state and church (LaSalle, Cadillac, DeSoto). Names of the past twenty years, on the other hand, smack of wild, literally unbridled power (Mustang, Bronco, Pinto), or proud outcasts (Maverick), or the government's historical opponents (Cherokee, Navajo), or figures on the fringe of legitimate authority (Ranger). Ads often make the appeal specific. A recent example, showing a Mustang heading for a mountain horizon, urged customers to "put everything else behind you," and the Jeep Cherokee was touted as "the get-away machine *your* family has been waiting for."[19] Images of such vehicles far from any pavement, atop southwestern buttes and skittering the edges of arroyos, are visual expressions of the same idea. Motorcycles offered an even more individualistic vision of the lone rider loose from family and companions. Early in the 1970s Harley-Davidson was calling one of its models "The Great American Freedom Machine." Its ad showed a man reclining and reading by a pup tent in the desert, a wilderness solitaire with his bike poised in the foreground. "So when things hassle you," the text read, "throw some stuff on your SX-175, kick her down, and move out to where you can get some freedom and solitude."[20]

But the problem again appears: get away to where? These machines, like the railroads, are marvels of the twin revolutions of industry and transportation that Americans have applauded for conquering the West. (Besides, many resources to make and run cars have come from taming the wild country.) The problem is kept comfortably out-of-focus, however. The lure in these ads is not some specific stretch of the untamed West but the *idea* of spontaneous movement into a generically western landscape. Witness, for instance, this recent fictional testimony for a Suzuki Sidekick:

> We were cruisin' Highway 34 when Lenny said, "Take the left fork." "Why?" I asked. Lenny's answer, "Why not?" My husband the navigator. The kids spotted icicles on the shady side of the rocks. More advice from Lenny: "Take the trail between those two big boulders." I was dubious. But Lenny repeated, "Why not?" adding, "the Sidekick is built to go just about anywhere." So off we went. Four wheelin' uphill. Plenty of power from its 16-valve engine. Lenny was in all his glory. "Go left." An old Doobie Brothers cassette played. A deer bounded by just to our right. I checked the mirror to see if the kids saw her, but they were asleep. "This Sidekick is almost too comfortable," I whispered. Lenny winked at me and said, "Pull over under that tree." I smiled and answered, "Why not?"[21]

The second category of advertisements concentrates on the West as a story. In particular it draws on the mythic tradition of pioneers who overcome formidable challenges and hardships, a test that brings out their best and tempers the emerging steel of their characters. The West here is not so much a landscape as a series of opportunities to be realized and threats to be faced down.

Businesses turned to this theme with special enthusiasm during the 1930s and 1940s, years of crisis when Americans were looking for reminders of their abilities and for assurances that dangers would be survived. When possible, advertisers associated their products with contemporary episodes of muscling western lands into submission. International Trucks boasted of doing 80 percent of the heavy hauling that humbled the Colorado River at Boulder Dam, the world's largest. During wartime some companies tried to draw on the pride and power associated with working the West. Allis-Chalmers, a manufacturer of industrial equipment, including farm machinery, juxtaposed photographs of a modern cowboy roping a steer and a soldier herding prisoners of war. These twin roundups of "American Beef [and] Axis Bullies" illustrated the corporation's part in feeding the world and trouncing the enemy.[22] In retrospect such unblushing confidence could have ironic overtones. A 1942 ad depicted a family leaving their home on the Great Plains, the father shaking his fist at a towering cloud of dust over their barren farm. The scene, of course, was from the dust bowl, the region's most dramatic lesson in environmental fragility and the disastrous consequences of trying to make over the West. Here, however, it was used for quite another purpose: selling air filters.[23]

This ad suggested, once again, the contradictions inherent in using the western myth in today's America. Even with a few dams still to build, the West as frontier story was finished by the 1940s, just as the West as wild place was subdued and, in an alarming number of cases, despoiled. How and where, then, could advertisers link their products to that heroizing process the public continued to regard so fondly?

At work here was a dilemma that reveals much about the myth's contemporary appeal while also bringing sharply into focus the unique place held by these ads within modern expressions of the Western. As most of the other chapters in this book point out, western-related art forms of this century have been powerfully nostalgic. Movies, songs, art, and illustrations often have hearkened back to an earlier imagined time when Americans supposedly lived by virtues—among others, an unswerving integrity, a spit-in-your-eye individualism, and a simple and unsullied honesty with others and themselves—that have disappeared in our modern age of soft living, conformity, dollar chasing, and moral drift. Westerns often have looked fondly backward and frequently considered modern America dangerously degenerate. That poses no problem in moviemaking and the composition of songs. To the contrary, those media are splendidly fit for nostalgic expression.

Advertising, however, is a different matter. Americans enjoy fantasizing about a past world of superior virtue—until, that is, they go shopping, at which point they demand the most up-to-date results of the most forward-looking technology. The ad exec must pitch the goods as "new" and "improved" (the terms are used synonymously) and appeal to the public's fascination with being modern.[24] Indeed, many ads seem to sell not so much a product as a feeling of participating in progress and the forces of change. This leaves advertisers with an obvious difficulty. They naturally hope to use the undeniable appeal of the western myth, but the images from that myth derive from the Old West, a time that recedes, year by year, from the up-to-date America that the makers of ads market. In fact, the accomplishments of modern life that advertisers celebrate and sell—technological wizardry, globe-shrinking transportation, mass communication, and the fruits of big business, to name only a few—are the very forces the public believes obliterated the Old West and ushered in a way of life that the myth condemns.

So here is the rub: how to use the old to sell the new? And even tougher, how to invoke a vanished way of life to sell what has caused that way of life to vanish?

One frequent answer has been to keep the Old West alive by blurring over distinctions between that imagined Golden Age and the present. Some ads simply asserted a connection, however tenuous, with the frontier, then moved quickly to modern applications. A full-page ad in a 1920 issue of the *Saturday Evening Post* began with a tribute to the Conestoga wagon, "the ship of the trackless prairie and the trails that led courageous men and unfaltering women through rugged, sullen mountain country, to the promised land of virgin plenty." What was being sold here? Not wagons, land, or freighting but Masury paints, which were claimed to have been used on some prairie schooners and now, "more than abreast of the times," were leading the nation "into the gold country of accomplishment."[25] Nearly thirty years later Du Pont was showing how nylon products could be used in the Old West's most famous task, roping cattle, as well as in making modern luggage and evening dresses. The Railroad Express Agency took pride that their employees were still protecting every shipment, just as they had against the Dalton Boys in Indian Territory.[26]

A common variation recalled (and trivialized) the tradition of the West as the hard land of suffering. A bulldogger told how Bayer Aspirin eased his aches. Chapstick's long-running campaign as the balm for "outdoor lips" often used images of hard-worked, sunburned cowboys. "The Indian bit the dust . . . but the dust bit *me!*" testified the movie actress Maureen O'Hara about the tribulations of working on desert location filming *Comanche Territory.* Jergens lotion, however, turned her dry skin soft and lovely in time for romantic close-ups.[27] In these ways advertisers tried to establish some immediate and practical application of their products with the accomplishments, jobs, and ordeals associated with the story of the Old West.

Some businesses, by redefining and updating the meaning of opportunity, said that the Old West was still out there, a land of untapped veins of investment and unplowed financial sod where today's risk-taking pioneer could prove his or her stuff. A 1983 issue of *Forbes* featured a splashy, three-page layout with a Frederic Remington painting, a photograph of galloping cowboys, and, in bold black letters, the claim that "once again the American frontier is in the West." The ad's subject was US West, a gigantic communications company spun off from the divestiture of the Bell Telephone system. The company claimed to be "out to win its spurs" in a region of vast resources, blossoming population, and booming trade, and it invited investors to throw in with the enterprise. Ten years earlier Western Bancorporation had made a similar appeal for anyone looking for ways to plant money into Washington and Oregon: "There's more to us than $16 billion. There's the West!"[28]

These strategies held no hope, however, for businesses selling products with little, if any, direct connection to the West. For these concerns another approach was needed. "We think of pioneers as those courageous people who . . . fought their way through forest, across prairie and desert," a 1953 ad mused. But one industry—"INSURANCE!"—had always displayed the "courage and vision needed to expand our economic frontiers" and has continued to do so.[29] The essential point here was a set of traits associated with the pioneer West, not the region itself or any of its environmental or social specifics. Through these traits a business could take on a positive "western" appeal without even showing how it helped in roping cattle or relieving sun-chapped skin.

Invariably this association was reinforced visually. In a television commercial in the mid-1960s Chevrolet put a convertible atop Utah's Castle Rock, hundreds of feet above the desert floor. The ad was successful enough to reproduce in print. The copy beneath this "unforgettable sight that symbolizes an attitude" used phrases familiar to any reader of pulp Westerns—"bold," "restless search," "keen," "fierce pride"—to praise a corporate philosophy, "the Chevrolet Way," that demanded the best of its engineers and workers.[30] So, too, with other ads: a cowboy astride a bucking horse symbolizing an electrical supply firm's manly taming of the wild, potentially dangerous forces of electricity; a magnificent team pulling a buckboard full of computers against a mountain backdrop ("We call 'em . . . WORKHORSES"); and eighty-one cowpunchers at a roundup, all with different styles of Bulova self-winding watches, "each handsome as a dude rancher, rugged as a prairie dog."[31]

As these ads loosened their connections to any tasks directly associated with the western story, they often turned inward. Like cars offering a spirit of breaking free, products could promise a *feeling* of the pioneer hero's accomplishment and transformation, as long as western icons were invoked in meeting challenges of today. Echoing a tribute to the Colt .45 revolver, the Rogers Peet Company, "a pioneer in ready-made men's clothes," praised its suit as "the great equalizer" in the modern business world, the "best weapon of attack" for the young executive needing confidence "for the job, the women, the ego."[32]

Ads from the third category draw on the first two, yet they are distinct. In this last type the West is not mainly a place or a story. It is a style.

Both of the first two sorts of western-related ads encountered the same problems: how to tap the western myth's powerful emotional appeal in a world with less and less similarity to the Old West of the popular imagination? How to sell things—railroad travel, cars, and forces of modernization—that in fact hastened the demise of that mythic place and story? The answer, in both cases, was much the same. Besides insisting, with decreasing success, that in some ways the Old West had managed to survive, the ads relied on abstraction. They stepped away from troublesome particulars—of a place that was gone and a story that was over—into vaguer territory. With the help of an icon or image, an ad attributed to its product a western "spirit," some hallowed virtue from the familiar myth that was then applied to a modern-day task or psychological need. A car possessed the pioneer spirit of boldness and liberation; a watch or computer, the frontiersman's pragmatic toughness and stamina.

The West as style took this process of abstraction one step further, removing any pretense that a product's western virtues could be applied in any way to any immediate purpose. Instead, some mythic quality was attributed to the basic nature of what was being sold. That quality and the object were inseparable, almost interchangeable; in a sense the product *became* its "western" attribute.

As always the point was made through mythically resonant images and language. With the Alamo as a backdrop, L&M cigarettes were dubbed "The Proud Smoke . . . Product of a Proud Land," and Budweiser beer, through a picture of two weatherworn cowboys at day's end, was recommended "For Everyone Who Stands His Ground Sunup to Sundown."[33] As these cases illustrate, the West as style was especially suited for items of exclusively personal use, with no application to anything beyond the body. Making a western virtue the essence of what was sold allowed an unprecedented intimacy between purchaser and product. Customers were not using some special quality to accomplish anything. They were consuming it—in the case of cigarettes and liquor, literally breathing and swallowing the fantasy, making it a part of themselves.

The most familiar instance of this category—and the longest-running use of the West in advertising—is the Marlboro Man. First marketed in 1923, Marlboro cigarettes sold sluggishly until 1954, when their manufacturer, Philip Morris, added a filter, introduced a "crush-proof" box, and began a new ad campaign featuring a series of rugged men meant to exude what an executive called "masculine confidence." One of these, a cowboy, proved far and away the most appealing, and after some experimentation, Philip Morris began using this figure exclusively in 1964. Twelve years later Marlboro was the best-selling cigarette in the United States and the world (fig. 10.1). These ads have epitomized the mythic West as place and story. The Marlboro Man works in Marlboro Country, a land of majestic mountains and wild, wide spaces. How he looks and what he does tell of a life that has made him supremely independent, utterly at ease in Eden, self-contained, as tough as his saddle. He is a clear, pure note. Anyone responding to these ads is buying an uncompromised dream of westering.[34]

In other ads that use the West as style, however, the myth's contradictions still creep in. The strategy is most effective with products, like tobacco and alcoholic beverages, that are not tied to modern America and consequently can be fantasized backward into the frontier's Golden Age. More modern goods have more of a problem. A Daniel Mink ad for the Original Cowboy wristwatch, water resistant to 105 feet and sold at Saks Fifth Avenue, dilutes its serious tone ("steeped in Western legacy") with tongue-in-cheek touches ("Horse optional") (fig. 10.2), and ads for more technologically advanced creations, such as satellite dishes, play the style even more for light comedy.[35] The approach works well in selling coffee. But hot tubs?[36]

Unlike ads of the first two categories, the problem here is not in trying to make a product work some modern task in a way evocative of the Old West. The contradiction is all within the consumer. Ads are appealing to customers who want to feel advanced and in sync with the latest trends while in touch with virtues of a receding past, in the same way that Americans have always celebrated both the wilderness and the pioneer's conquest of it. This mix of impulses appears most clearly in the two industries that have used the West as style most enthusiastically—clothing and cosmetics. In both cases, significantly, the goods are among the most highly individualized of the marketplace. Choosing a wardrobe and applying makeup are acts of self-definition, so a jacket or eyeliner is ideally suited for advertisers appealing to a consumer hoping to wear the myth, to make those western traits part of him- or herself.

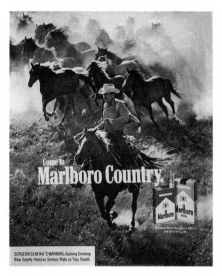

Figure 10.1. The Marlboro Man became a popular icon during the cold war era, portraying the American cowboy as the quintessential, rugged individualist. (Ball State University Photo Services.)

Figure 10.2. Western images are used to advertise the "Original Cowboy Watch" by Daniel Mink. (Ball State University Photo Services.)

The early 1980s saw a surge in popularity of western men's fashions. As booted and denim-clad models crowded the advertising sections of magazines, some images stressed a Marlboro-like machismo, as in the ad with a hand (holding a cigar and sporting a "Let's Rodeo" ring) casually about to flick a scorpion from a Nocono boot. But the message in other ads was murkier. In offering "shirts that speak out" Arrow showed several young men on a Great Basin salt flat wearing loudly colored shirts and looks of stony determination. The cut of the shirts is western casual, and the models stand like gunfighters, yet the men have an undeniable worldliness and coifed sophistication. It is an image in search of a balance between past and present.[37] A more recent campaign for Colours menswear made the point more explicitly. Its model is no Marlboro Man but a young rancher with a graduate degree in business who is shown working on horseback, relaxing in a bunkhouse, and arriving from his accounting office.[38]

Women's clothing and cosmetics, too, have lately been marketed through western themes. This has been a major departure from previous practice. Western advertising always had been pitched to men or to families. Appeals made exclusively to women had been rare indeed until the 1980s. Then, as magazines such as *Cosmopolitan* and *Glamour* began publishing modestly feminist articles, western motifs began to appear in their advertisements. The connection was clear enough. As women's claims to an expanding independence entered the mainstream of popular culture, mythic values that had been men's alone—pride, self-reliance, standing tough, individualism, breaking free in search of a new start—suddenly fit the commercial needs of both sexes. A reader could even see women rodeo champions endorsing beer.[39]

The women's ads have shared the conflicts of the men's and have added their own. They appeal to a newly independent woman who, for instance, still pursues traditional definitions of beauty, in the same way that mass-circulation women's magazines have blended a new assertiveness with older visions of the feminine (fig. 10.3). (A recent issue of *Cosmopolitan* contained articles entitled "Getting Your Own Way" and "Glorify Your Bosom!")[40] And as with men's fashions, the appeal of the Old West somehow must be reconciled with the need to feel up to date and aligned with modern trends. Early in the decade Estée Lauder offered a line of lipstick, blush, and nail polish in "The Colors of the Great American Desert." The corresponding ads featured a woman in native-pioneer dress beside an unsaddled horse in a southwestern landscape. Within a few years Maybelline was marketing its Indian Glaze collection and Revlon, its Santa Fe cosmetics.[41] The immediate selling point of all three was supposed to be their range of muted colors from the desert palette, but the stance and trappings of the models mixed elements of freedom and self-confidence with an exotic sensuality, long associated in popular culture with Indian women and with white females who had "gone native." In case the western setting implied provinciality, Revlon offered lipsticks in "the colors of the Great Plains. But with a dropdead worldliness."

Models of women's clothing always exude sophistication, sometimes wearing tradition-oriented dress but often sporting brightly colored boots, rhinestone-studded hats, and leather skirts and blouses, slightly outrageous styles that strive to establish a woman's variation on an old theme, one that gently mocks the genre's macho roots while announcing that women are going their own way.[42] Ads for Lady Stetson fragrances summed up this approach. Featuring smartly dressed women in chic cowboy hats, they called their cologne "A Declaration of Independence" and told customers, "Lady . . . you're free! Country proud. . . . You're an American phenomenon" (fig. 10.4).[43]

The master of advertising through western style has been Ralph Lauren. No one else has exploited traditional themes better while working so artfully with that balance between old and new. Lauren's distinctive western look is a stylistic weave of elegance and simplicity. His sophisticated design and the groomed, insouciant models assure customers that these are not clothes for rubes. Yet the shirts, jackets, and pants, especially when advertised around corrals and chuck wagons, have a back-to-basics informality that seems to thumb its nose at high fashion while suggesting something like sartorial innocence. Like other images of escape from regimentation, his ads have a strong suggestion of a loose, freewheeling individualism, but the Lauren Man is a buckaroo with eastern savvy, Jay Gatsby in Marlboro Country.

By the mid-1980s Lauren had expanded his domain to fragrances, shoes, and home furnishings. He also remained highly visible, a kind of living advertisement of the possibility of moving between two worlds. Whether photographed on his Colorado ranch or at a Manhattan opening, the Brooklyn-born Lauren seemed always the elegant cowboy in some combination of slightly faded jeans, cotton work shirt, boots, and sheepherder's jacket.[44] His message—that the West is a yearning that any man, in Wyoming or Hoboken, can satisfy by wearing its style—was stated clearly in a 1979 ad for his then new cologne: "The West . . . It's an image of men who are real and proud. Of freedom and independence we all would like to feel. . . . Chaps is a cologne a man can put on as easily as a worn leather jacket or a pair of jeans. Chaps, it's the West. The West you would like to feel inside of yourself."[45]

Figure 10.3. This 1995 advertisement suggests that modern women can be independent like cowboys, yet still feminine and sexy, if they wear western fashions by Cherokee Leather. (Ball State Photo Services.)

Figure 10.4. A recent ad for Lady Stetson perfume demonstrates that in an era of equal rights, women can also acquire the freedom and individualism associated with cowboys. (Ball State University Photo Services.)

In what must be one of the unlikeliest cases of American matchmaking, these ads have married Horace Greeley to Charles Revson. "With directness and decision," they offer dreams with their blue jeans and sell hope with their aftershave. The product and the myth—and in the case of Lauren, the creator—have become one. In purchasing L&Ms a smoker buys not just cigarettes but pride. Paying for beer or perfume, a man or woman is consuming and declaring an independence and a toughness. Through abstraction—that is, by disengaging what is being sold from the West as a tangible place or as a story with actual consequences—mythic values can be used in marketing just about anything: herbal teas and houses, bathrobes and financial advice. Ironically, the less connection the myth has had to any practical realities of national life, the broader have been its possibilities in selling things to the American people.

This tendency toward abstraction has helped western ads to maintain their positive tone. In other expressions of the western myth, especially since the early 1960s, a far darker view of the American and frontier past has intruded. Effective ads, however, must be relentlessly upbeat. Consequently, western-related advertisements foster the illusion that, even in a modern world that has taken a wrong turn, whatever good there was of the Old West can somehow be expressed with the right vest, a dash of cologne, or a dab of perfume. In that sense advertising is the most positive contemporary expression of the western myth.

Even when abstracted into pure style, however, the myth still is shot through with contradictions. It cannot be otherwise, since it is drawn from a national culture with deeply ambivalent attitudes toward past and future, tradition and progress. It speaks for a public that celebrates conquest of the wild places while mourning their passing, a society that takes as its heroes men who destroy what has made them heroic.

Because the Western's values are logically and emotionally at war with one another, they have posed certain practical difficulties for advertisers. But in another sense, this is not a problem that calls for any solution. To put it mildly, Americans have shown no interest in resolving it. Rather, these contradictions show how a diverse people have drawn on deceptively simple images and stories to meet their complex, changing needs. If on one level the western myth is a simple moral tale of white and black hats, on another it is profoundly paradoxical and full of ambiguities that resist simple description.

Nowhere is this complexity more apparent than in western adland, that country where families ride mechanical mavericks and men wear business suits like six-shooters. Its scenes and stories are one dialect of our national rhetoric, a language as strangely and variously mixed as the people who speak it.

Notes

I would like to thank Dr. Katherine Villard for allowing me access to her splendid collection of advertisements with western themes. I also thanks Ms. Michelle Davidson and Mr. Michael Strickland for their help in research and for their insights and ideas.

1. Daniel J. Boorstin, *Democracy and Its Discontents: Reflections on Everyday America* (New York, 1971), 26–42.

2. Ibid., 32.

3. Daniel A. Pope, "The Development of National Advertising, 1865–1920," Ph.D. diss., Columbia University, 1973; cited in Vincent Vinikas, *Soft Soap, Hard Sell: American Hygiene in an Age of Advertisement* (Ames, Iowa, 1992), 119.

4. Horace Greeley, "The Philosophy of Advertising," *The Merchant's Magazine*, November 1850, 582.

5. Quoted in Michael Schudson, *Advertising, the Uneasy Persuasion: Its Dubious Impact on American Society* (New York, 1984), 129.

6. Supposedly comic images included, for instance, American Indian women carrying men, papooselike, to a Hilton Hotel (*Life,* February 1, 1943); a man puffing smoke signals on a Benson and Hedges cigarette (*Life,* June 14, 1968); a warrior scalping a man as an appeal to buy dandruff shampoo (*Sports Illustrated,* September 10, 1962); and an endorsement of breakfast cereal as "heap good" (*Life,* May 4, 1962). Although not as common as the comic, images of the Indian male as a figure of idealized dignity also appeared. See the ad for Pontiac automobiles (*Life,* July 26, 1936) and another from the Advertising Council, featuring the well-known Native American actor Iron Eyes Cody, appealing for support in a campaign against pollution and littering (*Sports Illustrated,* October 23, 1972).

7. *Life,* October 4, 1948; *Life,* August 4, 1941.

8. *Life,* July 7, 1958, and September 12, 1955. A common variation has been the use of cartoon characters, relentlessly cute and speaking in western vernacular. For a few of the many examples, including some in cartoons, see *Saturday Evening Post,* August 29, 1936; *Time,* September 10, 1956; and *Life,* June 21, 1943, July 2, 1951, October 6, 1952, and April 15, 1957.

9. *Time,* April 12, 1926; *Life,* September 6, 1948, and April 7, 1967. Alberta advertisement in Katherine Villard Collection, copy in possession of the author. For a look at how one southwestern city advertised itself, see Alex Jay Kimmelman, "Luring the Tourist to Tucson: Civic Promotion during the 1920s," *Journal of Arizona History* 28, no. 2 (Summer 1987): 135–54.

10. On distinctively American approaches to travel, see Daniel J. Boorstin, *The Image: A Guide to Pseudo-Events in America* (New York, 1972), 77–117.

11. *Collier's,* May 23, 1914; *Time,* April 12, 1926; *Atlantic Monthly,* December 1940, ads in unpaginated advertising section.

12. For a few of the many examples of railroad advertisements of the West, see *Vanity Fair,* April 1930; *Time,* February 8, 1932; *Life,* April 5, 1937; and *New Yorker,* May 17, 1952. On dude ranches and publicity for them, see Lawrence R. Borne, *Dude Ranching: A Complete History* (Albuquerque, N.Mex., 1983).

13. For a fascinating study of the Santa Fe's campaign, see T. C. McLuhan, *Dream Tracks: The Railroad and the American Indian, 1890–1930* (New York, 1985).

14. *Time,* February 8, 1932; *Collier's,* May 23, 1914.

15. An ad for the CIT plan for financing is in *Life,* September 3, 1956. For asphalt and cement ads, see *Saturday Evening Post,* July 4, 1959, and November 7, 1959.

16. *Saturday Evening Post,* April 24, 1926.

17. *Life,* November 5, 1971; *Time,* May 1, 1972, and June 5, 1972.

18. *Saturday Evening Post,* February 5, 1927.

19. *Time,* February 17, 1986, and September 17, 1973.

20. *Sports Illustrated,* December 7, 1973.

21. *Elle,* February 1992.

22. *Time,* July 27, 1936, and June 21, 1943.

23. *Time,* March 23, 1942.

24. For an extended discussion of this function of advertising, and of the ad man as "an exuberant apostle of modernity, see Roland Marchand, *Advertising the American Dream: Making Way for Modernity, 1920–1940* (Berkeley, Calif., 1985).

25. *Saturday Evening Post,* February 21, 1920.

26. *Life,* November 8, 1948; *Time,* May 19, 1952.

27. *Life,* October 1, 1947, March 1, 1948, March 6, 1950, and January 5, 1962.

28. *Forbes,* July 18, 1983; *Newsweek,* August 13, 1973.

29. *Time,* November 23, 1953.

30. *Life,* February 4, 1966.

31. *Time,* March 23, 1942; *Fortune,* January 23, 1984; *Life,* April 12, 1963.

32. *Time,* September 5, 1956.

33. The L&M ad, which appeared in several major magazines in the spring of 1976, is reprinted in Susan Prendergast Schoelwer, *Alamo Images: Changing Perceptions of a Texas Experience* (Dallas, 1985), 171; the Budweiser commercial is in the Villard collection. In a similar reference Old Grand Dad bourbon, "the spirit of America," was claimed as the favorite of the stalwart men who faced the blistering western deserts (depicted in a Thomas Ives photograph) and then toasted their adversary at day's end (*Time,* March 26, 1984).

34. Its remarkable success and longevity has brought the Marlboro campaign far more attention than any other aspect of western themes in advertis-

ing. See Leo Burnett, "The Marlboro Story: How One of America's Most Popular Filter Cigarettes Got That Way," *New Yorker,* November 15, 1958, 41–43; "Marlboro Won Success by Big Newspaper Ads," *Editor and Publisher,* December 6, 1958; Bruce A. Lohof, "The Higher Meaning of Marlboro Cigarettes," in *The Popular Culture Reader,* ed. Jack Nachbar and John Wright, 233–42 (Bowling Green, Ohio, 1977); and John G. Blair, "Cowboys, Europe, and Smoke: Marlboro in the Saddle," in *The American West as Seen by Europeans and Americans,* ed. Rob Kroes, 360–83 (Amsterdam, 1989).

35. *Vogue,* November 1987; *The Robb Report: The Magazine for Connoisseurs,* July 1983.

36. See the ad for Maxwell House coffee, featuring a western couple relaxing at dusk by a campfire, in *Cosmopolitan,* September 1983. For cowboys in hot tubs, see *Arkansas Times,* September 1983, and Lonn Taylor and Ingrid Maar, eds., *The American Cowboy* (Washington D.C., 1983), 172.

37. Taylor and Maar, *The Cowboy,* 169; *Sports Illustrated,* March 8, 1971.

38. *Sports Illustrated,* October 8, 1990. An article on western styles and advertisements in the *New York Times'* most recent annual survey of men's fashions noted this duality. The distinguishing feature of "western wear's new maturity" was the appearance of clothes "looking as brand-iron hot on a subway platform as they do against a Texas horizon." The style "welcomes gutsiness as long as the image isn't taken too seriously." See "No Cows, No Boys," in the *New York Times Magazine,* part 2, "Mens' Fashions of the Times," September 13, 1992, 59–61.

39. *Cosmopolitan,* April 1992.

40. Ibid.

41. *New Yorker,* February 16, 1981; *Glamour,* July 1984; *Vogue,* April 1984.

42. See, for instance, the collection of fashions and ads entitled "Best Westerns," in *Madmoiselle,* July 1992, 142–47.

43. *Cosmopolitan,* September 1986; *Madmoiselle,* May 1992.

44. On Lauren see "Ralph Lauren's Achievement," *Atlantic,* August 1987, 70–73; "You Are What You Wear," *Forbes,* April 21, 1986, 94–98; "Ralph Lauren—Looking Back," *Madmoiselle,* May 1992, 156–59.

45. Taylor and Maar, *The Cowboy,* 173.

Suggestions for Further Reading

POPULAR AND COMMERCIAL ART

Anderson, Nancy, and Linda Ferber. *Albert Bierstadt: Art and Enterprise.* New York, 1990.

Fox, Stephen. *The Mirror Makers: A History of American Advertising and Its Creators.* New York, 1984.

Getlein, Frank. *The Lure of the Great West.* Waukesha, Wis., 1973.

Goetzmann, William H., and William N. Goetzmann. *The West of the Imagination.* New York, 1986.

Kinsey, Joni L. *Thomas Moran and the Surveying of the American West.* Washington, D.C., 1992.

Marchand, Roland. *Advertising the American Dream: Making Way for Modernity, 1920–1940.* Berkeley, Calif., 1985.

Pope, Daniel. *The Making of Modern Advertising.* New York, 1983.

Prown, Jules David, et al., *Discovered Lands, Invented Pasts: Transforming Visions of the American West.* New Haven, Conn., 1992.

Rossi, Paul A., and David C. Hunt. *The Art of the Old West.* New York, 1971.

Schudson, Michael. *Advertising, the Uneasy Persuasion: Its Dubious Impact on American Society.* New York, 1984.

Shapiro, Michael Edward, and Peter H. Hassrick, eds. *Frederic Remington: The Masterworks.* St. Louis, 1988.

Taft, Robert. *Artists and Illustrators of the Old West, 1850–1900.* Princeton, N.J., 1953.

Trenton, Patricia, and Peter H. Hassrick. *The Rocky Mountains: A Vision for Artists in the Nineteenth Century.* Norman, Okla., 1983.

Truettner, William H. *The Natural Man Observed: A Study of Catlin's Indian Gallery.* Washington, D.C., 1979.

Truettner, William H., ed. *The West as America: Reinterpreting Images of the Frontier.* Washington, D.C., 1991.

Wood, James N. *Era of Exploration: The Rise of Landscape Photography in the American West, 1860–1885.* Boston, 1975.

Contributors

THOMAS L. ALTHERR is a professor of history and American studies at Metropolitan State College of Denver. The author or editor of numerous works in American social and cultural history, Professor Altherr is currently working on a book about the creation of national parks in the trans-Mississippi West.

RICHARD AQUILA is a professor of history and director of the American studies program at Ball State University, Muncie, Indiana. He is a specialist in American social and cultural history, and his publications include *The Iroquois Restoration* (1983) and *That Old Time Rock & Roll* (1989).

KENNETH J. BINDAS is an assistant professor of history at Kent State University, Trumbull Campus. He has written articles about popular music and American culture for *Western Historical Quarterly*, the *Historian* and other journals. He is the editor of *America's Musical Pulse: Popular Music in Twentieth-Century Society* (1992).

WILLIAM BLOODWORTH is a professor of English and president of Augusta College in Georgia. He has published books on Upton Sinclair and Max Brand, as well as several articles on western American literature.

CHRISTINE BOLD is an associate professor of English at the University of Guelph, Canada. Her publications include articles and reviews about the West and literature, as well as a book, *Selling the Wild West: Popular Western Fiction, 1860–1960* (1987).

JONI L. KINSEY is an assistant professor of art history at the University of Iowa. A specialist on western art, she has written essays on various western artists for William H. Truettner, ed. *The West as America: Reinterpreting Images of the Frontier, 1820–1920* (1991). Her most recent work is *Thomas Moran and the Surveying of the American West* (1992).

JOHN H. LENIHAN, an associate professor of history at Texas A&M University, is the author of numerous articles and papers dealing with recent American cultural and intellectual history. His publications include *Showdown: Confronting Modern America in the Western Film* (1980).

ELLIOTT WEST, a professor of history at the University of Arkansas, is the author or editor of numerous works on the American West. His publications include *The Saloon on the Rocky Mountain Mining Frontier* (1979), *Growing Up with the Country: Childhood on the Far Western Frontier* (1989), and *The Way to the West: Essays on the Central Plains* (1995).

RAY WHITE is the chair of the history department at Ball State University. He is the author of a number of articles and papers dealing with the American West and Western movies. Professor White's most recent work is *Roy Rogers and Dale Evans: A Bio-Bibliography* (forthcoming).

GARY A. YOGGY is a professor of history at Corning Community College, Corning, New York. The author of "When Television Wore Six-Guns: Cowboy Heroes on TV," in Archie P. McDonald, ed., *Shooting Stars: Heroes and Heroines of Western Film* (1987), he recently published a book about television Westerns entitled *Riding the Video Range* (1995).

Index

F 596 .W28 1996

Wanted dead or alive